Cases and Materials on Criminal Law

Authors

Deborah Davies

Nicola Monaghan

Katharine Matheson

Consultant Editor(s)

Deborah Davies

Editor-in-Chief

Christopher Costigan

First edition July 2010

Fifth edition July 2015

Published ISBN: 9781 4727 3397 9

Previous ISBN: 9781 4727 2120 4

British Library Cataloguing-in-Publication Data
A catalogue record for this book is available
from the British Library

Published by
BPP Learning Media Ltd
BPP House, Aldine Place
London W12 8AA
www.bpp.com/learningmedia

Printed in the United Kingdom by
Charlesworth Press

Flanshaw Way
Flanshaw Lane
Wakefield
WF2 9LP

Your learning materials, published by BPP
Learning Media Ltd, are printed on paper
obtained from traceable sustainable sources.

Extracts from the Law Reports, the Weekly Law
Reports and the Industrial Cases Reports are
reproduced by permission of:

The Incorporated Council of Law Reporting for
England and Wales, Megarry House,
119 Chancery Lane, London WC2A 1PP

Extracts from the All England Reports, and other
LexisNexis titles are reproduced by permission of
LexisNexis which is a trading name of, Reed
Elsevier (UK) Limited, Registered office, 1-3 Strand,
London WC2N 5JR

Extracts from Westlaw publications (including
journal articles) are reproduced with permission of
Thomson Reuters (Legal) Limited, Registered Office,
100 Avenue Road, London NW3 3PF

Contents

Table of Cases

A

B

C

D

F

H

J

M

P

R

S

T

Y

1

General Principles of Criminal Law: Actus Reus

Topic List

1.1 Causation

When crimes (whether committed by a positive act or an omission) require the occurrence of a particular consequence it is necessary to prove that the accused has caused that consequence both in fact and in law.

1.1.1 Factual Causation

In determining whether there is a factual link between the defendants act and the prohibited harm the jury must consider whether the resulting prohibited harm would have occurred irrespective of the defendant's act(s). It can be addressed by posing the question, 'but for the defendant's actions would the harm have occurred at that time and in that way?'

R v White [1910] 2 KB 124

Panel: Alverstone CJ, Bray and Pickford JJ

Facts: The defendant wished to kill his mother (the victim) for, it was suggested, financial gain. He added what he believed to be a deadly poison to his mother's bed time drink. Medical evidence showed that the mother did not die from the poison but from an unrelated heart attack. The defendant's appeal against conviction for attempted murder was dismissed by the Court of Appeal.

MR JUSTICE BRAY

...[T]he mother was found dead in a sitting posture on a sofa in a sitting-room in her house. There was a round table standing two feet from the sofa, on the further side of which was a wine glass three parts filled with a liquid made up of a drink called nectar and, as was afterwards shewn, containing two grains of cyanide of potassium. There were also on the table a nectar bottle, two lumps of sugar, and a spoon. There was no evidence to shew that she had taken any of this liquid, and the result of the post mortem examination and of the analysis of the contents of the stomach and of the contents of the wine glass was to shew that she had not died from poisoning by cyanide of potassium, but that death was most probably caused by syncope or heart failure, due to fright or some other external cause, and further that the quantity of cyanide of potassium in the wine glass was, even if she had taken the whole, insufficient to cause her death.

The defendant's act was not in fact the cause of his mother's death, she would have died anyway.

1.1.2 Legal Causation

The effect of applying the 'but for' test can be extremely broad in its scope and therefore potentially too harsh. The criminal law limits liability to when the defendant is not just the factual cause but also the legal cause of the consequence. Therefore the court in *R v Cheshire* [1991] 1 WLR 844 held that this would be the case if proven that the defendant's act or omission was an "operating and substantial" cause of the prohibited harm.

This will be the case if it is proved that the defendant's contribution was more than 'de minimis' (see *R v Kimsey* [1996] Crim LR 35) and there has been no break in the chain of causation. The courts have been asked to consider a number of situations which should be deemed a *novus actus interveniens*. The courts have been reluctant to do so.

1.1.3 Intervention of a Third Party

R v Pagett (1983) 76 Cr App R 279

Panel: Goff LJ, Cantley and Farquharson JJ

Facts: Police officers were trying to arrest the appellant, David Keith Pagett. Pagett armed himself with a shotgun in an attempt to evade arrest and used his 16 year old pregnant girlfriend (Gail Kinchen) as a human shield. Pagett shot at the police officers, who returned fire striking Gail Kinchen. She died. Pagett was convicted of her manslaughter. His appeal was dismissed by the Court of Appeal.

LORD JUSTICE ROBERT GOFF

The question of law relates to the direction given by the learned judge to the jury in respect of the count of murder, and the alternative count of manslaughter, of Gail Kinchen.

We turn to the first ground of appeal, which is that the learned judge erred in directing the jury that it was for him to decide *as a matter of law* whether by his unlawful and deliberate acts the appellant caused or was a cause of Gail Kinchen's death. It is right to observe that this direction of the learned judge followed upon a discussion with counsel, in the absence of the jury; though the appellant, having dismissed his own counsel, was for this purpose without legal representation. In the course of this discussion, counsel for the prosecution referred the learned judge to a passage in Professor Smith and Professor Hogan's Criminal Law (4th edn (1978), page 272), which reads as follows: "Causation is a question of both fact and law. D's act cannot be held to be the cause of an event if the event would have occurred without it. The act, that is, must be a *sine qua non* of the event and whether it is so is a question of fact. But there are many acts which are *sine qua non* of a homicide and yet are not either in law, or in ordinary parlance, the cause of it. If I invite P to dinner and he is run over and killed on the way, my invitation may be a *sine qua non* of his death, but no one would say I killed him and I have not caused his death in law. Whether a particular act which is a *sine qua non* of an alleged *actus reus* is also a cause of it is a question of law. Where the facts are admitted the judge may direct the jury that a particular act did, or did not, cause a particular result."

In cases of homicide, it is rarely necessary to give the jury any direction on causation as such. Of course, a necessary ingredient of the crimes of murder and manslaughter is that the accused has by his act caused the victim's death. But how the victim came by his death is usually not in dispute. What is in dispute is more likely to be some other matter: for example, the identity of the person who committed the act which indisputably caused the victim's death; or whether the accused had the necessary intent; or whether the accused acted in self-defence, or was provoked. Even where it is necessary to direct the jury's minds to the question of causation, it is usually enough to direct them simply that in law the accused's act need not be the sole cause, or even the main cause, of the victim's death, it being enough that his act contributed significantly to that result. It is right to observe in passing, however, that even this simple direction is a direction of law relating to causation, on the basis of which the jury are bound to act in concluding whether the prosecution has established, as a matter of fact, that the accused's act did in this sense cause the victim's death. Occasionally, however, a specific issue of causation may arise. One such case is where, although an act of the accused constitutes a causa sine qua non of (or necessary condition for) the death of the victim, nevertheless the intervention of a third person may be regarded as the sole cause of the victim's death, thereby relieving the accused of criminal responsibility. Such intervention, if it has such an effect, has often been described by lawyers as a novus actus interveniens. We are aware that this time-honoured Latin term has been the subject of criticism. We are also aware that attempts have been made to translate it into English; though no simple translation has proved satisfactory, really because the Latin term has become a term of art which conveys to lawyers the crucial feature that there has not merely been an intervening act of another person, but that that act was so independent of the act of the accused that it should be regarded in law as the cause of the victim's death, to the exclusion of the act of the accused.

 Alert

 Alert

Now the whole subject of causation in the law has been the subject of a well-known and most distinguished treatise by Professors Hart and Honorâ, *Causation in the Law.* Passages from this book were cited to the learned judge, and were plainly relied upon by him; we, too, wish to express our indebtedness to it. It would be quite wrong for us to consider in this judgment the wider issues discussed in that work. But, for present purposes, the passage which is of most immediate relevance is to be found in Chapter XII, in which the learned authors consider the circumstances in which the intervention of a third person, not acting in concert with the accused, may have the effect of relieving the accused of criminal responsibility. The criterion which they suggest should be applied in such circumstances is whether the intervention is voluntary, i.e. whether it is "free, deliberate and informed." We resist the temptation of expressing the judicial opinion whether we find ourselves in complete agreement with that definition; though we certainly consider it to be broadly correct and supported by authority. Among the examples which the authors give of non-voluntary conduct, which is not effective to relieve the accused of responsibility, are two which are germane to the present case, *viz.* a reasonable act performed for the purpose of self-preservation, and an act done in performance of a legal duty.

 Alert

There can, we consider, be no doubt that a reasonable act performed for the purpose of self-preservation, being of course itself an act caused by the accused's own act, does not operate as a novus actus interveniens. If authority is needed for this almost self-evident proposition, it is to be found in such cases as *Pitts* (1842) C. & M. 284, and *Curly* (1909) 2 Cr App R 96. In both these cases, the act performed for the purpose of self-preservation consisted of an act by the victim in attempting to escape from the

 Alert

 Link
See also Acts of Victim later in this chapter

violence of the accused, which in fact resulted in the victim's death. In each case it was held as a matter of law that, if the victim acted in a reasonable attempt to escape the violence of the accused, the death of the victim was caused by the act of the accused. Now one form of self-preservation is self-defence; for present purposes, we can see no distinction in principle between an attempt to escape the consequences of the accused's act, and a response which takes the form of self-defence.

Furthermore, in our judgment, if a reasonable act of self-defence against the act of the accused causes the death of a third party, we can see no reason in principle why the act of self-defence, being an involuntary act caused by the act of the accused, should relieve the accused from criminal responsibility for the death of the third party. Of course, it does not necessarily follow that the accused will be guilty of the murder, or even of the manslaughter, of the third party; though in the majority of cases he is likely to be guilty at least of manslaughter. Whether he is guilty of murder or manslaughter will depend upon the question whether all the ingredients of the relevant offence have been proved; in particular, on a charge of murder, it will be necessary that the accused had the necessary intent.

1.1.4 Medical Treatment

R v Cheshire [1991] 1 WLR 844

Panel: Beldam LJ, Boreham and Auld JJ

Facts: The appellant, David William Cheshire, shot a man in his thigh and stomach during an argument. Following extensive surgery the victim was transferred to intensive care where he developed respiratory problems and required the insertion of a tracheotomy tube into his windpipe. The victim continued to suffer from breathing difficulties. He was seen by several surgeons before his death who, it transpired mistakenly, diagnosed that his breathing difficulty was due to anxiety attacks. In fact a post mortem uncovered that the victim's windpipe had become blocked due to a narrowing near the tracheotomy scar (a fairly rare but not unknown condition). The appellant's appeal was dismissed by the Court of Appeal.

LORD JUSTICE BELDAM

Whilst medical treatment unsuccessfully given to prevent the death of a victim with the care and skill of a competent medical practitioner will not amount to an intervening cause, it does not follow that treatment which falls below that standard of care and skill will amount to such a cause. As Professors Hart and Honore comment, (in their work: Causation in the Law, 2nd edn (1985)) treatment which falls short of the standard expected of the competent medical practitioner is unfortunately only too frequent in human experience for it to be considered abnormal in the sense of extraordinary. Acts or omissions of a doctor treating the victim for injuries he has received at the hands of a defendant may conceivably be so extraordinary as to be capable of being regarded as acts independent of the conduct of the defendant but it is most unlikely that they will be.

We have not been referred to any English authority in which the terms of the direction which should be given to a jury in such a case have been considered. We were referred to *R v Jordan* (1956) 40 Cr App R 152 in which the appellant who had been convicted of murder sought leave to call further evidence about the cause of the victim's death. The application was granted and evidence was received by the court that the stab wound from which the victim died eight days later was not the cause of the victim's death. The deceased had died from the effects of sensitivity to Terramycin which had been given to him after his intolerance to it was established and in abnormal quantity. The court considered that the introduction into the system of the victim of a substance shown to be poisonous to him and in quantities which were so great as to result in pulmonary oedema leading to pneumonia were factors which ought to have been before the jury and which in all probability would have affected their decision.

Jordan's case was described in the later case of *R v Smith* [1959] 2 QB 35 as a very particular case dependent upon its exact facts. The appellant in *Smith* had been convicted at court-martial of the murder of another soldier by stabbing him. The victim had been dropped twice while being taken to the medical reception station and was subsequently given treatment which was said to be incorrect and harmful. Lord Parker CJ, giving the judgment of the court-martial appeal court, rejected a contention that his death did not result from the stab wound. He said, at pages 42–43:

> "It seems to the court that if at the time of death the original wound is still an operating cause and a substantial cause, then the death can properly be said to be the result of the wound, albeit that some other cause of death is also operating. Only if it can be said that the original wounding is merely the setting in which another cause operates can it be said that the death does not result from the wound. Putting it in another way, only if the second cause is so overwhelming as to make the original wound merely part of the history can it be said that the death does not flow from the wound."

Both these cases were considered by this court in *R v Malcherek* [1981] 1 WLR 690, in which it had been argued that the act of a doctor in disconnecting a life support machine had intervened to cause the death of the victim to the exclusion of injuries inflicted by the appellants. In rejecting this submission Lord Lane CJ, after considering *R v Jordan* and *R v Smith*, said:

> "In the view of this court, if a choice has to be made between the decision in *R v Jordan* and that in *R v Smith*, which we do not believe it does (*R v Jordan* being a very exceptional case), then the decision in *R v Smith* is to be preferred."

[There are] difficulties in formulating and explaining a general concept of causation but what we think does emerge from this and the other cases is that when the victim of a criminal attack is treated for wounds or injuries by doctors or other medical staff attempting to repair the harm done, it will only be in the most extraordinary and unusual case that such treatment can be said to be so independent of the acts of the defendant that it could be regarded in law as the cause of the victim's death to the exclusion of the defendant's acts.

Alert

In a case in which the jury have to consider whether negligence in the treatment of injuries inflicted by the defendant was the cause of death we think it is sufficient for the judge to tell the jury that they must be satisfied that the Crown have proved that the acts of the defendant caused the death of the deceased adding that the defendant's acts need not be the sole cause or even the main cause of death it being sufficient that his acts contributed significantly to that result. Even though negligence in the treatment of the victim was the immediate cause of his death, the jury should not regard it as excluding the responsibility of the defendant unless the negligent treatment was so independent of his acts, and in itself so potent in causing death, that they regard the contribution made by his acts as insignificant.

It is not the function of the jury to evaluate competing causes or to choose which is dominant provided they are satisfied that the defendant's acts can fairly be said to have made a significant contribution to the victim's death. We think the word "significant" conveys the necessary substance of a contribution made to the death which is more than negligible.

1.1.5 The 'Thin Skull Rule'

This principle establishes that the defendant must take his victim as he finds him. Meaning the whole victim, including his beliefs.

R v Blaue [1975] 1 WLR 1411

Panel: Lawton LJ, Thompson and Shaw JJ

Facts: The defendant, Ronald Konrad Blaue, attacked and stabbed the victim after she refused to have sexual intercourse with him. Due to the extensive nature of the injuries, the surgeon directed that the victim required a blood transfusion. The victim was a practising Jehovah Witness and therefore declined the transfusion as this was contrary to her religious beliefs. As a result the victim died. The defendant was convicted of manslaughter. The Court of Appeal dismissed the defendant's appeal against conviction.

LORD JUSTICE LAWTON

...Counsel then appearing for the defendant invited the judge to direct the jury to acquit the defendant generally on the count of murder. His argument was that her refusal to have a blood transfusion had broken the chain of causation between the stabbing and her death. As an alternative he submitted that the jury should be left to decide whether the chain of causation had been broken. Counsel for the prosecution submitted that the judge should direct the jury to convict, because no facts were in issue and when the law was applied to the facts there was only one possible verdict, namely, manslaughter by reason of diminished responsibility.

When the judge came to direct the jury on this issue he did so by telling them that they should apply their common sense. He then went on to tell them they would get some help from the cases to which counsel had referred in their speeches, *R v Smith* [1959] 2 QB 35 and *R v Holland* (1841) 2 Mood & R 351. ...

In *R v Holland*, the defendant in the course of a violent assault, had injured one of his victim's fingers. A surgeon had advised amputation because of the danger to life through complications developing. The advice was rejected. A fortnight later the victim died of lockjaw. Maule J. said, at page 352: "the real question is, whether in the end the wound inflicted by the prisoner was the cause of death." That distinguished judge left the jury to decide that question as did the judge in this case. They had to decide it as juries always do, by pooling their experience of life and using their common sense. They would not have been handicapped by a lack of training in dialectic or moral theology.

The physical cause of death in this case was the bleeding into the pleural cavity arising from the penetration of the lung. This had not been brought about by any decision made by the deceased but by the stab wound.

 Alert

Counsel for the defendant tried to overcome this line of reasoning by submitting that the jury should have been directed that if they thought the deceased's decision not to have a blood transfusion was an unreasonable one, then the chain of causation would have been broken. At once the question arises — reasonable by whose standards? Those of Jehovah's Witnesses? Humanists? Roman Catholics? Protestants of Anglo-Saxon descent? The man on the Clapham omnibus? But he might well be an admirer of Eleazar who suffered death rather than eat the flesh of swine (2 Maccabees, ch 6, vv 18–31) or of Sir Thomas More who, unlike nearly all his contemporaries, was unwilling to accept Henry VIII as Head of the Church in England. Those brought up in the Hebraic and Christian traditions would probably be reluctant to accept that these martyrs caused their own deaths.

As was pointed out to counsel for the defendant in the course of argument, two cases, each raising the same issue of reasonableness because of religious beliefs, could produce different verdicts depending on where the cases were tried. A jury drawn from Preston, sometimes said to be the most Catholic town in England, might have different views about martyrdom to one drawn from the inner suburbs of London. Counsel for the defendant accepted that this might be so: it was, he said, inherent in trial by jury. It is not inherent in the common law as expounded by Sir Matthew Hale and Maule J. It has long been the policy of the law that those who use violence on other people must take their victims as they find them. This in our judgment means the whole man, not just the physical man. It does not lie in the mouth of the assailant to say that his victim's religious beliefs which inhibited him from accepting certain kinds of treatment were unreasonable. The question for decision is what caused her death. The answer is the stab wound. The fact that the victim refused to stop this end coming about did not break the casual connection between the act and death.

 Alert

See also the cases of *R v Hayward* (1908) 21 Cox CC 692 and *R v McKechnie* (1992) 94 Cr App R 51.

1.1.6 Acts of the Victim: Escape Cases

R v Roberts (1972) 56 Cr App R 95

Panel: Stephenson LJ, Thompson and Bridge JJ

Facts: The victim had accepted a lift from the appellant, Kenneth Joseph Roberts. As they were driving the appellant grabbed the victim and tried to assault her. The victim escaped the attack by jumping out of the moving car, sustaining injury. The appellant was convicted of assault occasioning actual bodily harm. The Court of Appeal dismissed his appeal.

LORD JUSTICE STEPHENSON

[The argument] Counsel for the appellant has pursued before us is that the Chairman was wrong in law when he told the jury "if you are satisfied that he tried to pull off her coat and as a result she jumped out of the moving car, then your verdict is Guilty." He failed to tell the jury that they must be satisfied that the cause of her injuries was the action of the appellant, and not the fact that she was under the influence of alcohol, or any other reason. Then he goes on to submit that the learned Chairman was wrong in failing to tell the jury that they must be satisfied that the appellant foresaw that she might jump out as a result of his touching her, before they convicted.

We have been helpfully referred to a number of reported cases, some well over a century old, of women jumping out of windows, or jumping or throwing themselves into a river, as a consequence of threats of violence or actual violence. The most recent case is the case of Lewis [1970] Crim LR 647. An earlier case is that of Beech (1912) 7 Cr App R 197, which was a case of a woman jumping out of a window and injuring herself, and of a man who had friendly relations with her, whom she knew and might have had reason to be afraid of, being prosecuted for inflicting grievous bodily harm upon her, contrary to section 20 of the Offences against the Person Act. In that case the Court of Criminal Appeal (at page 200) approved the direction given by the trial judge in these terms: "Will you say whether the conduct of the prisoner amounted to a threat of causing injury to this young woman, was the act of jumping the natural consequence of the conduct of the prisoner, and was the grievous bodily harm the result of the conduct of the prisoner?" That, said the Court, was a proper direction as far as the law went, and they were satisfied that there was evidence before the jury of the prisoner causing actual bodily harm to the woman. "No-one could say," said Darling J. when giving the judgment of the Court, "that if she jumped from the window it was not a natural consequence of the prisoner's conduct. It was a very likely thing for a woman to do as the result of the threats of a man who was conducting himself as this man indisputably was."

This Court thinks that that correctly states the law, and that counsel for the appellant was wrong in submitting to this Court that the jury must be sure that a defendant, who is charged either with inflicting grievous bodily harm or assault occasioning actual bodily harm, must foresee the actions of the victim which result in the grievous bodily harm, or the actual bodily harm. That, in the view of this Court, is not the test. The test is: Was it the natural result of what the alleged assailant said and did, in the sense that it was something that could reasonably have been foreseen as the consequence of what he was saying or doing? As it was put in one of the old cases, it had got to be shown to be his act, and if of course the victim does something so "daft," in the words of the appellant in this case, or so unexpected, not that this particular assailant did not actually foresee it but that no reasonable man could be expected to foresee it, then it is only in a very remote and unreal sense a consequence of his assault, it is really occasioned by a voluntary act on the part of the victim which could not reasonably be foreseen and which breaks the chain of causation between the assault and the harm or injury.

 Alert

This test was subsequently approved and added to in the following case.

R v Williams & Davis [1992] 1 WLR 380

Panel: Stuart-Smith LJ, Waterhouse and Morland JJ

Facts: The victim, who was hitch-hiking to Glastonbury music festival, accepted a lift from the appellants, Barry Anthony Williams and Frank O'Neil Davis. It was alleged that the appellants tried to rob the victim, who jumped from the moving car and died from the resultant head injury.

LORD JUSTICE STUART-SMITH

The necessary causal link can be traced through the old cases and also the judgments of Stephenson L.J. in *R v Roberts* (1971) 56 Cr App R 95 and *R v Mackie* (1973) 57 Cr App R 453.

The jury should consider two questions: first, whether it was reasonably foreseeable that some harm, albeit not serious harm, was likely to result from the threat itself; and, secondly, whether the deceased's reaction in jumping from the moving car was within the range of responses which might be expected from a victim placed in the situation which he was. The jury should bear in mind any particular characteristic of the victim and the fact that in the agony of the moment he may act without thought and deliberation.

 Link

See also The Thin Skull Rule

1.1.7 Acts of the Victim: Refusal of Medical Treatment

R v Dear [1996] Crim LR 595

Panel: Rose LJ, Hidden and Buxton JJ

Facts: The appellant, Dear, and the victim were drinking companions. Dear's young daughter alleged that the victim had sexually assaulted her and told her father this. Dear slashed the victim with a knife cutting him severely. Two days later the victim died as a result of the wounds inflicted. The appellant argued that the chain of causation had been broken between his act of inflicting the wounds and the victim's death because the victim had committed suicide. It was alleged he had done so either by reopening the wounds or, if the wounds had reopened themselves by failing to staunch the blood flow from the wounds after they had reopened. (The evidence was not particularly clear on this point.) Dear thus asserted that the victim had caused his own death and that he was not the cause of death.

LORD JUSTICE ROSE

The case on causation advanced by the defence was, as we have indicated, that the deceased had or may have committed suicide by deliberately reopening his wounds or failing to tend them when they had reopened, and that he may have done so for a reason unconnected with the defendant's conduct, in particular, shame at his own behaviour in relation to the girl.

In our judgment the principal question raised by this appeal can be clearly answered by reference to four decisions of this Court and one textbook. ... [Lord Justice Rose set out *R v Smith* and continued]

In *Blaue*, at page 1415G, Lawton LJ said - and we have already referred to this passage but it bears repeating:

> "It does not lie in the mouth of the assailant to say that his victim's religious beliefs which inhibited him from accepting certain kinds of treatment were unreasonable. The question for decision is what caused the death. The answer is the stab wound."

In *R v Malcherek* [1981] 2 All ER 422, [1981] 1 WLR 690 the defendant inflicted serious brain damage. The victim required a life support machine which the doctors, several days later, turned off and death followed. The trial judge withdrew causation from the jury and an appeal on the ground that the doctors caused the death was dismissed. It was held that the injury inflicted by the defendant was an operating and substantial cause of death and it was immaterial whether or not the doctors also caused the death. Lord Lane CJ said at page 696H:

> "There may be occasions, although they will be rare, where the original injury has ceased to operate as a cause at all, but in the ordinary case if the treatment is given bona fide by competent and careful medical practitioners, then evidence will not be admissible to show that the treatment would not have been administered in the same way by other medical practitioners. In other words, the fact that the victim has died, despite or because of medical treatment for the initial injury given by careful and skilled medical practitioners, will not exonerate the original assailant from responsibility for the death."

In *Cheshire* (1991) 93 Cr App Rep 251, to which we have already referred, the defendant shot a man who died two months later in hospital from a rare complication due to medical negligence. This Court held that it is not for the jury to evaluate competing causes of death provided that they are satisfied that the accused's action contributed significantly to death: see the judgment of Beldam LJ page 258.

At page 342 of the Seventh Edition of Criminal Law by Smith & Hogan, after a review of the relevant authorities in relation to death caused by medical treatment, the authors conclude as follows:

"...the following propositions at present represent the law.

(i) Medical evidence is admissible to show that the medical treatment of a wound was the cause of death and that the wound itself was not. This is so whether or not the wound is mortal.

(ii) If a wound was an operating and substantial cause of death, the defendant is guilty of homicide, however badly the wound was treated. (3) If a wound was not an operating and substantial case of death (ie, it was effectively healed) but the victim was killed by, eg, the inadvertent admission of deadly poison by a nurse, the wrongful administration of terremycin, or the ill-treatment of a tracheotomy, the defendant may or may not be guilty of homicide."

With that passage we agree.

At the top of page 343 the learned authors in discussing "The Effect of Neglect by the Injured Person" say this:

"The common law rule is that neglect or maltreatment by the injured person of himself does not exempt the defendant from liability for his ultimate death."

With that also we agree.

The real question in this case, as in Smith, Blaue and Malcherek, was, as the judge correctly directed the jury, whether the injuries inflicted by the defendant were an operating and significant cause of the death. It is immaterial whether some other cause was also operating.

 Alert

The correct approach in the criminal law is that enunciated in Smith and the other authorities to which we have referred: were the injuries inflicted by the defendant an operating and significant cause of death? That question, in our judgment, is necessarily answered, not by philosophical analysis, but by common sense according to all the circumstances of the particular case.

In the present case the cause of the deceased's death was bleeding from the artery which the defendant had severed. Whether or not the resumption or continuation of that bleeding was deliberately caused by the deceased, the jury were entitled to find that the defendant's conduct made an operative and significant contribution to the death.

1.1.8 Acts of the Victim: Drug Administration

The question of whether following the defendant's supply of drugs, the victim's self administration of the drugs can break the chain of causation has long vexed the courts. The matter has now finally been resolved.

R v Kennedy (No 2) [2008] 1 AC 269

Panel: Lord Bingham of Cornhill, Lord Rodger of Earlsferry, Baroness Hale of Rochmond, Lord Carswell and Lord Mance

Facts: The appellant prepared a heroin fix for the victim. The appellant then handed the syringe over to the victim who injected himself. The victim then stopped breathing and subsequently died. The defendant was convicted of manslaughter. Initially the Court of Appeal upheld this conviction, but the case was subsequently referred back to the Court of Appeal by the Criminal Case Review Commission and eventually reached the House of Lords.

LORD BINGHAM OF CORNHILL

The question certified by the Court of Appeal (Criminal Division) for the opinion of the House neatly encapsulates the question raised by this appeal:

> "When is it appropriate to find someone guilty of manslaughter where that person has been involved in the supply of a class A controlled drug, which is then freely and voluntarily self-administered by the person to whom it was supplied, and the administration of the drug then causes his death?"

To establish the crime of unlawful act manslaughter it must be shown, among other things not relevant to this appeal: (1) that the defendant committed an unlawful act; (2) that such unlawful act was a crime (R v Franklin (1883) 15 Cox CC 163; R v Lamb [1967] 2 QB 981; R v Dias [2002] 2 Cr App R 96, para 9); and (3) that the defendant's unlawful act was a significant cause of the death of the deceased: R v Cato [1976] 1 WLR 110, 116–117. There is now, as already noted, no doubt but that the appellant committed an unlawful (and criminal) act by supplying the heroin to the deceased. But the act of supplying, without more, could not harm the deceased in any physical way, let alone cause his death. As the Court of Appeal observed in R v Dalby [1982] 1 WLR 425, "the supply of drugs would itself have caused no harm unless the deceased had subsequently used the drugs in a form and quantity which was dangerous". So, as the parties agree, the charge of unlawful act manslaughter cannot be founded on the act of supplying the heroin alone.

The parties are further agreed that an unlawful act of the appellant on the present facts must be found, if at all, in a breach of s 23 of the Offences against the Persons Act 1861.

The criminal law generally assumes the existence of free will. The law recognises certain exceptions, in the case of the young, those who for any reason are not fully responsible for their actions, and the vulnerable, and it acknowledges situations of duress and necessity, as also of deception and mistake. But, generally speaking, informed adults of sound mind are treated as autonomous beings able to make their own decisions how they will act, and none of the exceptions is relied on as possibly applicable in this case. Thus D is not to be treated as causing V to act in a certain way if V makes a voluntary and informed decision to act in that way rather than another.

There are many classic statements to this effect. In his article "Finis for Novus Actus?" [1989] CLJ 391, Professor Glanville Williams wrote:

> "I may suggest reasons to you for doing something; I may urge you to do it, tell you it will pay you to do it, tell you it is your duty to do it. My efforts may perhaps make it very much more likely that you will do it. But they do not cause you to do it, in the sense in which one causes a kettle of water to boil by putting it on the stove. Your volitional act is regarded (within the doctrine of responsibility) as setting a new 'chain of causation' going, irrespective of what has happened before."

In chapter XII of *Causation in the Law*, 2nd edn (1985), page 326, Hart & Honoré wrote:

> "The free, deliberate, and informed intervention of a second person, who intends to exploit the situation created by the first, but is not acting in concert with him, is normally held to relieve the first actor of criminal responsibility."

This statement was cited by the House with approval in *R v Latif* [1996] 1 WLR 104. The principle is fundamental and not controversial.

The answer to the certified question is: "In the case of a fully-informed and responsible adult, never." The appeal must be allowed and the appellant's conviction for manslaughter quashed. The appellant must have his costs, here and below, out of central funds.

 Alert

Much of the difficulty and doubt which have dogged the present question has flowed from a failure, at the outset, to identify the unlawful act on which the manslaughter count is founded. It matters little whether the act is identified by a separate count or counts under s 23, or by particularisation of the manslaughter count itself. But it would focus attention on the correct question, and promote accurate analysis of the real issues, if those who formulate, defend and rule on serious charges of this kind were obliged to consider how exactly, in law, the accusation is put.

1.1.9 Which test do you use?

The Court of Appeal made it clear in the recent case of **R v Girdler**, that it is the specific facts of the case, which will dictate which test is to be used to determine legal causation.

R v Girdler [2009] EWCA Crim 2666

Panel: Hooper LJ, Langstaff and Williams JJ

Facts: The appellant, Dean Girdler, was driving along a stretch of the A3, which consisted of four lanes, when he collided with a black taxi cab. As a result of the collision, the black taxi was shunted sideways into the fast lane. Some ongoing cars managed to avoid colliding with the black taxi, however one car did hit the taxi. Both drivers died. The appellant was convicted of causing death by dangerous driving of the driver of the black taxi, (the jury were unable to reach a verdict for the death of the driver of the second car). The issue before the Court of Appeal was whether the appellant, by the initial impact, could be held to be the legal cause of the second collision and subsequent deaths.

LORD JUSTICE HOOPER

29. Although there was in the present case an issue about the taxi driver's rear lights, the important issue concerned the conduct of a third party, Catherine Cunningham whose collision with the taxi was the immediate cause of the taxi driver's death.

30. What, in our view, the jury needed in this case was a simple test to decide whether the driving of Catherine Cunningham was, as the defendant contended, such a new and intervening act that it could not be said that the appellant caused either the death of the taxi driver or her death.

31. In Pagett (1983) 76 Cr App R 279 the Court approved the following passage from Hart and Honoré, Causation in the Law (2nd edn, 1985), Chapter 12, Criminal Law: Causing Harm at page 326:

The free deliberate and informed intervention of a second person, who intends to exploit the situation created by the first, but is not acting in concert with him, is normally held to relieve the first actor of criminal responsibility.

32. Examples of new and intervening acts may be found in Kennedy [2007] UKHL 38; [2008] 1 AC 269; [2008] 1 Cr App R 19 and in Rafferty [2007] EWCA Crim 1846 (neither of which were cited in argument before us).

33. Lord Bingham giving the considered opinion of the appeal committee that the appellant was not guilty of manslaughter said:

14. The criminal law generally assumes the existence of free will. The law recognises certain exceptions, in the case of the young, those who for any reason are not fully responsible for their actions, and the vulnerable, and it acknowledges situations of duress and necessity, as also of deception and mistake. But, generally speaking, informed adults of sound mind are treated as autonomous beings able to make their own decisions how they will act, and none of the exceptions is relied on as possibly applicable in this case. Thus D is not to be treated as causing V to act in a certain way if V makes a voluntary and informed decision to act in that way rather than another.

15. Questions of causation frequently arise in many areas of the law, but causation is not a single, unvarying concept to be mechanically applied without regard to the context in which the question arises. That was the point which Lord Hoffmann, with the express concurrence of three other members of the House, was at pains to make in *Environment Agency (formerly National Rivers Authority) v Empress Car Co (Abertillery) Ltd* [1999] 2 AC 22. The House was not in that decision purporting to lay down general rules governing causation in criminal law. It was construing, with reference to the facts of the case before it, a statutory provision

 Alert

imposing strict criminal liability on those who cause pollution of controlled waters. Lord Hoffmann made clear that (p 29E-F) common sense answers to questions of causation will differ according to the purpose for which the question is asked; that (p 31E) one cannot give a common sense answer to a question of causation for the purpose of attributing responsibility under some rule without knowing the purpose and scope of the rule; that (p 32B) strict liability was imposed in the interests of protecting controlled waters; and that (p 36A) in the situation under consideration the act of the defendant could properly be held to have caused the pollution even though an ordinary act of a third party was the immediate cause of the diesel oil flowing into the river. It is worth underlining that the relevant question was the cause of the pollution, not the cause of the third party's act.

16. The committee would not wish to throw any doubt on the correctness of Empress Car. But the reasoning in that case cannot be applied to the wholly different context of causing a noxious thing to be administered to or taken by another person contrary to section 23 of the 1861 Act. In *R v Finlay* [2003] EWCA Crim 3868 (8 December 2003) V was injected with heroin and died. D was tried on two counts of manslaughter, one on the basis that he had himself injected V, the second on the basis that he had prepared a syringe and handed it to V who had injected herself. The jury could not agree on the first count but convicted on the second. When rejecting an application to remove the second count from the indictment, the trial judge ruled, relying on Empress Car, that D had produced a situation in which V could inject herself, in which her self-injection was entirely foreseeable and in which self-injection could not be regarded as something extraordinary. He directed the jury along those lines. The Court of Appeal upheld the judge's analysis and dismissed the appeal. It was wrong to do so. Its decision conflicted with the rules on personal autonomy and informed voluntary choice to which reference has been made above. In the decision under appeal the Court of Appeal did not follow *R v Finlay* in seeking to apply Empress Car, and it was right not to do so.

34. Applying Kennedy, if the immediate cause of the death is the "free, deliberate, and informed" intervention of another person, then the chain of causation will be broken. There are, it seems to us, problems in applying that test in this case. Miss Cunningham's driving which led to the collision with the taxi driver cannot readily be described as falling within that category even if her driving was careless or dangerous (and we are not saying that it was).

35. If the only test were to be the "free, deliberate, and informed" test, then a driver who by his dangerous driving causes a minor accident pushing another car on to the hard shoulder would be automatically be liable for causing death by dangerous driving if the driver of a vehicle travelling at speed on the hard shoulder accidentally collided with the car on the hard shoulder whatever the circumstances, provided the jury took the view that the "more than a trifling link" test was satisfied. In our view juries needed a tailored direction to help them decide, in the appropriate case, whether there has been a new and intervening act or event.

36. In devising such a test we remind ourselves that the offences of causing death by dangerous and careless driving will punish the conduct of a person who has not intended or necessarily foreseen the consequences of his driving. Such a person is in a very different position to a person who has intended to kill or cause serious bodily harm or who has the *mens rea* for manslaughter. As Lord Hoffman said in the Empress Car case (page 29 F and 31E):

   …common sense answers to questions of causation will differ according to the purpose for which the question is asked. Questions of causation often arise for the purpose of attributing responsibility to someone, for example, so as to blame him for something which has happened.

   …one cannot give a common sense answer to a question of causation for the purpose of attributing responsibility under some rule without knowing the purpose and scope of the rule.

37. What we need is a form of words which sets out a test (comparatively easy to apply) which places an outside limit on the culpability of a driver in circumstances where there is more than a trifling link between the dangerous (or careless) driving and a death. It seeks to exclude consequences which are simply "too remote" from the driver's culpable conduct.

 Alert

38. Help in devising such a test comes from the passage in Smith and Hogan to which we have made reference. In paragraphs 4.5.6 and 4.5.6.1 (at pages 78–79) the author states that a person will not have caused something to have happened if a natural event which is not reasonably foreseeable was the immediate cause of the event. The test receives support from Clause 17(2)(c) of the Draft Criminal Code for England and Wales Law Comm. No 177 (1989). It also has similarities to the test to be applied when the defendant's unlawful and violent acts are said to have caused another person to suffer injuries in the course of escaping from those acts, see *R v Williams* (1992) 95 Cr App R 1.

 Alert

42. In practice we do not think that there is much difference in cases like the present between a reasonable foreseeability test and the test propounded by Lord Hoffmann but, on balance, we prefer the objective test of reasonable foreseeability in a case like the present where the defendant's case is that there was a new and supervening act or event. We bear in mind that Lord Bingham, in Kennedy, said in the passage which we have already set out in full (paragraph 33 above) that:

   The House was not in that decision purporting to lay down general rules governing causation in criminal law.

43. We are of the view that the words "reasonably foreseeable" whilst apt to describe for a lawyer the appropriate test, may need to be reworded to ease the task of a jury. We suggest that a jury could be told, in circumstances like the present where the immediate cause of death is a second collision, that if they were sure that the defendant drove dangerously and were sure that his dangerous driving was more than a slight or trifling link to the death(s) then:

the defendant will have caused the death(s) only if you are sure that it could sensibly have been anticipated that a fatal collision might occur in the circumstances in which the second collision did occur.

The judge should identify the relevant circumstances and remind the jury of the prosecution and defence cases. If it is thought necessary it could be made clear to the jury that they are not concerned with what the defendant foresaw.

1.2 Omissions

Although the law usually only imposes criminal liability on those who complete a prohibited positive act, there are instances where a person can be liable for failing to act when under a legal duty to do so.

Legal duties to act can exist in statute. However, they can also exist at common law. What follows are examples of when a duty to act has been held to arise at common law.

1.2.1 Voluntary Assumption of a Duty of Care

R v Stone; R v Dobinson [1977] QB 354

Panel: Geoffrey Lane LJ, Nield and Croom-Johnson JJ

Facts: The victim, Fanny Stone, went to live with the appellants, John Edward Stone (the victim's brother) and Gwendoline Dobinson (John Stone's partner). Both appellants suffered from learning and other physical disabilities. The victim suffered from anorexia nervosa. She would often decline to eat and stayed in her rooms for days. Eventually her condition deteriorated to the point where she was confined to her bed. The appellants failed to secure medical assistance even when asked to do so by neighbours. The appellants were convicted of gross negligence manslaughter. Their appeals were dismissed by the Court of Appeal.

LORD JUSTICE GEOFFREY LANE

There is no dispute, broadly speaking, as to the matters on which the jury must be satisfied before they can convict of manslaughter in circumstances such as the present. They are (1) that the defendant undertook the care of a person who by reason of age or infirmity was unable to care for himself; (2) that the defendant was grossly negligent in regard to his duty of care; (3) that by reason of such negligence the person died. It is submitted on behalf of the appellants that the judge's direction to the jury with regard to the first two items was incorrect.

At the close of the prosecution case submissions were made to the judge that there was no, or no sufficient evidence that the appellants, or either of them, had chosen to undertake the care of Fanny.

That contention was advanced by Mr Coles before this court as his first ground of appeal. He amplified the ground somewhat by submitting that the evidence which the judge had suggested to the jury might support the assumption of a duty by the appellants does not, when examined, succeed in doing so. He suggests that the situation here is unlike any reported case. Fanny came to this house as a lodger. Largely, if not entirely due to her own eccentricity and failure to look after herself or feed herself properly, she became increasingly infirm and immobile and eventually unable to look after herself. Is it to be said, asks Mr Coles rhetorically, that by the mere fact of becoming infirm and helpless in these circumstances she casts a duty on her brother and the appellant Dobinson to take steps to have her looked after or taken to hospital? The suggestion is that, heartless though it may seem, this is one of those situations where the appellants were entitled to do nothing; where no duty was cast upon them to help, any more than it is cast upon a man to rescue a stranger from drowning, however easy such a rescue might be.

This court rejects that proposition. Whether Fanny was a lodger or not she was a blood relation of the appellant Stone; she was occupying a room in his house; the appellant Dobinson had undertaken the duty of trying to wash her, of taking such food to her as she required. There was ample evidence that each appellant was aware of the poor condition she was in by mid-July. It was not disputed that no effort was made to summon an ambulance or the social services or the police despite the entreaties of Mrs Wilson and Mrs West. A social worker used to visit Cyril. No word was spoken to him. All these were matters which the jury were entitled to take into account when considering whether the necessary assumption of a duty to care for Fanny had been proved.

Alert

This was not a situation analogous to the drowning stranger. They did make efforts to care. They tried to get a doctor; they tried to discover the previous doctor. The appellant Dobinson helped with the washing and the provision of food. All these matters were put before the jury in terms which we find it impossible to fault. The jury were entitled to find that the duty had been assumed. They were entitled to conclude that once Fanny became helplessly infirm, as she had by July 19, the appellants were, in the circumstances, obliged either to summon help or else to care for Fanny themselves.

R v Gibbins & Proctor (1919) 13 Cr App R 134

Panel: Darling, McCardie and Salter JJ

Facts: The appellants, Walter Gibbins and Edith Rose Proctor were lovers. Gibbins and his daughter, Nelly Gibbins (the victim) moved in to live with Proctor and her children. Gibbins worked and provided Proctor with sufficient money to take care of the whole family. This Proctor did with the exception of Nelly whom she had taken a dislike. Proctor kept Nelly in a room upstairs, away from the others where she was neglected. Nelly subsequently died of starvation. The appellants were convicted of her murder. The Court of Appeal dismissed their appeals.

MR JUSTICE DARLING

But the misdirection here complained of is on a crucial matter, where he told the jury what they must find in order to convict either prisoner of murder.

There remains the question whether the judge misdirected the jury on a point of law. Had he done so on a really material point we should quash the conviction, unless it came within the proviso to s 4(1). But the misdirection here complained of is on a crucial matter, where he told the jury what they must find in order to convict either prisoner of murder. He said, "The charge against the prisoners is, in the first place, that they killed this child Nelly, or caused her death, by malice aforethought. That means they intended she should die and acted so as to produce that result." If that is a misdirection it is one in favour of the prisoners. "In dealing with that you will of course remember, and it is my duty to tell you, that very rarely will people say when they do such a thing that they intended to produce such a result. Sometimes they do say that they killed a person and intended to do so, but rarely, and as a rule you have to judge of persons' intentions from their acts, they being reasonable persons, and there is no suggestion here at all that either of these prisoners was in any way insane, being reasonable persons you have to deal with, you must judge of them as understanding the nature of the act they are doing, and if you think that one or other of those prisoners wilfully and intentionally withheld food from that child so as to cause her to weaken and to cause her grievous bodily injury, as the result of which she died, it is not necessary for you to find that she intended or he intended to kill the child then and there. It is enough if you find that he or she intended to set up such a set of facts by withholding food or anything as would in the ordinary course of nature lead gradually but surely to her death." In our opinion that direction simply fulfils the conditions which a judge should observe in directing the jury in such a case as this.

The case of Proctor is plainer. She had charge of the child. She was under no obligation to do so or to live with Gibbins, but she did so, and receiving money, as it is admitted she did, for the purpose of supplying food, her duty was to see that the child was properly fed and looked after, and to see that she had medical attention if necessary. We agree with what Lord Coleridge CJ said in *Instan* above: "There is no case directly in point, but it would be a slur upon, and a discredit to the administration of, justice in this country if there were any doubt as to the legal principle, or as to the present case being within it. The prisoner was under a moral obligation to the deceased from which arose a legal duty towards her; that legal duty the prisoner has wilfully and deliberately left unperformed, with the consequence that there has been an acceleration of the death of the deceased owing to the non-performance of that legal duty." Here Proctor took upon herself the moral obligation of looking after the children; she was *de facto*, though not *de jure*, the wife of Gibbins and had excluded the child's own mother. She neglected the child undoubtedly, and the evidence shows that as a result the child died. So a verdict of manslaughter at least was inevitable.

 Alert

 Alert

See also *R v Instan* [1893] 1 QB 450, *R v Ruffell* [2003] 2 Cr App R (S) 53 and *R v Nicholls* (1874) 13 Cox CC75. It can be seen from these cases that the basis on which the courts have held that such a legal duty exists is not always clear.

1.2.2 Creating a Dangerous Situation

R v Miller [1983] 2 AC 161

Panel: Lord Diplock, Lord Keith of Kinkel, Lord Bridge of Harwich, Lord Brandon of Oakbrook and Lord Brightman

Facts: James Miller, the defendant, was living in an unoccupied house. One night he lit a cigarette and then lay down on a mattress. However, he fell asleep before he had finished the cigarette and awoke to find the mattress smouldering. Miller did nothing to extinguish the fire. Rather he moved to another room and fell asleep. The house caught fire. Miller was convicted of arson. His appeal was dismissed by the Court of Appeal but he was given leave to appeal to the House of Lords who certified the following question of law:

"Whether the actus reus of the offence of arson is present when a defendant accidentally starts a fire and thereafter, intending to destroy or damage property belonging to another or being reckless as to whether any such property will be destroyed or damaged, fails to take any steps to extinguish the fire or prevent damage to such property by that fire?"

LORD DIPLOCK

The first question is a pure question of causation; it is one of fact to be decided by the jury in a trial upon indictment. It should be answered "No" if, in relation to the fire during the period starting immediately before its ignition and ending with its extinction, the role of the accused was at no time more than that of a passive bystander. In such a case the subsequent questions to which I shall be turning would not arise. The conduct of the parabolical priest and Levite on the road to Jericho may have been indeed deplorable, but English law has not so far developed to the stage of treating it as criminal; and if it ever were to do so there would be difficulties in defining what should be the limits of the offence.

If on the other hand the question, which I now confine to: "Did a physical act of the accused start the fire which spread and damaged property belonging to another?" is answered "Yes," as it was by the jury in the instant case, then for the purpose of the further questions the answers to which are determinative of his guilt of the offence of arson, the conduct of the accused, throughout the period from immediately before the moment of ignition to the completion of the damage to the property by the fire, is relevant; so is his state of mind throughout that period.

Since arson is a result-crime the period may be considerable, and during it the conduct of the accused that is causative of the result may consist not only of his doing physical acts which cause the fire to start or spread but also of his failing to take measures that lie within his power to counteract the danger that he has himself created. and if his conduct, active or passive, varies in the course of the period, so may his state of mind at the time of each piece of conduct. If at the time of any particular piece of conduct by the accused that is causative of the result, the state of mind that actuates his conduct falls within the description of one or other of the states of mind that are made a

Link

See Causation earlier in this chapter

necessary ingredient of the offence of arson by s 1(1) of the Criminal Damage Act 1971 (i.e. intending to damage property belonging to another or being reckless as to whether such property would be damaged). I know of no principle of English criminal law that would prevent his being guilty of the offence created by that subsection. Likewise I see no rational ground for excluding from conduct capable of giving rise to criminal liability, conduct which consists of failing to take measures that lie within one's power to counteract a danger that one has oneself created, if at the time of such conduct one's state of mind is such as constitutes a necessary ingredient of the offence. I venture to think that the habit of lawyers to talk of "actus reus," suggestive as it is of action rather than inaction, is responsible for any erroneous notion that failure to act cannot give rise to criminal liability in English law.

Alert

No one has been bold enough to suggest that if, in the instant case, the accused had been aware at the time that he dropped the cigarette that it would probably set fire to his mattress and yet had taken no steps to extinguish it he would not have been guilty of the offence of arson, since he would have damaged property of another being reckless as to whether any such property would be damaged.

I cannot see any good reason why, so far as liability under criminal law is concerned, it should matter at what point of time before the resultant damage is complete a person becomes aware that he has done a physical act which, whether or not he appreciated that it would at the time when he did it, does in fact create a risk that property of another will be damaged; provided that, at the moment of awareness, it lies within his power to take steps, either himself or by calling for the assistance of the fire brigade if this be necessary, to prevent or minimise the damage to the property at risk.

Generally it is accepted that it is right to impose criminal liability for failing to act when obliged to do so. The scope of such obligations remains a matter for debate.

Further Reading

Ashworth A 'The scope of Criminal Liability for Omissions' (1989) 105 *LQR* 424

Hart H and Honore T 'Causation in the Law' (2nd edition, 1985) Oxford University Press

Williams G 'Criminal Omissions - The Conventional View' (1991) 107 *LQR* 86

2

General Principles of Criminal Law: Mens Rea

Topic List

2.1 Intention

Intention is the *mens rea* term which covers the most culpable state of mind. It is the mental element required for many crimes, including murder and an offence under the Offences Against the Person Act 1861 s 18 and attempts to commit these substantive offences.

2.1.1 The Basic Meaning of Intention

The dictionary definition of intention is purpose or aim. In criminal law this is referred to as direct intent and is the meaning employed in the majority of situations. In most circumstances the judge should tell the jury to give the word its ordinary meaning. However, the judge may explain that this meaning differs from 'motive' or 'desire'.

R v Moloney [1985] AC 105

Panel: Lord Hailsham of St. Marylebone LC, Lord Fraser of Tullybelton, Lord Edmund-Davies, Lord Keith of Kinkel and Lord Bridge of Harwich

Facts: The appellant (Moloney) and the victim, his step father, were both drunk and had been competing to see who could load and draw a shot gun faster. The appellant shot and killed the victim and was convicted of murder. He appealed on the basis that the trial judge had given an incorrect definition of intention. The appeal was dismissed by the Court of Appeal, but allowed by the House of Lords.

LORD BRIDGE OF HARWICH

The golden rule should be that, when directing a jury on the mental element necessary in a crime of specific intent, the judge should avoid any elaboration or paraphrase of what is meant by intent, and leave it to the jury's good sense to decide whether the accused acted with the necessary intent, unless the judge is convinced that, on the facts and having regard to the way the case has been presented to the jury in evidence and argument, some further explanation or elaboration is strictly necessary to avoid misunderstanding. In trials for murder or wounding with intent, I find it very difficult to visualise a case where any such explanation or elaboration could be required, if the offence consisted of a direct attack on the victim with a weapon, except possibly the case where the accused shot at A and killed B, which any first year law student could explain to a jury in the simplest of terms. Even where the death results indirectly from the act of the accused, I believe the cases that will call for a direction by reference to foresight of consequences will be of extremely rare occurrence. I am in full agreement with the view expressed by Viscount Dilhorne that, in *Reg. v Hyam* [1975] AC 55, 82 itself, if the issue of intent had been left without elaboration, no reasonable jury could have failed to convict. I find it difficult to understand why the prosecution did not seek to support the conviction, as an alternative to their main submission, on the ground that there had been no actual miscarriage of justice.

I do not, of course, by what I have said in the foregoing paragraph, mean to question the necessity, which frequently arises, to explain to a jury that intention is something quite distinct from motive or desire. But this can normally be quite simply explained by reference to the case before the court or, if necessary, by some homely example. A man who at London Airport, boards a plane which he knows to be bound for Manchester, clearly intends to travel to Manchester, even though Manchester is the last place he wants to be and his motive for boarding the plane is simply to escape pursuit. The possibility that the plane may have engine trouble and be diverted to Luton does not affect the matter. By boarding the Manchester plane, the man conclusively demonstrates his intention to go there, because it is a moral certainty that that is where he will arrive.

2.1.2 The Wider Meaning of Intention

It has been recognised that intention can mean something more than aim and purpose. This wider meaning is often referred to as 'oblique intent'. The wider meaning of intention should only be considered in the absence of direct intention. Furthermore, a defendant will only be capable of having oblique intent if his purpose is to achieve a result other than the one being considered.

R v Moloney [1985] AC 105

Panel: Lord Hailsham of St. Marylebone LC, Lord Fraser of Tullybelton, Lord Edmund-Davies, Lord Keith of Kinkel and Lord Bridge of Harwich

LORD BRIDGE OF HARWICH

I am firmly of opinion that foresight of consequences, as an element bearing on the issue of intention in murder, or indeed any other crime of specific intent, belongs, not to the substantive law, but to the law of evidence. Here again I am happy to find myself aligned with my noble and learned friend, Lord Hailsham of St. Marylebone LC, in *Reg. v Hyam* [1975] AC 55, where he said, at page 65: "Knowledge or foresight is at the best material which entitles or compels a jury to draw the necessary inference as to intention." A rule of evidence which judges for more than a century found of the utmost utility in directing juries was expressed in the maxim: "A man is presumed to intend the natural and probable consequences of his acts." In *Director of Public Prosecutions v Smith* [1961] AC 290 your Lordships' House, by treating this rule of evidence as creating an irrebuttable presumption and thus elevating it, in effect, to the status of a rule of substantive law, predictably provoked the intervention of Parliament by section 8 of the Criminal Justice Act 1967 to put the issue of intention back where it belonged, viz., in the hands of the jury, "drawing such inferences from the evidence as appear proper in the circumstances." I do not by any means take the conjunction of the verbs "intended or foresaw" and "intend or foresee" in that section as an indication that Parliament treated them as synonymous; on the contrary, two verbs were needed to connote two different states of mind.

I think we should now no longer speak of presumptions in this context but rather of inferences. In the old presumption that a man intends the natural and probable consequences of his acts the important word is "natural." This word conveys the idea that in the ordinary course of events a certain act will lead to a certain consequence unless something unexpected supervenes to prevent it. One might almost say that, if a consequence is natural, it is really otiose to speak of it as also being probable.

Section 8 of the Criminal Justice Act 1967 leaves us at liberty to go back to the decisions before that of this House in *Director of Public Prosecutions v Smith* [1961] AC 290 and it is here, I believe, that we can find a sure, clear, intelligible and simple guide to the kind of direction that should be given to a jury in the exceptional case where it is necessary to give guidance as to how, on the evidence, they should approach the issue of intent.

I know of no clearer exposition of the law than that in the judgment of the Court of Criminal Appeal (Lord Goddard CJ, Atkinson and Cassels JJ.) delivered by Lord Goddard CJ in *Rex v Steane* [1947] KB 997 where he said, at page 1004:

> "No doubt, if the prosecution prove an act the natural consequence of which would be a certain result and no evidence or explanation is given, then a jury may, on a proper direction, find that the prisoner is guilty of doing the act with the intent alleged, but if on the totality of the evidence there is room for more than one view as to the intent of the prisoner, the jury should be directed that it is for the prosecution to prove the intent to the jury's satisfaction, and if, on a review of the whole evidence, they either think that the intent did not exist or they are left in doubt as to the intent, the prisoner is entitled to be acquitted."

In the rare cases in which it is necessary to direct a jury by reference to foresight of consequences, I do not believe it is necessary for the judge to do more than invite the jury to consider two questions. First, was death or really serious injury in a murder case (or whatever relevant consequence must be proved to have been intended in any other case) a natural consequence of the defendant's voluntary act? Secondly, did the defendant foresee that consequence as being a natural consequence of his act? The jury should then be told that if they answer yes to both questions it is a proper inference for them to draw that he intended that consequence.

R v Nedrick [1986] 1 WLR 1025

Panel: Lord Lane CJ, Leggatt and Kennedy JJ

Facts: The appellant (Nedrick) had a grudge against a woman. He went to her house during the night, poured paraffin through her letter box and set it alight. The woman's 12-year old son died in the ensuing fire. Nedrick was convicted of murder and appealed on the ground that the judge had misdirected the jury as to the meaning of intention. The Court of Appeal allowed the appeal.

LORD LANE CJ

Where the charge is murder and in the rare cases where the simple direction is not enough, the jury should be directed that they are not entitled to infer the necessary intention, unless they feel sure that death or serious bodily harm was a virtual certainty (barring some unforeseen intervention) as a result of the defendant's actions and that the defendant appreciated that such was the case.

Where a man realises that it is for all practical purposes inevitable that his actions will result in death or serious harm, the inference may be irresistible that he intended that result, however little he may have desired or wished it to happen. The decision is one for the Jury to be reached upon a consideration of all the evidence.

R v Woollin [1999] 1 AC 82

Panel: Lord Browne-Wilkinson, Lord Nolan, Lord Steyn, Lord Hoffmann and Lord Hope of Craighead

Facts: The appellant (Woollin) lost his temper with his three month old son and threw him onto a hard surface. The baby suffered a fractured skull and subsequently died. Woollin was convicted of murder and appealed as a result of the judge's direction on the meaning of intention. The Court of Appeal dismissed his appeal. The House of Lords allowed the appeal.

LORD STEYN

[Lord Steyn repeated the direction given by Lord Lane in *Nedrick*] The effect of the critical direction is that a result foreseen as virtually certain is an intended result.

The direct attack on Nedrick

It is now possible to consider the Crown's direct challenge to the correctness of *Nedrick*. First, the Crown argued that Nedrick prevents the jury from considering all the evidence in the case relevant to intention. The argument is that this is contrary to the provisions of section 8 of the Act of 1967. This provision reads:

"A court or jury, in determining whether a person has committed an offence - (a) shall not be bound in law to infer that he intended or foresaw a result of his actions by reasons only of its being a natural and probable consequence of those actions; but (b) shall decide whether he did intend or foresee that result by reference to all the evidence, drawing such inferences from the evidence as appear proper in the circumstances."

Paragraph (a) is an instruction to the judge and is not relevant to the issues on this appeal. The Crown's argument relied on paragraph (b) which is concerned with the function of the jury. It is no more than a legislative instruction that in considering their findings on intention or foresight the jury must take into account all relevant evidence: see Professor Edward Griew, "States of Mind, Presumptions and Inferences," in Criminal Law: Essays in Honour of J. C. Smith (1987), pages 68, 76-77. *Nedrick* is undoubtedly concerned with the mental element which is sufficient for murder. So, for that matter, in their different ways were *Smith*, *Hyam*, *Moloney* and *Hancock* . But, as Lord Lane CJ emphasised in the last sentence of *Nedrick*, at page 1028: "The decision is one for the jury to be reached upon a consideration of all the evidence." *Nedrick* does not prevent a jury from considering all the evidence: it merely stated what state of mind (in the absence of a purpose to kill or to cause serious harm) is sufficient for murder. I would therefore reject the Crown's first argument.

In the second place the Crown submitted that *Nedrick* is in conflict with the decision of the House in *Hancock*. Counsel argued that in order to bring some coherence to the process of determining intention Lord Lane CJ specified a minimum level of foresight, namely virtual certainty. But that is not in conflict with the decision in *Hancock* which, apart from disapproving Lord Bridge's "natural consequence" model direction, approved *Moloney* [1985] AC 905 in all other respects. and in *Moloney* Lord Bridge said, at page 925, that if a person foresees the probability of a consequence as little short of overwhelming, this "will suffice to establish the necessary intent." Nor did the House in *Hancock* rule out the framing of model directions by the Court of Appeal for the assistance of trial judges. I would therefore reject the argument that the guidance given in *Nedrick* was in conflict with the decision of the House in *Hancock*.

The Crown did not argue that as a matter of policy foresight of a virtual certainty is too narrow a test in murder. Subject to minor qualifications, the decision in *Nedrick* was widely welcomed by distinguished academic writers: see Professor JC Smith QC's commentary on Nedrick [1986] Crim LR 742, 743-744; Glanville Williams, "The Mens Rea for Murder: Leave it Alone" (1989) 105 LQR 387; JR Spencer, "Murder in the Dark: A Glimmer of Light?" [1986] CLJ 366-367; Ashworth, Principles of Criminal Law , 2nd edn (1995), page 172. It is also of interest that it is very similar to the threshold of being aware "that it will occur in the ordinary course of events" in the Law Commission's draft Criminal Code (see Criminal Law: Legislating the Criminal Code: Offences against the Person and General Principles, Law Com. No. 218 (1993) (Cm. 2370), Appendix A (Draft Criminal Law Bill with Explanatory Notes), pages 90-91): compare also Professor JC Smith QC, "A Note on 'Intention'" [1990] Crim LR 85, 86. Moreover, over a period of 12 years since *Nedrick* the test of foresight of virtual certainty has apparently caused no practical difficulties. It is simple and clear. It is true that it may exclude a conviction of murder in the often cited terrorist example where a member of the bomb disposal team is killed. In such a case it may realistically be said that the terrorist did not foresee the killing of a member of the bomb disposal team as a virtual certainty. That may be a consequence of not framing the principle in terms of risk-taking. Such cases ought to cause no substantial difficulty since immediately below murder there is available a verdict of manslaughter which may attract in the discretion of the court a life sentence. In any event, as Lord Lane CJ eloquently argued in a debate in the House of Lords, to frame a principle for particular difficulties regarding terrorism "would produce corresponding injustices which would be very hard to eradicate:" Hansard (H.L. Debates), 6 November 1989, col. 480. I am satisfied that the *Nedrick* test, which was squarely based on the decision of the House in *Moloney*, is pitched at the right level of foresight.

The argument that *Nedrick* has limited application

The Court of Appeal [1997] 1 Cr App R 97, 107 held that the phrase a "virtual certainty" should be confined to cases where the evidence of intent is limited to admitted actions of the accused and the consequences of those actions. It is not obligatory where there is other evidence to consider. The Crown's alternative submission on the appeal was to the same effect. This distinction would introduce yet another complication into a branch of the criminal law where simplicity is of supreme importance. The distinction is dependent on the vagaries of the evidence in particular cases. Moreover, a jury may reject the other evidence to which the Court of Appeal refers. and in preparing his summing up a judge could not ignore this possibility. If the Court of Appeal's view is right, it might compel a judge to pose different tests depending on what evidence the jury accepts. For my part, and with the greatest respect, I have to say that this distinction would be likely to produce great practical difficulties. But, most importantly, the distinction is not based on any principled view regarding the mental element in murder. Contrary to the view of the Court of Appeal, I would also hold that section 8(b) of the Act of 1967 does not compel such a result.

In my view the ruling of the Court of Appeal was wrong. It may be appropriate to give a direction in accordance with *Nedrick* in any case in which the defendant may not have desired the result of his act. But I accept the trial judge is best placed to decide what direction is required by the circumstances of the case.

The disposal of the present appeal

It follows that the judge should not have departed from the *Nedrick* direction. By using the phrase "substantial risk" the judge blurred the line between intention and recklessness, and hence between murder and manslaughter. The misdirection enlarged the scope of the mental element required for murder. It was a material misdirection. At one stage it was argued that the earlier correct direction "cured" the subsequent incorrect direction. A misdirection cannot by any means always be cured by the fact that the judge at an earlier or later stage gave a correct direction. After all, how is a jury to choose between a correct and an incorrect direction on a point of law? If a misdirection is to be corrected, it must be done in the plainest terms: Archbold, Criminal Pleading, Evidence & Practice, 1998 edn, page 411, para. 4-374.

That is, however, not the end of the matter. For my part, I have given anxious consideration to the observation of the Court of Appeal that, if the judge had used the phrase "a virtual certainty," the verdict would have been the same. In this case there was no suggestion of any other ill treatment of the child. It would also be putting matters too high to say that on the evidence before the jury it was an open-and-shut case of murder rather than manslaughter. In my view the conviction of murder is unsafe. The conviction of murder must be quashed.

The status of *Nedrick*

In my view Lord Lane CJ's judgment in *Nedrick* provided valuable assistance to trial judges. The model direction is by now a tried-and-tested formula. Trial judges ought to continue to use it. On matters of detail I have three observations, which can best be understood if I set out again the relevant part of Lord Lane's judgment. It was:

> "(A) When determining whether the defendant had the necessary intent, it may therefore be helpful for a jury to ask themselves two questions. (1) How probable was the consequence which resulted from the defendant's voluntary act? (2) Did he foresee that consequence? If he did not appreciate that death or serious harm was likely to result from his act, he

cannot have intended to bring it about. If he did, but thought that the risk to which he was exposing the person killed was only slight, then it may be easy for the jury to conclude that he did not intend to bring about that result. On the other hand, if the jury are satisfied that at the material time the defendant recognised that death or serious harm would be virtually certain (barring some unforeseen intervention) to result from his voluntary act, then that is a fact from which they may find it easy to infer that he intended to kill or do serious bodily harm, even though he may not have had any desire to achieve that result . . . (B) Where the charge is murder and in the rare cases where the simple direction is not enough, the jury should be directed that they are not entitled to infer the necessary intention, unless they feel sure that death or serious bodily harm was a virtual certainty (barring some unforeseen intervention) as a result of the defendant's actions and that the defendant appreciated that such was the case. (C) Where a man realises that it is for all practical purposes inevitable that his actions will result in death or serious harm, the inference may be irresistible that he intended that result, however little he may have desired or wished it to happen. The decision is one for the jury to be reached upon a consideration of all the evidence."   (Lettering added.)

First, I am persuaded by the speech of my noble and learned friend, Lord Hope of Craighead, that it is unlikely, if ever, to be helpful to direct the jury in terms of the two questions set out in (A). I agree that these questions may detract from the clarity of the critical direction in (B). Secondly, in their writings previously cited Glanville Williams, Professor Smith and Andrew Ashworth observed that the use of the words "to infer" in (B) may detract from the clarity of the model direction. I agree. I would substitute the words "to find." Thirdly, the first sentence of (C) does not form part of the model direction. But it would always be right for the judge to say, as Lord Lane CJ put it, that the decision is for the jury upon a consideration of all the evidence in the case.

2.1.2.1 Oblique Intention: Intention or Evidence of Intention

Most academic commentary on oblique intention comes to the conclusion that it should be included in the definition of intention rather being merely evidence of intention.

This is explained clearly in the following extract from an article by Alan Norrie.

Oblique intention and legal politics, Alan Norrie [1989] Crim LR 989

In making the radical distinction between foresight and intention discussed above, Lord Bridge claimed that the accused's foresight had a role to play in the law of evidence. Where the defendant foresees the side-consequence as a natural (morally certain) consequence of his act, "it is a proper inference for [the jury] to draw that he intended that consequence." [[1985] 1 All ER 1025, 1039] Can Lord Bridge logically say this if foresight is different from intention?

We are taking here of an inference from a set of facts to the existence of a mental state. We may infer or deduce from facts a1, a2, a3, etc., the existence of mental state

A, for facts a1,-a3 are empirical observations consistent with (establishing the existence of) mental state A. But we cannot infer from the same facts the existence of mental state B where A and B are distinct and different, for facts a1,-a3 are inconsistent with (do not establish the existence of) mental state B. Where intention connotes direct intention plus foresight of moral certainty (oblique intention) evidence of such foresight is evidence from which intention can be inferred. 58 Where intention excludes in its definition such foresight no evidence of such foresight can possibly constitute it. Accordingly, ... for an inference from foresight of moral certainty to be relevant to intention, intention must be constitutable by such foresight, i.e. qua oblique intent.

Norrie sees intention as the package of what will come about as a result of the defendant's desires.

Intention, desire and oblique intention

The relevance of this philosophical discussion becomes apparent when we consider the rationale for a doctrine of oblique intent. Oblique intention only becomes a problem for ordinary usage if one separates intention from desire, for one then loses the possibility of seeing what was intended as being that which possesses a "desirability characteristic," as being part of a "package" of desires. Williams is wrong to say that oblique intention involves a departure from the ordinary usage of "intention," for oblique intention can quite naturally be seen as a species of intention once one realises that what is intended is that which is desired in the broad "package" sense of the term. Williams writes: "If I drive over you because I am in a hurry and you will not get out of the way, I drive over you intentionally, and it would be no use my saying that my sole intention was to make progress." Indeed not, but Williams gives the example to illustrate a situation where desire does not go with intent, whereas given his espousal of the "package" view of desire, it does. I want to drive over you as part of a package which includes my making progress. Your injury is not my direct desire, but it has a "desirability characteristic" in the broader context. Oblique intention, which includes the intention of means necessary to ends and of necessary side consequences to ends, connotes desire in the broad sense outlined above.

It was thought that the Court of Appeal in *R v Nedrick* stated oblique intention as being evidence of intention because it felt bound by the House of Lords judgement in *R v Moloney*.

Sir John Smith, commenting on *R v Woollin* in the *Criminal Law Review* noted the subtle changes made to the *Nedrick* test.

Case and Comment on *R v Woollin*, Sir John Smith [1998] Crim L R 890

The direction proposed in *Nedrick* is approved with one important modification. The *Nedrick* direction tells the jury that "they are not entitled to infer the necessary intention, unless they feel sure that death or serious bodily harm was a virtual certainty ... and that the defendant appreciated that such was the case." Lord Steyn and Lord Hope agree that the substitution of "find" for "infer" would be an improvement. Indeed, it will and should get away from the strange and much criticised notion of inferring one state of mind from another. After *Nedrick* some of us hoped that a perceptive jury would ask some unlucky judge what was the state of mind they were required to find proved which was not purpose but was something more than foresight of virtual certainty? – a question to which there appears to be no answer. It does not seem ever to have happened – juries somehow – no one knows how – got by. The present decision nearly eliminates the possibility, but not quite. A jury might still fairly ask "We are all quite sure that D knew that it was virtually certain that his act would cause death. You tell us we are entitled to find that he intended it. Are we bound to find that? Some of us want to and some do not. How should we decide?" The implication appears to be that, even now, they are not so bound. But why not? At one point Lord Steyn says of *Nedrick* "The effect of the critical direction is that a result foreseen as virtually certain is an intended result." If that is right, the only question for the jury is, "Did the defendant foresee the result as virtually certain?" If he did, he intended it. That, it is submitted is what the law should be; and it now seems that we have at last moved substantially in that direction. The *Nedrick* formula, however, even as modified ("entitled to find"), involves some ambiguity with the hint of the existence of some ineffable, undefinable, notion of intent, locked in the breasts of the jurors.

However, the test given in *R v Woollin* is still in the negative, so a jury which considers the defendant saw a result as virtually certain, is not compelled to decide he intended it. The Court of Appeal has come to the conclusion that oblique intention remains merely evidence of intention.

R v Matthews; R v Alleyn [2003] EWCA Crim 192, [2003] 2 Cr App R 30

Panel: Rix LJ, Crane and Maddison JJ

Facts: The defendants were part of a gang which pushed the victim from a bridge into a river. They knew that the victim could not swim. The victim drowned. The defendant were convicted of murder and appealed on the grounds that the judge had directed the jury that foresight of virtual certainty constituted intention rather than evidence of intention. The appeal was dismissed.

LORD JUSTICE RIX

...Professor Smith cites Lord Lane speaking in the debate on the report of the House of Lords Select Committee on Murder (HL Paper, 78-I, 1989) as follows:

"...in *Nedrick* the court was obliged to phrase matters as it did because of earlier decisions in your Lordships' House by which it was bound. We had to tread very gingerly indeed in order not to tread on your Lordships' toes. As a result, *Nedrick* was not as clear as it should have been. However, I agree with the conclusions of the committee that 'intention' should be defined in the terms set out in para. 195 of the report on page 50. That seems to me to express clearly what in *Nedrick* we failed properly to explain."

42. The definition referred to, as Smith & Hogan goes on to explain, is that stated in cl.18(b) of the Draft Code (itself referred to by Lord Steyn in *Woollin*) as follows:

    "A person acts 'intentionally' with respect to ... a result when he acts either in order to bring it about or being aware that it will occur in the ordinary course of events."

43. In our judgment, however, the law has not yet reached a definition of intent in murder in terms of appreciation of a virtual certainty. Lord Lane was speaking not of what was decided in *Nedrick* (or in the other cases which preceded it) nor of what was thereafter to be decided in *Woollin*, but of what the law in his opinion should be, as represented by the cl.18(b) definition. Similarly, although the law has progressively moved closer to what Professor Smith has been advocating (see his commentaries in the Criminal Law Review on the various cases discussed above), we do not regard *Woollin* as yet reaching or laying down a substantive rule of law. On the contrary, it is clear from the discussion in *Woollin* as a whole that *Nedrick* was derived from the existing law, at that time ending in *Moloney* and *Hancock*, and that the critical direction in *Nedrick* was approved, subject to the change of one word.

44. In these circumstances we think that the judge did go further than the law as it stands at present permitted him to go in redrafting the *Nedrick / Woollin* direction into a form where, as Mr Coker accepts (although we have some doubt about this), the jury were directed to find the necessary intent proved provided they were satisfied in the case of any defendant that there was appreciation of the virtual certainty of death. This is to be contrasted with the form of the approved direction which is in terms of "not entitled to find the necessary intention, unless ..."

45. Having said that, however, we think that, once what is required is an appreciation of virtual certainty of death, and not some lesser foresight of merely probable consequences, there is very little to choose between a rule of evidence and one of substantive law. It is probably this thought that led Lord Steyn to say that a result foreseen as virtually certain is an intended result. Lord Bridge had reflected the same thought when he had said, in *R v Moloney* (1985) 81 Cr App R 93, 101, [1985] AC 905, 920C, that if the defendant there had had present to his mind, when he pulled the trigger, that his gun was pointing at his stepfather's head at a distance of six feet and "its inevitable consequence", then "the inference was inescapable, using words in their ordinary, everyday meaning, that he intended to kill his stepfather."

Lord Lane had also spoken in *Nedrick* of an irresistible inference.

46. We also think that on the particular facts of this case, reflected in the judge's directions, the question of the appellants' intentions to save Jonathan from drowning highlight the irresistible nature of the inference or finding of intent to kill, once the jury were sure both that the defendants appreciated the virtual certainty of death "(barring some attempt to save him)" and that at the time of throwing Jonathan from the bridge they then "had no intentions of saving him". If the jury

were sure that the appellants appreciated the virtual certainty of Jonathan's death when they threw him from the bridge and also that they then had no intention of saving him from such death, it is impossible to see how the jury could not have found that the appellants intended Jonathan to die.

2.1.2.2 A Note on the Test in *R v Woollin*

It is generally accepted that the test for oblique intention should not require the result to be virtually certain. It should be enough that the defendant foresaw the result as virtually certain. This is the line which has been adopted in the Draft Criminal Code.

Case and Comment on *R v Woollin*, Sir John Smith [1998] Crim L R 890

Must the result be, in fact, virtually certain? *Nedrick* says that it must and that is not altered by the present case. It is submitted that virtual certainty in fact should not be (indeed, one might venture to say, is not) a condition of intention because intention is a state of mind and a person may well believe a result to be certain when in fact it is not. D points a pistol at V's heart at point-blank range and pulls the trigger. He believes V will be shot dead. But, unknown to D, his gun has been unloaded, or V is wearing a bullet-proof vest. The result is not certain–indeed, it certainly will not occur–but it is undoubtedly intended. Of course, if the result is virtually certain in the circumstances known to D, that is persuasive evidence that he knew it was, and therefore intended the result. This point may not be of great practical importance; but it involves a confusion of evidence of facts with the facts to be proved: and that ought to be avoided.

2.2 Recklessness

Most crimes can be committed intentionally or recklessly. This is partly the result of the courts having interpreted the word 'maliciously' as it appears in older statutes to mean intentionally or recklessly. Criminal damage, assault, battery and the offences under the Offences Against the Person Act 1861 ss 47 and 20 are some examples of crimes for which the mens rea is intention or recklessness.

Recklessness is the taking of an unjustifiable risk. For many years there were two different types of recklessness. These where known as *Cunningham* recklessness and *Caldwell* recklessness. Some crimes required one type and some the other. Since the House of Lords decision in *R v G* [2003] UKHL 50, [2004] 1 AC 1034, *Caldwell* recklessness is no longer used.

R v Cunningham [1957] 2 Q B

Panel: Byrne, Slade and Barry JJ

Facts: Cunningham had torn open a gas meter to steal the money which it contained. In doing so he had fractured a gas pipe. Gas seeped into the next door flat and endangered the lives of the occupants. He was charged with an offence under the Offences Against the Person Act 1861 s 23, in that he had maliciously administered a noxious thing so as to endanger life. He was convicted and appealed on the ground that the trial judge had misdirected the jury as to the meaning of the word 'maliciously'.

His appeal was dismissed. The Court of Appeal defined malice as intention or recklessness and gave a definition of recklessness.

MR JUSTICE BYRNE

We have considered those cases, and we have also considered, in the light of those cases, the following principle which was propounded by the late Professor C. S. Kenny in the first edition of his Outlines of Criminal Law published in 1902 and repeated at page 186 of the 16th edition edited by Mr JW Cecil Turner and published in 1952:

"In any statutory definition of a crime, malice must be taken not in the old vague sense of wickedness in general but as requiring either (1) An actual intention to do the particular kind of harm that in fact was done; or (2) recklessness as to whether such harm should occur or not (i.e., the accused has foreseen that the particular kind of harm might be done and yet has gone on to take the risk of it). It is neither limited to nor does it indeed require any ill will towards the person injured." The same principle is repeated by Mr Turner in his 10th edition of Russell on Crime at page 1592.

We think that this is an accurate statement of the law.

R v G and Another [2003] UKHL 50, [2004] 1 AC 1034

Panel: Lord Bingham of Cornhill, Lord Browne-Wilkinson, Lord Steyn, Lord Hutton and Lord Rodger of Earlsferry

Facts: The appellants were boys aged 11 and 12 who had been camping out for the night. In the early hours of the morning they went to a yard behind a supermarket and set some piles of newspapers alight. They thought the papers would burn out on the concrete floor and left the yard whilst the papers were still burning. The fire spread to the shop and did £1 million pounds worth of damage. The boys were convicted of arson using the *Caldwell* test for recklessness. They appealed on the ground that, because of their age, the risk of damage would not have been obvious to them even if they had thought about it. The Court of Appeal rejected the appeal. The defendant further appealed.

LORD BINGHAM OF CORNHILL

1.   My Lords, the point of law of general public importance certified by the Court of Appeal to be involved in its decision in the present case is expressed in this way:

"Can a defendant properly be convicted under section 1 of the Criminal Damage Act 1971 on the basis that he was reckless as to whether property was destroyed or damaged when he gave no thought to the risk but, by reason of his age and/or personal characteristics the risk would not have been obvious to him, even if he had thought about it?"

The appeal turns on the meaning of "reckless" in that section. This is a question on which the House ruled in *R v Caldwell* [1982] AC 341, a ruling affirmed by the House in later decisions. The House is again asked to reconsider that ruling.

[Lord Bingham then referred to the facts, the trial and the law before the Criminal Damage Act 1971]

The 1971 Act

12. In its second programme of law reform the Law Commission, then under the chairmanship of Scarman J, envisaged the codification of the criminal law. As part of that project it examined a number of specific offences, among them the law of malicious damage, on which it published its Working Paper No 23 in April 1969. This described the Malicious Damage Act 1861, despite five later amending statutes, as "unsatisfactory": paragraph 2. In a brief statistical introduction the Law Commission drew attention, in paragraph 9, to the prevalence of malicious damage offences among the youngest criminal age group (the 10 to 14-year-olds) as well as among other juveniles, and to the fact that more than half of those convicted of the most serious offence (arson) were under 21. In a section on "The Mental Element" the Law Commission referred to a working party which was formulating draft propositions on the mental element in crime and observed, in paragraph 31:

"For the present purpose, we assume that the traditional elements of intention, knowledge and recklessness (in the sense of foresight and disregard of consequences or awareness and disregard of the likelihood of the existence of circumstances) will continue to be required for serious crime."

In paragraph 33 of the working paper the Law Commission identified "Intent to do the forbidden act or recklessness in relation to its foreseen consequences" as the "essential mental element in the existing malicious damage offences" and quoted with apparent approval the passage from *R v Cunningham* [1957] 2 QB 396 which is set out in paragraph 10 above. The Law Commission considered that the word "maliciously" should be avoided (paragraph 34) and favoured its replacement by "wilful or reckless": paragraph 64. It proposed (paragraph 68) that the new group of offences should require "traditional mens rea, in the sense of intention or recklessness in relation to prescribed consequences, and, where appropriate, knowledge or recklessness in relation to prescribed circumstances". The working paper does not suggest that the law as then understood was thought to be leading to unjustified acquittals. In a published comment on the working paper, Professor Brian Hogan wrote [1969] Crim LR 283, 288:

"What is implicit in 'maliciously' in the present law will appear explicitly as intention or recklessness in the new code. No doubt the meanings ascribed to intention and recklessness in the codification of the general principles will be applied mutatis mutandis to offences of damage to property."

13. In its Report on Offences of Damage to Property (Law Com No 29) published in July 1970, the Law Commission broadly followed, in respects relevant to this appeal, the lines of the working paper. On the mental element of criminal damage offences the Law Commission said, in paragraph 44:

"In the area of serious crime (in contrast to offences commonly described as 'regulatory offences' in which the test of culpability may be negligence, or even a test founded on strict liability) the elements of intention, knowledge or recklessness have always been required as a basis of liability. The tendency is to extend this basis to a wider range of offences and to limit the area of offences where a lesser mental element is required. We consider, therefore, that the same elements as are required at present should be retained, but that they should be expressed with greater simplicity and clarity. In particular, we prefer to avoid the use of such a word as 'maliciously', if only because it gives the impression that the mental element differs from that which is imposed in other offences requiring traditional mens rea. It is evident from such cases as *R v Cunningham* and *R v Mowatt* that the word can give rise to difficulties of interpretation. Furthermore, the word 'maliciously' conveys the impression that some ill-will is required against the person whose property is damaged."

It does not appear from the report that the Law Commission's consultation had elicited any complaint that the existing law was unduly favourable to defendants. Annexed to the report was a draft Bill: in this clause 1(1) and (2) were exactly as enacted in the 1971 Act, but what became section 1(3) was omitted. On 16 June 1970, a month before this report was published, the Law Commission had published its Working Paper No 31, General Principles: The Mental Element in Crime. In that working paper a definition of recklessness was proposed, on page 48:

"A person is reckless if—(a) knowing that there is a risk that an event may result from his conduct or that a circumstance may exist, he takes that risk, and (b) it is unreasonable for him to take it having regard to the degree and nature of the risk which he knows to be present."

In the 1971 Act as passed all except six sections of the Malicious Damage Act 1861, a lengthy Act, were repealed, very much as the Law Commission had proposed.

[Lord Bingham then noted that the term 'recklessness' in the Act was originally interpreted as in *Cunningham*.]

17. *R v Caldwell* [1982] AC 341 was a case of self-induced intoxication. The defendant, having a grievance against the owner of the hotel where he worked, got very drunk and set fire to the hotel where guests were living at the time. He was indicted upon two counts of arson. The first and more serious count was laid under section 1(2) of the 1971 Act, the second count under section 1(1). He pleaded guilty to the second count but contested the first on the ground that he had been so drunk at the time that the thought there might be people in the hotel had never crossed his mind. His conviction on count 1 was set aside by the Court of Appeal which certified the following question:

"Whether evidence of self-induced intoxication can be relevant to the following questions—(a) Whether the defendant intended to endanger the life of another; and (b) Whether the defendant was reckless as to whether the life of another would be endangered, within the meaning of section 1(2)(b) of the Criminal Damage Act 1971."

[His Lordship considered the issues in the case and then quoted Lord Diplock, giving what became known as the test for *Caldwell* recklessness.]

In a passage which has since been taken to encapsulate the law on this point, and which has founded many jury directions (including that in the present case) Lord Diplock then said, at page 354:

"In my opinion, a person charged with an offence under section 1(1) of the Criminal Damage Act 1971 is 'reckless as to whether any such property would be destroyed or damaged' if (1) he does an act which in fact creates an obvious risk that property will be destroyed or damaged and (2) when he does the act he either has not given any thought to the possibility of there being any such risk or has recognised that there was some risk involved and has none the less gone on to do it. That would be a proper direction to the jury; cases in the Court of Appeal which held otherwise should be regarded as overruled."

[His Lordship considered the cases following *Caldwell* and then came to the following conclusions as to how 'recklessness' should be defined in the Criminal Damage Act.]

28. The task confronting the House in this appeal is, first of all, one of statutory construction: what did Parliament mean when it used the word "reckless" in section 1(1) and (2) of the 1971 Act? In so expressing the question I mean to make it as plain as I can that I am not addressing the meaning of "reckless" in any other statutory or common law context. In particular, but perhaps needlessly since "recklessly" has now been banished from the lexicon of driving offences, I would wish to throw no doubt on the decisions of the House in *R v Lawrence* (Stephen) [1982] AC 510 and *R v Reid* [1992] 1 WLR 793.

29. Since a statute is always speaking, the context or application of a statutory expression may change over time, but the meaning of the expression itself cannot change. So the starting point is to ascertain what Parliament meant by "reckless" in 1971. As noted above in paragraph 13, section 1 as enacted followed, subject to an immaterial addition, the draft proposed by the Law Commission. It cannot be supposed that by "reckless" Parliament meant anything different from the Law Commission. The Law Commission's meaning was made plain both in its Report (Law Com No 29) and in Working Paper No 23 which preceded it. These materials (not, it would seem, placed before the House in *R v Caldwell* [1982] AC 341) reveal a very plain intention to replace the old-fashioned and misleading expression "maliciously" by the more familiar expression "reckless" but to give the latter expression the meaning which *R v Cunningham* [1957] 2 QB 396 and Professor Kenny had given to the former. In treating this authority as irrelevant to the construction of "reckless" the majority fell into understandable but clearly demonstrable error. No relevant change in the mens rea necessary for proof of the offence was intended, and in holding otherwise the majority misconstrued section 1 of the Act.

30. That conclusion is by no means determinative of this appeal. For the decision in *R v Caldwell* was made more than 20 years ago. Its essential reasoning was unanimously approved by the House in *R v Lawrence* [1982] AC 510. Invitations to reconsider that reasoning have been rejected. The principles laid down have been applied on many occasions, by Crown Court judges and, even more frequently, by justices. In the submission of the Crown, the ruling of the House works well and causes no injustice in practice. If Parliament had wished to give effect to the intention of the Law Commission it has had many opportunities, which it has not taken, to do so. Despite its power under Practice Statement (Judicial Precedent) [1966] 1 WLR 1234 to depart from its earlier decisions, the House should be very slow to do so, not least in a context such as this.

31. These are formidable arguments, deployed by Mr Perry with his habitual skill and erudition. But I am persuaded by Mr Newman for the appellants that they should be rejected. I reach this conclusion for four reasons, taken together.

32. First, it is a salutary principle that conviction of serious crime should depend on proof not simply that the defendant caused (by act or omission) an injurious result to another but that his state of mind when so acting was culpable. This, after all, is the meaning of the familiar rule actus non facit reum nisi mens sit rea. The most obviously culpable state of mind is no doubt an intention to cause the injurious result, but knowing disregard of an appreciated and unacceptable risk of causing an injurious result or a deliberate closing of the mind to such risk would be readily accepted as culpable also. It is clearly blameworthy to take an obvious and significant risk of causing injury to another. But it is not clearly blameworthy to do something involving a risk of injury to another if (for reasons other than self-induced intoxication: *R v Majewski* [1977] AC 443) one genuinely does not perceive the risk. Such a person may fairly be accused of stupidity or lack of imagination, but neither of those failings should expose him to conviction of serious crime or the risk of punishment.

33. Secondly, the present case shows, more clearly than any other reported case since *R v Caldwell*, that the model direction formulated by Lord Diplock (see paragraph 18 above) is capable of leading to obvious unfairness. As the excerpts quoted in paragraphs 6-7 reveal, the trial judge regretted the direction he (quite rightly) felt compelled to give, and it is evident that this direction offended the jury's sense of fairness. The sense of fairness of 12 representative citizens sitting as a jury (or of a smaller group of lay justices sitting as a bench of magistrates) is the bedrock on which the administration of criminal justice in this country is built. A law which runs counter to that sense must cause concern. Here, the appellants could have been charged under section 1(1) with recklessly damaging one or both of the wheelie-bins, and they would have had little defence. As it was, the jury might have inferred that boys of the appellants' age would have appreciated the risk to the building of what they did, but it seems clear that such was not their conclusion (nor, it would appear, the judge's either). On that basis the jury thought it unfair to convict them. I share their sense of unease. It is neither moral nor just to convict a defendant (least of all a child) on the strength of what someone else would have

apprehended if the defendant himself had no such apprehension. Nor, the defendant having been convicted, is the problem cured by imposition of a nominal penalty.

34. Thirdly, I do not think the criticism of *R v Caldwell* [1982] AC 34 expressed by academics, judges and practitioners should be ignored. A decision is not, of course, to be overruled or departed from simply because it meets with disfavour in the learned journals. But a decision which attracts reasoned and outspoken criticism by the leading scholars of the day, respected as authorities in the field, must command attention. One need only cite (among many other examples) the observations of Professor John Smith [1981] Crim LR 392 , 393-396, and Professor Glanville Williams in "Recklessness Redefined" [1981] CLJ 252. This criticism carries greater weight when voiced also by judges as authoritative as Lord Edmund-Davies and Lord Wilberforce in *R v Caldwell* itself, Robert Goff LJ in *Elliott v C* [1983] 1 WLR 939 and Ackner LJ in *R v R* (Stephen Malcolm) 79 Cr App R 334. The reservations expressed by the trial judge in the present case are widely shared. The shopfloor response to *R v Caldwell* may be gauged from the editors' commentary, to be found in Archbold Pleading, Evidence and Practice in Criminal Cases, 41st ed (1982), pages 1009-1010, paras 17-25 . The editors suggested that remedial legislation was urgently required.

35. Fourthly, the majority's interpretation of "reckless" in section 1 of the 1971 Act was, as already shown, a misinterpretation. If it were a misinterpretation that offended no principle and gave rise to no injustice there would be strong grounds for adhering to the misinterpretation and leaving Parliament to correct it if it chose. But this misinterpretation is offensive to principle and is apt to cause injustice. That being so, the need to correct the misinterpretation is compelling.

36. It is perhaps unfortunate that the question at issue in this appeal fell to be answered in a case of self-induced intoxication. For one instinctively recoils from the notion that a defendant can escape the criminal consequences of his injurious conduct by drinking himself into a state where he is blind to the risk he is causing to others. In *R v Caldwell* [1982] AC 341 it seems to have been assumed (see paragraph 18 above) that the risk would have been obvious to the defendant had he been sober. Further, the context did not require the House to give close consideration to the liability of those (such as the very young and the mentally handicapped) who were not normal reasonable adults. The overruling by the majority of *R v Stephenson* [1979] QB 695 does however make it questionable whether such consideration would have led to a different result.

37. In the course of argument before the House it was suggested that the rule in *R v Caldwell* might be modified, in cases involving children, by requiring comparison not with normal reasonable adults but with normal reasonable children of the same age. This is a suggestion with some attractions but it is open to four compelling objections. First, even this modification would offend the principle that conviction should depend on proving the state of mind of the individual defendant to be culpable. Second, if the rule were modified in relation to children on grounds of their immaturity it would be anomalous if it were not

also modified in relation to the mentally handicapped on grounds of their limited understanding. Third, any modification along these lines would open the door to difficult and contentious argument concerning the qualities and characteristics to be taken into account for purposes of the comparison. Fourth, to adopt this modification would be to substitute one misinterpretation of section 1 for another. There is no warrant in the Act or in the travaux préparatoires which preceded it for such an interpretation.

38. A further refinement, advanced by Professor Glanville Williams in his article "Recklessness Redefined" [1981] CLJ 252, 270-271, adopted by the justices in *Elliott v C* [1983] 1 WLR 939 and commented upon by Robert Goff LJ in that case is that a defendant should only be regarded as having acted recklessly by virtue of his failure to give any thought to an obvious risk that property would be destroyed or damaged, where such risk would have been obvious to him if he had given any thought to the matter. This refinement also has attractions, although it does not meet the objection of principle and does not represent a correct interpretation of the section. It is, in my opinion, open to the further objection of over-complicating the task of the jury (or bench of justices). It is one thing to decide whether a defendant can be believed when he says that the thought of a given risk never crossed his mind. It is another, and much more speculative, task to decide whether the risk would have been obvious to him if the thought had crossed his mind. The simpler the jury's task, the more likely is its verdict to be reliable. Robert Goff LJ's reason for rejecting this refinement was somewhat similar: *Elliott v C*, page 950.

39. I cannot accept that restoration of the law as understood before *R v Caldwell* [1982] AC 341 would lead to the acquittal of those whom public policy would require to be convicted. There is nothing to suggest that this was seen as a problem before *R v Caldwell*, or (as noted above in paragraphs 12 and 13) before the 1971 Act. There is no reason to doubt the common sense which tribunals of fact bring to their task. In a contested case based on intention, the defendant rarely admits intending the injurious result in question, but the tribunal of fact will readily infer such an intention, in a proper case, from all the circumstances and probabilities and evidence of what the defendant did and said at the time. Similarly with recklessness: it is not to be supposed that the tribunal of fact will accept a defendant's assertion that he never thought of a certain risk when all the circumstances and probabilities and evidence of what he did and said at the time show that he did or must have done.

40. In his printed case, Mr Newman advanced the contention that the law as declared in *R v Caldwell* was incompatible with article 6 of the European Convention on Human Rights . While making no concession, he forebore to address legal argument on the point. I need say no more about it.

41. For the reasons I have given I would allow this appeal and quash the appellants' convictions. I would answer the certified question obliquely, basing myself on clause 18(c) of the Criminal Code Bill annexed by the Law Commission to its Report on Criminal Law: A Criminal Code for England and Wales and Draft Criminal Code Bill, vol 1 (Law Com No 177, April 1989):

"A person acts recklessly within the meaning of section 1 of the Criminal Damage Act 1971 with respect to—(i) a circumstance when he is aware of a risk that it exists or will exist; (ii) a result when he is aware of a risk that it will occur; and it is, in the circumstances known to him, unreasonable to take the risk."

Chief Constable of Avon and Somerset Constabulary v Shimmen (1987) 84 Cr App R 7

Panel: Watkins LJ and Taylor J

Facts: The defendant, Shimmen, and four friends had spent the evening at a club in Bristol. They had all consumed alcohol. After they left the club, Shimmen, who was described as a 'skilled and experienced practitioner of the Korean art of self defence' was demonstrating his martial arts skills by a plate glass window. One of his kicks broke the window. He was charged with criminal damage, but acquitted by the County of Avon justices. This was because, although he had initially recognised the risk of damaging the window, he had aimed off and thought he had eliminated the risk. The Divisional Court of the Queen's Bench allowed an appeal by the prosecutor and remitted the case to the justices with a direction to convict. Although the test for recklessness at the time was *Caldwell* recklessness, the part of that test being considered is the current definition of recklessness.

MR JUSTICE TAYLOR

Applying those examples to the present case, it seems to me that on the findings of the justices and more particularly, as I shall indicate in a moment, on the evidence which they exhibited to their case, this defendant did recognise the risk. It was not a case of his considering the possibility and coming to the conclusion that there was no risk. What he said to the justices in cross-examination should be quoted. He said: "I thought I might break the window but then I thought I will not break the window ... I thought to myself, the window is not going to break." A little later on he said: "I weighed up the odds and thought I had eliminated as much risk as possible by missing by two inches instead of two millimetres."

The specific finding of the justices, at para. 5(c) of the case, was as follows: "... the defendant perceived there could be a risk of damage but after considering such risk concluded that no damage would result." It seems to me that what this case amounts to is as follows; that this defendant did perceive, which is the same as Lord Diplock's word "recognise," that there could be a risk, but by aiming off rather more than he normally would in this sort of display, he thought he had minimized it and therefore no damage would result. In my judgment, that is far from saying that he falls outside the state of mind described by Lord Diplock in these terms, "... has recognised that there was some risk involved and has nonetheless gone on to do it."

In my judgment, therefore, whatever may be the situation in a hypothetical case such as that of M. as detailed by Professor Griew, which may need to be considered on another occasion, so far as this case is concerned, the justices were wrong in coming to the conclusion that this was not recklessness by reason of what the defendant had put forward.

To establish recklessness it is necessary to identify the risk which the defendant saw, and then consider whether that risk was an unreasonable one to take. The requirement that the risk be unreasonable is to be judged objectively, albeit with reference to the circumstances known to the defendant, and one important consideration will be whether the defendant's actions had social utility. The court considered that Shimmen thought he had eliminated most of the risk, but saw that a tiny risk remained. Presumably it concluded that it is not reasonable to take even a tiny risk of damaging another's property in such circumstances.

2.3 Transferred Malice

The doctrine of transferred malice states that if D does the actus reus of a crime with the appropriate mens rea, the mens rea can be transferred from the victim D had in mind, to the actual victim. It also applies in criminal damage where the mens rea can be transferred from the property D had in mind to the property he actually damaged.

However the defendant must have the mens rea of the crime charged. It was held in *R v Pembliton* (1872-75) LR 2 CCR 119, in which a stone thrown at some people missed the people and broke a window, that it is not possible to transfer the mens rea from one type of crime (that of an offence against the person) to another crime (that of damaging property).

R v Latimer (1886) LR 17 QBD 359

Panel: Lord Coleridge CJ, Lord Esher MR, Bowen LJ, Field and Manisty JJ

Facts: Latimer had been arguing with a man called Chapple. He took off his belt and swung it at Chapple. The belt rebounded off Chapple and hit the victim, cutting open her face. Latimer was convicted of malicious wounding contrary to the Offences Against the Person Act 1861 s 20. Latimer appealed, citing the case of *R v Pembliton*.

LORD COLERIDGE CJ

We are of opinion that this conviction must be sustained. It is common knowledge that a man who has an unlawful and malicious intent against another, and, in attempting to carry it out, injures a third person, is guilty of what the law deems malice against the person injured, because the offender is doing an unlawful act, and has that which the judges call general malice, and that is enough. Such would be the case if the matter were res integra; but it is not so, for *Rex v Hunt* is an express authority on the point. There a man intended to injure A., and said so, and, in the course of doing it, stabbed the wrong man, and had clearly malice in fact, but no intention of injuring the man who was stabbed. He intended to do an unlawful act, and in course of doing it the consequence was that somebody was injured. But the words of the statute under which the prisoner is indicted carry the case against him further still, because 24 & 25 Vict. c. 100, s 18, enacts that "whosoever shall unlawfully and maliciously cause any grievous bodily harm to any person" with malicious intent, shall be guilty of felony; then s 20 leaves out the intent, and says, "whosoever shall unlawfully and maliciously wound or inflict any grievous bodily harm upon any other person ... shall be guilty of a misdemeanour." The language of s 18 and of s 20 is different, and the present conviction is under s 20 and not under s 18.

The Master of the Rolls has pointed out to me that these sections are in substitution for and in correction of the earlier statutes, in which the unlawful act must be done with intent to injure "such person," making it necessary that the intent should be against the person injured, whereas in 24 & 25 Vict. c. 100, the words "such person" are left out, for s 18 says, "any person," and s 20 "any other person." So, but for *Reg. v Pembliton*, there would not have been the slightest difficulty. Does that case make any difference? I think not, and, on consideration, that it was quite rightly decided. But it is clearly distinguishable, because the indictment in *Reg. v Pembliton* was on the Act making unlawful and malicious injury to property a statutory offence punishable in a certain way, and the jury expressly negatived, and the facts expressly negatived, any intention to do injury to property, and the Court held that under the Act making it an offence to injure any property there must be an intent to injure property. *Reg. v Pembliton*, therefore, does not govern the present case, and on no other ground is there anything to be said for the prisoner.

2.4 Coincidence of Actus Reus and Mens Rea

The general rule is that all the elements of the crime must occur at the same time, so the defendant must have the mens rea at the precise time he commits the actus reus. The courts have used various methods to get round this principle. These can be seen in the cases below.

2.4.1 The Continuing Act Theory

The actus reus is seen as a continuing act, and whilst the defendant did not have the mens rea at the beginning of that act, it is sufficient for him to have formed the mens rea whilst the act continues.

Fagan v Commissioner of Metropolitan Police [1969] 1 QB 439

Panel: Lord Parker CJ, James and Bridge JJ

Facts: A policeman asked Fagan to pull his car over to the kerb. Fagan drove onto the policeman's foot. There was some doubt as to whether Fagan had initially realised the car was on the policeman's foot, but when the policeman shouted 'Get off, you are on my foot', Fagan turned off the ignition and told the policeman he could wait. Eventually he reversed off the foot. He was convicted of assaulting a policeman in the execution of his duty, contrary to the Police Act 1964 s 51. The Divisional Court of the Queen's Bench used the continuing act theory to dismiss the appeal.

MR JUSTICE JAMES

To constitute the offence of assault some intentional act must have been performed: a mere omission to act cannot amount to an assault. Without going into the question whether words alone can constitute an assault, it is clear that the words spoken by the appellant could not alone amount to an assault: they can only shed a light on the appellant's action. For our part we think the crucial question is whether in this case the act of the appellant can be said to be complete and spent at the moment of time when the car wheel came to rest on the foot or whether his act is to be regarded as a continuing act operating until the wheel was removed. In our judgment a distinction is to be drawn between acts which are complete - though results may continue to flow - and those acts which are continuing. Once the act is complete it cannot thereafter be said to be a threat to inflict unlawful force upon the victim. If the act, as distinct from the results thereof, is a continuing act there is a continuing threat to inflict unlawful force. If the assault involves a battery and that battery continues there is a continuing act of assault.

For an assault to be committed both the elements of actus reus and mens rea must be present at the same time. The "actus reus" is the action causing the effect on the victim's mind (see the observations of Park B. in *Regina v St. George*. The "mens rea" is the intention to cause that effect. It is not necessary that mens rea should be present at the inception of the actus reus; it can be superimposed upon an existing act. On the other hand the subsequent inception of mens rea cannot convert an act which has been completed without mens rea into an assault.

In our judgment the Willesden magistrates and quarter sessions were right in law. On the facts found the action of the appellant may have been initially unintentional, but the time came when knowing that the wheel was on the officer's foot the appellant (1) remained seated in the car so that his body through the medium of the car was in contact with the officer, (2) switched off the ignition of the car, (3) maintained the wheel of the car on the foot and (4) used words indicating the intention of keeping the wheel in that position. For our part we cannot regard such conduct as mere omission or inactivity.

There was an act constituting a battery which at its inception was not criminal because there was no element of intention but which became criminal from the moment the intention was formed to produce the apprehension which was flowing from the continuing act. The fallacy of the appellant's argument is that it seeks to equate the facts of this case with such a case as where a motorist has accidentally run over a person and, that action having been completed, fails to assist the victim with the intent that the victim should suffer.

We would dismiss this appeal.

2.4.2 The Transaction Principle

The acts of the accused can be seen as a series of acts making up one transaction. In these circumstances it is sufficient for the defendant to have the mens rea at some point during those transaction.

Meli v The Queen [1954] 1 LR 228

Panel: Lord Goddard CJ, Lord Reid and Mr L M D De Silva

Facts: This was an appeal to the Privy Council from the High Court of Basutoland. The appellants had a preconceived plan to kill the victim. They took the victim to a hut where they gave him beer and then hit him over the head. Thinking that they had killed him, they then rolled him over a low cliff, to make it look as if he had died in an accident. Medical evidence showed that the victim had not been killed by the blow to the head, but had died of exposure at the bottom of the cliff. The appellants appealed against their conviction for murder on the ground that there was no coincidence of actus reus and mens rea.

LORD REID

The point of law which was raised in this case can be simply stated. It is said that two acts were necessary and were separable: first, the attack in the hut; and, secondly, the placing of the body outside afterwards. It is said that, while the first act was accompanied by mens rea, it was not the cause of death; but that the second act, while it was the cause of death, was not accompanied by mens rea; and on that ground it is said that the accused are not guilty of any crime except perhaps culpable homicide.

It appears to their Lordships impossible to divide up what was really one transaction in this way. There is no doubt that the accused set out to do all these acts in order to achieve their plan and as parts of their plan; and it is much too refined a ground of judgment to say that, because they were under a misapprehension at one stage and thought that their guilty purpose and been achieved before in fact it was achieved, therefore they are to escape the penalties of the law. Their Lordships do not think that this is a matter which is susceptible of elaboration. There appears to be no case either in South Africa or England, or for that matter elsewhere, which resembles the present. Their Lordships can find no difference relevant to the present case between the law of South Africa and the law of England, and they are of opinion that by both laws there could be no separation such as that for which the accused contend, so as to reduce the crime from murder to a lesser crime, merely because the accused were under some misapprehension for a time during the completion of their criminal plot.

R v Le Brun [1992] QB 61

Panel: Lord Lane CJ, Auld and Judge JJ

Facts: The appellant and his wife were walking home after having dinner with friends. The case was decided on the basis that they had argued and the appellant had hit his wife on the chin, probably rendering her unconscious. He had then tried to drag her home to avoid detection and had accidently let her fall onto the pavement. The fall fractured her skull and killed her. He was convicted of manslaughter and appealed.

LORD LANE CJ

The question can be perhaps framed in this way. There was here an initial unlawful blow to the chin delivered by the appellant. That, again on what must have been the jury's finding, was not delivered with the intention of doing really serious harm to the wife. The guilty intent accompanying that blow was sufficient to have rendered the appellant guilty of manslaughter, but not murder, had it caused death. But it did not cause death. What caused death was the later impact when the wife's head hit the pavement. At the moment of impact the appellant's intention was to remove her, probably unconscious, body to avoid detection. To that extent the impact may have been accidental. May the earlier guilty intent be joined with the later non-guilty blow which caused death to produce in the conglomerate a proper verdict of manslaughter?

It has usually been in the previous decisions in the context of murder that the problem has arisen. We have had our attention directed to a Privy Council case, *Meli v The Queen* [1954] 1 WLR 228. It is to be observed that two members of the Judicial Committee on that occasion were Lord Goddard CJ and Lord Reid. The facts of the case were these. The appellants, all in accordance with their preconceived plan, took a man to a hut, gave him beer so that he was partially intoxicated and then struck him over the head. They thought he was dead. They took what they thought was his lifeless body, rolled it over a cliff, and then dressed up the scene as though the whole affair was an accident. In fact the man was not dead. It was established from medical evidence that the final cause of his death was exposure. He had been left at the bottom of the cliff over which he had been rolled.

At their trial for murder the appellants contended that the two acts were separate acts, and that, while the first act was accompanied by a guilty mind, it was not the cause of death. The second act, while it was the cause of death, was not accompanied by the guilty mind. Therefore they were not guilty of murder, a similar situation to that which exists in the present case.

Lord Reid delivering the judgment of the Judicial Committee said, at page 230:

> "It appears to their Lordships impossible to divide up what was really one transaction in this way. There is no doubt that the accused set out to do all these acts in order to achieve their plan and as parts of their plan; and it is much too refined a ground of judgment to say that, because they were under a misapprehension at one stage and thought that their guilty purpose had been achieved before in fact it was achieved, therefore they are to escape the penalties of the law."

That decision of course is not binding upon us. It is of very persuasive authority and it was adopted by another division of this court in 1975 in *Reg. v Moore* [1975] Crim LR 229.

However, it will be observed that the present case is different from the facts of those two cases in that death here was not the result of a preconceived plan which went wrong, as was the case in those two decisions which we have cited. Here the death, again assuming the jury's finding to be such as it must have been, was the result of an initial unlawful blow, not intended to cause serious harm, in its turn causing the appellant to take steps possibly to evade the consequences of his unlawful act. During the taking of those steps he commits the actus reus but without the mens rea necessary for murder or manslaughter. Therefore the mens rea is contained in the initial unlawful assault, but the actus reus is the eventual dropping of the head on to the ground.

Normally the actus reus and mens rea coincide in point of time. What is the situation when they do not? Is it permissible, as the prosecution contend here, to combine them to produce a conviction for manslaughter?

The answer is perhaps to be found in the next case to which we were referred, and that was *Reg. v Church* [1966] 1 QB 59. In that case the defendant was charged with the murder of a woman whose body was found in a river. The cause of death was drowning. The defendant had it seemed attacked the woman and rendered her semi-conscious. He thought she was dead and in his panic he threw her into the river. He was acquitted of murder but convicted of manslaughter. Edmund Davies J., giving the judgment of this court, said, at page 70:

"the conclusion of this court is that an unlawful act causing the death of another cannot, simply because it is an unlawful act, render a manslaughter verdict inevitable. For such a verdict inexorably to follow, the unlawful act must be such as all sober and reasonable people would inevitably recognise must subject the other person to, at least, the risk of some harm resulting therefrom, albeit not serious harm. . . . In the light of *Meli v The Queen* [1954] 1 WLR 228 it is conceded on behalf of the appellant that, on the murder charge, the trial judge was perfectly entitled to direct the jury, as he did: 'Unless you find that something happened in the course of this evening between the infliction of the injuries and the decision to throw the body into the water, you may undoubtedly treat the whole course of conduct of the accused as one.' But for some reason not clear to this court, appellant's counsel denies that such an approach is possible when one is considering a charge of manslaughter. We fail to see why. We adopt as sound Dr. Glanville Williams' view in his book, Criminal Law, 2nd edn (1961), page 174, that, 'If a killing by the first act would have been manslaughter, a later destruction of the supposed corpse should also be manslaughter.' Had Mrs Nott [the victim] died of her initial injuries a manslaughter verdict might quite conceivably have been returned on the basis that the accused inflicted them under the influence of provocation or that the jury were not convinced that they were inflicted with murderous intent. All that was lacking in the direction given in this case was that, when the judge turned to consider manslaughter, he did not again tell the jury that they were entitled (if they thought fit) to regard the conduct of the appellant in relation to Mrs Nott as constituting throughout a series of acts which culminated in her death, and that, if that was how they regarded the accused's behaviour, it mattered not whether he believed her to be alive or dead when he threw her in the river."

> It seems to us that where the unlawful application of force and the eventual act causing death are parts of the same sequence of events, the same transaction, the fact that there is an appreciable interval of time between the two does not serve to exonerate the defendant from liability. That is certainly so where the appellant's subsequent actions which caused death, after the initial unlawful blow, are designed to conceal his commission of the original unlawful assault.

In *Meli v The Queen* the Privy Council held that the series of acts could be viewed as one transaction because they followed an antecedent plan. In both *R v Church* and *R v Le Brun* there was no antecedent plan. What enabled the courts to view the series of acts as one transaction was the fact that in each case the act which caused the death was designed to cover up an original unlawful act which was done with the mens rea for the crime charged.

2.4.3 Causation

Sometimes an apparent problem of lack of coincidence of actus reus and mens rea may disappear when applying the rules of causation. It may be that the act done with the mens rea can be seen as the act which caused death.

R v Le Brun [1992] QB 61

LORD LANE CJ

> It would be possible to express the problem as one of causation. The original unlawful blow to the chin was a causa sine qua non of the later actus reus. It was the opening event in a series which was to culminate in death: the first link in the chain of causation, to use another metaphor. It cannot be said that the actions of the appellant in dragging the victim away with the intention of evading liability broke the chain which linked the initial blow with the death.

Further Reading

Amirthalingam K 'Caldwell Recklessness is Dead, Long Live Mens Rea's Fecklessness' (2004) 67(3) *MLR* 491

Ashworth A Commentary on *R v G* [2004] *Crim LR* 369

Kugler I 'Conditional Oblique Intention' [2004] *Crim LR* 284

Norrie A 'After Woollin' [1999] *Crim LR* 532

3

Homicide I: Voluntary Manslaughter

Topic List

3.1 The Defence of Loss of Control

The Coroners and Justice Act 2009 (CJA) abolished the old defence of provocation and replaced it with a defence of loss of control. You should refer to ss 54 and 55 when reading this section. This new defence has recently been considered by the Court of Appeal.

R v Clinton, Parker and Evans [2012] EWCA Crim 2

Panel: Judge LCJ, Henriques adn Gloster JJ

This co-joined appeal relates to three defendants, all convicted for the murder of their wives. The issue for the Court of Appeal centred on the availability of this defence in cases concerning sexual infedility. The Court took this opportunity to review this new defence.

3.1.1 The Loss of Control

Section 54(2) expressly removes the requirement from the defence of provocation that the loss of self control should be sudden. In *R v Clinton* the court of appeal made it clear that Parliament has replaced the old defence of provocation with this new defence of loss of control and that is the new law from which we are to work on.

THE LORD CHIEF JUSTICE

The first component

10. For present purposes, subsection 1(a) , which addresses the first ingredient, is self explanatory. The killing must have resulted from the loss of self control. The loss of control need not be sudden, but it must have been lost. That is essential. Before reaching the second ingredient, the qualifying trigger, there is a further hurdle, that the defendant must not have been acting in a "considered" desire for revenge. The possible significance of "considered" arises in the appeal of Evans . In the broad context of the legislative structure, there does not appear to be very much room for any "considered" deliberation. In reality, the greater the level of deliberation, the less likely it will be that the killing followed a true loss of self control.

It is still thought that cases on provocation may still be useful in establishing what is required for a loss of self control. Therefore it is likely that the loss of control need not be complete and that there is no requirement for the defendant to be in a state of automatism. Guidance on this can be sought from the case of *Richens, based on the old law.*

R v Richens [1994] 98 Cr App R 43

Panel: Lord Taylor CJ, Hutchison and Holland JJ

Facts: Richens and his girlfriend Sabrina spent the night at the victim's house. Sabrina told Richens that the victim had raped her. Two weeks later Richens and Sabrina went to the victim's house and Richens challenged the victim about the rape. The victim claimed that Sabrina had been a willing participant. Richens became enraged and stabbed the victim to death. Richens was convicted and appealed on several grounds, one of which was that the trial judge had directed the jury that, for the defence of provocation, there had to be a total loss of control.

LORD TAYLOR CJ

In the critical passage in his summing-up the learned judge was plainly seeking to convey to the jury that loss of self-control meant something more than mere loss of temper. If he thought, in order to illuminate this distinction, that a more homely or readily understandable paraphrase of Devlin J.'s words was required, it would have been perfectly proper to emphasise that the test was not "loss of temper" but "a sudden and temporary loss of self-control which resulted in the defendant's being unable to restrain himself from doing what he did." Unfortunately, however, the learned judge went further than this. Three times he spoke of "complete loss of control": and (which is it seems to us the more telling criticism) he twice qualified the phrase, first with the words "to the extent where you really do not know what you are doing"; and (immediately after introducing the *Duffy* formulation) with the words: "It might be slightly better put that his mind is no longer master of his body, because he has so far lost control, he really does not know what he is doing."

It is, of course, necessary to look at this passage in the summing-up as a whole, and to consider it in the context of the facts of the case and the nature of the issues before the jury. We were invited to say that, so viewed, there was no material misdirection, since the overall message the jury would have received was that provocation involved more than mere loss of temper but less than automatism. It could be argued that the jury would have understood the phrase "not know what he is doing" as referring not to complete lack of awareness but as involving a failure by the appellant to appreciate the full import, in terms of legal or moral responsibility or consequences, of his actions. We are, accordingly, invited to say that there was not here a material misdirection.

It was also a requirement under the old law that where a person acts out of revenge he will not have lost his self control. This is now in statutory form in s 54(4). The case of *Ibrams and Greggory* sets out an example of when this could arise.

R v Ibrams and Gregory (1982) 74 Cr App R 154

Panel: Lawton LJ, Bingham and McCowan JJ

Facts: The victim had tortured, bullied and terrorised the two appellants and Ibrams's fiancée for several weeks. On two occasions the police had been informed, but had taken no action. The Lord Chief Justice described the victim's behaviour as appalling and as a result showed a wish that the appellants should obtain parole reasonably early. In order to stop the bullying the appellants devised a plot to attack the victim at night. They stabbed him with an axe and a knife while he was asleep and killed him. At their trial the judge had withdrawn the issue of provocation from the jury on the grounds that there was no loss of self control.

LORD JUSTICE LAWTON

Here the last act of provocation was on Sunday, October 7. It was not in any way suggested that the dead man had provoked anybody on the night of his death. In fact, when Gregory and Ibrams went into the bedroom he was asleep. The first blow he received was inflicted on him by Gregory, and it dazed him but did not knock him unconscious. He was able to sit up in bed, and he was then attacked by Ibrams. Nothing happened on the night of the killing which caused Ibrams to lose his self-control. There having been a plan to kill Monk, his evidence that when he saw him all the past came to his mind does not, in our judgment, provide any evidence of loss of self-control.

In our judgment, the matter is really concluded by the summing-up to the jury of Devlin J. (as he then was) in *Duffy* [1949] 1 All ER 932, which was approved by the Court of Criminal Appeal. There is a passage in the summing-up so approved which is referred to time and time again in cases and in the textbooks; but, whether we look at the whole of the summing-up or at those parts of it which were approved by the Court of Criminal Appeal, it appears that there was another passage which is directly relevant to the facts of this case. The part which has been referred to many times with approval, and in particular with the approval of this Court in *Whitfield* (1976) 63 Cr App R 39, 42, is as follows:

> "Provocation is some act or series of acts done by the dead man to the accused which would cause in any reasonable person and actually causes in the accused, a sudden and temporary loss of self-control, rendering the accused so subject to passion as to make him for the moment not master of his mind."

That passage refers to "a sudden and temporary loss of self-control," which has to be of such a kind as to make the accused for the moment not master of his mind.

Later in the same summing-up, in another passage which was also approved by the Court of Criminal Appeal in *Duffy* (supra), are these words: ([1949] 1 All ER at p. 932H)

> "Indeed, circumstances which induce a desire for revenge are inconsistent with provocation, since the conscious formulation of a desire for revenge means that a person has had time to think, to reflect, and that would negative a sudden temporary loss of self-control, which is of the essence of provocation."

 Alert

Mr Hytner has pointed out to us that this gross bullying and terrorising had almost certainly impaired the judgment of Ibrams, Gregory and Andronik, but that impairment of judgment is not the same as loss of self-control. Impairment of judgment led them, on the Wednesday following Sunday, October 7, to plan Monk's death or, if Ibrams's version is right, to do him grievous bodily harm. They carried out the plan. They were masters of their minds when carrying it out, because they worked out the details with considerable skill; and in pursuing the plan as they did on the Friday night they were still masters of their own minds. They were doing what they had planned to do. When they went into Monk's bedroom and Gregory struck the first blow that again was pursuant to the plan which had been worked out, and they were masters of their own minds.

It follows, in our judgment, that McNeill J. was right in ruling that there was no evidence of loss of self-control. In those circumstances the appeal will be dismissed.

The Court wishes to say that this case is a most unusual one, and had it not been for the appalling criminal behaviour of the dead man these two appellants would not today be serving sentences of life imprisonment for murder. It is to be hoped that a copy of this judgment will be sent to the appropriate department of the Home Office and that the parole board will as soon as possible be alerted to the very unusual and very disturbing facts of this case.

Section 54(2) states that the loss of self control does not have to be sudden. Therefore a defendant will not be prevented from running the defence by the fact that he lost his self control some time after the qualifying trigger. The Court of Appeal has examined in the case below the relevance of a time delay between the provocative act (now the qualifying trigger) and the loss of self control.

R v Ahluwalia [1992] 4 All ER 889

Panel: Lord Taylor CJ, Swinton Thomas and Judge JJ

Facts: Mrs Ahluwalia had been verbally and physically abused by her husband for many years. One night, as he slept, she poured petrol over him and set him alight. He died from his burns. She was convicted of murder after the trial judge had directed the jury that a sudden and temporary loss of self control was required for the defence of provocation. She appealed on several grounds, one of which was that this was a misdirection.

LORD TAYLOR CJ

Nevertheless, it is open to the judge, when deciding whether there is any evidence of provocation to be left to the jury and open to the jury when considering such evidence, to take account of the interval between the provocative conduct and the reaction of the defendant to it. Time for reflection may show that after the provocative conduct made its impact on the mind of the defendant, he or she kept or regained self-control. The passage of time following the provocation may also show that the subsequent attack was planned or based on motives, such as revenge or punishment, inconsistent with the loss of self-control and therefore with the defence of provocation. In some cases, such an interval may wholly undermine the defence of provocation; that, however, depends entirely on the facts of the individual case and is not a principle of law.

Mr Robertson referred to the phrase "cooling off period" which has sometimes been applied to an interval of time between the provocation relied upon and the fatal act. He suggests that although in many cases such an interval may indeed be a time for cooling and regaining self-control so as to forfeit the protection of the defence, in others the time lapse has an opposite effect. He submits, relying on expert evidence not before the trial judge, that women who have been subjected frequently over a period to violent treatment may react to the final act or words by what he calls a "slow-burn" reaction rather than by an immediate loss of self-control.

We accept that the subjective element in the defence of provocation would not as a matter of law be negatived simply because of the delayed reaction in such cases, provided that there was at the time of the killing a "sudden and temporary loss of self-control" caused by the alleged provocation. However, the longer the delay and the stronger the evidence of deliberation on the part of the defendant, the more likely it will be that the prosecution will negative provocation.

In the present case, despite the delay after the last provocative act or words by the deceased, and despite the appellant's apparent deliberation in seeking and lighting the petrol, the trial judge nevertheless left the issue of provocation to the jury. His references to "sudden and temporary loss of self-control" were correct in law. He did not suggest to the jury that they should or might reject the defence of provocation because the last provocative act or word of the deceased was not followed immediately by the appellant's fatal acts.

We consider that the learned judge's direction was in accordance with the well established law and cannot be faulted.

The Court did, however, reduce the offence from murder to manslaughter on the grounds of diminished responsibility.

3.1.2 Qualifying trigger

Much of the judgment in **Clinton** and others deals with the prohibition contained in s 55(6)(c).

THE LORD CHIEF JUSTICE

The second component

11. The qualifying trigger provisions are self contained in section 55. There is no point in pretending that the practical application of this provision will not create considerable difficulties. Sections 55(3) and (4) define the circumstances in which a qualifying trigger may be present. The statutory language is not bland. In section 55(3) it is not enough that the defendant is fearful of violence. He must fear serious violence. In subsection (4)(a) the circumstances must not merely be grave, but extremely so. In subsection (4)(b) it is not enough that the defendant has been caused by the circumstances to feel a sense of grievance. It must arise from a justifiable sense not merely that he has been wronged, but that he has been seriously wronged. By contrast with the former law of provocation, these provisions, as Mr Michael Birnbaum QC, on behalf of Clinton submitted, have raised the bar. We have been used to a much less prescriptive approach to the provocation defence.

12. Mr Birnbaum submitted, and we think correctly, that the defendant himself must have a sense of having been seriously wronged. However even if he has, that is not the end of it. In short, the defendant cannot invite the jury to acquit him of

 Alert

murder on the ground of loss of control because he personally sensed that he had been seriously wronged in circumstances which he personally regarded as extremely grave. The questions whether the circumstances were extremely grave, and whether the defendant's sense of grievance was justifiable, indeed all the requirements of section 55(4)(a) and (b), require objective evaluation.

Alert

13. The process of objective evaluation in each individual case is hugely complicated by the prohibitions in section 55(6) which identifies a number of features which are expressly excluded from consideration as qualifying triggers. Thus the defendant, who, looking for trouble to the extent of inciting or exciting violence loses his control, does not qualify. In effect self induced loss of control will not run. The most critical problem, however, which lies at the heart of the Clinton appeal, is subsection 6(c), "sexual infidelity".

14. This provision was described by Mr Andrew Edis QC, who acted for the prosecution in each of the appeals, as a "formidably difficult provision": so indeed it is. On the face of the statutory language, however grave the betrayal, however humiliating, indeed however provocative in the ordinary sense of the word it may be, sexual infidelity is to be disregarded as a qualifying trigger. Nevertheless, other forms of betrayal or humiliation of sufficient gravity may fall within the qualifying triggers specified in section 55(4). What, therefore, is the full extent of the prohibition?

15. We highlight some of the matters raised in argument to illustrate some of the potential problems. This list is not comprehensive. The forensic analysis could have gone on much longer, and so, for that matter, could this judgment.

16. We immediately acknowledge that the exclusion of sexual infidelity as a potential qualifying trigger is consistent with the concept of the autonomy of each individual. Of course, whatever the position may have been in times past, it is now clearly understood, and in the present context the law underlines, that no one (male or female) owns or possesses his or her spouse or partner. Nevertheless daily experience in both criminal and family courts demonstrates that the breakdown of relationships, whenever they occur, and for whatever reason, is always fraught with tension and difficulty, with the possibility of misunderstanding and the potential for apparently irrational fury. Meanwhile experience over many generations has shown that, however it may become apparent, when it does, sexual infidelity has the potential to create a highly emotional situation or to exacerbate a fraught situation, and to produce a completely unpredictable, and sometimes violent response. This may have nothing to do with any notional "rights" that the one may believe that he or she has over the other, and often stems from a sense of betrayal and heartbreak, and crushed dreams.

17. Mr Birnbaum drew attention to and adopted much of the illuminating and critical commentary by Professor Ormerod at pages 520–522 in Smith and Hogan's Criminal Law. To begin with, there is no definition of "sexual infidelity". Who and what is embraced in this concept? Is sexual infidelity to be construed narrowly so as to refer only to conduct which is related directly and exclusively to sexual

activity? Only the words and acts constituting sexual activity are to be disregarded: on one construction, therefore, the effects are not. What acts relating to infidelity, but distinguishable from it on the basis that they are not "sexual", may be taken into account? Is the provision directly concerned with sexual infidelity, or with envy and jealousy and possessiveness, the sort of obsession that leads to violence against the victim on the basis expressed in the sadly familiar language, "if I cannot have him/her, then no one else will/can"? The notion of infidelity appears to involve a relationship between the two people to which one party may be unfaithful. Is a one-night-stand sufficient for this purpose?

18. Take a case like *R v Stingel* [1990] 171 CLR 312, an Australian case where a jealous stalker, who stabbed his quarry when he found her, on his account, having sexual intercourse. He does not face any difficulty with this element of the offence, just because, so far as the stalker was concerned, there was no sexual infidelity by his victim at all. Is the jealous spouse to be excluded when the stalker is not? In *R v Tabeel Lewis* ... an 18 year old Jehovah's Witness killed his lover, a 63 year old co-religionist, because on one view, he was ashamed of the consequences, if she carried out her threat to reveal their affair to the community. She was not sexually unfaithful to him, but he killed her because he feared that she would betray him, not sexually, but by revealing their secret. Mr Birnbaum asked rhetorically, why should the law exclude one kind of betrayal by a lover but not another?

19. Mr Edis agreed that "sexual infidelity" is not defined. He suggested that its ambit is not confined to "adultery" and that no marriage or civil partnership ceremony or any formal arrangement is required to render the violent reaction of the defendant to the sexual infidelity of the deceased impermissible for the purposes of a qualifying trigger. He suggested however that the concept of "infidelity" involves a breach of mutual understanding which is to be inferred within the relationship, as well as any of the more obvious expressions of fidelity, such as those to be found in the marriage vows. Notwithstanding their force, these considerations do not quite address the specific requirement that the infidelity to be disregarded must be "sexual" infidelity. The problem was illustrated when Mr Edis postulated the example of a female victim who decided to end a relationship and made clear to her former partner that it was at an end, and whether expressly or by implication, that she regarded herself as free to have sexual intercourse with whomsoever she wanted. After the end of the relationship, any such sexual activity could not sensibly be called "infidelity". If so, for the purposes of any qualifying trigger, it would not be caught by the prohibition in section 55(6)(c). In such a case the exercise of what Mr Edis described as her sexual freedom might possibly be taken into account in support of the defence, if she was killed by her former partner, whereas, if notwithstanding her disillusionment with it, she had attempted to keep the relationship going, while from time to time having intercourse with others, it could not.

20. Mr Birnbaum and Mr Edis could readily have identified a large number of situations arising in the real world which, as a result of the statutory provision, would be productive of surprising anomalies. We cannot resolve them in advance. Whatever

the anomalies to which it may give rise, the statutory provision is unequivocal: loss of control triggered by sexual infidelity cannot, on its own, qualify as a trigger for the purposes of the second component of this defence. This is the clear effect of the legislation.

21. The question however is whether it is a consequence of the legislation that sexual infidelity is similarly excluded when it may arise for consideration in the context of another or a number of other features of the case which are said to constitute an appropriate permissible qualifying trigger. The issue is complex.

22. To assist in its resolution, Mr Edis drew attention to the formal guidance issued by the Crown Prosecution Service on this issue. This provides that "it is the issue of sexual infidelity that falls to be disregarded under sub-section (6)(c) . However certain parts of the case may still amount to a defence under section 55(4) ". The example is given of the defendant who kills her husband because he has raped her sister (an act of sexual infidelity). In such a case the act of sexual infidelity may be disregarded and her actions may constitute a qualifying trigger under section 55(4) .

23. This example is interesting as far as it goes, and we understand it to mean that the context in which sexual infidelity may arise may be relevant to the existence of a qualifying trigger, but in truth it is too easy. Any individual who witnesses a rape may well suffer temporary loss of control in circumstances in which a qualifying trigger might well be deemed to be present, although in the case of a rape of a stranger, insufficient to cause the defendant to have a sense of being seriously wronged personally. A much more formidable and difficult example would be the defendant who kills her husband when she suddenly finds him having enthusiastic, consensual sexual intercourse with her sister. Taken on its own, the effect of the legislation is that any loss of control consequent on such a gross betrayal would be totally excluded from consideration as a qualifying trigger. Let us for the purposes of argument take the same example a little further. The defendant returns home unexpectedly and finds her spouse or partner having consensual sexual intercourse with her sister (or indeed with anyone else), and entirely reasonably, but vehemently, complains about what has suddenly confronted her. The response by the unfaithful spouse or partner, and/or his or her new sexual companion, is to justify what he had been doing, by shouting and screaming, mercilessly taunting and deliberately using hurtful language which implies that she, not he, is responsible for his infidelity. The taunts and distressing words, which do not themselves constitute sexual infidelity, would fall to be considered as a possible qualifying trigger. The idea that, in the search for a qualifying trigger, the context in which such words are used should be ignored represents an artificiality which the administration of criminal justice should do without. And if the taunts by the unfaithful partner suggested that the sexual activity which had just been taking place was infinitely more gratifying than any earlier sexual relationship with the defendant, are those insults – in effect using sexual infidelity to cause deliberate distress — to be ignored? On the view of the legislation advanced for our consideration by Mr Edis, they must be. Yet, in most criminal cases, as our recent judgment in the context of the riots and public order demonstrates, context is critical.

24. We considered the example of the wife who has been physically abused over a long period, and whose loss of self control was attributable to yet another beating by her husband, but also, for the first time, during the final beating, taunts of his sexual activities with another woman or other women. And so, after putting up with years of violent ill-treatment, what in reality finally caused the defendant's loss of control was hurtful language boasting of his sexual infidelity. Those words were the final straw. Mr Edis invited us to consider (he did not support the contention) whether, on a narrow interpretation of the statutory structure, if evidence to that effect were elicited (as it might, in cross-examination), there would then be no sufficient qualifying trigger at all. Although the persistent beating might in a different case fall within the provisions for qualifying triggers in section 55(4)(a) and (b), in the case we are considering, the wife had endured the violence and would have continued to endure it but for the sudden discovery of her husband's infidelity. On this basis the earlier history of violence, as well as the violence on the instant occasion, would not, without reference to the claims of sexual infidelity, carry sufficient weight to constitute a qualifying trigger. Yet in the real world the husband's conduct over the years, and the impact of what he said on the particular occasion when he was killed, should surely be considered as a whole.

25. We addressed the same issue in discussion about the impact of the words "things said" within subsection 55(6)(c). Everyone can understand how a thing done may constitute sexual infidelity, but this argument revolved around finding something "said" which "constituted" sexual infidelity. Mr Edis accepted that no utterance, as such, could constitute sexual infidelity, at any rate as narrowly construed. Professor Ormerod suggests the example of a defendant hearing a wife say to her lover, "I love you". On close examination, this may or may not provide evidence of sexual infidelity. However it does not necessarily "constitute" it, and whether it does or not depends on the relationship between the parties, and the person by whom and to whom and the circumstances in which the endearment is spoken. It may constitute a betrayal without any sexual contact or intention. Mr Birnbaum raised another question. He pointed out that in the case of Clinton, Mrs Clinton confessed to having had an affair on the day before she was killed, but earlier she boasted that she had had sex with five men. If the boast, intended to hurt, was simply untrue, how could those words "constitute" infidelity?

26. We are required to make sense of this provision. It would be illogical for a defendant to be able to rely on an untrue statement about the victim's sexual infidelity as a qualifying trigger in support of the defence, but not on a truthful one. Equally, it would be quite unrealistic to limit its ambit to words spoken to his or her lover by the unfaithful spouse or partner during sexual activity. In our judgment things "said" includes admissions of sexual infidelity (even if untrue) as well as reports (by others) of sexual infidelity. Such admissions or reports will rarely if ever be uttered without a context, and almost certainly a painful one. In short, the words will almost invariably be spoken as part of a highly charged discussion in which many disturbing comments will be uttered, often on both sides.

27. We must briefly return to the second example suggested by Professor Ormerod, that is the defendant telling his spouse or partner that he or she loves someone else. As we have said, this may or may not provide evidence of sexual infidelity. But it is entirely reasonable to assume that, faced with such an assertion, the defendant will ask who it is, and is likely to go on to ask whether they have already had an affair. If the answer is "no" there would not appear to be any sexual infidelity. If the answer is "yes", then obviously there has been. If the answer is "no", but it is perfectly obvious that the departing spouse intends to begin a full relationship with the new partner, would that constitute sexual infidelity? And is there a relevant distinction between the defendant who believes that a sexual relationship has already developed, and one who believes that it has not, but that in due course it will. Situations arising from overhearing the other party to a relationship saying "I love you", or saying to the defendant, "I love someone else", simple enough words, will give rise to manifold difficulties in the context of the prohibition on sexual infidelity as a qualifying trigger.

28. This discussion of the impact of the statutory prohibition in section 55(6)(c) arises, we emphasise, in the context, not of an academic symposium, but a trial process in which the defendant will be entitled to give evidence. There is no prohibition on the defendant telling the whole story about the relevant events, including the fact and impact of sexual infidelity. To the contrary: this evidence will have to be considered and evaluated by the jury. That is because notwithstanding that sexual infidelity must be disregarded for the purposes of the second component if it stands alone as a qualifying trigger, for the reasons which follow it is plainly relevant to any questions which arise in the context of the third component, and indeed to one of the alternative defences to murder, as amended in the 2009 Act, diminished responsibility.

29. We shall return to the question whether, notwithstanding that it must be disregarded if it is the only qualifying trigger, a thing done or said which constitutes sexual infidelity is properly available for consideration in the course of evaluating any qualifying trigger which is not otherwise prohibited by the legislation.

This defence has been further examined by the Court of Appeal, especially in relation to the first qualifying trigger: fear of serious violence.

R v Dawes, Hatter and Bowyer [2013] EWCA Crim 322

Panel: The Lord Chief Justice, Rafferty LJ and Simon J

Facts: These were 3 appeals against conviction for murder. All three appeals questioned the availability of the defence of loss of control.

THE LORD CHIEF JUSTICE

When considering the first element and whether there has been a loss of control, the Court of Appeal has confirmed the ability to take into account previous events.

54. We can now turn to the first requirement, that is that the defendant's acts or omissions in doing, or in being a part of, the killing resulted from his loss of self control. Provided there was a loss of control, it does not matter whether the loss was sudden or not. A reaction to circumstances of extreme gravity may be delayed. Different individuals in different situations do not react identically, nor respond immediately. Thus for the purposes of the new defence, the loss of control may follow from the cumulative impact of earlier events. For the purposes of this first ingredient, the response to what used to be described as "cumulative provocation" requires consideration in the same way as it does in relation to cases in which the loss of control is said to have arisen suddenly. Given the changed description of this defence, perhaps "cumulative impact" is the better phrase to describe this particular feature of the first requirement.

The Court of Appeal did not feel the need to discuss the issue of the third element of this defence in any detail as no issues seem to arise on the facts of the appeal.

55. For present purposes, we can deal briefly with the third ingredient of the defence, that a person of D's sex and age, with a normal degree of tolerance and self-restraint and in the circumstances of D, that is all of his circumstances other than those bearing on his general capacity for tolerance or self-restraint, might have reacted or behaved in the same or a similar way. In this judgment, no further elaboration is appropriate.

The Court of Appeal then went on to carry out a detailed examination of what is required for a defendant to rely on the argument that he reacted due to fear of serious violence from the victim.

56. The crucial questions in the present appeals involve an examination of the qualifying triggers defined in s 54(1)(b) as elaborated in s 55, that is the second ingredient of the defence. To the extent explained in *Clinton*, sexual infidelity is to be disregarded. By contrast, if the loss of self control is attributable to D's fear of serious violence from the victim against him or some other identified person, the qualifying trigger may be present. A further qualifying trigger applies if the loss of self control is attributed to a thing or things done or said, or both, which constituted circumstances of an extremely grave character, and causes the defendant to have a justifiable sense of being seriously wronged. As the legislation recognises in s 55(5) there are unlikely to be many cases where the only feature of the evidence relating to the qualifying trigger in the context of fear of violence will arise in total isolation from things done or said within s 55(4). In most cases the qualifying trigger based on a fear of violence will almost inevitably to include consideration of things said and done, in short, a combination of the features identified in s 55(3) and (4).

57. Neither qualifying trigger in s 55(6)(a) and (b) is available to the defendant who has deliberately sought to provide himself with an excuse to use violence by inciting, or encouraging or manufacturing a situation for this purpose.

58. There was some debate about the continuing authority, if any, of *Johnson* [1989] 89 Cr App R 148, decided in the context of the former provocation defence. In that case the court rejected the submission "that the mere fact that a defendant caused a

reaction in others, which in turn led him to lose his self-control, should result in the issue of provocation being outside a jury's consideration". In our judgment, for the purposes of the loss of control defence, the impact of *Johnson* is now diminished, but not wholly extinguished by the new statutory provisions. One may wonder (and the judge would have to consider) how often a defendant who is out to incite violence could be said to "fear" serious violence; often he may be welcoming it. Similarly, one may wonder how such a defendant may have a justifiable sense of being seriously wronged if he successfully incites someone else to use violence towards him. Those are legitimate issues for consideration, but as a matter of statutory construction, the mere fact that in some general way the defendant was behaving badly and looking for and provoking trouble does not of itself lead to the disapplication of the qualifying triggers based on s 55(3)(4) and (5) unless his actions were intended to provide him with the excuse or opportunity to use violence. As *Johnson* no longer fully reflects the appropriate principle, further reference to it is inappropriate. The relevant principle is identified in the present judgment.

59. The loss of control defence is not self-defence, but there will often be a factual overlap between them. It will be argued on the defendant's behalf that the violence which resulted in the death of the deceased was, on grounds of self-defence, not unlawful. This defence is now governed by s 76 of the Criminal Justice and Immigration Act 2008. In the context of violence used by the defendant there are obvious differences between the two defences and they should not be elided. These are summarised in *Smith and Hogan, 13th edition,* at page 135. The circumstances in which the defendant, who has lost control of himself, will nevertheless be able to argue that he used reasonable force in response to the violence he feared, or to which he was subjected, are likely to be limited. But even if the defendant may have lost his self-control, provided his violent response in self-defence was not unreasonable in the circumstances, he would be entitled to rely on self defence as a complete defence. S 55(3) is focussed on the defendant's fear of *serious* violence. We underline the distinction between the terms of the qualifying trigger in the context of loss of control with self-defence, which is concerned with the threat of violence in any form. Obviously, if the defendant genuinely fears serious violence then, in the context of self-defence, his own response may legitimately be more extreme. Weighing these considerations, it is likely that in the forensic process those acting for the defendant will advance self-defence as a complete answer to the murder charge, and on occasions, make little or nothing of the defendant's response in the context of the loss of control defence. As we have already indicated, the decision taken on forensic grounds (whether the judge believes it to be wise or not) is not binding on the judge and, provided the statutory conditions obtain, loss of control should be left to the jury. Almost always, we suggest, the practical course, if the defence is to be left, is to leave it for the consideration of the jury after it has rejected self-defence.

60. As noted in *Clinton*, viewed overall, the eventual legislation which found its way into ss 54 and 55 of the 2009 Act did not closely follow the overall recommendations of the Murder, Manslaughter and Infanticide (Law Commission No. 309). Nevertheless, as the Law Commission noted, in the context of the

former defence of provocation, the judge was bound to leave the defence if there was evidence that the defendant was provoked to lose self-control, however improbable the defence may have appeared. In the view of the Law Commission 5.15:

"The current position does not serve the interests of justice because the need to put the defence to the jury in these circumstances increases the likelihood that an unmeritorious claim may succeed"

At 5.16 it was proposed that the trial judge should have the task of "filtering out purely speculative and wholly unmeritorious claims". We see a direct link between this recommendation and the legislative provisions in s 55(3), (4) and (5). Their effect is that the circumstances in which the qualifying triggers will arise is much more limited than the equivalent provisions in the former provocation defence. The result is that some of the more absurd trivia which nevertheless required the judge to leave the provocation defence to the jury will no longer fall within the ambit of the qualifying triggers defined in the new defence. This is unsurprising. For the individual with normal capacity of self-restraint and tolerance, unless the circumstances are extremely grave, normal irritation, and even serious anger do not often cross the threshold into loss of control.

61. The presence, or otherwise, of a qualifying trigger is not defined or decided by the defendant and any assertions he may make in evidence, or any account given in the investigative process. S 55(3) directly engages the defendant's fear of serious violence. As we have explained, in this type of case s 55(4) will almost inevitably arise for consideration. Unless the defendant has a sense of being *seriously* wronged s 55(4) has no application. Even if it does, there are two distinctive further requirements. The circumstances must be *extremely* grave and the defendant's sense of being seriously wronged by them must be *justifiable*. In our judgment these matters require objective assessment by the judge at the end of the evidence and, if the defence is left, by the jury considering their verdict. If it were otherwise it would mean that a qualifying trigger would be present if the defendant were to give an account to the effect that, "the circumstances were extremely grave to me and caused me to have what I believed was a justifiable sense that I had been seriously wronged". If so, when it is clear that the availability of a defence based on the loss of control has been significantly narrowed, one would have to question the purpose of s 55(3), (4) and (5).

 Alert

All three appeals were dismissed.

3.1.3 Circumstances of the Defendant

Section 54(1)(c) provides a requirement for the defence 'that a person of the defendant's sex and age, with a normal degree of tolerance and self restraint, in the circumstances of the defendant might have reacted in a similar way'. This is very like the requirement for provocation, but is slightly wider, in that it allows all the circumstances to be taken into account, rather than just those circumstances and characteristics which effect the gravity of the provocation.

Clarification of the requirement in s 54(1)(c) is to be found in 54(3). The Explanatory Note to the Coroners and Justice Act 2009 said about 54(3):

> 'Subsection (3) supplements subsection (1)(c) by clarifying that the reference to the defendant's circumstances in that subsection means all of those circumstances except those whose only relevance to the defendant's conduct is that they impact upon the defendant's general level of tolerance and self-restraint. Thus, a defendant's history of abuse at the hands of the victim could be taken into account in deciding whether an ordinary person might have acted as the defendant did, whereas the defendant's generally short temper could not. Consequently, when applying the test in subsection (1)(c) the jury will consider whether a person of the defendant's sex and age with an ordinary level of tolerance and self-restraint and in the defendant's specific circumstances (in the sense described earlier in this paragraph) might have acted as the defendant did.'

Does this mean any circumstances at all, or does this retain the distinction between those that go to the gravity of the "provocation" and general characteristics (as per *DPP v Camplin* [1978] AC 705, A-G for Jersey v Holley).

Under the old law those circumstances and characteristics which effect the gravity of the provocation were deemed to l be particularly relevant.

DPP v Camplin [1978] AC 705

Panel: Lord Diplock, Lord Morris of Borth-y-Gest, Lord Simon of Glaisdale, Lord Fraser of Tullybelton and Lord Scarman.

Facts: Khan, raped Camplin, who was a 15 year old boy, and then laughed at him. Camplin hit Khan over the head with a chapatti pan, splitting his skull. Khan died. The trial judge had directed the jury that they must consider whether a reasonable adult would have done what Camplin did. The Court of Appeal allowed his appeal on the ground that the jury should have been directed to consider what a reasonable 15 year old boy would have done. The Director of Public Prosecutions appealed. The House of Lords confirmed that the test required consideration of a reasonable 15 year old. It went on to consider what other characteristics should be taken into account, and concluded, those which effected the gravity of the provocation should also be given to the reasonable man.

LORD MORRIS OF BORTH-y-GEST

In my view it would now be unreal to tell a jury that the notional 'reasonable man' is someone without the characteristics of the accused: it would be to intrude into their province. A few examples may be given. If the accused is of particular colour or particular ethnic origin and things are said which to him are grossly insulting it would be utterly unreal if the jury had to consider whether the words would have provoked a man of different colour or ethnic origin - or to consider how such a man would have acted or reacted. The question would be whether the accused if he was provoked only reacted as even any reasonable man in his situation would or might have reacted. If the accused was ordinarily and usually a very unreasonable person, the view that on a particular occasion he acted just as a reasonable person would or might have acted would not be impossible of acceptance.

Lord Diplock noted that taunts will often be more provocative if they are true.

LORD DIPLOCK

[T]he gravity of verbal provocation may well depend upon the particular characteristics or circumstances of the person to whom a taunt or insult is addressed. To taunt a person because of his race, his physical infirmities or some shameful incident in his past may well be considered by the jury to be more offensive to the person addressed, however equable his temperament, if the facts on which the taunt is founded are true than it would be if they were not.

In **Clinton**, the Court of Appeal endorsed a direction given in the trial of Parker which repeated s 54(1)(c) with no elaboration, albeit that there were no characteristics necessarily relevant there. Does this suggest that the matter is now to be left to the jury to decide what circumstances are appropriate to take into account?

THE LORD CHIEF JUSTICE

The Third Component

30....This third ingredient is related to the requirement, that even faced with situations which may amount to a qualifying trigger, the defendant is nevertheless expected to exercise a degree of self control. For this purpose the age and sex of the defendant is relevant. Perhaps a very immature defendant will be less likely to be able to exercise the self control which might be exercised by an adult. The defendant's reaction (that is what he actually did, rather than the fact that he lost his self control) may therefore be understandable in the sense that another person in his situation and the circumstances in which he found himself, might have reacted in the same or in a similar way.

The Court of Appeal does make clear that, providing that s 55(6)(c) does not on the facts prevent a qualifying trigger being present, sexual infidelity is one of the circumstances that can be taken into account.

31. For present purposes the most significant feature of the third component is that the impact on the defendant of sexual infidelity is not excluded. The exclusion in section 55(6)(c) is limited to the assessment of the qualifying trigger. In relation to the third component, that is the way in which the defendant has reacted and lost control, "the circumstances" are not constrained or limited. Indeed, section 54(3) expressly provides that reference to the defendant's circumstances extends to "all" of the circumstances except those bearing on his general capacity for tolerance and self-restraint. When the third component of the defence is examined it emerges that, notwithstanding section 55(6)(c) , account may, and in an appropriate case, should be taken of sexual infidelity.

It is highly likely that the circumstances to be considered for s 54(1)(c) will include those which the defendant had brought on himself and those which are disreputable, such as paedophilia, alcoholism and drug addition. This was the case with provocation at common law.

R v Morhall [1996] AC 90

Panel: Lord Goff of Chieveley, Lord Browne-Wilkinson, Lord Slynn of Hadley, Lord Nicholls of Birkenhead and Lord Steyn

Facts: Morhall was addicted to glue. The victim, together with Morhall's girlfriend and another friend, had nagged Morhall about his glue sniffing addiction. They did this throughout the day and into the evening, by which time Morhall was high on glue. Eventually Morhall picked up a hammer and hit the victim on the head. Morhall was pulled away by a friend and the victim went to his bedroom, but Morhall followed and stabbed him several times with a knife. The victim died. Morhall was convicted of murder. The Court of Appeal held that a disreputable characteristic such as glue sniffing could not be given to the reasonable man for the test in provocation in that it was inconsistent with the very concept of a reasonable man.

LORD GOFF OF CHIEVELEY

Second, in an appropriate case, it may be necessary to refer to other circumstances affecting the gravity of the provocation to the defendant which do not strictly fall within the description 'characteristics,' as for example the defendant's history or the circumstances in which he is placed at the relevant time (see *Reg. v Camplin*, at p. 717C-D, per Lord Diplock, where he referred to 'the particular characteristics or circumstances' of the defendant, and at p. 727D, per Lord Simon of Glaisdale, who referred to 'the entire factual situation,' including the characteristics of the defendant.) At all events in the present case, when the judge turned to the second and objective inquiry, he was entitled to direct the jury that they must take into account the entire factual situation (and in particular the fact that the provocation was directed at a habitual glue sniffer taunted with his habit) when considering the question whether the provocation was enough to cause a man possessed of an ordinary man's power of self control to act as the defendant did.

However, the point can be taken further. Among the characteristics stated to be excluded from consideration on the approach favoured by the Court of Appeal is that of being a paedophile. But suppose that a man who has been in prison for a sexual offence, for example rape, has after his release been taunted by another man with reference to that offence. It is difficult to see why, on ordinary principles, his characteristic or history as an offender of that kind should not be taken into account as going to the gravity of the provocation. The point is well made by Professor Smith in his commentary on the present case [1993] Crim LR 957, 958:

> 'Suppose that an old lag, now trying to go straight, is taunted with being 'a jailbird.' This might be extremely provoking, especially if it reveals his murky past to new friends or employers unaware of it. It really would not make much sense to ask the jury to consider the effect of such provocation on a man of good character.'

In truth, the mere fact that a characteristic of the defendant is discreditable does not exclude it from consideration, as was made plain by Lord Diplock in *Reg. v Camplin* when, at p. 717D, he referred to a shameful incident in a man's past as a relevant characteristic for present purposes. Indeed, even if the defendant's discreditable conduct causes a reaction in another, which in turn causes the defendant to lose his self-control, the reaction may amount to provocation: see *Edwards v The Queen* [1973] AC 648, a case concerned with a hostile reaction to his blackmailer by a man whom he was trying to blackmail, and *Reg. v Johnson (Christopher)* [1989] 1 WLR 740 in which *Edwards v The Queen* was followed and applied by the Court of Appeal. These cases are, in my opinion, inconsistent with the decision of the Court of Appeal in the present case.

Of course glue-sniffing (or solvent abuse), like indulgence in alcohol or the taking of drugs, can give rise to a special problem in the present context, because it may arise in more than one way. First, it is well established that, in considering whether a person having the power of self-control to be expected of an ordinary person would have reacted to the provocation as the defendant did, the fact (if it be the case) that the defendant was the worse for drink at the time should not be taken into account, even though the drink would, if taken by him, have the effect of reducing an ordinary person's power of self-control. It is sometimes suggested that the reason for this exclusion is that drunkenness is transitory and cannot therefore amount to a characteristic. But I doubt whether that is right. Indeed some physical conditions (such as eczema) may be transitory in nature and yet can surely be taken into account if the subject of taunts. In *Reg. v Camplin* [1978] AC 705, 726F, Lord Simon of Glaisdale considered that drunkenness should be excluded as inconsistent with the concept of the reasonable man in the sense of a man of ordinary self-control; but it has to be recognised that, in our society, ordinary people do sometimes have too much to drink. I incline therefore to the opinion that the exclusion of drunkenness in this context flows from the established principle that, at common law, intoxication does not of itself excuse a man from committing a criminal offence, but on one or other of these bases it is plainly excluded. At all events it follows that, in a case such as the present, a distinction may have to be drawn between two different situations. The first occurs where the defendant is taunted with his addiction (for example, that he is an alcoholic, or a drug addict, or a glue-sniffer), or even with having been intoxicated (from any cause) on some previous occasion. In such a case, however discreditable such condition may be, it may where relevant be taken into account as going to the gravity of the provocation. The second is the simple fact of the defendant being intoxicated - being drunk, or high with drugs or glue - at the relevant time, which may not be so taken into account, because that, like displaying a lack of ordinary self-control, is excluded as a matter of policy. Although the distinction is a fine one, it will, I suspect, very rarely be necessary to explain it to a jury. Drunkenness itself may be a not unusual feature of cases raising the issue of provocation, as occurred, for example, in *Reg. v Newell* (1980) 71 Cr App R 331, where the drunkenness of the defendant was rightly excluded as irrelevant. But none of the counsel in the present case had any experience, or indeed knowledge, of a case other than the present in which addiction as such was the subject of verbal taunts or insults said to constitute provocation, with the effect that the addiction was therefore relevant

Alert

as going to the gravity of the provocation. The present case may therefore be compared with *Reg. v Newell*, in which the defendant's chronic alcoholism was excluded from consideration because 'it had nothing to do with the words by which it is said that he was provoked:' see page 340, per Lord Lane CJ I only wish to add a warning that the court's strong reliance in that case on the judgment of North J. in *Reg. v McGregor* [1962] NZLR 1069 must be regarded with caution, having regard to the reservations expressed with regard to that judgment by the Court of Appeal of New Zealand in *Reg. v McCarthy* [1992] 2 NZLR 550, 557-558, per Cooke P. delivering the judgment of the court, part of which is quoted by Professor Smith [1993] Crim LR 957, 958 in his commentary on the present case. In particular, I wish to record my concern that the Court of Appeal in *Reg. v Newell* may have placed too exclusive an emphasis on the word 'characteristic,' as a result of relying on the judgment of North J. in *Reg. v McGregor*, where North J. was construing a statute in which that word was used.

It follows from what I have said that I am, with all respect, unable to accept the reasoning, or the conclusion, of the Court of Appeal. The answer to the question of law posed for consideration by your Lordships' House is apparent from what I have said earlier in this speech. In my opinion, the judge should have directed the jury to take into account the fact of the defendant's addiction to glue-sniffing when considering whether a person with the ordinary person's power of self-control would have reacted to the provocation as the defendant did. The judge failed so to direct the jury in the first passage which I have quoted from the summing up. Furthermore in my opinion his reference to the defendant's addiction in the second passage was ambiguous. This was because it did not make clear whether the defendant's addiction to glue-sniffing was a characteristic which went to the gravity of the provocation to be taken into account when considering whether a person having the power of self-control to be expected of an ordinary person would have reacted to the provocation as the defendant did, or whether it was only to be taken into account when considering whether, as the judge put it, the allegedly provoking conduct caused the defendant to lose his self-control. It follows that, since it is accepted that no question of the exercise of the proviso arises in the present case, the conviction of the defendant for murder must be quashed and a conviction of manslaughter substituted.

The House of Lords in *DPP v Camplin* had held that the reasonable man should have ordinary powers of self control. This has been replicated in s 54(1)(c) which requires 'a normal degree of tolerance and self restraint.'

This means that sometimes a factor, such as intoxication or glue sniffing, will be a relevant circumstance, but will not be taken into account as effecting the normal man's tolerance and self restraint. A similar situation occurred under the law of provocation.

A-G for Jersey v Holley [2005] UKPC 23, [2005] 2 AC 580

Panel: Lord Bingham of Cornhill, Lord Nicholls of Birkenhead, Lord Hoffmann, Lord Hope of Craighead, Lord Scott of Foscote, Lord Rodger of Earlsferry, Lord Walker of Gestingthorpe, Baroness Hale of Richmond and Lord Carswell

Facts: Holley and the victim were both alcoholics who had lived together for many years. During which time there were numerous arguments which usually involved the victim making derogatory comments which effected Holley's self esteem. On several occasions Holley inflicted violence on the victim and had served prison sentences as a result. On the day in question they drank for most of the morning and spent the afternoon chopping wood with an axe and drinking larger. The victim went to the pub and when she returned she told Holley she had just had sex with another man. He picked up the axe and hit her several times. By the time the case reached the Privy Council the issue was whether the test for provocation was that from *DPP v Camplin* or the later House of Lords case of *R v Smith*. The Privy Council sat with an especially enlarged Board, so that its decision could clarify English law definitively. It decided that the test in *DPP v Camplin* was the correct test.

Lord Nicholls explained how the matter of intoxication would be dealt with by that test.

LORD NICHOLLS OF BIRKENHEAD

Their Lordships mention some ancillary points. The first is relevant to the facts in the present case It concerns application of the principles discussed above in circumstances where the defendant acted under the influence of alcohol or drugs and, therefore, at a time when his level of self-control may have been reduced. If the defendant was taunted on account of his intoxication, that may be a relevant matter for the jury to take into account when assessing the gravity of the taunt to the defendant. But the defendant's intoxicated state is not a matter to be taken into account by the jury when considering whether the defendant exercised ordinary self-control. The position is the same, so far as provocation is concerned, if the defendant's addiction to alcohol has reached the stage that he is suffering from the disease of alcoholism.

3.2 The Defence of Diminished Responsibility

The Coroners and Justice Act 2009 has also altered the defence of diminished responsibility found in the Homicide Act 1957 s 2.

3.2.1 Abnormality of Mental Functioning

Baroness Murphy, a psychiatrist, said in the debate on the bill in the House of Lords:

'Overall the concept of abnormal mental functioning is better than the current concept of abnormality of mind because it emphasises processes rather than a static idea'.

Apart from the emphasis on the functioning of the mind, it is probable that the term differs little from the previous 'abnormality of mind'. This term was defined in the case below.

R v Byrne [1960] 2 QB 396

Panel: Lord Parker CJ, Hilbery and Diplock JJ

Facts: Byrne had strangled a girl at a YMCA hostel and then mutilated her body. He pleaded diminished responsibility on the grounds that he was unable to resist his abnormal sexual urges. The judge directed the jury that such urges could not amount to an abnormality of mind. Byrne appealed and the Court of Appeal reduced his conviction for murder to manslaughter.

Alert

> LORD PARKER
>
> "Abnormality of mind," which has to be contrasted with the time-honoured expression in the *M'Naughten* Rules "defect of reason," means a state of mind so different from that of ordinary human beings that the reasonable man would term it abnormal. It appears to us to be wide enough to cover the mind's activities in all its aspects, not only the perception of physical acts and matters, and the ability to form a rational judgment as to whether an act is right or wrong, but also the ability to exercise will power to control physical acts in accordance with that rational judgment. The expression "mental responsibility for his acts" points to a consideration of the extent to which the accused's mind is answerable for his physical acts which must include a consideration of the extent of his ability to exercise will power to control his physical acts.

Whether the accused was at the time of the killing suffering from any "abnormality of mind" in the broad sense which we have indicated above is a question for the jury. On this question medical evidence is no doubt of importance, but the jury are entitled to take into consideration all the evidence, including the acts or statements of the accused and his demeanour. They are not bound to accept the medical evidence if there is other material before them which, in their good judgment, conflicts with it and outweighs it.

3.2.2 Recognised Medical Condition

The Homicide Act 1957 s 2(1)(a) requires the abnormality arise from a recognised medical condition. This is a much clearer and in one sense, wider definition than under the old law. However it has long been recognised, that the old law allowed juries to return a verdict of manslaughter in those difficult cases where the defendant was not mentally ill, but the jury felt it would be wrong to return a murder conviction. Examples include *R v Ireland* (1983) The Times 26th March where a 'slave son', who had been kept in a kennel and horsewhipped by his parents, was allowed the defence when he shot them and *R v Eeles* (1972) The Times 22nd November where the defence was available to a man who had been tormented for years by his three mad neighbours and shot them all. Professor Glanville Williams concluded in his textbook 'In short the defence of diminished responsibility is interpreted in accordance with the morality of the case rather than as an application of psychiatric concepts.'

R D MacKay [2010] Crim L R 290

On the requirement that the abnormality must arise from a recognised medical condition.

> Clearly, therefore, it is not limited to recognised mental disorders and must include conditions like epilepsy, sleep disorders and diabetes. In short, this is a concept which is capable of covering any and all medical conditions and as such is wider than the bracketed causes in s 2(1) of the 1957 Act which it replaces. These bracketed causes were open to criticism in that they were not psychiatrically recognised and their meaning had taxed the courts. However, it was clear that to succeed in a plea under

s 2(1) the abnormality of mind had to fall within one or more of these bracketed causes, thus restricting the plea's availability. There is no such restriction relating to the scope of "recognised medical condition" in s 52 of the Coroners and Justice Act 2009, so it is to the new plea's other requirements which one must turn for this. Before doing so, however, three additional remarks may be made about "recognised medical condition".

First, although it has been suggested above that this concept is wider than its counterpart in the original s 2(1) of the 1957 Act, there is ironically a danger that–because it focuses exclusively on the need for a defined and demonstrable condition which is medically recognised–it may fail to include those "mercy killing" cases which currently qualify for a diminished responsibility plea. The reason for this is that because the wording of the current plea is so obscure, the court and the experts are sometimes able to enter into a benevolent conspiracy, thus permitting the psychiatric evidence to be stretched so as "to produce a greater range of exemption from liability for murder than its terms really justify". In short, therefore–having regard to the difficulty which psychiatrists experienced in bringing such cases within "abnormality of mind" under the original s 2 of the 1957 Act – the concept of "recognised medical condition" may exacerbate this difficulty. Secondly, in his article on the new loss of control plea, Alan Norrie makes it clear that as this new plea is narrower than the provocation plea which it replaces, cases such as *Humphreys* (emotional immaturity) and *Acott* (low intelligence) are unlikely to fall within its scope. And the same is likely to be true in relation to s 52 of the Coroners and Justice Act 2009, as its requirements including the need for a "recognised medical condition" – lack the flexibility of the original s 2 of the 1957 Act, which it turn often permitted both pleas to be combined; a defence strategy which is now much less likely to succeed owing to the fact that both new pleas are drafted in a manner which militates against possible overlap. Finally, by whom does the condition need to be recognised? Most of us can "recognise" certain conditions of a medical nature. Presumably, however, what is meant here is that in order to fall within s 52 of the Coroners and Justice Act 2009, it must be a professionally accepted medical condition; although such recognition it seems will no longer be restricted to those with psychiatric expertise but will include, where relevant, all other branches of the medical profession and psychologists.

3.2.3 Substantial Impairment of Defendant's Ability

The Homicide Act 1957 s 2(1A) (as amended) requires a substantial impairment of the defendant's ability to do either understand the nature of his conduct; form a rational judgment or exercise self-control. The word substantial was used in the old law. There is no need for the impairment to be total, but it has been held that the word means considerably more than trivial.

R v Lloyd [1967] 1 QB 175

Panel: Edmund Davies, Fenton Atkinson and Lyell JJ

Facts: Lloyd strangled his wife. Two doctors gave evidence that he was suffering from a mental abnormality, but neither would go so far as to say his mental responsibility was substantially impaired. Lloyd was convicted and appealed on the basis that 'substantially' meant more than trivial, and he was covered by this definition.

MR JUSTICE EDMUND DAVIES

Mr Justice Edmund Davies quoted the trial judge's direction on substantial, a definition the court was later to adopt.

> "Fourthly, this word 'substantial,' members of the jury. I am not going to try to find a parallel for the word 'substantial.' You are the judges, but your own common sense will tell you what it means. This far I will go. Substantial does not mean total, that is to say, the mental responsibility need not be totally impaired, so to speak, destroyed altogether. At the other end of the scale substantial does not mean trivial or minimal. It is something in between and Parliament has left it to you and other juries to say on the evidence, was the mental responsibility impaired, and, if so, was it substantially impaired?"

Alert

Mr Davies [the appellant's counsel] says "substantially" can mean one of two things; it can mean that the impairment was real and not illusory, or it may mean that it was of considerable amount. The judge, he says, should have assisted the jury that the meaning of the word "substantially" was real or, I suppose, really impaired. But Mr Davies, being confronted then by the difficulty that with that interpretation the word "substantially" in the section would appear to be superfluous, says:

> "What I really mean by that is that 'substantially' means 'more than trivial,' and as in the present case the doctors had said with one voice that the impairment here was not minimal, was not trivial, therefore, the defence of diminished responsibility was made out."

This court is wholly unable to accept that submission. The word "substantially" obviously is inserted in the Act with a view to carrying some meaning. It does carry a meaning. This court is quite unable to see that the direction given to the jury on the meaning of this word, can validly be criticised, and finds itself in a difficulty of saying that any distinction can be validly drawn between the direction given in the instant case and that approved of by this court in *Reg. v Simcox*. Of course, the words employed are not identical, but the substance of the direction in both the instant case and that of *Simcox* seems to this court to be for all substantial purposes indistinguishable the one from the other. I quote from the judgment of this court in *Simcox* by Lord Parker CJ: "All four experts were of the opinion that this appellant suffered from an abnormality of mind, and that abnormality of mind arose from inherent causes, the name given to the abnormality being paranoid personality. Not one of them, however, would go to the length of saying that as a result of that abnormality the appellant's mental responsibility was substantially impaired. They used words to the effect that the impairment was moderate, that it was harder for him to control his actions, that the degree of paranoid personality was, as one doctor said, persistent and strong. Those and other expressions were used, but not one of the mental experts felt that he could say that the impairment was substantial. In those circumstances the jury, after what this court considers to be a most admirable and fair summing-up, refused to return a verdict of manslaughter, but returned a verdict of capital murder."

Then, quoting from the direction of the trial judge, Finnemore J., we have this passage:

> "Members of the jury, the real thing you may think here is this word 'substantially,' and we will come to it in a moment. Neither doctor called for the defence obviously liked the word, and it may be so, but that is the word in the Act of Parliament, that is the word you have got to use, and I expect you will not have as much difficulty as some people might have. There is no scientific precise test. That cannot be and never can in human conduct, otherwise we should not need juries or anybody, and if you will allow me to say so, I think you should look at it in a broad common-sense way and ask yourselves, having heard what the doctors have said, having made up your minds about it, knowing what this man did, knowing the whole story, 'Do we think, looking at it broadly as common-sense people, there was a substantial impairment of his mental responsibility in what he did?' If the answer to that is 'yes,' then you find him not guilty of murder, but guilty of manslaughter. If the answer to that is 'no,' there may be some impairment, but we do not think it was substantial, we do not think it was something which really made any great difference, although it may have made it harder to control himself, to refrain from crime, then you would find him guilty as he is charged in the only charge to this indictment!"

Then this court, having quoted that passage, had this to say: "The court can see no ground whatever for criticising the judge for dealing with the word 'substantial' in that way." This court adopts those words in the present case and can see no ground whatever for criticising the direction given by the judge to the jury as to the manner in which they were here invited to approach the interpretation of the word "substantially."

The factors in s 2(1A) come from the case of *R v Byrne* [1960] 2 QB 396 (see above). In that case Lord Parker said an abnormality of mind was wide enough to cover the mind's activities in all its aspects, and then gave the three examples which have been adopted by Parliament. Now it is just these three examples which will be included.

R D MacKay [2010] Crim L R 290

[T]he new plea's approach of spelling out what abilities need to be impaired inevitably means that "abnormality of mental functioning" is now narrower than "abnormality of mind" in that the only activities of the mind which are included are the three specified things in subs.(1A) of the 1957 Act as amended. In addition, there is a legitimate concern that these three specified things will, taken together, prove to be more limited in scope than those which fell within the original plea. This was certainly the view of Baroness Murphy who, during debate on the Bill in the House of Lords, put forward an amendment to allow for,

"...distortion of thinking or perception as a basis for a successful plea of diminished responsibility where the defendant was able to exercise self-control".

This would have more readily accommodated those whose mental disorder substantially impairs his or her perception of reality. It might also have included those with personality disorders, a condition which is now unlikely to fall within the new plea unless the defendant's ability to exercise self-control can be proved to have been substantially impaired. In any event, this amendment was roundly rejected by the Attorney General who said:

"In the unlikely event of cases arising where a defendant's perception of reality is substantially impaired but his ability to understand the nature of his conduct, form a rational judgment and exercise self-control are not, we do not consider that he should benefit from the partial defence as these issues go right to the heart of the case for reduced responsibility in homicide cases where there is an abnormality of mental function."

However, what this remark fails to acknowledge is that under the original s 2 of the 1957 Act there was nothing in principle to prevent a substantial impairment of perception of reality from falling within its scope owing to the flexibility/obscurity of the plea's drafting.

The recent decision of the Court of Appeal as to when alcoholism might substantially impair mental responsibility will also be helpful in applying the new law.

R v Stewart [2009] EWCA Crim 593, [2009] 1 WLR 2507

Panel: Lord Judge CJ, Wyn Williams and Holroyde JJ

Facts: Stewart and the victim, who both suffered from alcohol dependency syndrome, were sleeping rough near Marble Arch. Stewart had drunk a considerable amount of alcohol when he battered the victim to death.

LORD JUDGE CJ

Whether or not brain damage is discernible, alcohol dependency syndrome is a disease (ICD-10) or disorder of the mind (DSM-IV-TR). It is not excluded from the operation of s 2 of the Homicide Act 1957. If the defence of diminished responsibility is to operate according to its statutory structure, the law must take account of advances in medical knowledge. Nevertheless, when the issue arises, it must be addressed in the context of a further principle, that the voluntary consumption of alcohol, and the defendant's voluntary intoxication, does not provide a defence to murder, although it may, in an extreme case, bear on the question of the defendant's intent (R v Sheehan and Moore (1974) 60 Cr App R 308). These principles have to be reconciled.

Alcoholism varies greatly in its nature and extent. As with other conditions, it involves different levels of severity. A heavy drinker does not necessarily suffer from alcohol dependency syndrome and someone suffering from it may very well have lengthy periods when he is either sober or when his mental responsibility is not significantly impaired by alcohol. Thus, for example, in the present case, the appellant's condition did not preclude sensible, intelligent discussions both with a doctor and his probation officer not long before he killed the deceased. One of the criteria for ICD-10 purposes includes the "difficulty", not, we emphasise, the impossibility of controlling the use of alcohol, and DCM-IV-TR acknowledges that unsuccessful efforts to cut down or control alcohol abuse may be an indication of the presence of the disorder, and, in other words, would allow for temporary improvements without undermining the overall diagnosis of alcohol dependency syndrome. In short, even if the diagnosis is agreed and correct, not every alcoholic is suffering from such abnormality of mind that his mental responsibility for his actions at the time of the killing is or must be treated as if it were substantially impaired. Thus, although the condition is a disease encompassed by s 2 of the 1957 Act, [and is also included in the definition in s 2(1)(a) of the 1957 Act (as amended)] the defence is not established simply on the basis of a diagnosis of alcohol dependency syndrome.

Lord Judge CJ then noted that for alcoholism to amount to an abnormality of mind there is no longer a requirement that there should be brain damage or the drinking should be involuntary.

The consumption of vast amounts of alcohol may therefore reduce murder to manslaughter, first, when the effect of the intoxication is so extreme that the prosecution has failed to prove the necessary intent to kill or cause grievous bodily harm (R v Sheehan and Moore) and second, assuming that the necessary intent is proved notwithstanding the consumption of alcohol, on the basis of diminished responsibility, provided the defendant proves that he was suffering from such abnormality of mind induced by the disease or illness of alcohol dependency syndrome that his mental responsibility for his actions in doing the killing was substantially impaired.

Lord Judge CJ then considered the first two requirements for the defence under the old law.

Finally, and assuming that the particular defendant's alcohol dependency syndrome did indeed constitute an abnormality of mind due to disease or illness, which was present at the time of the killing, directions about whether the defendant's mental responsibility for what he did was substantially impaired should be addressed in conventional terms. The jury should be assisted with the concept of substantial impairment, and may properly be invited to reflect on the difference between a failure by the defendant to resist his impulses to behave as he actually did, and an inability consequent on it to resist them.

In answering these questions, the jury should be directed to consider all the evidence, including the opinions of the medical experts. The issues likely to arise in this kind of case and on which they should be invited to form their own judgment will include (a) the extent and seriousness of the defendant's dependency, if any, on alcohol (b) the extent to which his ability to control his drinking or to choose whether to drink or not, was reduced, (c) whether he was capable of abstinence from alcohol, and if so, (d) for how long, and (e) whether he was choosing for some particular reason, such as a birthday celebration, to decide to get drunk, or to drink even more than usual. Without seeking to be prescriptive about considerations relevant to an individual case, the defendant's pattern of drinking in the days leading to the day of the killing, and on the day of the killing itself, and notwithstanding his consumption of alcohol, his ability, if any, to make apparently sensible and rational decisions about ordinary day to day matters at the relevant time, may all bear on the jury's decision whether diminished responsibility is established in the context of this individual defendant's alcohol dependency syndrome.

We acknowledge that this decision will rarely be easy. Indeed it is fair to say that diminished responsibility has always raised complex and difficult issues for the jury, not least because the defence usually involves conflicting medical evidence addressing legal, not medical concepts, for a jury of lay persons to decide. The jury is often called upon to confront problems relating to the operation of the mind with which they will be unfamiliar. Nevertheless the resolution of these problems continues to be the responsibility of the jury, and when addressing their responsibility they are inevitably required to make the necessary judgments not just on the basis of expert medical opinion but also by using their collective common sense and insight into the practical realities which underpin the individual case.

3.2.4 Causation

The 1957 Act s 2(1B) provides that there must be a causal link between the abnormality of mental function which substantially impairs D's ability and the killing. It must be a 'significant contributory factor'. This accords with the old law, where the abnormality of mind did not need to be the sole reason for the killing.

R v Dietschmann [2003] UKHL 10, [2003] 1 AC 1209

Panel: Lord Nicholls of Birkenhead, Lord Lloyd of Berwick, Lord Hutton, Lord Hobhouse of Woodborough and Lord Rodger of Earlsferry

Facts: At the time of the killing Dietschmann was suffering from severe depression caused by the death of his aunt, with whom he had been having a physical and emotional relationship. He was also intoxicated. Dietschmann kicked and punched the victim to death because he thought the victim had broken a watch the aunt gave him before she died. The judge directed the jury that the defence of diminished responsibility was not available to him if he would not have killed had he not been drunk. He was convicted of murder and appealed.

The Court of Appeal certified the following question of general public importance:

"(1) Does a defendant seeking to prove a defence of diminished responsibility under section 2(1) of the Homicide Act 1957 in a case where he had taken drink prior to killing the victim, have to show that if he had not taken drink (a) he would have killed as in fact he did; and (b) he would have been under diminished responsibility when he did so? (2) If not, what direction ought to be given to a jury as to the approach to be taken to self-induced intoxication which was present at the material time in conjunction with an abnormality of mind which falls within section 2(1) of the 1957 Act?"

LORD HUTTON

Lord Hutton approved the decision in *R v Gittens* [1984] QB 698

Therefore four points clearly emerge from the judgment of the Court of Appeal in *R v Gittens* [1984] QB 698 :

(i) Where a defendant suffers from an abnormality of mind arising from arrested or retarded development of mind or inherent causes or induced by disease or injury and has also taken drink before the killing, the abnormality of mind and the effect of the drink may each play a part in impairing the defendant's mental responsibility for the killing.

(ii) Therefore the task for the jury is to decide whether, despite the disinhibiting effect of the drink on the defendant's mind, the abnormality of mind arising from a cause specified in subsection 2(1) nevertheless substantially impaired his mental responsibility for his fatal acts.

(iii) Accordingly it is not correct for the judge to direct the jury that unless they are satisfied that if the defendant had not taken drink he would have killed, the defence of diminished responsibility must fail. Such a direction is incorrect because it fails to recognise that the abnormality of mind arising from a cause specified in the subsection and the effect of the drink may each play a part in impairing the defendant's mental responsibility for the killing.

(iv) The direction given by the judge in *R v Turnbull (Launcelot)* 65 Cr App R 242 should not be followed.

Lord Hutton then considered further relevant cases and concluded:

Therefore I would answer the first part of the certified question in the negative. As regards the second part of the question, without attempting to lay down a precise form of words as the judge's directions are bound to depend to some extent on the facts of the case before him, I consider that the jury should be directed along the following lines:

"Assuming that the defence have established that the defendant was suffering from mental abnormality as described in section 2, the important question is: did that abnormality substantially impair his mental responsibility for his acts in doing the killing? You know that before he carried out the killing the defendant had had a lot to drink. Drink cannot be taken into account as something which contributed to his mental abnormality and to any impairment of mental responsibility arising from that abnormality. But you may take the view that both the defendant's mental abnormality and drink played a part in impairing his mental responsibility for the killing and that he might not have killed if he had not taken drink. If you take that view, then the question for you to decide is this: has the defendant satisfied you that, despite the drink, his mental abnormality substantially impaired his mental responsibility for his fatal acts, or has he failed to satisfy you of that? If he has satisfied you of that, you will find him not guilty of murder but you may find him guilty of manslaughter. If he has not satisfied you of that, the defence of diminished responsibility is not available to him."

The recent death of Professor Sir John Smith is a great loss to the world of legal scholarship, especially in the field of criminal law, and in suggesting the direction set out above I am fortified by the consideration that it would be in general conformity with the direction suggested by him as an alternative approach to the problem in his commentary on the judgment of the Court of Appeal in the present case [2002] Crim LR 132, 136:

"You may think that all of these factors (including his drunkenness) played a part in causing D to act as he did. The only factor which the law recognises as capable of diminishing his mental responsibility is the mental abnormality described by the expert witnesses. If you are satisfied on the balance of probabilities that this abnormality existed and played such a part in his actions as, in your opinion, substantially to diminish his mental responsibility for those acts, you will find him not guilty of murder ..."

Accordingly, for the reasons which I have given, I would remit the case to the Court of Appeal for that court to decide whether to allow the appeal and quash the conviction for murder and order a new trial or to substitute a verdict of guilty of manslaughter for the verdict of murder found by the jury and to pass an appropriate sentence for that offence.

Further Reading

Dell S 'Diminished Responsibility Reconsidered' [1982] *Crim LR* 809

McKay R 'The Coroners and Justice Act 2009 – partial defences to murder (2) The new diminished responsibility plea' [2010] *Crim LR* 290

Norrie A 'The Coroners and Justice Act 2009 – partial defences to murder (1) Loss of control' [2010] *Crim LR* 275

4

Homicide II: Involuntary Manslaughter

Topic List

Introduction

Involuntary manslaughter is a generic term to describe those types of manslaughter where the defendant kills without the mens rea for murder. The two main types are unlawful act manslaughter, sometimes referred to as constructive manslaughter, and gross negligence manslaughter.

4.1 Unlawful Act Manslaughter

In this type of manslaughter the victim is killed as a result of an unlawful act. The current requirements arise from a House of Lords decision.

Director of Public Prosecutions v Newbury and Jones [1977] AC 500

Panel: Lord Diplock, Lord Simon of Glaisdale, Lord Kilbrandon, Lord Salmon and Lord Edmund-Davies

Facts: Two fifteen year old boys pushed a paving stone over a railway bridge into the path of a train. It went through the driver's cab and killed a guard. They were convicted of manslaughter.

LORD SALMON

The learned trial judge did not direct the jury that they should acquit the appellants unless they were satisfied beyond a reasonable doubt that the appellants had foreseen that they might cause harm to someone by pushing the piece of paving stone off the parapet into the path of the approaching train. In my view the learned trial judge was quite right not to give such a direction to the jury. The direction which he gave is completely in accordance with established law, which, possibly with one exception to which I shall presently refer, has never been challenged. In *Rex v Larkin* (1942) 29 Cr App R 18, Humphreys J. said, at page 23:

> "Where the act which a person is engaged in performing is unlawful, then if at the same time it is a dangerous act, that is, an act which is likely to injure another person, and quite inadvertently the doer of the act causes the death of that other person by that act, then he is guilty of manslaughter"

I agree entirely with Lawton L.J. that that is an admirably clear statement of the law which has been applied many times. It makes it plain (a) that an accused is guilty of manslaughter if it is proved that he intentionally did an act which was unlawful and dangerous and that that act inadvertently caused death and (b) that it is unnecessary to prove that the accused knew that the act was unlawful or dangerous. This is one of the reasons why cases of manslaughter vary so infinitely in their gravity. They may amount to little more than pure inadvertence and sometimes to little less than murder.

 Alert

The four requirements have been succinctly set out by the Court of Appeal.

R v Goodfellow (1986) 83 Cr App R 23

Panel: Lord Lane CJ, Boreham and Taylor JJ

Facts: Goodfellow lived in a council house. He wanted to be rehoused as he was having trouble with his neighbours. However, he knew that his rent arrears made this unlikely. He planned to set fire to his house, making it appear as if one of the neighbours had attacked the house with a petrol bomb. He lived with his wife and three children and also had a girlfriend, whom he arranged should be in the house that night to help rescue the children. The fire got out of control and Goodfellow's wife, girlfriend and one of his children died. He was convicted of manslaughter. On his appeal against conviction, it was held he could be liable for both reckless manslaughter (the predecessor to gross negligence manslaughter) and unlawful act manslaughter.

LORD LANE CJ

The questions which the jury have to decide on the charge of manslaughter of this nature are: (1) Was the act intentional? (2) Was it unlawful? (3) Was it an act which any reasonable person would realise was bound to subject some other human being to the risk of physical harm, albeit not necessarily serious harm? (4) Was that act the cause of death?

4.1.1 An Intentional Act

All that is required for this element is that the act, which is unlawful, dangerous and caused death, should be done intentionally.

4.1.2 An Unlawful Act

4.1.2.1 An unlawful act is required for this type of manslaughter

R v Lamb [1967] 3 WLR 888

Panel: Sachs LJ, Lyell and Geoffrey Lane JJ

Facts: As a joke Lamb pointed a gun at his friend and pulled the trigger. The gun fired and killed the friend. The bullets in the gun were not opposite the barrel and Lamb had no idea that on the pulling of the trigger the cylinder housing the bullets would rotate and the gun would fire. He was convicted of manslaughter. The trial judge had not directed the jury to consider whether Lamb had the mens rea for the offence of assault.

LORD JUSTICE SACHS

Unfortunately, however, he [the trial judge] fell into error as to the meaning of the word "unlawful" in that passage and pressed upon the jury a definition with which experienced counsel for the Crown had disagreed during the trial and which he found himself unable to support on the appeal. The trial judge took the view that the pointing of the revolver and the pulling of the trigger was something which could of itself be unlawful even if there was no attempt to alarm or intent to injure. This view is exemplified in a passage in his judgment which will be cited later.

It was no doubt on that basis that he had before commencing his summing-up stated that he was not going to "involve the jury in any consideration of the niceties of the question whether or not the" action of the "accused did constitute or did not constitute an assault"; and thus he did not refer to the defence of accident or the need for the prosecution to disprove accident before coming to a conclusion that the act was unlawful.

Mr Mathew, however, had at all times put forward the correct view that for the act to be unlawful it must constitute at least what he then termed "a technical assault." In this court moreover he rightly conceded that there was no evidence to go to the jury of any assault of any kind. Nor did he feel able to submit that the acts of the defendant were on any other ground unlawful in the criminal sense of that word. Indeed no such submission could in law be made: if, for instance, the pulling of the trigger had had no effect because the striking mechanism or the ammunition had been defective no offence would have been committed by the defendant.

Another way of putting it is that mens rea, being now an essential ingredient in manslaughter (compare *Andrews v Director of Public Prosecutions* and *Reg. v Church*), that could not in the present case be established in relation to the first ground except by proving that element of intent without which there can be no assault. It is perhaps as well to mention that when using the phrase "unlawful in the criminal sense of that word" the court has in mind that it is long settled that it is not in point to consider whether an act is unlawful merely from the angle of civil liabilities. That was first made clear in the "*Brighton Pier*" case (*Reg. v Franklin*) The relevant extracts from that and from later judgments are collected in Russell on Crime, 11th edn (1958), pages 651-658.

 Alert

The whole of that part of the summing-up which concerned the first ground was thus vitiated by misdirections based on an erroneous concept of the law; and the strength with which that ground was put to the jury no doubt stemmed from the firm view of the trial judge, expressed more than once in the course of the discussion on law in relation to the undisputed facts: "How can there be a defence to the charge of manslaughter? Manslaughter requires no intent."

4.1.2.2 The unlawful act cannot be based on an act, such as driving, which is intrinsically lawful and becomes unlawful only because it is performed negligently

Andrews v Director of Public Prosecutions [1937] AC 576

Panel: Lord Atkin, Viscount Finlay, Lord Thankerton, Lord Wright and Lord Roche.

Facts: Andrews had killed a pedestrian whilst driving a van dangerously. He appealed against conviction. When the case reached the House of Lords it was confirmed that he was guilty of gross negligence manslaughter, but it was stated that he could not be liable for unlawful act manslaughter.

LORD ATKIN

In particular at the beginning of his charge to the jury he began with the statement that if a man kills another in the course of doing an unlawful act he is guilty of manslaughter, and then proceeded to ascertain what the unlawful act was by considering s 11 of the Road Traffic Act, 1930. If the summing-up rested there, there would have been misdirection. There is an obvious difference in the law of manslaughter between doing an unlawful act and doing a lawful act with a degree of carelessness which the Legislature makes criminal. If it were otherwise a man who killed another while driving without due care and attention would ex necessitate commit manslaughter

4.1.2.3 An unlawful omission will not suffice

R v Lowe [1973] 2 WLR 481

Panel: Phillimore LJ, Cusack and Mars-Jones JJ

Facts: Lowe was charged jointly with Marshall, the mother his five children. He was said to be of low intelligence and she was educationally subnormal. He had known his baby daughter was ill, but had not called a doctor. The baby died of dehydration and gross emaciation. The jury had found him guilty of cruelty to a child by wilfully neglecting it so as to cause unnecessary suffering or injury to health contrary to the Children and Young Persons Act 1933 s 1(1), but not guilty of what was then called negligence manslaughter and required proof of recklessness. The trial judge held that if the crime he was guilty of had caused death, he must also be liable for unlawful act manslaughter. The Court of Appeal upheld his conviction under s 1(1), but said he would not be liable for constructive (unlawful act) manslaughter.

LORD JUSTICE PHILLIMORE

Now in the present case the jury negatived recklessness. How then can mere neglect, albeit wilful, amount to manslaughter? This court feels that there is something inherently unattractive in a theory of constructive manslaughter. It seems strange that an omission which is wilful solely in the sense that it is not inadvertent and the consequences of which are not in fact foreseen by the person who is neglectful should, if death results, automatically give rise to an indeterminate sentence instead of the maximum of two years which would otherwise be the limit imposed.

We think that there is a clear distinction between an act of omission and an act of commission likely to cause harm. Whatever may be the position with regard to the latter it does not follow that the same is true of the former. In other words, if I strike a child in a manner likely to cause harm it is right that, if the child dies, I may be charged with manslaughter. If, however, I omit to do something with the result that it suffers injury to health which results in its death, we think that a charge of manslaughter should not be an inevitable consequence, even if the omission is deliberate.

4.1.3 Dangerous

The test comes from the case of *R v Church* [1966] 1 QB 59 and has been confirmed by The House of Lords in *DPP v Newbury and Jones* [1977] AC 500

R v Church **[1966] 1 QB 59**

Panel: Edmund-Davies, Marshall and Widgery JJ

Facts: Church had a fight with the victim after she had mocked him for failing to satisfy her sexually. He knocked her unconscious. After trying to rouse her for some time, he concluded she was dead. He panicked and threw her into a river. In fact she was alive and later died by drowning. Church was convicted of manslaughter and appealed on a number of grounds, one of which was that the trial judge had directed the jury that all that needed to be proved for unlawful act manslaughter was that the unlawful act caused death.

MR JUSTICE EDUMUND-DAVIES

...[T]he conclusion of this court is that an unlawful act causing the death of another cannot simply because it is an unlawful act, render a manslaughter verdict inevitable. For such a verdict inexorably to follow, the unlawful act must be such as all sober and reasonable people would inevitably recognise must subject the other person to, at least, the risk of some harm resulting therefrom, albeit not serious harm.

However the Court decided that the verdict was not unsafe and upheld the conviction.

4.1.3.1 What constitutes harm?

This has been considered by The Court of Appeal.

R v Dawson, Nolan and Walmsley **(1985) 81 Cr App R 150**

Panel: Watkins LJ, Wood J and Sir John Thompson

Facts: Dawson, Nolan and Walmsley went to a petrol filling station at around midnight. The attendant, Mr Black, was behind a protective glass screen. Dawson had a stocking over his face and pointed a fake gun at Mr Black. Walmsley's face was covered by a balaclava and he held a pickaxe handle which he banged on the counter as he demanded cash. Mr Black pushed a panic button, at which point the gang ran off. Later Mr Black, who had previously had heart trouble, was found to have died from a heart attack.

LORD JUSTICE WATKINS

It has, in our experience, been generally understood that the harm referred to in the second element of the offence of manslaughter, namely, the unlawful act, must be one that all sober and reasonable people would realise was likely to cause some, albeit not serious, harm, means physical harm. We observe that in Smith and Hogan, Criminal Law (5th edn, 1983) at page 319, the authors state:

> "Whether frightening is itself 'harm', so that an act which is likely only to frighten amounts to manslaughter if it in fact kills, is less clear. In *Reid* (1975) 62 Cr App R 109, causing fright by threats to use firearms was regarded as harm. P was in fact shot dead and whether the court would have taken the same view if the guns had not been loaded and P had died of fright is open to question."

However, there seems to us to be no sensible reason why shock produced by fright should not come within the definition of harm in this context. From time to time one hears the expression "frightened to death" without thinking that the possibility of such event occurring would be an affront to reason or medical knowledge. Shock can produce devastating and lasting effects, for instance upon the nervous system. That is surely harm, i.e. injury to the person. Why not harm in this context?

[The trial judge had said:]

> 'I direct you that if an act puts a person in such terror that he or she may suffer emotional or physical disturbance which is detrimental then that disturbance is harm within the meaning of what you have to consider. If, therefore, you conclude that all sober and reasonable people, which means you, because it is your standards that have got to be applied, could only come to the conclusion that the result of the threats with the pickaxe handle and the firearm in the middle of the night was likely to be that inevitably there was a risk that Mr Black would be put in such terror that he would suffer some such disturbance which would be bad for him, then that can be harm and the second element that you have to find is made out."

These directions have been roundly attacked as being wholly erroneous. It was argued that, contrary to an indication given by him to counsel, the judge in that passage directed the jury that a definition of harm was "emotional disturbance which is detrimental produced by terror." He had, as we have seen from a transcript of discussion between him and counsel, intended to direct the jury that a definition of harm for present purposes was emotional and physical disturbance produced by terror. We think it was unfortunate that the judge, probably through inadvertence, used the disjunctive "or". As it was, the jury were left with a choice. Which they chose and acted upon we cannot tell. If they acted upon the basis that emotional disturbance was enough to constitute harm then, in our judgment, they would have done so upon a misdirection. Emotional disturbance does not occur to us as sensibly descriptive of injury or harm to the person through the operation of shock produced by terror or fright; moreover, we do not think the word "detrimental" assists to clarify whatever the expression "emotional disturbance" is meant to convey. The further phrase used, namely, "some such disturbance which would be bad for him" is likewise not helpful.

In his endeavours to give the jury appropriate guidance upon the meaning of harm within the facts of this case the judge was sailing uncharted seas. We have every sympathy with him. Unfortunately we think that what he said, other than the use of the phrase "physical disturbance which is detrimental" (this was, we think, by itself, though easier to understand, inadequate) could have led the jury to contemplate merely a disturbance of the emotions as harm sufficient for the purpose of the second element when clearly, in our view, it is not.

In our judgment, a proper direction would have been that the requisite harm is caused if the unlawful act so shocks the victim as to cause him physical injury.

 Alert

4.1.3.2 What knowledge does the reasonable man have?

R v Dawson, Nolan and Walmsley (1985) 81 Cr App R 150

Panel: Watkins LJ, Wood J and Sir John Thompson

Facts: the trial judge had directed the jury that when considering whether the reasonable man would have inevitably recognised the risk of some harm, the reasonable man would know the facts that they knew. The jury knew that Mr Black had heart problems. The Court of Appeal held this direction to be wrong.

LORD JUSTICE WATKINS

We look finally at the direction, "That is to say all reasonable people who knew the facts that you know." What the jury knew included, of course, the undisputed fact that the deceased had a very bad heart which at any moment could have ceased to function. It may be the judge did not intend that this fact should be included in the phrase "the facts that you know." If that was so, it is regrettable that he did not make it clear. By saying as he did, it is argued "including the fact that the gun was a replica" and so on, the jury must have taken him to be telling them that all facts known to them, including the heart condition, should be taken into account in performing what is undoubtedly an objective test. We think there was a grave danger of that.

This test can only be undertaken upon the basis of the knowledge gained by a sober and reasonable man as though he were present at the scene of and watched the unlawful act being performed and who knows that, as in the present case, an unloaded replica gun was in use, but that the victim may have thought it was a loaded gun in working order. In other words, he has the same knowledge as the man attempting to rob and no more. It was never suggested that any of these appellants knew that their victim had a bad heart. They knew nothing about him.

A jury must be informed by the judge when trying the offence of manslaughter what facts they may and those which they may not use for the purpose of performing the test in the second element of this offence. The judge's direction here, unlike the bulk of an admirable summing-up, lacked that necessary precision and in the form it was given may, in our view, have given the jury an erroneous impression of what knowledge they could ascribe to the sober and reasonable man.

For these reasons we see no alternative to quashing the convictions for manslaughter as unsafe and unsatisfactory. The appeal against the convictions for manslaughter is therefore allowed.

It is worth noting that Dawson, Nolan, and Walmsley were acquitted because the trial judge had misdirected the jury. The Court of Appeal did not find that the unlawful act was not dangerous. Indeed it is highly likely that a jury would find the robbery to be dangerous by the correct test.

R v Watson [1989] 1 WLR 684

Panel: Lord Lane CJ, Farquharson and Potts JJ

Facts: Watson and an accomplice broke into the house of an 87 year old man who lived alone by throwing a brick through the window and then entering his house. The man woke up and Watson verbally abused him but left without stealing anything. The man had a heart condition and died soon afterwards. Watson was convicted but appealed on two grounds. Firstly, that he would not have known of the man's age and frailty on entry, which is when he committed the burglary, and secondly that the death could have been caused by the arrival of the police or the council to repair the window.

LORD LANE CJ

Reference was made to the explanation of how a burglary could cause death in someone with heart disease.

Dr West, who was called on behalf of the prosecution, had performed the autopsy. He was sure that the burglary was the cause of death. He described for the benefit of the jury how excitement causes the production of adrenalin making the heart beat faster. The heart therefore needs more blood and oxygen, but is unable to obtain it if there is a chronic heart disease, as there was here, with the result that the arteries leading to the heart are substantially narrowed. The heart then begins to beat irregularly, it eventually stops beating and thus death ensues.

The first ground of appeal was dismissed.

The first point taken on behalf of the appellant is this. When one is deciding whether the sober and reasonable person (the bystander) would realise the risk of some harm resulting to the victim, how much knowledge of the circumstances does one attribute to the bystander? The appellant contends that the unlawful act here was the burglary as charged in the indictment.

The charge was laid under section 9(1)(a) of the Theft Act 1968, the allegation being that the appellant had entered the building as a trespasser with intent to commit theft. Since that offence is committed at the first moment of entry, the bystander's knowledge is confined to that of the defendant at that moment. In the instant case there was no evidence that the appellant, at the moment of entry, knew the age or physical condition of Mr Moyler or even that he lived there alone.

The judge clearly took the view that the jury were entitled to ascribe to the bystander the knowledge which the appellant gained during the whole of his stay in the house and so directed them. Was this a misdirection? In our judgment it was not. The unlawful act in the present circumstances comprised the whole of the burglarious intrusion and did not come to an end upon the appellant's foot crossing the threshold or windowsill. That being so, the appellant (and therefore the bystander) during the course of the unlawful act must have become aware of Mr Moyler's frailty and approximate age, and the judge's directions were accordingly correct. We are supported in this view by the fact that no one at the trial seems to have thought otherwise.

The second ground of this appeal was successful. The Court decided that the judge, by telling the jury in answer to a question during their deliberations, that it did not matter whether the death had been caused by the initial burglary or the arrival of the emergency services, had stated that the chain of causation had not been broken. Counsel for the defendant had been denied a chance to argue this point, so the verdict was unsafe. It is argued by Diane Birch in her commentary on the case, [1989] Crim LR 734, that such a predictable event as the emergency services arriving would never break the chain of causation.

In *R v Dawson* Watkins LJ first stated that a sober and reasonable man would have the knowledge he would have gained had he been present at the scene and watched the unlawful act being performed. Unfortunately, he then stated that the reasonable man would have the knowledge of the defendant and no more. This could be a different amount of knowledge. If the defendant were intoxicated, unobservant or of low intelligence, he might not have noticed facts which a sober and reasonable man would have noticed. Given that the test for 'dangerous' is widely acknowledged to be an objective one, it is submitted that the first statement should represent the law. The following case could be said to bear this out.

R v Ball [1989] Crim LR 730

Panel: Stuart-Smith LJ, Hobhouse and Leggatt JJ

Facts: The victim had stored a Land Rover on Ball's land with Ball's consent. Ball decided it had been there too long and sold it. The victim and two men arrived at Ball's house and asked to see the Land Rover. Ball, who had severe hearing and speech defects, behaved aggressively and followed them down the garden path with a gun. The victim was seen running towards a wall and, as she was climbing over it, Ball shot her and killed her. Ball kept live and blank cartridges in his overall pocket in his house and had grabbed a handful of cartridges when he picked up the gun, intending to frighten the victim. He claimed that, because he had been frightened by the two men, he had not noticed the difference in weight between the live and blank cartridges and he believed the cartridges to be blank. He was convicted of manslaughter and appealed on the ground that the judge had misdirected the jury in telling them not to consider Ball's belief that the cartridge was blank.

The following is not a verbatim record of the judgement, but a summary from the only report of the case which is in Criminal Law Review.

He had used his own cartridges and loaded the gun himself; no other agency was involved. In manslaughter arising from an unlawful and dangerous act, the accused's state of mind was relevant only to establish (a) that the act was committed intentionally;

and (b) that it was an unlawful act (*DPP v Newbury* 62 Cr App R 291). Once (a) and (b) were established, the question whether the act was dangerous was to be judged not by the appellant's appreciation but by that of the sober and reasonable man, and it was impossible to impute into his appreciation the mistaken believe that what he was doing was not dangerous because he thought he had a blank cartridge in the chamber. At that stage, his intention, foresight or knowledge was irrelevant.

In *R v Ball* the reasonable man was given knowledge of circumstances which existed well before the commission of the offence – the fact that the defendant had mixed blank and live cartridges in his overall pocket. It has been cogently argued that if the defendant knows of a fact which makes the victim more vulnerable, the reasonable man should also be given this knowledge.

Professor Sir John Smith commenting on *R v Ball* [1989] Crim LR 730

The test is whether all sober and reasonable people would recognise that the act was dangerous. In *Dawson* – a case involving the killing of a filling station attendant with a weak heart in the course of a robbery – Watkins L.J. said:

"this test can only be undertaken upon the basis of the knowledge gained by a sober and reasonable man as though he were present at the scene of and watched the unlawful act being performed ... he has the same knowledge as the man attempting to rob and no more."

The sober and reasonable man cannot be treated as having come on the scene at the moment of the fatal act with no knowledge of any earlier events. His knowledge must surely include awareness of the preparatory acts done by the defendant–in the present case his taking up a handful of cartridges from a pocket which he knew to contain both live ones and blanks. It was this act which made the subsequent pulling of the trigger dangerous and the sober and reasonable person would have recognised it as such.

The present court says: "But in our judgment *Dawson's* case goes no further than showing that the sober and reasonable man must look at the unlawful act to see if it is dangerous and not at the peculiarities of the victim." It is submitted, however, that the peculiarities of the victim are not different in principle from other circumstances. In determining whether the act was "dangerous" a peculiarity of the victim rendering him particularly vulnerable will be relevant if it is known to the defendant, or would be known to the sober and reasonable man in his situation. In *Dawson* the victim's severe heart condition was irrelevant not because it was a "peculiarity of the victim" but because it was unknown to the defendant and would not have been apparent to the sober and reasonable observer of the whole course of the defendant's conduct.

4.1.4 Causation

The act which is intentional, unlawful and dangerous must also cause death and the usual rules of causation apply here. See Chapter 1.

4.2 Gross Negligence Manslaughter

There is an alternative type of manslaughter. Over the years it has been called 'reckless manslaughter' and 'gross negligence manslaughter' and various tests have been given to establish fault. The law has now become settled by House of Lords decision in *R v Adomako* [1995] 1 AC 171 which established the existence of and set out the test for gross negligence manslaughter. This type of manslaughter can be committed by an omission. It can also be committed by a lawful act, performed negligently.

R v Adomako [1995] 1 AC 171

Panel: Lord Mackay of Clashfern LC, Lord Keith of Kinkel, Lord Goff of Chieveley, Lord Browne-Wilkinson and Lord Woolf

Facts: Adomako was an anaesthetist taking part in an eye operation. During the operation a disconnection occurred in the endotrachial tube which caused the supply of oxygen to the patient to cease. An alarm bell, monitoring the patient's blood pressure, sounded and Adomako checked some of the equipment, but not the relevant tube. The patient died. Adomako conceded that he had been negligent. The issue was whether he had committed a crime. The case went to the House of Lords which had to decide the test for manslaughter in such cases. It decided that the test of *Caldwell* recklessness, given in *R v Lawrence* and *R v Seymour* was not appropriate to establish liability for manslaughter.

LORD MACKAY OF CLASHFERN LC

Lord Mackay referred to the test for manslaughter given by Lord Hewart CJ in *R v Bateman* (1925) 19 Cr App Rep 8.

'To support an indictment for manslaughter the prosecution must prove the matters necessary to establish civil liability (except pecuniary loss), and, in addition, must satisfy the jury that the negligence or incompetence of the accused went beyond a mere matter of compensation and showed such disregard for the life and safety of others as to amount to a crime against the state and conduct deserving punishment.'

He then referred to the case of *Andrews v DPP* [1937] AC 576.

In my opinion the law as stated in these two authorities is satisfactory as providing a proper basis for describing the crime of involuntary manslaughter. Since the decision in Andrews was a decision of your Lordships' House, it remains the most authoritative statement of the present law which I have been able to find and although its relationship to *Reg. v Seymour* [1983] 2 AC 493 is a matter to which I shall have to return, it is a decision which has not been departed from. On this basis in my opinion the ordinary principles of the law of negligence apply to ascertain whether or not the defendant has been in breach of a duty of care towards the victim who has died. If such breach of duty is established the next question is whether that breach of duty caused the death of the victim. If so, the jury must go on to consider whether that breach of duty should be characterised as gross negligence and therefore as a crime. This will depend on the seriousness of the breach of duty committed by the defendant in

 Alert

all the circumstances in which the defendant was placed when it occurred. The jury will have to consider whether the extent to which the defendant's conduct departed from the proper standard of care incumbent upon him, involving as it must have done a risk of death to the patient, was such that it should be judged criminal.

It is true that to a certain extent this involves an element of circularity, but in this branch of the law I do not believe that is fatal to its being correct as a test of how far conduct must depart from accepted standards to be characterised as criminal. This is necessarily a question of degree and an attempt to specify that degree more closely is I think likely to achieve only a spurious precision. The essence of the matter which is supremely a jury question is whether having regard to the risk of death involved, the conduct of the defendant was so bad in all the circumstances as to amount in their judgment to a criminal act or omission.

In the past, gross negligence manslaughter had required either a risk of death or a risk to the safety of others and reckless manslaughter could have been satisfied by considering a risk of causing serious bodily harm or a risk to the health and welfare of the victim. It was not completely clear whether the test in *R v Adomako* requires a risk of death. This has now been confirmed in a series of Court of Appeal decisions.

R v Misra and Srivastava [2004] EWCA Crim 2375 [2005] 1 Cr App R 21

Panel: Judge LJ, Treacy and Bean JJ

Facts: The victim had undergone surgery to repair a tendon in his knee. Afterwards it became infected. The poisons built up in his body and he died from toxic shock. Misra and Scrivastava were senior housemen involved in his post operative care at the hospital. The case against them depended on negligence. They had failed to recognise the classic signs of the victim's infection, had not given him antibiotics which would have cured it, looked at the result of his blood tests or asked for help from senior colleagues. The court stated that a risk of death was necessary for liability.

LORD JUSTICE JUDGE

The decision of the House of Lords in *Adomako* clearly identified the ingredients of manslaughter by gross negligence. In very brief summary, confirming *Andrews v Director of Public Prosecutions* (1938) 26 Cr App R 34, [1937] AC 576, the offence requires, first, death resulting from a negligent breach of the duty of care owed by the defendant to the deceased; second, that in negligent breach of that duty, the victim was exposed by the defendant to the risk of death; and third, that the circumstances were so reprehensible as to amount to gross negligence.

 Alert

No issue arises whether both appellants owed a duty of care to the deceased, or were negligently in breach of it. There was however helpful argument about the nature of the relevant risk. Was it, as the judge directed the jury in the present case, "serious risk to life", or was it much broader, extending to serious risk to safety as well as life? In its original formulation in *R v Bateman* (1926) 19 Cr App R 8, Lord Hewitt CJ referred to "disregard to the life and safety of others" in the sense of serious injury. In *Seymour*, the risk was confined to the risk of death. In *R v Stone* (1977) 64 Cr App R 186,

[1977] QB 554 and *R v West London Coroner, Ex p. Grey* [1988] QB 467 reference was made to risks in broader terms, extending to health and welfare. Although Lord Mackay of Clashfern spoke in approving terms of these decisions in a different context, it is clear that his approval was directed to the deployment of the word "reckless". He was not addressing, and it would have been inconsistent with his own analysis of the legal principles if he were approving, the wider basis for identifying risk described in *Stone and West London Coroner Ex p. Grey*. It is also striking that Lord Mackay did not expressly adopt or approve the broader formulation of risk made by Lord Taylor of Gosforth CJ in *Prentice*. Since *Adomako*, this issue has been addressed in this court, in *R v Singh (Gurphal)* [1999] Crim LR 582 and the Divisional Court in *Lewin v Crown Prosecution Service* [2002] EWHC 1049 (Admin), unreported, May 24, 2002. In *Singh*, this Court strongly approved the trial judge's direction in a case of manslaughter by gross negligence that "the circumstances must be such that a reasonably prudent person would have foreseen a serious and obvious risk not merely of injury, even serious injury, but of death". In *Lewin*, the Divisional Court applied that direction.

Mr David Perry, on behalf of the Attorney General, informed us that, as a matter of policy, when making a decision whether to prosecute for this offence in cases like the present, the Director of Public Prosecutions looks for evidence of an obvious risk of death, and that, if the extent of the risk were limited to the obvious risk of serious injury, and no more, prosecution would not follow.

The editors of Blackstone's Criminal Practice suggest that the law needs clarification, and that, if it were clarified, some "degree of symmetry" between murder and manslaughter would be achieved if, for the purposes of gross negligence manslaughter, the risk should extend to grievous bodily harm. Professor Smith took the contrary view, suggesting that "if we are to have an offence of homicide by gross negligence at all, it seems right that it should be ... limited. The circumstances must be such that a reasonably prudent person would have foreseen a serious risk, not merely of injury, even serious injury, but of death".

There will, of course, be numerous occasions when these distinctions are entirely theoretical. From time to time, however, they will be of great significance, not only to the decision whether to prosecute, but also to the risk of conviction of manslaughter. In our judgment, where the issue of risk is engaged, *Adomako* demonstrates, and it is now clearly established, that it relates to the risk of death, and is not sufficiently satisfied by the risk of bodily injury or injury to health. In short, the offence requires gross negligence in circumstances where what is at risk is the life of an individual to whom the defendant owes a duty of care.

 Alert

Further Reading

Birch D 'Commentary on *R v Watson*', [1989] *Crim LR* 734

Gardner S 'Manslaughter by Gross Negligence' (1995) 111 *LQR* 22

Keating H 'The Restoration of a Serious Crime' [1996] *Crim LR* 535

Wasik M 'Form and Function in the Law of Involuntary Manslaughter' [1994] *Crim LR* 883

The Law Commission Report 1995 (Law Comm no 237) Legislating the Criminal Code: Involuntary Manslaughter

5

Non Fatal Offences Against the Person

Topic List

5.1 Assault

Assault is a common law offence which was defined in *Fagan v Metropolitan Police Commissioner* [1969] 1 QB 439 as 'intentionally or recklessly causing another person to apprehend immediate and unlawful personal violence.'

5.1.1 Form of Assault

R v Ireland, R v Burstow [1998] AC 147

Panel: Lord Goff of Chieveley, Lord Slynn of Hadley, Lord Steyn, Lord Hope of Craighead and Lord Hutton

Statute: Offences Against the Person Act 1861 s 47

Facts: This was a conjoined appeal to the House of Lords. One of the appellants, Ireland, had made numerous silent telephone calls to three women. As a result these women had suffered psychological damage. Ireland was convicted of assault occasioning actual bodily harm contrary to Offences Against the Person Act 1861 s 47. He appealed on the basis that there was no assault, as required for this offence. It was argued on his behalf that silence, or indeed words alone, cannot constitute an assault.

LORD STEYN

It is now necessary to consider whether the making of silent telephone calls causing psychiatric injury is capable of constituting an assault under section 47. The Court of Appeal, as constituted in *Reg. v Ireland* case, answered that question in the affirmative. There has been substantial academic criticism of the conclusion and reasoning in *Reg. v Ireland*: see Archbold News, Issue 6, 12 July 1996; Archbold's Criminal Pleading, Evidence & Practice, Supplement No. 4 (1996), pages 345-347; Smith and Hogan, Criminal Law, 8th edn (1996), 413; 'Assault by Telephone' by Jonathan Herring [1997] CLJ 11 and 'Assault' [1997] Crim LR 434 , 435-436. Counsel's arguments, broadly speaking, challenged the decision in *Reg. v Ireland* on very similar lines. Having carefully considered the literature and counsel's arguments, I have come to the conclusion that the appeal ought to be dismissed.

The starting point must be that an assault is an ingredient of the offence under section 47. It is necessary to consider the two forms which an assault may take. The first is battery, which involves the unlawful application of force by the defendant upon the victim. Usually, section 47 is used to prosecute in cases of this kind. The second form of assault is an act causing the victim to apprehend an imminent application of force upon her: see *Fagan v Metropolitan Police Commissioner* [1969] 1 QB 43 , 444d-e.

One point can be disposed of, quite briefly. The Court of Appeal was not asked to consider whether silent telephone calls resulting in psychiatric injury is capable of constituting a battery. But encouraged by some academic comment it was raised before your Lordships' House. Counsel for Ireland was most economical in his argument on the point. I will try to match his economy of words. In my view it is not feasible to enlarge the generally accepted legal meaning of what is a battery to include the circumstances of a silent caller who causes psychiatric injury.

It is to assault in the form of an act causing the victim to fear an immediate application of force to her that I must turn. Counsel argued that as a matter of law an assault can never be committed by words alone and therefore it cannot be committed by silence. The premise depends on the slenderest authority, namely, an observation by Holroyd J. to a jury that 'no words or singing are equivalent to an assault:' *Rex v Meade and Belt* (1823) 1 Lew. 184. The proposition that a gesture may amount to an assault, but that words can never suffice, is unrealistic and indefensible. A thing said is also a thing done. There is no reason why something said should be incapable of causing an apprehension of immediate personal violence, e.g. a man accosting a woman in a dark alley saying, 'Come with me or I will stab you.' I would, therefore, reject the proposition that an assault can never be committed by words.

That brings me to the critical question whether a silent caller may be guilty of an assault. The answer to this question seems to me to be 'Yes, depending on the facts.' It involves questions of fact within the province of the jury. After all, there is no reason why a telephone caller who says to a woman in a menacing way 'I will be at your door in a minute or two' may not be guilty of an assault if he causes his victim to apprehend immediate personal violence. Take now the case of the silent caller. He intends by his silence to cause fear and he is so understood. The victim is assailed by uncertainty about his intentions. Fear may dominate her emotions, and it may be the fear that the caller's arrival at her door may be imminent. She may fear the possibility of immediate personal violence. As a matter of law the caller may be guilty of an assault: whether he is or not will depend on the circumstance and in particular on the impact of the caller's potentially menacing call or calls on the victim. Such a prosecution case under section 47 may be fit to leave to the jury. and a trial judge may, depending on the circumstances, put a common sense consideration before the jury, namely what, if not the possibility of imminent personal violence, was the victim terrified about? I conclude that an assault may be committed in the particular factual circumstances which I have envisaged. For this reason I reject the submission that as a matter of law a silent telephone caller cannot ever be guilty of an offence under section 47. In these circumstances no useful purpose would be served by answering the vague certified question in *Reg. v Ireland*.

LORD HOPE

In this case the appellant pled guilty to three contraventions of section 47 of the Act of 1861. He admitted to having made numerous telephone calls to three women, during which he remained silent when the women answered the telephone. These calls lasted sometimes for a minute or so, and sometimes for several minutes. On some occasions they were repeated over a relatively short period. There is no doubt that this conduct was intended to distress the victims, each of whom suffered as a result from symptoms of such a kind as to amount to psychiatric injury. But, for the appellant to be guilty of an offence contrary to section 47 of the Act of 1861, he must be held to have committed an act which amounts to an assault.

Plainly there was no element of battery, although counsel for the Crown made brief submissions to the contrary, as at no time was there any kind of physical contact between the appellant and his victims. As Swinton Thomas LJ observed in the Court of

Appeal [1997] QB 114, 119d, that is a fact of importance in this case. But it is not an end of the matter, because as he went on to say it has been recognised for many centuries that putting a person in fear may amount to what in law is an assault. This is reflected in the meaning which is given to the word 'assault' in Archbold Criminal Pleading, Evidence & Practice (1997), p. 1594, para. 19-66, namely that an assault is any act by which a person intentionally or recklessly causes another to apprehend immediate and unlawful violence. This meaning is well vouched by authority: see *Reg. v Venna* [1976] QB 421; *Reg. v Parmenter* [1992] 1 AC 699, 740f, per Lord Ackner.

The question is whether such an act can include the making of a series of silent telephone calls. Counsel for the appellant said that such an act could not amount to an assault under any circumstances, just as words alone could not amount to an assault. He also submitted that, in order for there to be an assault, it had to be proved that what the victim apprehended was immediate and unlawful violence, not just a repetition of the telephone calls. It was not enough to show merely that the victim was inconvenienced or afraid. He said that the Court of Appeal had fallen into error on this point, because they had proceeded on the basis that it was sufficient that when the victims lifted the telephone they were placed in immediate fear and suffered the consequences which resulted in psychiatric injury. The court had not sufficiently addressed the question whether the victims were apprehensive of immediate and unlawful violence and, if so, whether it was that apprehension which had caused them to sustain the bodily injury.

I agree that a passage in the judgment of the Court of Appeal [1997] QB 114, 122c-g suggests that they had equated the apprehension of immediate and unlawful violence with the actual psychiatric injury which was suffered by the victims. I also agree that, if this was so, it was an incorrect basis from which to proceed. But in the penultimate sentence in this passage Swinton Thomas LJ said that in the court's judgment repetitive telephone calls of this nature were likely to cause the victim to apprehend immediate and unlawful violence. Furthermore, as the appellant pled guilty to these offences, the question whether that apprehension caused the psychiatric injury did not need to be explored in evidence. The important question therefore is whether the making of a series of silent telephone calls can amount in law to an assault.

There is no clear guidance on this point either in the statute or in the authorities. On the one hand in *Rex v Meade and Belt* (1823) 1 Lew. 184 Holroyd J. said that no words or singing can amount to an assault. On the other hand in *Reg. v Wilson* [1955] 1 WLR 493, 494 Lord Goddard CJ said that the appellant's words, 'Get out knives' would itself be an assault. The word 'assault' as used in section 47 of the Act of 1861 is not defined anywhere in that Act. The legislation appears to have been framed on the basis that the words which it used were words which everyone would understand without further explanation. In this regard the fact that the statute was enacted in the middle of the last century is of no significance. The public interest, for whose benefit it was enacted, would not be served by construing the words in a narrow or technical way. The words used are ordinary English words, which can be given their ordinary meaning in the usage of the present day. They can take account of changing circumstances both as regards medical knowledge and the means by which one person can cause bodily harm to another.

The fact is that the means by which a person of evil disposition may intentionally or recklessly cause another to apprehend immediate and unlawful violence will vary according to the circumstances. Just as it is not true to say that every blow which is struck is an assault some blows, which would otherwise amount to battery, may be struck by accident or in jest or may otherwise be entirely justified so also it is not true to say that mere words or gestures can never constitute an assault. It all depends on the circumstances. If the words or gestures are accompanied in their turn by gestures or by words which threaten immediate and unlawful violence, that will be sufficient for an assault. The words or gestures must be seen in their whole context.

In this case the means which the appellant used to communicate with his victims was the telephone. While he remained silent, there can be no doubt that he was intentionally communicating with them as directly as if he was present with them in the same room. But whereas for him merely to remain silent with them in the same room, where they could see him and assess his demeanour, would have been unlikely to give rise to any feelings of apprehension on their part, his silence when using the telephone in calls made to them repeatedly was an act of an entirely different character. He was using his silence as a means of conveying a message to his victims. This was that he knew who and where they were, and that his purpose in making contact with them was as malicious as it was deliberate. In my opinion silent telephone calls of this nature are just as capable as words or gestures, said or made in the presence of the victim, of causing an apprehension of immediate and unlawful violence.

 Alert

Whether this requirement, and in particular that of immediacy, is in fact satisfied will depend on the circumstances. This will need in each case, if it is disputed, to be explored in evidence. But that step was not necessary in this case as the appellant was prepared to plead guilty to having committed the offence. I would therefore answer the certified question in the affirmative and dismiss this appeal also.

5.1.2 Immediate

One of the requirements of an assault is that the apprehension should be of being inflicted with personal violence immediately. The courts have not interpreted 'immediate' to mean instantaneous.

Smith v Chief Superintendent, Woking Police Station (1983) 76 Cr App R 234

Panel: Kerr LJ and Glidewell J

Facts: Smith entered the enclosed garden of a house at night and looked through the window of a ground floor bedroom at the victim who was in a nightdress. He pressed his face against the glass for several seconds. The victim recognised Smith and was terrified. Smith was charged under the Vagrancy Act 1824 s 4 which required the defendant to be in an enclosed garden for an unlawful purpose. The unlawful purpose relied upon was assault. He appealed on the ground that there was no evidence he had the mens rea for assault.

LORD JUSTICE KERR

It is also common ground that the definition of an assault as stated, for instance, in Archbold (41st edn), para. 20-114, is correct in law: "An assault is any act which intentionally—or recklessly—causes another to apprehend immediate and unlawful violence." It is stated later on in the passage that there must be, on the part of the defendant, a hostile intent calculated to cause apprehension in the mind of the victim.

In the present case, on the findings which I have summarised, there was quite clearly an intention to cause fear, an intention to frighten, and that intention produced the intended effect as the result of what the defendant did, in that it did frighten and indeed terrify Miss Mooney to the extent that she screamed. It is not a case where she was merely startled or surprised or ashamed to be seen in her nightclothes; she was terrified as the result of what the defendant deliberately did, knowing and either intending or being reckless as to whether it would cause that fear in her.

Ultimately, as it seems to me, the only point taken by Mr Denny which requires some consideration is whether there was a sufficient apprehension, within the definition which I have read, of immediate and unlawful violence. He takes the point that there is no finding here that what Miss Mooney was terrified of was some violence, and indeed some violence which can be described as immediate. However, as it seems to me, Mr Greenbourne is right when he submits, really in the form of a question: "What else, other than some form of immediate violence, could Miss Mooney have been terrified about?"

When one is in a state of terror one is very often unable to analyse precisely what one is frightened of as likely to happen next. When I say that, I am speaking of a situation such as the present, where the person who causes one to be terrified is immediately adjacent, albeit on the other side of a window. Mr Denny relied on a sentence in Smith and Hogan's Criminal Law (4th edn), page 351, where an illustration is given as follows: "There can be no assault if it is obvious to P"—the complainant—"that D"—the defendant—"is unable to carry out his threat, as where D shakes his fist at P who is safely locked inside his car." That may be so, but those are not the facts of the present case.

In the present case the defendant intended to frighten Miss Mooney and Miss Mooney was frightened. As it seems to me, there is no need for a finding that what she was frightened of, which she probably could not analyse at that moment, was some innominate terror of some potential violence. It was clearly a situation where the basis of the fear which was instilled in her was that she did not know what the defendant was going to do next, but that, whatever he might be going to do next, and sufficiently immediately for the purposes of the offence, was something of a violent nature. In effect, as it seems to me, it was wholly open to the justices to infer that her state of mind was not only that of terror, which they did find, but terror of some immediate violence. In those circumstances, it seems to me that they were perfectly entitled to convict the defendant who had gone there, as they found, with the intention of frightening her and causing her to fear some act of immediate violence, and therefore with the intention of committing an assault upon her. Accordingly, I would dismiss this appeal.

In *R v Ireland, R v Burstow*, Lord Steyn equated immediate with imminent.

> LORD STEYN
>
> After all, there is no reason why a telephone caller who says to a woman in a menacing way 'I will be at your door in a minute or two' may not be guilty of an assault if he causes his victim to apprehend immediate personal violence. Take now the case of the silent caller. He intends by his silence to cause fear and he is so understood. The victim is assailed by uncertainty about his intentions. Fear may dominate her emotions, and it may be the fear that the caller's arrival at her door may be imminent. She may fear the possibility of immediate personal violence.

5.1.3 The Victim's Apprehension

Assault is unusual in that the actus reus depends on the mental state of the victim. There can be no assault if the victim is deaf so does not hear the defendant's words, or if the victim is asleep or blind, so does not see the defendant's actions. In *R v Lamb* [1967] 2 QB 981, where the defendant pointed a gun at the victim and pulled the trigger, there was no actus reus or mens rea of assault as neither party thought the gun would fire a bullet.

On the other hand, if the defendant causes the victim to apprehend immediate unlawful personal violence, this will constitute the actus reus of assault, despite the defendant not intending to carry out his threat, or not having the means to carry out his threat. In *Logdon v DPP* [1976] Crim LR 121 there was an assault where the defendant threatened the victim with a replica gun, which the defendant knew was a replica, but the victim believed was real.

What is required is an apprehension of personal violence, rather than fear. So if the victim believes he will be hit, but is not afraid of this, the actus reus will be present. However, fear by itself is not enough. The Court of Appeal in *R v Ireland* [1997] QB 114 confused fear with an apprehension of personal violence.

Assault occasioning actual bodily harm - psychological damage, Professor Sir John Smith [1997] Crim LR 435

> This decision is forcefully criticised by the late Professor Edward Griew in Archbold News, July 12, 1996, and by the editors of Archbold itself, Archbold Supp. 19-166.
>
> Assault. The so-called "classic" definition of assault derives from the first edition of Smith and Hogan, Criminal Law (1965), page 262: "An assault is any act by which D intentionally or (possibly) recklessly, causes P to apprehend immediate and unlawful personal violence." (Following *Venna* [1976] QB 421, we have since been able to drop "possibly"–see, e.g. 8th edn, page 410.) This definition, which owes much to the important article by Dr JWC Turner, "Assault at Common Law" (1927) 7 CLJ 56, was adopted, almost verbatim, but without acknowledgment by James J., delivering the judgment with Lord Parker CJ agreed in *Fagan v Metropolitan Police Commissioner* [1968] 3 All ER 442 at 445, DC From there it eventually found its way into Archbold (38th edn, 1973, s 2634) and other books, superseding the antiquated and

misleading definitions previously found in those works and, as noted in the present case, it was approved in *Savage and Parmenter* [1992] 1 AC 699 at 740.

The court accepts this definition, as it was, no doubt, bound to do but thereafter seems (i) to confuse causing fear (which the appellant did) with causing apprehension of immediate violence (which he did not) and (ii) wrongly to equate the causing of harm which he did) with the infliction of violence (which he neither did nor threatened). The causing of harm and the infliction of violence are by no means the same thing. The court says:

> "... if the Crown can prove that the victims have sustained actual bodily harm, in this case psychological harm, and the accused must have intended the victims to sustain such harm or been reckless as to whether they did sustain such harm, and that harm resulted from an act or acts of the appellant, namely telephone calls followed by silence, it is open to the jury to find that he has committed an assault."

If that is a description of any offence, it is a description of a battery, not the assault which the court professes to be discussing. It refers to an injury actually inflicted, not one apprehended. Assault and battery are two distinct crimes, with a different actus reus and a different mens rea. It is essential to distinguish between them. A judgment which drifts between one and the other is bound to get into difficulties. To take the corresponding definition of battery from Smith and Hogan: a battery–"consists in the infliction of unlawful personal violence by D upon P." The appellant may certainly be taken to have inflicted harm on his victim but it could scarcely be described as "personal violence."

The actus reus of an assault typically occurs when P thinks, "I am about to receive a punch on the nose." Are we to imagine that P, on picking up the telephone, thinks "I am about to suffer a psychological injury"? Surely the idea is as ludicrous as that the appellant had mens rea, i.e. that he was thinking "This'll cause him to think he's in for a nervous shock!"

As for authorities, the court quoted extensively from the judgment of Kerr LJ in *Smith v Chief Superintendent, Woking Police Station* (assault by looking through the window of a bedsitting room at P in her night clothes with intent to frighten her) but did not quote the passage in which Kerr LJ limited his decision to a case where D "is immediately adjacent, albeit on the other side of a window." Kerr LJ distinguished, without dissenting from, the opinion in the fourth edition of Smith and Hogan that "there can be no assault if it is obvious to P that D is unable to carry out his threat, as where he shakes his fist at P who is safely locked inside his car."

Barton v Armstrong is a first instance ruling in a civil action in New South Wales in which Taylor J. was emphatic that the "threatening act must put the victim in immediate fear or apprehension of violence." He said "Physical violence and death can be produced by acts done at a distance by people who are out of sight and by agents hired for that purpose. I do not think that these, if they result in apprehension of physical violence in the mind of a reasonable person, are outside the protection of the criminal law." That is perfectly acceptable–but far removed from the present case. In *Knights* (1988) A Crim R 314, CCA, NSW, it appears that telephonic threats were held not to amount to criminal assault because they were not threats of immediate violence.

5.1.4 Mens Rea

The mens rea is intention or recklessness. The Court of Appeal in *R v Venna* [1976] QB 421 held this to be *Cunningham* recklessness. This was confirmed by the House of Lords in *R v Savage; R v Parmenter* [1992] 1 AC 714. So the defendant must see the risk that his actions will cause the victim to apprehend immediate unlawful personal violence.

5.2 Battery

Battery is a common law offence which was defined in *Fagan v Metropolitan Police Commissioner* [1969] 1 QB 439 as 'the actual intended use of unlawful force to another person without his consent'.

5.2.1 Force

The merest touching amounts to force. It was held in *R v Thomas* (1985) 81 Cr App R 331 that the touching can be through clothing.

Collins v Wilcock (1984) 79 Cr App R 229

Panel: Robert Goff LJ and Mann J

Facts: Wilcock and another police officer were on duty when they saw two women in the street whom they believed to be prostitutes soliciting for business. One of the women was a known prostitute. They asked the women to get into their police car so they could talk to them. The known prostitute did so, but the other, Collins, refused. She swore at the police officers and walked off. Wilcock got out of the car and put a hand on Collins' arm to restrain her. Collins swore again and scratched the police officer's arm with her fingernails. Collins was convicted of assaulting a police constable in the execution of her duty. On appeal the conviction was overturned. It was held that the police officer was not engaged in arresting Collins at the time, and that her act of putting her hand on Collins's arm was a battery.

LORD JUSTICE ROBERT GOFF

The law draws a distinction, in terms more easily understood by philologists than by ordinary citizens, between an assault and a battery. An assault is an act which causes another person to apprehend the infliction of immediate, unlawful, force on his person; a battery is the actual infliction of unlawful force on another person. Both assault and battery are forms of trespass to the person. Another form of trespass to the person is false imprisonment, which is the unlawful imposition of constraint upon another's freedom of movement from a particular place. The requisite mental element is of no relevance in the present case.

We are here concerned primarily with battery. The fundamental principle, plain and incontestable, is that every person's body is inviolate. It has long been established that any touching of another person, however slight, may amount to a battery. So Holt CJ held in 1704 that "the least touching of another in anger is a battery": see *Cole v Turner* (1704) Mod. 149. The breadth of the principle reflects the fundamental nature of the interest so protected; as Blackstone wrote in his Commentaries on the Laws of England, "the law cannot draw the line between different degrees of violence, and therefore totally prohibits the first and lowest stage of it; every man's person being sacred, and no other having a right to meddle with it, in any the slightest manner" (3 Bl.Com. 120). The effect is that everybody is protected not only against physical injury but against any form of physical molestation.

 Alert

That the force need not be applied directly is illustrated by the case below.

Director of Public Prosecutions v K (A Minor) [1990] 1 WLR 1067

Panel: Parker LJ and Tudor Evans J

Statute: Offences Against the Person Act 1861 s 47

Facts: K, aged 15, took some concentrated sulphuric acid out of a chemistry lesson to the school lavatory where he proceeded to test its reaction on some paper. When he heard footsteps approaching he panicked and poured the acid into a hand drier. The air nozzle on the drier was pointing upwards. The next person to turn the drier on had acid blown onto his face. This caused a permanent scar. The defendant was charged with assault occasioning actual bodily harm contrary to Offences against the Person Act 1861 s 47. The magistrates found that K did not possess the mens rea for a battery. The prosecution appealed and was successful in the Divisional Court.

LORD JUSTICE PARKER

The second of the two questions is perhaps not very happily worded but in my judgment there can be no doubt that if a defendant places acid into a machine with the intent that it shall, when the next user switches the machine on, be ejected onto him and do him harm there is an assault [meaning assault or battery, so here battery] when the harm is done. The position was correctly and simply stated by Stephen J. in *Reg. v Clarence* (1888) 22 QBD 23, 45:

> "If a man laid a trap for another into which he fell after an interval, the man who laid it would during the interval be guilty of an attempt to assault,[meaning assault or battery, so here battery] and of an actual assault as soon as the man fell in."

This illustration was also referred to by Wills J. in the same case in relation to section 20 of the Act of 1861. Wills J. there also referred to *Reg. v Martin* (1881) 8 QBD 54, saying, at page 36:

"The prisoner in that case did what was certain to make people crush one another, perhaps to death, and the grievous bodily harm was as truly inflicted by him as if he had hurled a stone at somebody's head."

In the same way a defendant, who pours a dangerous substance into a machine, just as truly assaults the next user of the machine as if he had himself switched the machine on. So, too, in my judgment would he be guilty of an assault [meaning assault or battery, so here battery] if he was guilty of relevant recklessness.

This case was subsequently overruled by the Court of Appeal, but not on the ground that there was no actus reus.

5.2.2 Consent

Battery requires an absence of consent, and much of the touching which occurs in everyday life is impliedly consented to.

Collins v Wilcock (1984) 79 Cr App R 229

Panel: Robert Goff LJ and Mann J

LORD JUSTICE ROBERT GOFF

But so widely drawn a principle must inevitably be subject to exceptions. For example, children may be subjected to reasonable punishment; people may be subjected to the lawful exercise of the power of arrest; and reasonable force may be used in self-defence or for the prevention of crime. But, apart from these special instances where the control or constraint is lawful, a broader exception has been created to allow for the exigencies of everyday life. Generally speaking, consent is a defence to battery; and most of the physical contacts of ordinary life are not actionable because they are impliedly consented to by all who move in society and so expose themselves to the risk of bodily contact. So nobody can complain of the jostling which is inevitable from his presence in, for example, a supermarket, an underground station or a busy street; nor can a person who attends a party complain if his hand is seized in friendship, or even if his back is (within reason) slapped (see *Tuberville v Savage* (1669) 1 Mod. 3). Although such cases are regarded as examples of implied consent, it is more common nowadays to treat them as falling within a general exception embracing all physical contact which is generally acceptable in the ordinary conduct of daily life. We observe that, although in the past it has sometimes been stated that a battery is only committed where the action is "angry or revengeful, or rude or insolent" (see 1 Hawkins Pleas of the Crown, ch 62, s 2), we think that nowadays it is more realistic, and indeed more accurate, to state the broad underlying principle, subject to the broad exception.

Among such forms of conduct, long held to be acceptable, is touching a person for the purpose of engaging his attention, though of course using no greater degree of physical contact than is reasonably necessary in the circumstances for that purpose. So, for example, it was held by the Court of Common Pleas in 1807 that a touch by a constable's staff on the shoulder of a man who had climbed on a gentleman's railing to gain a better view of a mad ox, the touch being only to engage the man's attention,

 Alert

did not amount to a battery (see *Wiffin v Kincard* (1807) 2 Bos. & Pul. N.R. 471): for another example, see *Coward v Baddeley* (1859) 4 H. & N. 478. But a distinction is drawn between a touch to draw a man's attention, which is generally acceptable, and a physical restraint, which is not. So we find Parke B. observing in *Rawlings v Till* (1837) 3 M. & W. 28, with reference to *Wiffin v Kincard*, that "there the touch was merely to engage a man's attention, not to put a restraint upon his person" (see page 29 of the report). Furthermore, persistent touching to gain attention in the face of obvious disregard may transcend the norms of acceptable behavior, and so be outside the exception. We do not say that more than one touch is never permitted: for example, the lost or distressed may surely be permitted a second touch, or possibly even more, on a reluctant or impervious sleeve or shoulder, as may a person who is acting reasonably in the exercise of a duty. In each case, the test must be whether the physical contact so persisted in has in the circumstances gone beyond generally acceptable standards of conduct; and the answer to that question will depend upon the facts of the particular case.

 Alert

5.2.3 Mens Rea

The mens rea is intention or recklessness. The Court of Appeal in *R v Venna* [1976] QB 421 held this to be *Cunningham* recklessness. This was confirmed by the House of Lords in *R v Savage; R v Parmenter* [1992] 1 AC 714. So the defendant must see the risk that his actions will inflict unlawful force on another person without their consent.

5.3 Assault Occasioning Actual Bodily Harm: s 47

5.3.1 Actual Bodily Harm

The principal definitions which the courts have given to actual bodily harm are referred to by Mr Justice Maurice Kay in the case below.

T v Director of Public Prosecutions [2003] EWHC 266 (Admin), [2003] Crim LR 622

Panel: Maurice Kay J

Statute: Offences Against the Person Act 1861 s 47

Facts: T, a minor, was in a gang which had attacked the victim. The victim fell to the ground and T was seen by a police officer to kick the victim in the head. The victim momentarily lost consciousness and remembered nothing until being woken by the police officer. A Youth Court convicted T of assault occasioning actual bodily harm contrary to Offences Against the Person Act 1861 s 47 and he appealed on the ground that a momentary loss of consciousness did not amount to actual bodily harm.

MR JUSTICE MAURICE KAY

4. The question posed by the justices for the opinion of this court is expressed in this way:

   "Whether momentary loss of consciousness is sufficient to make out the offence of Assault Occasioning Actual Bodily Harm contrary to sec. 47 of The Offences Against the Person Act 1861."

5. In his submissions on behalf of the appellant, Mr Hearnden focuses on the well-known passage from the judgment of the Court of Appeal given by Swift J in *R v Donovan* [1934] 2 KB 498. It contains this passage at page 509:

   "For this purpose we think that 'bodily harm' has its ordinary meaning and includes any hurt or injury calculated to interfere with the health or comfort of the prosecutor. Such hurt or injury need not be permanent, but must, no doubt, be more than merely transient and trifling."

   Mr Hearnden's approach is to focus on the word "transient". Taking that word and its deployment in *Donovan* as a starting point, he then synonymises it with the word "momentary", by reference to certain respected dictionaries, and submits that a momentary loss of consciousness cannot be actual bodily harm because it is, by definition, merely transient.

6. In my judgment that is a flawed approach. I go back to the specific words of section 47. The words "actual bodily harm" are not defined in the Act and there is no reason why they should have been; they were and are everyday words. In *R v Chan-Fook* [1994] 2 All England Reports 552 at 557D it was stated of the words "actual bodily harm":

   "These are three words of the English language which require no elaboration and in the ordinary course should not receive any. The word 'harm' is a synonym for injury. The word 'actual' indicates that the injury (although there is no need for it to be permanent) should not be so trivial as to be wholly insignificant."

   In my view, it cannot be doubted that the loss of consciousness suffered by the victim in this case fell within the meaning of the word "harm". Nor can it be doubted that that harm was "bodily". It involved an injurious impairment to the victim's sensory functions. It is axiomatic that the bodily harm was "actual". In my judgment, on the plain words of the section, the justices were entitled to find that the assault carried out by the appellant had occasioned actual bodily harm.

7. I consider it inappropriate to approach the words used by the Court of Appeal in *Donovan* as though they were the words of a statute. As it happens, they do not even form part of the ratio of that case, the issue in which related to consent. However, they have been referred to frequently for many years. So too has the ruling given by Lynskey J in the case of *Miller*. He said at page 292:

   "I am satisfied that the second count [alleging assault occasioning actual bodily harm] is a valid one and must be left to the jury for their decision. The point has been taken that there is no evidence of bodily harm. The bodily harm alleged is said to be the result of the [defendant's] actions, and that is, if the jury accept the evidence, that he threw the wife down three times. There is evidence that afterwards she was in a hysterical and nervous condition, but it is said by counsel [for the defendant] that that is not 'actual bodily harm' ... There was a time when shock was not regarded as bodily hurt, but the day has gone by when that could be said. It seems to me now that if a person is caused hurt or injury resulting, not in any physical injury, but in an injury to her state of mind for the time being, that is within the definition of 'actual bodily harm', and on that point I would leave the case to the jury."

The issue in *Miller's case* was the hysterical and nervous condition to which the learned judge referred. The justices in the present case specifically relied upon the case of *Miller* and the passage to which I have just referred. In my judgment, they did not err by so doing. The important point, however, is that none of these authorities provides a gloss on the statute. What one has to do is to return to the statute itself.

8. However, I add this: even if one focuses on the words in *Donovan*, upon which Mr Hearnden relies, it is clear, as Mr Fields points out, that what the Court of Appeal was excluding from the definition of actual bodily harm was harm that was "transient and trifling", not "transient or trifling". Accordingly, to focus on transience to the exclusion of triviality is in itself an inappropriate exercise.

9. I am entirely satisfied that the justices did not fall into error. They were entitled to convict the appellant on the evidence of momentary loss of consciousness. Accordingly, this appeal is dismissed.

It has been confirmed by the House of Lords that bodily harm includes psychiatric injury.

R v Ireland, R v Burstow [1998] AC 147

LORD STEYN

It will now be convenient to consider the question which is common to the two appeals, namely, whether psychiatric illness is capable of amounting to bodily harm in terms of sections 18, 20 and 47 of the Act of 1861. The answer must be the same for the three sections.

The only abiding thing about the processes of the human mind, and the causes of its disorders and disturbances, is that there will never be a complete explanation. Psychiatry is and will always remain an imperfectly understood branch of medical science. This idea is explained by Vallar's psychiatrist in Iris Murdoch's The Message to the Planet:

'Our knowledge of the soul, if I may use that unclinical but essential word, encounters certain seemingly impassable limits, set there perhaps by the gods, if I may refer to them, in order to preserve their privacy, and beyond which it maybe not only futile but lethal to attempt to pass and though it is our duty to seek for knowledge, it is also incumbent on us to realise when it is denied us, and not to prefer a fake solution to no solution at all.'

But there has been progress since 1861 and courts of law can only act on the best scientific understanding of the day. Some elementary distinctions can be made. The appeals under consideration do not involve structural injuries to the brain such as might require the intervention of a neurologist. One is also not considering either psychotic illness or personality disorders. The victims in the two appeals suffered from no such conditions. As a result of the behaviour of the appellants they did not develop psychotic or psychoneurotic conditions. The case was that they developed mental disturbances of a lesser order, namely neurotic disorders. For present purposes the relevant forms of neurosis are anxiety disorders and depressive disorders. Neuroses must be distinguished from simple states of fear, or problems in coping with every day life. Where the line is to be drawn must be a matter of psychiatric judgment. But for present purposes it is important to note that modern psychiatry treats neuroses as recognisable psychiatric illnesses: see 'Liability for Psychiatric Injury,' Law Commission Consultation Paper No. 137 (1995) Part III (The Medical Background); Mullany and Hanford, Tort Liability for Psychiatric Damages (1993), discussion on 'The Medical Perspective,' at pages 24-42, and particularly at page 30, footnote 88. Moreover, it is essential to bear in mind that neurotic illnesses affect the central nervous system of the body, because emotions such as fear and anxiety are brain functions.

Lord Steyn then noted that the civil law does not distinguish between physical and mental illnesses.

The criminal law has been slow to follow this path. But in *Reg. v Chan-Fook* [1994] 1 WLR 689 the Court of Appeal squarely addressed the question whether psychiatric injury may amount to bodily harm under section 47 of the Act of 1861. The issue arose in a case where the defendant had aggressively questioned and locked in a suspected thief. There was a dispute as to whether the defendant had physically assaulted the victim. But the prosecution also alleged that even if the victim had suffered no physical injury, he had been reduced to a mental state which amounted to actual bodily harm under section 47. No psychiatric evidence was given. The judge directed the jury that an assault which caused an hysterical and nervous condition was an assault occasioning actual bodily harm. The defendant was convicted. Upon appeal the conviction was quashed on the ground of misdirections in the summing up and the absence of psychiatric evidence to support the prosecution's alternative case. The interest of the decision lies in the reasoning on psychiatric injury in the context of section 47. In a detailed and careful judgment given on behalf of the court Hobhouse LJ said, at page 695:

'The first question on the present appeal is whether the inclusion of the word 'bodily' in the phrase 'actual bodily harm' limits harm to harm to the skin, flesh and bones of the victim. . . . The body of the victim includes all parts of his body, including his organs, his nervous system and his brain.

Bodily injury therefore may include injury to any of those parts of his body responsible for his mental and other faculties.'

In concluding that 'actual bodily harm' is capable of including psychiatric injury Hobhouse LJ emphasised, at page 696:

'it does not include mere emotions such as fear or distress nor panic nor does it include, as such, states of mind that are not themselves evidence of some identifiable clinical condition.'

He observed that in the absence of psychiatric evidence a question whether or not an assault occasioned psychiatric injury should not be left to the jury.

The Court of Appeal, as differently constituted in *Reg. v Ireland* and *Reg. v Burstow*, was bound by the decision in *Reg. v Chan-Fook*. The House is not so bound. Counsel for the appellants in both appeals submitted that bodily harm in Victorian legislation cannot include psychiatric injury. For this reason they argued that *Reg. v Chan-Fook* was wrongly decided. They relied on the following observation of Lord Bingham of Cornhill CJ in *Reg. v Burstow* [1997] 1 Cr App R 144, 148-149:

'Were the question free from authority, we should entertain some doubt whether the Victorian draftsman of the 1861 Act intended to embrace psychiatric injury within the expressions 'grievous bodily harm' and 'actual bodily harm'.'

Nevertheless, Lord Bingham CJ observed that it is now accepted that in the relevant context the distinction between physical and mental injury is by no means clear cut. He welcomed the ruling in *Reg. v Chan-Fook*, at p. 149b. I respectfully agree. But I would go further and point out that, although out of considerations of piety we frequently refer to the actual intention of the draftsman, the correct approach is simply to consider whether the words of the Act of 1861 considered in the light of contemporary knowledge cover a recognisable psychiatric injury. It is undoubtedly true that there are statutes where the correct approach is to construe the legislation 'as if one were interpreting it the day after it was passed:' *The Longford* (1889) 14 PD 34. Thus in *The Longford* the word 'action' in a statute was held not to be apt to cover an Admiralty action in rem since when it was passed the Admiralty Court 'was not one of His Majesty's Courts of Law:' see pages 37, 38. Bearing in mind that statutes are usually intended to operate for many years it would be most inconvenient if courts could never rely in difficult cases on the current meaning of statutes. Recognising the problem Lord Thring, the great Victorian draftsman of the second half of the last century, exhorted draftsmen to draft so that 'An Act of Parliament should be deemed to be always speaking:' Practical Legislation (1902), page 83; see also Cross, Statutory Interpretation, 3rd edn (1995), page 51; Pearce and Geddes, Statutory Interpretation in Australia, 4th edn (1996), pages 90-93. In cases where the problem arises it is a matter of interpretation whether a court must search for the historical or original meaning of a statute or whether it is free to apply the current meaning of the statute to present day conditions. Statutes dealing with a particular grievance or problem may sometimes require to be historically interpreted. But the drafting technique of Lord Thring and his successors have brought about the situation that statutes will generally be found to be of the 'always speaking' variety: see *Royal College of Nursing of the United Kingdom v Department of Health and Social Security* [1981] AC 800 for an example of an 'always speaking' construction in the House of Lords.

The proposition that the Victorian legislator when enacting sections 18, 20 and 47 of the Act of 1861, would not have had in mind psychiatric illness is no doubt correct. Psychiatry was in its infancy in 1861. But the subjective intention of the draftsman is immaterial. The only relevant inquiry is as to the sense of the words in the context in which they are used. Moreover the Act of 1861 is a statute of the 'always speaking' type: the statute must be interpreted in the light of the best current scientific appreciation of the link between the body and psychiatric injury.

For these reasons I would, therefore, reject the challenge to the correctness of *Reg. v Chan-Fook* [1994] 1 WLR 689. In my view the ruling in that case was based on principled and cogent reasoning and it marked a sound and essential clarification of the law. I would hold that 'bodily harm' in sections 18, 20 and 47 must be interpreted so as to include recognisable psychiatric illness.

 Alert

5.3.2 Mens Rea

It was confirmed by the House of Lords in *R v Savage, R v Parmenter* [1992] 1 AC 699 that the only mens rea required for this offence is that required for the assault or the battery. It is not necessary to prove that the defendant intended or was reckless to the actual bodily harm.

5.4 Maliciously Wounding or Inflicting Grievous Bodily Harm: s 20

5.4.1 Wounding

C (A Minor) v Eisenhower [1984] QB 331

Panel: Robert Goff LJ and Mann J

Statute: Offences Against the Person Act 1861 s 20

Facts: The defendant, a 15-year old boy and another boy had acquired an air gun. The defendant fired it at the victim, rupturing internal blood vessels in the victim's eye. The defendant was charged with unlawfully and maliciously wounding contrary to the Offences against the Person Act 1861 s 20. He appealed on the basis that the victim had not suffered a wound.

LORD JUSTICE ROBERT GOFF

In later cases the matter was refined in two ways. First, in *Reg. v M'Loughlin* (1838) 8 Car. & P. 635, it was held by Coleridge J., other judges being present, that it must be the whole skin that is broken. He, of course, was referring to the fact that the human skin has two layers, an outer layer called the epidermis or the cuticle, and an under layer which is sometimes called the dermis or the true skin. In that case there was evidence of an abrasion of the skin, with blood issuing from it. It was made plain to the jury by Coleridge J. that:

> "if it is necessary to constitute a wound, that the skin should be broken, it must be the whole skin, and it is not sufficient to shew a separation of the cuticle only."

It was therefore not enough that there had been an abrasion affecting only the cuticle. There had to be a break in the continuity of the whole skin.

The second way in which the point was refined is to be found in two cases, *Rex v Shadbolt* (1833) 5 Car. & P. 504 and *Reg. v Waltham* (1849) 3 Cox CC 442. These cases show that there can be a break in the continuity of the skin sufficient to constitute a wound if the skin which was broken is the skin of an internal cavity of the body, being a cavity from the outer surface of the body where the skin of the cavity is continuous with the outer skin of the body. So, for example, in *Shadbolt* it was held that it was sufficient if there had been a break in the skin of the internal surface of the lips inside the mouth. In *Waltham*, which is possibly the most extreme of the cases cited to us, it was held by Cresswell J. that there would be a wounding if there had been a rupture of the lining membrane of the urethra causing a small flow of blood into the urine, because that membrane was of precisely the same character as that which lined the cheek and the internal skin of the lip.

Lord Justice Robert Goff then considered a case raised by counsel for the Crown in which the word 'wound' had been used in another context. He concluded that this case was not relevant.

In my judgment, having regard to the cases there is a continuous stream of authority - to which I myself can find no exception - which establishes that a wound is, as I have stated, a break in the continuity of the whole skin. I can see nothing in the authorities which persuades me to think otherwise. This has become such a well-established meaning of the word "wound" that in my judgment it would be very wrong for this court to depart from it.

 Alert

We now turn to the case stated for our consideration by the justices. The justices concluded that there was a wound because, although they described the injury as a bruise just below the left eyebrow with fluid filling the front part of his left eye for a time afterwards which abnormally contained red blood cells, they thought that the abnormal presence of red blood cells in the fluid in Martin Cook's left eye indicated at least the rupturing of a blood vessel or vessels internally; and this they thought was sufficient to constitute a wound for the purposes of section 20 of the Offences against the Person Act 1861.

In my judgment, that conclusion was not in accordance with the law. It is not enough that there has been a rupturing of a blood vessel or vessels internally for there to be a wound under the statute because it is impossible for a court to conclude from that evidence alone that there has been a break in the continuity of the whole skin. There may have simply been internal bleeding of some kind or another, the cause of which is not established. In these circumstances, the evidence is not enough, in my judgment, to establish a wound within the statute. In my judgment, the justices erred in their conclusion on the evidence before them. The question posed for the opinion of this court is whether, in the light of the facts found by the justices and the law applied to those facts, they were right to find the defendant guilty of the offence with which he had been charged, viz., the unlawful and malicious wounding of Martin Cook contrary to section 20 of the Offences against the Person Act 1861. I would answer that question in the negative.

5.4.2 Grievous Bodily Harm

The word 'grievous' was defined by the House of Lords in *DPP v Smith* [1961] AC 290 as 'really serious'. It has subsequently been held that the word 'really' adds little and can be omitted. The Court of Appeal in the case below gave several useful directions on what could constitute serious harm.

R v Bollom [2003] EWCA Crim 2846, [2004] 2 Cr App R 6

Panel: Lord Woolf CJ, Gibbs and Fulford JJ

Facts: Bollom was convicted of maliciously causing grievous bodily harm to his girlfriend's 17 month old daughter. He appealed on the grounds, *inter alia*, that the injuries did not constitute grievously bodily harm and that the judge should not have directed the jury that the child's age was a relevant factor in determining whether the injuries were serious.

MR JUSTICE FULFORD

52. Mr Davies, on behalf of the appellant, at para. 9 of his Advice and orally before us, submits that the injuries should be assessed without reference to the particular victim. He suggests the age, health or any other particular factors relating to the person harmed should be ignored when deciding whether the injuries amounted to really serious harm. We are unable to accept that proposition. To use this case as an example, these injuries on a 6 foot adult in the fullness of health would be less serious than on, for instance, an elderly or unwell person, on someone who was physically or psychiatrically vulnerable or, as here, on a very young child. In deciding whether injuries are grievous, an assessment has to be made of, amongst other things, the effect of the harm on the particular individual. We have no doubt that in determining the gravity of these injuries, it was necessary to consider them in their real context.

53. The next issue is whether, approached in that way, these injuries could properly be considered by a jury as grievous. The House of Lords has emphasised that "grievous bodily harm" should be given its ordinary and natural meaning, that of really serious bodily harm, and other definitions should be resisted: *Director of Public Prosecutions v Smith* [1961] AC 290. The ambit of grievous bodily harm is

therefore potentially wide, as is demonstrated by the inclusion, for instance, of psychiatric injury: *R v Ireland; R v Burstow* [1998] 1 Cr App R 177, [1998] AC 147. The prosecution do not have to prove that the harm was life-threatening, dangerous or permanent: *R v Ashman* (1858) 1 F&F 88. Moreover, there is no requirement in law that the victim should require treatment or that the harm should extend beyond soft tissue damage.

In this context, the appellant seeks to rely before this court on the statement of Dr Baden Powell, who did not give evidence at trial and who expresses the view that the injuries were all superficial in that they would heal spontaneously and would be most unlikely to leave any permanent damage. But as we have just observed, there is no pre-condition to a finding that the injuries amounted to grievous bodily harm that the victim should require treatment or that the harm would have lasting consequences. In those circumstances the statement of Dr Baden Powell adds nothing as regards this issue to the evidence before the court at trial. In our judgment, the judge was right to leave this decision to the jury so they could apply the standards of society as a whole in assessing the harm done to this young child. These injuries were sufficiently numerous and extensive to justify the jury's conclusion that they constituted grievous bodily harm. Apart from one matter addressed hereafter, the direction the judge gave to the jury in this regard, was balanced and appropriate:

"Now there is no definitive list of what amounts to serious harm; you have to look at the evidence and you have to decide. It is a question of fact for you to decide. The prosecution rely of course on what the paediatrician has said about Alex's injuries, the photographs and what you have heard and seen of the injuries. You may consider the number of bruises, their location, their size, the cuts, and of course you may consider Alex's age."

(In this regard the judge made a mistake of two months in the child's age, saying that she was fifteen months. We do not consider this to be significant.)

"Look at all the evidence. If you look at the individual cuts and bruises, you may think they would not merit, individually, the description of 'really serious harm'. But you can look at the totality of the injuries and then consider whether together they amount to really serious harm. It is a question of fact for you and, as you know, it is a matter of dispute. Bear this in mind. Any deliberate attack on a baby is a serious matter. What you have to decide is whether in this particular case the end result was serious injury to Alex. If you are not sure the injuries amounted to really serious harm to Alex you will return a verdict of not guilty to counts 1 and 2 and then you can go on directly to consider count 5."

54. However, what does give us cause for concern is that the judge failed to go on to direct the jury they had to be sure these injuries were caused as part of one continuous course of conduct constituting a single assault rather than during distinct and separate assaults. Given this case depended on circumstantial evidence and there was no direct evidence as to how the injuries were inflicted, this was a real rather than a fanciful issue. These injuries could have occurred at

any time over a number of hours, when, as we have observed, this child was alone in the house with a number of adults, who were mostly in various stages of intoxication. In addition, before the jury both defendants blamed Stuart McGregor. The prosecution for their part blamed the appellant. Accordingly, at trial there were cross-allegations with two people being accused, yet the judge never directed the jury that they must be sure that Stuart McGregor was not responsible for these injuries, or some of them, before they could convict the appellant. The closest the judge came to a direction of this kind was when she posed rhetorically to the jury the question: "Who inflicted these injuries?"

55. In our judgment therefore, it was incumbent on the judge to direct the jury that they had to be sure not only that these injuries, viewed collectively, constituted grievous bodily harm, but also that they had been inflicted as part of one assault rather than on different occasions as a part of separate assaults. The judge failed to give this latter direction, and as a result, particularly given the lack of direct evidence against the appellant, in our judgment the conviction under count 1 is unsafe.

 Alert

5.4.3 Mens Rea

The mens rea word in the statute is 'maliciously'. Its meaning was discussed in the case below, which has subsequently been approved by the House of Lords in *R v Savage; R v Parmenter* [1992] 1 AC 699

R v Mowatt [1968] 1 QB 421

Panel: Diplock LJ, Brabin and Waller JJ

Statute: Offences Against the Person Act 1861 s 20

Facts: Mowatt was with a friend who had taken £5 from the victim's pocket and run off. The victim chased the thief without success and then came back and grabbed Mowatt, demanding to know where his friend had gone. Mowatt hit the victim repeatedly, rendering him nearly unconscious. Mowatt claimed to be acting in self defence. The trial judge explained the meaning of unlawfully in the section, but gave no definition of maliciously and as a result Mowatt appealed.

LORD JUSTICE DIPLOCK

...[N]owhere in the summing-up did the judge mention the word "maliciously" or give the jury any directions as to its meaning. It was for this reason that the single judge gave leave to appeal against the defendant's conviction for unlawful wounding so that this court might be given an opportunity to consider to what extent it is necessary in a case of this kind to give to the jury express instructions upon the meaning of the word "maliciously" such as those as are discussed in *Reg. v Cunningham*.

"Unlawfully and maliciously" was a fashionable phrase of parliamentary draftsmen in 1861. It runs as a theme with minor variations throughout the Malicious Damage Act, 1861, and the Offences against the Person Act, passed in that year.

Reg. v Cunningham was a case under section 23 of the Offences against the Person Act, 1861, which provides:

> "Whosoever shall unlawfully and maliciously administer to or cause to be administered to or taken by any other person any poison or other destructive or noxious thing, so as thereby to endanger the life of such person, or so as thereby to inflict upon such person any grievous bodily harm, shall be guilty of felony."

The facts were very special. The appellant went to the cellar of a house and wrenched the gas meter from a gas pipe and stole it together with its contents, and gas seeped through the wall. The cellar was under a divided house, one part of which an elderly couple occupied, and one of them inhaled some gas and her life was endangered. He was indicted under section 23 of the Act of 1861. No doubt upon these facts the jury should be instructed that they must be satisfied before convicting the accused that he was aware that physical harm to some human being was a possible consequence of his unlawful act in wrenching off the gas meter. In the words of the court, "maliciously in a statutory crime postulates foresight of consequence," and upon this proposition we do not wish to cast any doubt. But the court in that case also expressed approval obiter of a more general statement by Professor Kenny, [Kenny's Outlines of Criminal Law, 18th edn (1962), page 202] which runs as follows:

> "in any statutory definition of a crime, 'malice' must be taken not in the old vague sense of wickedness in general, but as requiring either (1) an actual intention to do the particular kind of harm that in fact was done, or (2) recklessness as to whether such harm should occur or not (ie, the accused has foreseen that the particular kind of harm might be done, and yet has gone on to take the risk of it). It is neither limited to, nor does it indeed require, any ill will towards the person injured."

This generalisation is not, in our view, appropriate to the specific alternative statutory offences described in sections 18 and 20 of the Offences against the Person Act, 1861, and section 5 of the Prevention of Offences Act, 1851, and if used in that form in the summing-up is liable to bemuse the jury. In section 18 the word "maliciously" adds nothing. The intent expressly required by that section is more specific than such element of foresight of consequences as is implicit in the word "maliciously" and in directing a jury about an offence under this section the word "maliciously" is best ignored.

In the offence under section 20, and in the alternative verdict which may be given on a charge under section 18, for neither of which is any specific intent required, the word "maliciously" does import upon the part of the person who unlawfully inflicts the wound or other grievous bodily harm an awareness that his act may have the consequence of causing some physical harm to some other person. That is what is meant by "the particular kind of harm" in the citation from Professor Kenny. It is quite unnecessary that the accused should have foreseen that his unlawful act might cause physical harm of the gravity described in the section, i.e., a wound or serious physical injury. It is

 Alert

enough that he should have foreseen that some physical harm to some person, albeit of a minor character, might result.

Lord Justice Diplock decided that, had they been given a direction as to maliciously, no jury would have decided that the appellant did not see the risk of causing some harm to the victim. He therefore dismissed the appeal.

5.5 Administering Poison with Intent to Injure, Aggrieve or Annoy: s 24

5.5.1 Administer

R v Gillard (1988) 87 Cr App R 189

Panel: O'Connor LJ, McNeilland and Ognall JJ

Statute: Offences Against the Person Act 1861 s 24

Facts: Gillard was stopped at Newhaven and was found in possession of a gas pistol, gas cartridge and a gas spray. It was claimed that he intended these to be used in an attack on the doorman of a public house. The attack took place later that night when the victim was sprayed by three aerosols. Gillard was convicted of an offence under the Offences Against the Person Act 1861 s 24 and appealed.

MR JUSTICE McNEIL

The basis on which this appeal is brought, by leave of the single judge, is this: that upon the true construction of section 24 of the 1861 Act the word "administer" is not apt in law to encompass the spraying of CS gas from a canister into the face of a victim: that such conduct ought properly and only to be charged as assault, or, where the facts justify it, assault occasioning actual bodily harm.

Mr Justice McNeil then considered each party's arguments.

This Court does not accept that the words or purport of sections other than section 24 is relevant. A well established canon of construction is that if the words of a section are capable on their own of bearing a clear and ascertainable meaning there is no scope for reference over to other sections of the same statute: such recourse may only be had in the event of ambiguity or uncertainty or if that meaning is apparently inconsistent with the general intention of the statute. This is not the case here.

Where, in the view of this Court, the learned recorder was in error was in holding that "administering" and "taking" were to be treated effectively as synonymous or as conjunctive words in the section: on the contrary, the repeated use of the word "or" makes it clear that they are disjunctive. The word "takes" postulates some "ingestion" by the victim: "administer" must have some other meaning and there is no difficulty in including in that meaning such conduct as spraying the victim with noxious fluid or vapour, whether from a device such as a gas canister or, for example, hosing down with effluent. There is no necessity when the word "administer" is used to postulate any form of entry into the victim's body, whether through any orifice or by absorption: a court dealing with such a case should not have to determine questions of pathology such as, for example, the manner in which skin irritation results from exposure to CS gas or the manner in which the eye waters when exposed to irritant. The word "ingest" should be reserved to its natural meaning of intake into the digestive system and not permitted to obscure the statutory words.

In the view of this Court, the proper construction of "administer" in section 24 includes conduct which not being the application of direct force to the victim nevertheless brings the noxious thing into contact with his body.

 Alert

5.5.2 Poison, Destructive or Noxious Thing

R v Marcus [1981] 1 WLR 774

Panel: Shaw LJ, Tudor Evans and Sheldon JJ

Statute: Offences Against the Person Act 1861 s 24

Facts: Marcus put 8 sleeping pills in a bottle of milk on her neighbour's doorstep. She was convicted of attempting to administer a position, destructive and noxious thing contrary to Offences Against the Person Act 1861 s 24. She appealed on the ground that the jury had been misdirected as to the meaning of noxious. It was claimed on her behalf that a thing which is intrinsically harmless, such as a sleeping pill, could not become noxious or harmful by being given in excessive quantity. Secondly, it was argued that the word "noxious" means harmful and that the meaning is confined to injury to the body and cannot include harm involving an impairment of faculties, such as might occur whilst driving while sedated.

MR JUSTICE TUDOR EVANS

We are of the opinion that for the purposes of section 24 the concept of the "noxious thing" involves not only the quality or nature of the substance but also the quantity administered or sought to be administered. If the contention of the defendant is correct, then, on the assumption that the drugs were intrinsically harmless, it would follow that if the defendant had attempted to administer a dose of 50 tablets by way of the milk, an amount which, if taken, would have been potentially lethal, she would have committed no offence. We do not consider that such a result can follow from the language of section 24. The offence created by the section involves an intention to injure, aggrieve or annoy.

 Alert

We consider that the words "noxious thing" mean that the jury has to consider the very thing which on the facts is administered or sought to be administered both as to quality and as to quantity. The jury has to consider the evidence of what was administered or attempted to be administered both in quality and in quantity and to decide as a question of fact and degree in all the circumstances whether that thing was noxious. A substance which may have been harmless in small quantities may yet be noxious in the quantity administered. Many illustrations were put in the course of the argument: for example, to lace a glass of milk with a quantity of alcohol might not amount to administering a noxious thing to an adult but it might do so if given to a child.

...

We shall now consider the second submission for the appellant, that the word "noxious" means harmful in the sense of injury to bodily health. Counsel took us through the relevant sections of the Act. In a number of sections (including section 24) the words "poison or other destructive or noxious thing" appear. It was submitted that the meaning of the word "noxious" must take colour from the preceding words. We do not accept that construction. It seems to us, looking at the relevant sections, that the statute is dealing with offences in a declining order of gravity and that by "noxious" is meant something different in quality from and of less importance than poison or other destructive things.

...

In the course of his summing up, the judge quoted the definition of "noxious" from the Shorter Oxford English Dictionary, where it is described as meaning "injurious, hurtful, harmful, unwholesome." The meaning is clearly very wide. It seems to us that even taking its weakest meaning, if for example, a person were to put an obnoxious (that is objectionable) or unwholesome thing into an article of food or drink with the intent to annoy any person who might consume it, an offence would be committed. A number of illustrations were put in argument, including the snail said to have been in the ginger beer bottle (to adapt the facts in *Donoghue v Stevenson* [1932] AC 562). If that had been done with any of the intents in the section, it seems to us that an offence would have been committed.

5.5.3 Mens Rea

R v Hill (1985) 81 Cr App R 206

Panel: Robert Goff LJ, Mars-Jones and Drake JJ

Statute: Offences Against the Person Act 1861 s 24

Facts; Hill gave two young boys prescription only slimming pills which caused them to suffer diarrhoea and vomiting. One of the boys spent the night at his flat. Hill admitted he had homosexual pedophilic tendencies, but nothing untoward happened. The trial judge directed the jury that an intention to keep the boys awake would count as an intention to injure for the purposes of s 24, and Hill was convicted.

LORD JUSTICE ROBERT GOFF

We have no doubt that, in considering whether in any particular case the accused acted "with intent to injure", it is necessary to have regard not merely to his intent with regard to the effect which the noxious thing will have upon the person to whom it is administered, but to his whole object in acting as he has done. The accused may, in one case, administer the noxious thing with the intent that it would itself injure the person in question; but in another case he may have an ulterior motive, as for example when he administers a sleeping pill to a woman with an intent to rape her when she is comatose. In either case he will, in our judgment, have an intent to injure the person in question, within the words in the section. By way of contrast, if a husband puts a sleeping draught in his wife's nightcap, without her knowledge, because he is worried that she has been sleeping badly and wishes to give her a decent night's sleep, he will commit no offence. So, in each case it is necessary to ask the question: Did the accused have the intention, in administering the noxious thing, to injure the person in question? And in each case it is necessary to look, not just at his intention as regards the immediate effect of the noxious thing upon that person, but at the whole object of the accused. If his intention, so understood, is that the noxious thing should itself injure the person in question, then that is enough; but it will also be enough if he has an ulterior motive that the person should, as a result of taking the noxious thing, suffer injury. Within this latter category there will, in our judgment, fall those cases where the accused intends, in administering the noxious thing, thereby to achieve or facilitate an act of unlawful sexual interference with the person in question—unlawful, either because it is not consented to (as, for example, in the case of rape), or because the law forbids it (as, for example, in the case of sexual intercourse with girls under the age of 16, or of unlawful homosexual activity). In such cases the accused does, we consider, have an intent to injure the person in question within the meaning of those words in the section.

 Alert

5.6 Administering Poison so as to Endanger Life: s 23

5.6.1 Poison, Destructive or Noxious Thing

R v Cato, R v Morris, R v Dudley [1976] 1 WLR 110

Panel: Lord Widgery CJ, O'Connor and Jupp JJ

Statute: Offences Against the Person Act 1861 s 23

Facts: The appellants had been injecting each other and the victim with heroin. The victim subsequently died as a result of the heroin. The appellants were charged with manslaughter and with administering a noxious thing contrary to Offences Against the Person Act 1861 s 23. They appealed on the ground, *inter alia*, that the judge had misdirected the jury that heroin was a 'noxious' thing.

LORD WIDGERY CJ

What is a noxious thing, and in particular is heroin a noxious thing? The authorities show that an article is not to be described as noxious for present purposes merely because it has a potentiality for harm if taken in an overdose. There are many articles of value in common use which may be harmful in overdose, and it is clear on the authorities when looking at them that one cannot describe an article as noxious merely because it has that aptitude. On the other hand, if an article is liable to injure in common use, not when an overdose in the sense of an accidental excess is used but is liable to cause injury in common use, should it then not be regarded as a noxious thing for present purposes?

When one has regard to the potentiality of heroin in the circumstances which we read and hear about in our courts today we have no hesitation in saying that heroin is a noxious thing and we do not think that arguments are open to an accused person in a case such as the present, whereby he may say "Well, the deceased was experienced in taking heroin; his tolerance was high," and generally to indicate that the heroin was unlikely to do any particular harm in a particular circumstance. We think there can be no doubt, and it should be said clearly, that heroin is a noxious thing for the purposes of section 23 of the Act of 1861.

It is worth noting that Lord Widgery CJ said a substance could not be described a noxious, merely because it would do harm if taken in large quantities. He did not say that if a substance was administered in such large quantities that it would do harm, as were the sleeping pills in *R v Marcus*, it would not be noxious.

Further Reading

Bronitt S 'Spreading Disease and the Criminal Law' [1994] *Crim LR* 21

Gardner S 'Rationality ad the Rule of Law in Offences Against the Person' [1994] *CLJ* 502

Horder J 'Reconsidering Psychic Assault' [1998] *Crim LR* 392

Hirst M 'Assault, Battery and Indirect Violence' [1999] *Crim LR* 557

6

Theft

Topic List

8.1 Appropriation

There is a partial definition of appropriation under Theft Act 1968 s 3(1) which states that appropriation is "any assumption by a person of the rights of an owner". In *R v Morris* [1984] AC 320 the House of Lords held that an assumption of any of the rights of the owners is sufficient for appropriation. The prosecution does not have to prove that the defendant assumed all of the rights of the owner; an assumption of any single right will do.

R v Morris [1984] AC 320

Panel: Lord Fraser of Tullybelton, Lord Edmund-Davies, Lord Roskill, Lord Brandon of Oakbrook and Lord Brightman

Statute: Theft Act 1968 s 3(1)

Facts: The defendant removed price labels from goods in a shop and replaced them with labels showing cheaper prices. He then presented the goods at the checkout for payment and paid the lower prices. He was charged with theft under the Theft Act 1968 s 1(1) and convicted. His appeal to the Court of Appeal was dismissed but the defendant appealed to the House of Lords.

LORD ROSKILL

...My Lords, in his submissions for the appellants .. Mr Denison urged that on these simple facts neither appellant was guilty of theft ... because there was no appropriation by him before payment at the checkpoint sufficient to support a charge of theft, however dishonest his actions may have been in previously switching the labels. ...

My Lords, if these submissions be well founded it is clear that, however dishonest their actions, each respondent was wrongly convicted of theft. The question is whether they are well founded. The answer must depend upon the true construction of the relevant sections of the Act of 1968...

It is to be observed that the definition of "appropriation" in section 3(1) is not exhaustive. But section 1(1) and section 3(1) show clearly that there can be no conviction for theft contrary to section 1(1) even if all the other ingredients of the offence are proved unless "appropriation" is also proved.

 Alert

The starting point of any consideration ... must, I think, be the decision of this House in *Reg. v Lawrence (Alan)* [1972] AC 626. In the leading speech, Viscount Dilhorne expressly accepted the view of the Court of Appeal (Criminal Division) in that case that the offence of theft involved four elements, (1) a dishonest (2) appropriation (3) of property belonging to another, (4) with the intention of permanently depriving the owner of it. Viscount Dilhorne also rejected the argument that even if these four elements were all present there could not be theft within the section if the owner of the property in question had consented to the acts which were done by the defendant. That there was in that case a dishonest appropriation was beyond question and the House did not have to consider the precise meaning of that word in section 3(1). Mr Denison submitted that the phrase in section 3(1) "any assumption by a person of *the rights*"

(my emphasis) "of an owner amounts to an appropriation" must mean any assumption of "*all* the rights of an owner." Since neither respondent had at the time of the removal of the goods from the shelves and of the label switching assumed *all* the rights of the owner, there was no appropriation and therefore no theft. Mr Jeffreys for the prosecution, on the other hand, contended that *the* rights in this context only meant *any* of the rights. An owner of goods has many rights - they have been described as "a bundle or package of rights." Mr Jeffreys contended that on a fair reading of the subsection it cannot have been the intention that every one of an owner's rights had to be assumed by the alleged thief before an appropriation was proved and that essential ingredient of the offence of theft established.

My Lords, if one reads the words "the rights" at the opening of section 3(1) literally and in isolation from the rest of the section, Mr Denison's submission undoubtedly has force. But the later words "any later assumption of a right" in subsection (1) and the words in subsection (2) "no later assumption by him of rights" seem to me to militate strongly against the correctness of the submission. Moreover the provisions of section 2(1)(a) also seem to point in the same direction. It follows therefore that it is enough for the prosecution if they have proved in these cases the assumption by the respondents of any of the rights of the owner of the goods in question, that is to say, the supermarket concerned, it being common ground in these cases that the other three of the four elements mentioned in Viscount Dilhorne's speech in *Reg. v Lawrence (Alan)* had been fully established.

 Alert

My Lords, Mr Jeffreys sought to argue that any removal from the shelves of the supermarket, even if unaccompanied by label switching, was without more an appropriation. In one passage in his judgment in *Morris*'s case, the learned Lord Chief Justice appears to have accepted the submission, for he said [1983] QB 587, 596:

> "it seems to us that in taking the article from the shelf the customer is indeed assuming one of the rights of the owner - the right to move the article from its position on the shelf to carry it to the check-out."

The House of Lords had disagreed in the cases of *R v Lawrence* and *R v Morris* as to whether an act which was consented to by the owner could amount to an appropriation. The matter was resolved in the case of *R v Gomez* [1993] AC 442.

DPP v Gomez [1993] AC 442

Panel: Lord Keith of Kinkel, Lord Jauncey of Tullichettle, Lord Lowry, Lord Browne-Wilkinson and Lord Slynn of Hadley

Statute: Theft Act 1968 s 3(1)

Facts: The defendant was an assistant manager of an electrical shop. He accepted two stolen cheques from his co-accused in exchange for goods, knowing the cheques to be stolen. He deceived the manager of the store into authorising the transaction. As a result, he was convicted of theft under the Theft Act 1968 s 1(1). The Court of Appeal certified a point of law of general public importance for consideration by the House of Lords:

"When theft is alleged and that which is alleged to be stolen passes to the defendant with the consent of the owner, but that has been obtained by a false representation, has (a) an appropriation within the meaning of section 1(1) of the Theft Act 1968 taken place, or (b) must such a passing of property necessarily involve an element of adverse [interference] with or usurpation of some right of the owner?"

LORD KEITH OF KINKEL

My Lords, this appeal raises the question whether two decisions of your Lordships' House upon the proper construction of certain provisions of the Theft Act 1968 are capable of being reconciled with each other, and, if so, in what manner. The two decisions are *Reg. v Lawrence (Alan)* [1972] AC 626 and *Reg. v Morris (David)* [1984] AC 320. The question has given rise to much debate in subsequent cases and in academic writings. ...

In my opinion Lord Roskill [in *R v Morris*] was undoubtedly right when he said ... that the assumption by the defendant of any of the rights of an owner could amount to an appropriation within the meaning of section 3(1), and that the removal of an article from the shelf and the changing of the price label on it constituted the assumption of one of the rights of the owner and hence an appropriation within the meaning of the subsection. But there are observations in the [opinion] which, with the greatest possible respect to my noble and learned friend Lord Roskill, I must regard as unnecessary for the decision of the case and as being incorrect. In the first place, it seems to me that the switching of price labels on the article is in itself an assumption of one of the rights of the owner, whether or not it is accompanied by some other act such as removing the article from the shelf and placing it in a basket or trolley. No one but the owner has the right to remove a price label from an article or to place a price label upon it. If anyone else does so, he does an act, as Lord Roskill puts it, by way of adverse interference with or usurpation of that right. This is no less so in the case of the practical joker figured by Lord Roskill than in the case of one who makes the switch with dishonest intent. The practical joker, of course, is not guilty of theft because he has not acted dishonestly and does not intend to deprive the owner permanently of the article. So the label switching in itself constitutes an appropriation and so to have held would have been sufficient for the dismissal of both appeals. On the facts of the two cases it was unnecessary to decide whether, as argued by Mr Jeffreys, the mere taking of the article from the shelf and putting it in a trolley or other receptacle amounted to the assumption of one of the rights of the owner, and hence an appropriation. There was much to be said in favour of the view that it did, in respect that doing so gave the shopper control of the article and the capacity to exclude any other shopper from taking it. However, Lord Roskill expressed the opinion, at page 332, that it did not, on the ground that the concept of appropriation in the context of section 3(1) "involves not an act expressly or impliedly authorised by the owner but an act by way of adverse interference with or usurpation of those rights."

While it is correct to say that appropriation for purposes of section 3(1) includes the latter sort of act, it does not necessarily follow that no other act can amount to an appropriation and in particular that no act expressly or impliedly authorised by the owner can in any circumstances do so. Indeed, *Reg. v Lawrence* [1972] AC 626 is a clear decision to the contrary since it laid down unequivocally that an act may be an appropriation notwithstanding that it is done with the consent of the owner. It does not appear to me that any sensible distinction can be made in this context between consent and authorisation. ...

The actual decision in Morris was correct, but it was erroneous, in addition to being unnecessary for the decision, to indicate that an act expressly or impliedly authorised by the owner could never amount to an appropriation. ...

In my opinion it serves no useful purpose at the present time to seek to construe the relevant provisions of the Theft Act by reference to the report which preceded it, namely the Eighth Report of the Criminal Law Revision Committee on Theft and Related Offences (1966) (Cmnd. 2977) . The decision in *Lawrence* was a clear decision of this House upon the construction of the word "appropriate" in section 1(1) of the Act, which had stood for 12 years when doubt was thrown upon it by obiter dicta in *Morris*. Lawrence must be regarded as authoritative and correct, and there is no question of it now being right to depart from it. ...

My Lords, for the reasons which I have given I would answer branch (a) of the certified question in the affirmative and branch (b) in the negative, and allow the appeal. ...

LORD BROWNE-WILKINSON

In *Reg. v Lawrence* [1972] AC 626 Megaw LJ in the Court of Appeal [1971] 1 QB 373, 376 analysed the constituent elements of the offence created by section 1(1) of the Theft Act 1968 as being "(i) a dishonest (ii) appropriation (iii) of property belonging to another (iv) with the intention of permanently depriving the owner of it." This analysis was adopted and approved by this House and I do not intend to cast any doubt on it. But it should not be overlooked that elements (i) and (ii) (unlike elements (iii) and (iv)) are interlinked: element (i) (dishonest) is an adjectival description of element (ii) (appropriation). Parliament has used a composite phrase "dishonest appropriation." Thus it is not every appropriation which falls within the section but only an act which answers the composite description.

The fact that Parliament used that composite phrase - "dishonest appropriation" - in my judgment casts light on what is meant by the word "appropriation." The views expressed (obiter) by this House in *Reg. v Morris* [1984] AC 320 that "appropriation" involves an act by way of adverse interference with or usurpation of the rights of the owner treats the word appropriation as being tantamount to "misappropriation." The concept of adverse interference with or usurpation of rights introduces into the word appropriation the mental state of both the owner and the accused. So far as concerns the mental state of the owner (did he consent?), the Act of 1968 expressly refers to such consent when it is a material factor: see sections 2(1)(b), 11(1), 12(1) and 13. So far as concerns the mental state of the accused, the composite phrase in section 1(1) itself indicates that the requirement is dishonesty.

For myself, therefore, I regard the word "appropriation" in isolation as being an objective description of the act done irrespective of the mental state of either the owner or the accused. It is impossible to reconcile the decision in *Lawrence* (that the question of consent is irrelevant in considering whether there has been an appropriation) with the views expressed in *Morris*, which latter views in my judgment were incorrect.

Thus, the House of Lords confirmed the position of the law as stated in *Lawrence v MPC*, that consent is irrelevant to appropriation. *R v Morris* is no longer good law in this respect. Although it clarified the law in some respects, the decision in *DPP v Gomez* raised questions over whether a defendant could be guilty of theft of a valid gift. After a number of cases on this issue, the House of Lords determined that a gift could be stolen in *R v Hinks* [2001] 2 AC 241.

R v Hinks [2001] 2 AC 241

Panel: Lord Slynn of Hadley, Lord Jauncey of Tullichettle, Lord Steyn, Lord Hutton and Lord Hobhouse of Woodborough

Statute: Theft Act 1968 s 3(1)

Facts: The defendant made friends with a 53 year old man of limited intelligence. Every day over a period of about seven months, the defendant took the man to the building society where he withdrew £300 and this was deposited in the defendant's bank account. The total amount of money given to the defendant was £60,000. The man also gave the defendant his television set. The defendant was charged with theft under the Theft Act 1968 s 1(1) on the basis that she had "influenced, coerced and encouraged" the man to make these gifts to her. The defendant was convicted and appealed. The Court of Appeal dismissed her appeal against conviction by certified a point of law of general public importance for consideration by the House of Lords.

LORD STEYN

...The certified question before the House is as follows: "Whether the acquisition of an indefeasible title to property is capable of amounting to an appropriation of property belonging to another for the purposes of section 1(1) of the Theft Act 1968." In other words, the question is whether a person can "appropriate" property belonging to another where the other person makes him an indefeasible gift of property, retaining no proprietary interest or any right to resume or recover any proprietary interest in the property....

[I]t is immaterial whether the act was done with the owner's consent or authority. It is true of course that the certified question in *Gomez* referred to the situation where consent had been obtained by fraud. But the majority judgments do not differentiate between cases of consent induced by fraud and consent given in any other circumstances. The ratio involves a proposition of general application. Gomez therefore gives effect to section 3(1) of the Act by treating "appropriation" as a neutral word comprehending "any assumption by a person of the rights of an owner". If the law is as held in *Gomez*, it destroys the argument advanced on the present appeal, namely that an indefeasible gift of property cannot amount to an appropriation.

Counsel for the appellant submitted in the first place that the law as expounded in *Gomez* and *Lawrence* must be qualified to say that there can be no appropriation unless the other party (the owner) retains some proprietary interest, or the right to resume or recover some proprietary interest, in the property. Alternatively, counsel argued that "appropriates" should be interpreted as if the word "unlawfully" preceded it. Counsel said that the effect of the decisions in *Lawrence* and *Gomez* is to reduce the actus reus of theft to "vanishing point" (see *Smith & Hogan, Criminal Law,* 9th edn (1999), page 505). He argued that the result is to bring the criminal law "into conflict" with the civil law. Moreover, he argued that the decisions in *Lawrence* and *Gomez* may produce absurd and grotesque results. He argued that the mental requirements of dishonesty and intention of permanently depriving the owner of property are insufficient to filter out some cases of conduct which should not sensibly be regarded as theft....

[I]n such cases a prosecution is hardly likely and if mounted, is likely to founder on the basis that the jury will not be persuaded that there was dishonesty in the required sense. And one must retain a sense of perspective. At the extremity of the application of legal rules there are sometimes results which may seem strange. A matter of judgment is then involved. The rule may have to be recast. Sir John Smith has eloquently argued that the rule in question ought to be recast. I am unpersuaded. If the law is restated by adopting a narrower definition of appropriation, the outcome is likely to place beyond the reach of the criminal law dishonest persons who should be found guilty of theft. The suggested revisions would unwarrantably restrict the scope of the law of theft and complicate the fair and effective prosecution of theft. In my view the law as settled in *Lawrence* and *Gomez* does not demand the suggested revision. Those decisions can be applied by judges and juries in a way which, absent human error, does not result in injustice.

Counsel for the appellant further pointed out that the law as stated in *Lawrence* [1972] AC 626 and *Gomez* [1993] AC 442 creates a tension between the civil and the criminal law. In other words, conduct which is not wrongful in a civil law sense may constitute the crime of theft. Undoubtedly, this is so. The question whether the civil claim to title by a convicted thief, who committed no civil wrong, may be defeated by the principle that nobody may benefit from his own civil *or* criminal wrong does not arise for decision. Nevertheless there is a more general point, namely that the interaction between criminal law and civil law can cause problems: compare J Beatson and A P Simester, "Stealing One's Own Property" (1999) 115 LQR 372. The purposes of the civil law and the criminal law are somewhat different. In theory the two systems should be in perfect harmony. In a practical world there will sometimes be some disharmony between the two systems. In any event, it would be wrong to assume on a priori grounds that the criminal law rather than the civil law is defective. Given the jury's conclusions, one is entitled to observe that the appellant's conduct should constitute theft, the only available charge. The tension between the civil and the criminal law is therefore not in my view a factor which justifies a departure from the law as stated in Lawrence and Gomez. Moreover, these decisions of the House have a marked beneficial consequence. While in some contexts of the law of theft a judge cannot avoid explaining civil law concepts to a jury (e g in respect of section 2(1)(a)), the decisions of the House of Lords eliminate the need for such explanations in respect of appropriation. That is a great advantage in an overly complex corner of the law.

My Lords, if it had been demonstrated that in practice *Lawrence* and *Gomez* were calculated to produce injustice that would have been a compelling reason to revisit the merits of the holdings in those decisions. That is however, not the case. In practice the mental requirements of theft are an adequate protection against injustice. In these circumstances I would not be willing to depart from the clear decisions of the House in *Lawrence* and *Gomez*. This brings me back to counsel's principal submission, namely that a person does not appropriate property unless the other (the owner) retains, beyond the instant of the alleged theft, some proprietary interest or the right to resume or recover some proprietary interest. This submission is directly contrary to the holdings in *Lawrence* and *Gomez*. It must be rejected. The alternative submission is that the word "appropriates" should be interpreted as if the word "unlawfully" preceded it so that only an act which is unlawful under the general law can be an appropriation. This submission is an invitation to interpolate a word in the carefully crafted language of the 1968 Act. It runs counter to the decisions in *Lawrence* and *Gomez* and must also be rejected. It follows that the certified question must be answered in the affirmative.

 Alert

Thus, according to *R v Hinks*, a valid gift may be appropriated and therefore may be the subject of theft.

8.2 Belonging to Another

The property must belong to another. Under the Theft Act 1968 s 5(1), property belongs to anyone having possession or control of it, or a proprietary right or interest in it.

R v Woodman [1974] QB 754

Panel: Lord Widgery CJ, Ashworth and Mocatta JJ

Statute: Theft Act 1968 s 5(1)

Facts: The defendant took some scrap metal from a disused factory belonging to English China Clays. When the business at the factory had ceased, English China Clays had sold all the scrap metal at the site to the Bird group of companies. However, unknown to English China Clays, some had not been removed by the Bird group, and this was the scrap metal taken by the defendant. The factory was surrounded by a barbed-wire fence, intended to exclude trespassers and there were also signs instructing trespassers to keep out. The defendant was charged on an indictment of theft of scrap metal belonging to English China Clays. The recorder took the view that English China Clays did not have possession or control of the metal, so it did not belong to them for the purposes of the Theft Act.

LORD WIDGERY CJ

[I]t is the Theft Act 1968 which governs the matter, and so one must turn to see what it says. Section 1(1) provides: "A person is guilty of theft if he dishonestly appropriates property belonging to another." I need not go further because the whole of the debate turns on the phrase "belonging to another." Section 5(1) of the Act expands the meaning of the phrase in these terms:

> "Property shall be regarded as belonging to any person having possession or control of it, or having in it any proprietary right or interest...."

The recorder took the view that the contract of sale between English China Clays and the Bird group had divested English China Clays of any proprietary right to any scrap on the site. It is unnecessary to express a firm view on that point, but the court are not disposed to disagree with that conclusion that the proprietary interest in the scrap had passed. The recorder also took the view on the relevant facts that it was not possible to say that English China Clays were in possession of the residue of the scrap. It is not quite clear why he took that view. It may have been because he took the view that difficulties arose by reason of the fact that English China Clays had no knowledge of the existence of this particular scrap at any particular time. But the recorder did take the view that so far as control was concerned there was a case to go to the jury on whether or not this scrap was in the control of English China Clays, because if it was, then it was to be regarded as their property for the purposes of a larceny charge even if they were not entitled to any proprietary interest.

The contention before us today is that the recorder was wrong in law in allowing this issue to go to the jury. Put another way, it is said that as a matter of law English China Clays could not on these facts have been said to be in control of the scrap.

We have formed the view without difficulty that the recorder was perfectly entitled to do what he did, that there was ample evidence that English China Clays were in control of the site and had taken considerable steps to exclude trespassers as demonstrating the fact that they were in control of the site, and we think that in ordinary and straightforward cases if it is once established that a particular person is in control of a site such as this, then prima facie he is in control of articles which are on that site.

 Alert

The point was well put in an article written by no lesser person than Mr Wendell Holmes in his book *The Common Law* (1881), at pages 222, 223-224, dealing with possession. Considering the very point we have to consider here, he said, and I take the extract from *Hibbert v McKiernan* [1948] 2 KB 142, 147:

"'There can be no animus domini unless the thing is known of; but an intent to exclude others from it may be contained in a larger intent to exclude others from the place where it is, without any knowledge of the object's existence.... In a criminal case, the property in iron taken from the bottom of a canal by a stranger was held well laid in the canal company, although it does not appear that the company knew of it, or had any lien upon it. The only intent concerning the thing discoverable in such instances is the general intent which the occupant of land has to exclude the public from the land, and thus, as a consequence, to exclude them from what is upon it.'"

So far as this case is concerned, arising as it does under the Theft Act 1968, we are content to say that there was evidence of English China Clays being in control of the site and prima facie in control of articles upon the site as well. The fact that it could not be shown that they were conscious of the existence of this or any particular scrap iron does not destroy the general principle that control of a site by excluding others from it is prima facie control of articles on the site as well.

There has been some mention in argument of what would happen if in a case like the present, a third party had come and placed some article within the barbed-wire fence and thus on the site. The article might be an article of some serious criminal consequence such as explosives or drugs. It may well be that in that type of case the fact that the article has been introduced at a late stage in circumstances in which the occupier of the site had no means of knowledge would produce a different result from that which arises under the general presumption to which we have referred, but in the present case there was, in our view, ample evidence to go to the jury on the question of whether English China Clays were in control of the scrap at the relevant time. Accordingly, the recorder's decision to allow the case to go to the jury cannot be faulted and the appeal must be dismissed.

Parker v British Airways Board [1982] QB 1004

Panel: Eveleigh and Donaldson L.JJ. and Sir David Cairns

Facts: Parker found a gold bracelet in a British Airways Board lounge. The owner could not be found. This was a civil case to decide whether Parker or the British Airways Board was entitled to keep the bracelet. It is relevant for the law of Theft as the case hinged on whether the British Airways Board had possession and control of the bracelet at the time Parker found it.

DONALDSON LJ

On November 15, 1978, the plaintiff, Alan George Parker, had a date with fate - and perhaps with legal immortality. He found himself in the international executive lounge at terminal one, Heathrow Airport. and that was not all that he found. He also found a gold bracelet lying on the floor.

We know very little about the plaintiff, and it would be nice to know more. He was lawfully in the lounge and, as events showed, he was an honest man. Clearly he had not forgotten the schoolboy maxim "Finders keepers." But, equally clearly, he was well aware of the adult qualification "unless the true owner claims the article."

It was then noted that the owner could not be traced, but that the British Airways Board had sold the bracelet and kept the money. Donaldson LJ then considered whether it was entitled to do this.

The defendants, for their part, cannot assert any title to the bracelet based upon the rights of an occupier over chattels attached to a building. The bracelet was lying loose on the floor. Their claim must, on my view of the law, be based upon a manifest intention to exercise control over the lounge and all things which might be in it. The evidence is that they claimed the right to decide who should and who should not be permitted to enter and use the lounge, but their control was in general exercised upon the basis of classes or categories of user and the availability of the lounge in the light of the need to clean and maintain it. I do not doubt that they also claimed the right to exclude individual undesirables, such as drunks, and specific types of chattels such as guns and bombs. But this control has no real relevance to a manifest intention to assert custody and control over lost articles. There was no evidence that they searched for such articles regularly or at all.

*1019

Evidence was given of staff instructions which govern the action to be taken by employees of the defendants if they found lost articles or lost chattels were handed to them. But these instructions were not published to users of the lounge and in any event I think that they were intended to do no more than instruct the staff on how they were to act in the course of their employment.

It was suggested in argument that in some circumstances the intention of the occupier to assert control over articles lost on his premises speaks for itself. I think that this is right. If a bank manager saw fit to show me round a vault containing safe deposits and I found a gold bracelet on the floor, I should have no doubt that the bank had a better title than I, and the reason is the manifest intention to exercise a very high degree of control. At the other extreme is the park to which the public has unrestricted access during daylight hours. During those hours there is no manifest intention to exercise any such control. In between these extremes are the forecourts of petrol filling stations, unfenced front gardens of private houses, the public parts of shops and supermarkets as part of an almost infinite variety of land, premises and circumstances.

This lounge is in the middle band and in my judgment, on the evidence available, there was no sufficient manifestation of any intention to exercise control over lost property before it was found such as would give the defendants a right superior to that of the plaintiff or indeed any right over the bracelet. As the true owner has never come forward, it is a case of "finders keepers."

EVERLEIGH LJ

A person permitted upon the property of another must respect the lawful claims of the occupier as the terms upon which he is allowed to enter, but it is only right that those claims or terms should be made clear. What is necessary to do this must depend on the circumstances. Take the householder. He has the key to the front door. People do not enter at will. They come by very special invitation. They are not members of a large public group, even a restricted group of the public, as users of the executive lounge may be. I would be inclined to say that the occupier of a house will almost invariably possess any lost article on the premises. He may not have taken any positive steps to demonstrate his animus possidendi, but so firm is his control that the animus can be seen to attach to it. It is rather like the strong room of a bank, where I think it would be difficult indeed to suggest that a bracelet lying on the floor was not in the possession of the bank. The firmer the control, the less will be the need to demonstrate independently the animus possidendi.

The absence of both elements in *Bridges v Hawkesworth*, 21 LJQB 75, was emphasised by Lord Russell of Killowen CJ in *South Staffordshire Water Co. v Sharman* [1896] 2 QB 44, 47, when he said:

> "The shopkeeper did not know they had been dropped, and did not in any sense exercise control over them. The shop was open to the public, and they were invited to come there."

I do not myself support the criticism that has been levelled against Lord Russell of Killowen CJ's words by those who state broadly that the place makes no difference and call in support the words of Patteson J. in *Bridges v Hawkesworth*, 21 LJQB 75, 78: "... the learned judge was mistaken in holding that the place in which they were found makes any legal difference." He was not saying that the place is an irrelevant consideration. He was saying that there was nothing in the place where the notes were found to rebut the principle of "finders keepers." There was nothing special about it. It was open to the public. One could not infer any special conditions of entry. Earlier, however, he said, at page 78: "The notes never were in the custody of the defendant, nor within the protection of his house before they were found ..." I see in those words a recognition of the fact that other considerations might apply in the case of a private house. In the present case I have come to the conclusion that there is nothing so special in the place and no other evidence to indicate that the defendants, on whom is the burden of proof, in any way demonstrated that they possessed the intention to exercise exclusive control over lost property or that the permission to enter as a member of the travelling public, albeit having purchased the special privilege of the executive lounge, was upon the terms that the commonly

 Alert

Although theft requires the appropriation of property belonging to another, there is authority to suggest that a person can be guilty of stealing his own property.

R v Turner (No. 2) [1971] 1 WLR 901

Panel: Lord Parker CJ, Lord Widgery LJ and Bridge J

Statute: Theft Act 1968 s 5(1)

Facts: The defendant took his car to a garage to be repaired. The proprietor of the garage, Mr Brown, carried out the repairs to the car and left the car on the street. The defendant called at the garage to ask if the car was ready. He was told that it was except that it might also need to be tuned and that he could collect it the following day. The defendant said that he would return the following day and pay for the repairs then. Instead, the defendant used his spare key and took the car without paying the repair bill. He was convicted of theft and appealed.

LORD PARKER CJ

[W]hen it comes to this court two points, and two only, are taken. It is said in the first instance that while Mr Brown may have had possession or control in fact, that is not enough, and that it must be shown before it can be said that the property "belonged to" Mr Brown, those being the words used in section 1 (1) of the Theft Act 1968, that

that possession is, as it is said, a right superior to that in the defendant. It is argued from that in default of proof of a lien — and the judge in his summing up directed the jury that they were not concerned with the question of whether there was a lien — that Mr Brown was merely a bailee at will and accordingly that he had no sufficient possession.

The words "belonging to another" are specifically defined in section 5 of the Act, subsection (1) of which provides: "Property shall be regarded as belonging to any person having possession or control of it, or having in it any proprietary right or interest." The sole question was whether Mr Brown had possession or control.

This court is quite satisfied that there is no ground whatever for qualifying the words "possession or control" in any way. It is sufficient if it is found that the person from whom the property is taken, or to use the words of the Act, appropriated, was at the time in fact in possession or control. At the trial there was a long argument as to whether that possession or control must be lawful, it being said that by reason of the fact that this car was subject to a hire purchase agreement, Mr Brown could never even as against the defendant obtain lawful possession or control. As I have said, this court is quite satisfied that the judge was quite correct in telling the jury they need not bother about lien, and that they need not bother about hire purchase agreements. The only question was whether Mr Brown was in fact in possession or control.

 Alert

The second point that is taken relates to the necessity for proving dishonesty. Section 2(1) provides that: "A person's appropriation of property belonging to another is not to be regarded as dishonest...

if he appropriates the property in the belief that he has in law the right to deprive the other of it, on behalf of himself or of a third person;"

The judge said in his summing up:

> "Fourth and last, they must prove that the defendant did what he did dishonestly and this may be the issue which lies very close to the heart of this case."

He then went on to give them a classic direction in regard to claim of right, emphasising that it is immaterial that there exists no basis in law for such belief. He reminded the jury that the defendant had said categorically in evidence: "I believe that I was entitled in law to do what I did." At the same time he directed the jury to look at the surrounding circumstances. He said this:

> "The prosecution say that the whole thing reeks of dishonesty, and if you believe Mr Brown that the defendant drove the car away from Carlyle Road, using a duplicate key, and having told Mr Brown that he would come back tomorrow and pay, you may think the prosecution are right."

On this point Mr Herbert says that if in fact you disregard lien entirely, as the jury were told to do, then Mr Brown was a bailee at will and this car could have been taken back by the defendant perfectly lawfully at any time whether any money was due in regard to repairs or whether it was not. He says, as the court understands it, first that if there was that right, then there cannot be theft at all, and secondly that if and in so far as the mental element is relevant, namely belief, the jury should have been told that he had this right and be left to judge, in the light of the existence of that right, whether they thought he may have believed, as he said, that he did have a right.

The court, however, is quite satisfied that there is nothing in this point whatever. The whole test of dishonesty is the mental element of belief. No doubt, though the defendant may for certain purposes be presumed to know the law, he would not at the time have the vaguest idea whether he had in law a right to take the car back again, and accordingly when one looks at his mental state, one looks at it in the light of what he believed. The jury were properly told that if he believed that he had a right, albeit there was none, he would nevertheless fall to be acquitted. This court, having heard all that Mr Herbert has said, is quite satisfied that there is no manner in which this summing up can be criticised, and that accordingly the appeal against conviction should be dismissed.

Where a person is given property for a particular purpose and that person is under a legal obligation to deal with the property in that way, then the property belongs to another (see the Theft Act 1968 s 5(3)).

R v Hall [1973] QB 126

Panel: Edmund Davies, Stephenson LJJ and Boreham J

Statute: Theft Act 1968 s 5(3)

Facts: The defendant was a travel agent who took deposits from people for flights. However, he did not use the money to buy the flights, but instead put it in his business account. The flights never materialised and no refunds were given to customers. Ultimately, the money was used to pay off the company's creditors and the defendant went bankrupt. The defendant was convicted of theft and appealed. The Court of Appeal allowed the appeal and held that it had not been established that there was a legal duty on the defendant to deal with the money in a particular way. Thus, the Theft Act 1968 s 5(3) did not apply and the money did not belong to another for the purposes of theft.

LORD JUSTICE EDMUND DAVIES

[This case] turns on the application of section 5(3) of the Theft Act 1968 which provides that:

> "Where a person receives property from or on account of another, and is under an obligation to the other to retain and deal with that property or its proceeds in a particular way, the property or proceeds shall be regarded (as against him) as belonging to the other."

Mr Jolly submitted that in the circumstances ... there arose no such "obligation" upon the defendant. He referred us to a passage in the eighth report of the Criminal Law Revision committee (1966) (Cmnd. 2977), at page 127, which reads:

"Subsection (3) provides for the special case where property is transferred to a person to retain and deal with for a particular purpose and he misapplies it or its proceeds. An example would be the treasurer of a holiday fund. The person in question is in law the owner of the property; but the subsection treats the property, as against him, as belonging to the persons to whom he owes the duty to retain and deal with the property as agreed. He will therefore be guilty of stealing from them if he misapplies the property or its proceeds."

Mr Jolly submitted that the example there given is, for all practical purposes, identical with the actual facts in *Reg. v Pulham* (unreported) June 15, 1971, where, incidentally, section 5(3) was not discussed, the convictions there being quashed, as we have already indicated, owing to the lack of a proper direction as to the accused's state of mind at the time he appropriated. But he submits that the position of a treasurer of a solitary fund is quite different from that of a person like the defendant, who was in general, and genuine, business as a travel agent, and to whom people pay money in order to achieve a certain object - in the present cases, to obtain charter flights to America. It is true, he concedes, that thereby the travel agent undertakes a contractual obligation in relation to arranging flights and at the proper time paying the air line and any other expenses. Indeed, the defendant throughout acknowledged that this was so, though contending that in some of the seven cases it was the other party who was in breach. But what Mr Jolly resists is that in such circumstances the travel agent "is under an obligation" to the client "to retain and deal with ... in a particular way" sums paid to him in such circumstances.

...[W]hen a client goes to a firm carrying on the business of travel agents and pays them money, he expects that in return he will, in due course, receive the tickets and other documents necessary for him to accomplish the trip for which he is paying, and the firm are "under an obligation" to perform their part to fulfil his expectation and are liable to pay him damages if they do not. But, in our judgment, what was not here established was that these clients expected them "to retain and deal with that property or its proceeds in a particular way," and that an "obligation" to do this was undertaken by the defendant.

 Alert

We must make clear, however, that each case turns on its own facts. Cases could, we suppose, conceivably arise where by some special arrangement (preferably evidenced by documents), the client could impose upon the travel agent an "obligation" falling within section 5 (3). But no such special arrangement was made [here]...

It follows from this that, despite what on any view must be condemned as scandalous conduct by the defendant, in our judgment upon this ground alone this appeal must be allowed and the convictions quashed ...

This is not limited to commercial situations.

Davidge v Bunnett [1984] Crim LR 297

Panel: Ackner LJ and Taylor J

Statute: Theft Act 1968 s 5(3)

Facts: The defendant shared a flat with three other ladies upon agreement that the cost of the utility bills would be shared between them. On receipt of the gas bill, in the sum of £159.75, the defendant was given cheques to the sum of £109.75 towards the cost of the bill. The defendant cashed the cheques but spent the money on Christmas presents rather than pay the gas bill. The issue for the Divisional Court was whether the defendant was under a legal obligation to deal with the proceeds in a particular way.

LORD JUSTICE ACKNER

The subsection of the Theft Act 1968 relied upon by the prosecution was section 5, subsection (3), which reads as follows: "Where a person receives property from or on account of another, and is under an obligation to the other to retain and deal with that property or its proceeds in a particular way, the property or proceeds shall be regarded (as against him) as belonging to the other."

To my mind the position is a simple one. The Appellant was under an obligation to use the cheques or their proceeds in whatever way she thought fit, so long as they were applied pro tanto in the discharge of the gas bill within a reasonable time. For instance, Mr Power [the defendant's employer who cashed the cheques] could have paid the cheques into his own bank account and instead of providing cash to the Appellant have written out a cheque for £159.75, the amount of the account, given of course that he was provided in addition to the cheques with the sum of £50 by the Appellant. Alternatively, with the money received from Mr Power as the result of his cashing the cheques together with her own contribution, the Appellant could have acquired a bank draft. Alternatively, she could have opened a bank account in her own name, paid the proceeds of the three cheques into that account together with £50 of her own money and thereafter have drawn a cheque on that account for £159.75 in favour of the Gas Board. Hence the finding that she was not obliged to apply the actual bank notes she received from Mr Power to the discharge of the bill.

The Appellant's action in using the proceeds of the two cheques on Christmas presents was the very negation of her obligation to use them in one way or another in discharge of Miss Coshan's and Miss McFeely's indebtedness for gas they had used. In my judgment, when the Appellant received these cheques on account of those two ladies, she was under an obligation to deal with the proceeds of those cheques in a particular way, once she had cashed them, namely by applying them in payment of the gas bill, and accordingly, the proceeds must be regarded as against the Appellant as belonging to those ladies. There was never any issue with regard to the Appellant's dishonesty and, accordingly, I think she was rightly convicted and would therefore dismiss the appeal.

 Alert

8.3 Dishonesty

Dishonesty is a question of fact for the jury to determine. The positive test of dishonesty is set out in *R v Ghosh* [1982] QB 1053.

R v Ghosh [1982] QB 1053

Panel: Lord Lane CJ, Lloyd and Eastham JJ

Facts: The defendant was a consultant at a hospital. He claimed fees for operations which he had not carried out. He was charged with attempting to secure the execution of a valuable security by deception under the Theft Act 1968 s 20(2) and three counts of attempting to or obtaining property by deception under the Theft Act 1968 s 15(1). He was convicted and appealed to the Court of Appeal. The issue on appeal was the meaning of "dishonesty" under the Theft Act 1968.

LORD LANE CJ

A little later *Reg. v Feely* [1973] QB 530 came before a court of five judges. The case is often treated as having laid down an objective test of dishonesty for the purpose of section 1 of the Theft Act 1968. But what it actually decided was (i) that it is for the jury to determine whether the defendant acted dishonestly and not for the judge, (ii) that the word "dishonestly" can only relate to the defendant's own state of mind, and (iii) that it is unnecessary and undesirable for judges to define what is meant by "dishonestly."

It is true that the court said, at pages 537-538:

> "Jurors, when deciding whether an appropriation was dishonest, can be reasonably expected to, and should, apply the current standards of ordinary decent people."

It is that sentence which is usually taken as laying down the objective test. But the passage goes on:

In their own lives they have to decide what is and what is not dishonest. We can see no reason why, when in a jury box, they should require the help of a judge to tell them what amounts to dishonesty."

The sentence requiring the jury to apply current standards leads up to the prohibition on judges from applying *their* standards. That is the context in which the sentence appears. It seems to be reading too much into that sentence to treat it as authority for the view that "dishonesty can be established independently of the knowledge or belief of the defendant." If it could, then any reference to the state of mind of the defendant would be beside the point.

This brings us to the heart of the problem. Is "dishonestly" in section 1 of the Theft Act 1968 intended to characterise a course of conduct? Or is it intended to describe a state of mind? If the former, then we can well understand that it could be established independently of the knowledge or belief of the accused. But if, as we think, it is the latter, then the knowledge and belief of the accused are at the root of the problem.

Take for example a man who comes from a country where public transport is free. On his first day here he travels on a bus. He gets off without paying. He never had any intention of paying. His mind is clearly honest; but his conduct, judged objectively by what he has done, is dishonest. It seems to us that in using the word "dishonestly" in the Theft Act 1968, Parliament cannot have intended to catch dishonest conduct in that sense, that is to say conduct to which no moral obloquy could possibly attach. This is sufficiently established by the partial definition in section 2 of the Theft Act itself. All the matters covered by section 2(1) relate to the belief of the accused. Section 2(2) relates to his willingness to pay. A man's belief and his willingness to pay are things which can only be established subjectively. It is difficult to see how a partially subjective definition can be made to work in harness with the test which in all other respects is wholly objective.

If we are right that dishonesty is something in the mind of the accused (what Professor Glanville Williams calls "a special mental state"), then if the mind of the accused is honest, it cannot be deemed dishonest merely because members of the jury would have regarded it as dishonest to embark on that course of conduct.

So we would reject the simple uncomplicated approach that the test is purely objective, however attractive from the practical point of view that solution may be.

There remains the objection that to adopt a subjective test is to abandon all standards but that of the accused himself, and to bring about a state of affairs in which "Robin Hood would be no robber": *Reg. v Greenstein* [1975] 1 WLR 1353. This objection misunderstands the nature of the subjective test. It is no defence for a man to say "I knew that what I was doing is generally regarded as dishonest; but I do not regard it as dishonest myself. Therefore I am not guilty." What he is however entitled to say is "I did not know that anybody would regard what I was doing as dishonest." He may not be believed; just as he may not be believed if he sets up "a claim of right" under section 2(1) of the Theft Act 1968, or asserts that he believed in the truth of a misrepresentation under section 15 of the Act of 1968. But if he *is* believed, or raises a real doubt about the matter, the jury cannot be sure that he was dishonest.

In determining whether the prosecution has proved that the defendant was acting dishonestly, a jury must first of all decide whether according to the ordinary standards of reasonable and honest people what was done was dishonest. If it was not dishonest by those standards, that is the end of the matter and the prosecution fails.

Alert

If it was dishonest by those standards, then the jury must consider whether the defendant himself must have realised that what he was doing was by those standards dishonest. In most cases, where the actions are obviously dishonest by ordinary standards, there will be no doubt about it. It will be obvious that the defendant himself knew that he was acting dishonestly. It is dishonest for a defendant to act in a way which he knows ordinary people consider to be dishonest, even if he asserts or genuinely believes that he is morally justified in acting as he did. For example, Robin Hood or those ardent anti-vivisectionists who remove animals from vivisection laboratories are acting dishonestly, even though they may consider themselves to be morally justified in doing what they do, because they know that ordinary people would consider these actions to be dishonest.

Alert

Cases which might be described as borderline, such as *Boggeln v Williams* [1978] 1 WLR 873, will depend upon the view taken by the jury as to whether the defendant may have believed what he was doing was in accordance with the ordinary man's idea of honesty. A jury might have come to the conclusion that the defendant in that case was disobedient or impudent, but not dishonest in what he did.

So far as the present case is concerned, it seems to us that once the jury had rejected the defendant's account in respect of each count in the indictment (as they plainly did), the finding of dishonesty was inevitable, whichever of the tests of dishonesty was applied. If the judge had asked the jury to determine whether the defendant might have believed that what he did was in accordance with the ordinary man's idea of honesty, there could have only been one answer - and that is no, once the jury had rejected the defendant's explanation of what happened.

8.4 Intention to Permanently Deprive

S 6(1) states that even if a defendant does not intend the other to permanently lose the property, he will still have an intention to permanently deprive where he intends to treat the property as his own to dispose of regardless of the others rights.

Where the defendant intends only to temporarily deprive the owner of the property, the Theft Act 1968 the second half of s 6(1) requires consideration.

R v Lloyd [1985] QB 829

Panel: Lord Lane CJ, Farquharson and Tudor Price JJ

Statute: Theft Act 1968 s 6(1)

Facts: The defendant took film reels from a cinema, intending to copy the films and then return the reels. He was convicted of theft under the Theft Act 1968 and appealed. The Court of Appeal quashed his conviction on the basis that it had not been established that defendant had any intention to permanently deprive.

LORD LANE CJ

...[T]he first part of section 6(1) seems to us to be aimed at the sort of case where a defendant takes things and then offers them back to the owner for the owner to buy if he wishes. If the taker intends to return them to the owner only upon such payment, then, on the wording of section 6(1), that is deemed to amount to the necessary intention permanently to deprive...

It seems to us that in this case we are concerned with the second part of section 6(1), namely, the words after the semi-colon:

"and a borrowing or lending of it may amount to so treating it if, but only if, the borrowing or lending is for a period and in circumstances making it equivalent to an outright taking or disposal."

These films, it could be said, were borrowed by Lloyd from his employers in order to enable him and the others to carry out their "piracy" exercise.

Borrowing is ex hypothesi not something which is done with an intention permanently to deprive. This half of the subsection, we believe, is intended to make it clear that a

Alert

mere borrowing is never enough to constitute the necessary guilty mind unless the intention is to return the "thing" in such a changed state that it can truly be said that all its goodness or virtue has gone: for example *Reg. v Beecham* (1851) 5 Cox CC 181, where the defendant stole railway tickets intending that they should be returned to the railway company in the usual way only after the journeys had been completed. He was convicted of larceny. The judge in the present case gave another example, namely, the taking of a torch battery with the intention of returning it only when its power is exhausted.

That being the case, we turn to inquire whether the feature films in this case can fall within that category. Our view is that they cannot. The goodness, the virtue, the practical value of the films to the owners has not gone out of the article. The film could still be projected to paying audiences, and, had everything gone according to the conspirators' plans, would have been projected in the ordinary way to audiences at the Odeon Cinema, Barking, who would have paid for their seats. Our view is that those particular films which were the subject of this alleged conspiracy had not themselves diminished in value at all. What had happened was that the borrowed film had been used or was going to be used to perpetrate a copyright swindle on the owners whereby their commercial interests were grossly and adversely affected in the way that we have endeavoured to describe at the outset of this judgment. That borrowing, it seems to us, was not for a period, or in such circumstances, as made it equivalent to an outright taking or disposal. There was still virtue in the film.

The proposition that borrowing will only amount to an intention to permanently deprive if the intention is to return the thing in such a changed state that it can truly be said that all its goodness, virtue and practical value has gone, has been settled law since *R v Lloyd*. However, there has been much debate, judicial and academic, as to what other situations are covered by this phrase 'treating as his own to dispose of regardless of the other's rights'.

R v Cahill [1993] Crim LR 141

Panel: Russell LJ, Potts and Waterhouse JJ

Statute: Theft Act 1968 s 6(1)

Facts: The defendant, with another, had taken a bundle of newspapers from outside a shop. He stated that he believed the package to be lost property and intended to hand it into the local police station. The defendant was convicted of theft. He appealed on the ground, inter alia, that the trial judge had misdirected the jury as to what was required for s 6(1) to be established. The trial judge had said that if the defendants had an intention to treat the property as their own, regardless of the rights of the owner, that would amount to an intention to permanently deprive. The Court of Appeal held that this was a misdirection because the words 'to dispose of' had been omitted.

MR JUSTICE POTTS

In this connection it is helpful to refer to Professor Smith's book, the Law of Theft, sixth edition. At pages 72 and 73 of that volume the learned author analyses section 6 of the Theft Act. On page 73 (paragraph 133) there is the following passage:

> "The attribution of an ordinary meaning to the language of s 6 presents some difficulties. It is submitted, however, that an intention merely to use the thing as one's own is not enough and that 'dispose of' is not used in the sense in which a general might 'dispose of' his forces but rather in the meaning given by the Shorter Oxford Dictionary: 'To deal with definitely; to get rid off; to get done with, finish. To make over by way of sale or bargain, sell.'"

 Alert

Looking at the whole of the original direction given by the learned recorder and the learned recorder's answer to the specific question posed by the jury, we are satisfied that no adequate direction was given as to the effect of the words "dispose of" in the context of section 6.

R v Fernades [1996] 1 Cr App R 175

Panel: Auld LJ, Mantell and Sachs JJ

Statute: Theft Act 1968 s 6(1)

Facts: The defendant was a solicitor convicted of stealing money from his clients. For one of the counts of theft he had transferred money out of his client's account and invested it in a risky backstreet money lending business. One of his grounds of appeal was that the judge had wrongly used s 6(1) in his directions to the jury because that section had a limited meaning which did not cover the defendant's intention.

LORD JUSTICE AULD

The appellant's seventh ground of appeal, which went to both convictions of theft, was that the judge should not have introduced section 6(1) considerations because they had no application to the facts of the case. Mr Coward submitted that in each case the Crown had to prove an unwatered down intention permanently to deprive. He maintained that section 6(1) only applies to property such as a ticket which has been used and returned to its owner as a valueless piece of paper, or to a cheque which has been paid into an account and then returned, having lost all but its nominal value to the drawer or his bank. He relied upon *Warner* (1970) 55 Cr App R 93; *Lloyd, Bhuee and Ali* (1985) 81 Cr App R 182; and *Duru, Asghar & Khan* (1974) 58 Cr App R 151, C.A. In particular, he relied upon a passage from the judgment of Lord Lane, CJ, in *Lloyd*, considering an observation of Edmund-Davies LJ in *Warner* at pages 96–97, that section 6(1) does not water down the need to prove an intention permanently to deprive, but merely illustrates what can amount to such an intention. [Counsel for the appellant suggested that the trial judge's comments during the summing up] created a danger that the jury would equate what later turned out to have been an unwise and risky investment of the money with an intention, at the time of making it, permanently to deprive.

[With reference to *Lloyd*] Mr Coward submitted, in reliance upon those words, that the first limb of section 6(1) is restricted to a taking and re-sale or attempted re-sale to the owner, and that the second limb is restricted to a borrower's or lender's treatment of property in such a way as to render it valueless on return. He suggested that the judge's use of words, clearly taken from the first limb, was inappropriate because, on that restricted interpretation, this was not a first limb case, a taking and re-sale or attempted re-sale. He submitted that, at best for the prosecution, it was a second limb case, a borrowing, though not of the kind mentioned by Lord Lane; and the judge did not direct them about that.

Alert

In our view, section 6(1), which is expressed in general terms, is not limited in its application to the illustrations given by Lord Lane CJ in Lloyd. Nor, in saying that in most cases it would be unnecessary to refer to the provision, did Lord Lane suggest that it should be so limited. The critical notion, stated expressly in the first limb and incorporated by reference in the second, is whether a defendant intended "to treat the thing as his own to dispose of regardless of the other's rights". The second limb of subsection (1), and also subsection (2), are merely specific illustrations of the application of that notion. We consider that section 6 may apply to a person in possession or control of another's property who, dishonestly and for his own purpose, deals with that property in such a manner that he knows he is risking its loss.

In the circumstances alleged here, an alleged dishonest disposal of someone else's money on an obviously insecure investment, we consider that the judge was justified in referring to section 6.

The Director of Public Prosecutions v SJ, PI, RC [2002] EWHC 291 (Admin)

Panel: Mr Justice Silber

Statute: Theft Act 1968 s 6(1)

Facts: The defendants, boys of about 14, confronted a boy of the same age who attended a special needs school. One of the defendants took the victim's headphones, snapped them in two and then returned them. On a charge of robbery, the magistrates concluded that there was no case to answer as the prosecution had not established an intention to permanently deprive the boy of the headphones. The Director of Public Prosecution appealed by way of case stated.

MR JUSTICE SILBER

13. In the light of the wording of section 6(1) of the Theft Act 1968, the issue before this Court can be refined to being whether the respondents, by snatching and snapping the headphones before returning them, did not demonstrate their intention was to treat the headphones as their own to dispose of regardless of the rights of the owner so as to satisfy the requirement of intention to permanently deprive in section 1 of the Theft Act.

14. It is common ground between all the parties that no issue can be taken about whether the respondents were acting individually, because it is accepted that there was adequate evidence that this was a joint enterprise.

15. It is necessary to focus on the requirement that for there to be an intention to permanently deprive, the intention of the wrongdoers has to be to treat the article in question, namely the headphones, as their own, and this is important in the words of section 6(1) of the Theft Act "to dispose of". These words have a wide meaning, and the Court of Appeal approved in Cahill [1993] Crim LR 141 of the conclusion of Professor Sir John Smith, who had explained in relation to these words that:

"The words 'dispose of' are crucial and are, it is submitted, not used in the sense in which a general might 'dispose of' his forces, but rather than a meaning given by the Shorter Oxford Dictionary 'to deal with definitely; to get rid of; to get done with, finish. To make over by way of sale or bargain'."

16. This passage quoted from Professor Sir John Smith is now to be found in the 8th edition of his Book, The Law of Theft, at paragraph 2.132.

17. Of course, the intention of the respondents has to be inferred from their acts. It is common ground between the parties that once the headphones had been snapped by one of the respondents, they were in fact useless. I consider that anyone who snatches headphones from the owner of them and then renders them useless in that way could be considered as having demonstrated an intention to treat the headphones as his own to 'dispose of' regardless of the rights of the owner. The reason is that those acts of the respondents would, in the words of the passage from Sir John Smith's book that I have quoted, have dealt with the headphones definitely or got rid of them or would have finished them. Thus, it was not open to the magistrates to find no case to answer in relation to the requirement of intention to permanently deprive.

 Alert

18. This conclusion is supported by the view of Auld LJ, who, in giving the judgment of the Court of Appeal Criminal Division in Fernandes [1991] 1 Crim App R 175, 188, said (with my emphasis added) that:

"We consider that section 6 may apply to a person in possession or control of another's property who dishonestly and for his own purpose, deals with that property in such a manner that he knows he is risking its loss."

19. I do not believe that there is any difference between a person who knows that by his actions he risks the loss of the property of another, and another person who, as in the present case, snatches another person's property and then snaps them, with the result that he must have known that they then became of no use.

20. It was said on behalf of the third respondent that the goods have to be "completely exhausted" before they can be disposed of for the purposes of section 6 of the Theft Act. There is nothing in that statutory provision which indicates that the word "dispose" has to be so construed. No authorities were relied on in support of this contention, and it would run contrary to the approach adopted by

the Court of Appeal Criminal Division in Cahill and Fernandes, as I have explained. Thus, I cannot agree with that construction. In any event, I cannot understand how that concept could apply in the case of an item which is damaged so it has no conceivable use whatsoever. In the light of the careful findings of fact of the magistrates, I consider there was evidence on which a reasonable tribunal might be satisfied there was an intention to permanently deprive the owner of his headphones.

21. I have considered but have been unable to accept as having any probative value the, clear reasons given by the magistrates for finding there was no case to answer. They state that:

"We do not find there was sufficient evidence that the three boys had the intention to deprive [the owner] permanently of the headphones ... As we did not find the elements of the theft proved, we find there was no case to answer."

22. I agree with Mr Barnard, for the Director, that the magistrates appear to have applied the wrong test. By using the words "we do not find", they appear to be looking at the matter as they do at the end of a trial rather than on a submission for no case to answer. I have already indicated that the task for the magistrates was to see whether there was any evidence to prove an essential element of the alleged offence. That, of course, is a different test from the one that they applied, which was more appropriate to a decision at the conclusion of a trial.

23. Even so, the magistrates relied on three factors to determine whether there should be no case to answer. The first was that the headphones were returned immediately. I cannot share their view that this was a valid point, bearing in mind that it is settled law that the intention of the respondents has to be considered as at the time when the headphones were seized in the light of their conduct. In any event, as I have explained, the opening words of section 6(1) of the Theft Act 1968 give a wider meaning than might otherwise apply to the requirement of an intention to permanently deprive. They clearly envisage that a person who does not mean the other to permanently lose the thing may nevertheless be regarded as having the intention of permanently depriving the other of it if his intention is to treat the thing as his own to dispose of.

24. The second factor relied on by the magistrates was that the headphones were of no use on their own, but this was a point which, quite rightly, was conceded by counsel for two of the respondents as not being a valid point. I am unable to agree that this factor has any value and this factor is not an element of theft or a requirement of it. The goods stolen need not have any particular use on their own; after all, many offences can be committed simply out of a sense of malice, as might well have been the motive of the respondents in this case.

25. I ought to say that counsel for two of the respondents also did not seek to justify the third factor relied on by the magistrates, which was that the headphones were of low value whereas other items which were of higher value on the owner would have been worth stealing had they had the intention. This point presupposes that the only purpose of stealing is to obtain things of the highest value, and there is no

statutory or other requirement for that, especially as in this case the purpose of the offence appears to have been to punish the owner. I am unable to agree with the magistrates that this or any of the three factors relied on are relevant.

26. For all those reasons, the appeal of the Director of Public Prosecutions should be allowed, as the magistrates should not have found that there was no case to answer on the issue of whether the prosecution could establish an intention to permanently deprive the owner of the headphones. Thus, the question raised for this Court must be answered in the negative, as there was evidence on which a reasonable tribunal could have found that there was an intention to permanently deprive the owner of the headset and the magistrates should not have found no case to answer on that issue.

R v Mitchell [2008] EWCA Crim 850

Panel: Rix LJ, David Clarke J, His honour Judge Stewart QC (sitting as a judge of the Court of Appeal Criminal Division)

Statute: Theft Act s 6(1)

Facts: The victim was sitting in a BMW car in a country lane, talking on her mobile telephone. The defendant was in a car with three other men which was being pursued by the police. This car crashed into a concrete bollard near the victim's car. The men used a metal bar to break the BMW car windows. They dragged the victim out and drove off in the BMW. The BMW was found a few miles away 45 minutes later in a built up area with its hazard lights on. Mitchell's blood was found in the BMW and he was charged with robbery. The Court of Appeal reviewed the law on s 6(1).

RIX LJ

It goes without saying that robbery involves, and we are not giving the statutory definition at this point, the use of violence in the course of and for the purpose of a theft (see s 8(1) of the Theft Act 1968: "if he steals, and immediately before or at the time of doing so, and in order to do so") Theft involves s 1 Theft Act 1968 an intention permanently to deprive the owner of the property concerned. The question in this case was whether the facts laid by the prosecution established a case to go before the jury of violence in the pursuit of theft. Had there been an intention permanently to deprive Mr or Mrs Davis of ownership of the BMW?

12. There is a further section in the Theft Act upon which the prosecution relied for these purposes and that is s 6(1) which provides as follows:

"A person appropriating property belonging to another without meaning the other permanently to lose the thing itself is nevertheless to be regarded as having the intention of permanently depriving the other of it if his intention is to treat the thing as his own to dispose of regardless of the other's rights; and a borrowing or lending of it may amount to so treating it if, but only if, the borrowing or lending is for a period and in circumstances making it equivalent to an outright taking or disposal."

We are concerned essentially in this case with the section down to the semicolon. We will also, however, read s 6(2) because its provisions are also discussed in the jurisprudence of s 6 to which we will have to make mention. Section 6(2) provides:

> "Without prejudice to the generality of sub-section (1) above, where a person, having possession or control (lawfully or not) of property belonging to another, parts with the property under a condition as to its return which he may not be able to perform, this (if done for purposes of his own and without the other's authority) amounts to treating the property as his own to dispose of regardless of the other's rights."

13. There has been some discussion in cases, as will be seen, as to whether s 6 waters down or extends or only exemplifies the underlying requirement for theft of an intention permanently to deprive. Taking the wording of s 6(1) by itself without regard to authority it would seem that there is the possibility of a s 6 intention, that is to say an intention to treat the thing as his own to dispose of regardless of the other's rights, as somewhat extending the intention permanently to deprive, because the section begins with the hypothesis that property belonging to another has been taken "without meaning the other permanently to lose the thing itself". Although those words carefully avoid the word "intention", since the word "meaning" is used instead, or the word "deprived" since the word "lose" is used instead, nevertheless it would appear that the purpose of the section is to render a Defendant to be regarded or deemed as having the necessary s 1 intention of permanently depriving the owner of his property if the s 6(1) intention is established. Having said that, we observe that the jurisprudence discusses the extent to which s 6 goes beyond the essential underlying intention of permanently depriving the owner of his property.

14. A number of relevant authorities have been helpfully cited to us. We begin with *R v Warner* 55 Cr App Rep 93, [1971] Crim LR 114. That was a case in which one worker had been seen making off with the tools of a colleague which were very shortly thereafter found hidden under some scarves. It was only at trial that his real defence emerged; there had been a dispute between that Defendant and his colleague about a right of way affecting their properties which had got into the hands of solicitors and the Defendant was reacting to that dispute by removing his colleague's tools for what he insisted was only intended to be a short time, but the police had almost immediately become involved and he had lost his nerve about owning up.

15. The Crown had invoked s 6(1) of the Theft Act and the Defendant had been convicted. His appeal was allowed. Edmund Davies LJ referred to the Theft Act as "aspiring to remove legal subtleties devoid of merit". He referred to s 1 declaring that the intention of permanently depriving another of his property was an essential ingredient and said that nothing was to be found elsewhere in the Act which justified a conviction for theft in its absence. Turning then to s 6, which he considered had unfortunately confused the trial, Edmund Davies LJ said this (at 97):

"Its object is, in no way wise to cut down the definition of 'theft' contained in section 1. It is always dangerous to paraphrase a statutory enactment, but its apparent aim is to prevent specious pleas of a kind which have succeeded in the past by providing in effect, that it is no excuse for an accused person to plead absence of the necessary intention if it is clear that he appropriated another's property intending to treat it as his own, regardless of the owner's rights. Section 6 thus gives illustrations, as it were, of what can amount to the dishonest intention demanded by section 1(1). But it is a misconception to interpret it as watering down section 1."

16. The matter was revisited in *R v Lloyd* and others [1985] QB 829. That case involved a conspiracy to defraud the owners of the copyright of films by removing the film reels being shown in a cinema for as short a period as made it possible to have them copied onto a video master tape before having them returned surreptitiously back to the cinema from which they had been taken. The Defendants were charged with conspiracy to steal. Section 6 was relied on to make good the intention necessary to theft in circumstances where it had been plain that the whole point of the exercise was to get the film reels back to the cinema as soon as could be done. That was another case where use of s 6 had led to a conviction but where this court had to allow an appeal.

17. In a wide-ranging judgment, Lord Lane CJ, considered the background of s 6 both in the common law and since the enactment of the Theft Act. He cited JR Spencer in an article in [1977] Criminal Law Review 653 for describing s 6 as a provision which "sprouts obscurities at every phrase" and observed: "We are inclined to agree with him" 834B. He then referred to the passage in Warner (which we have cited). Next he referred to *R v Duru* [1974] 1 WLR 2, a case involving cheques which had been stolen, paid out to the thieves and then returned in the normal course of processing to their owners. It was submitted that the return of the cheques, albeit devoid of value to their owners once they had been paid, indicated the lack of the necessary intention under the Theft Act. But Megaw LJ at page 8 explained that although as a piece of paper the cheque remained, subject to a rubber stamp on it, the same as before, it had entirely ceased to be a thing in action, as it had been before it had been paid, had ceased to be in substance the same thing as it was before and had become worthless. In those circumstances if it had been necessary to look to s 6, said Megaw LJ, that could have been applied since it was plain "that the Defendants each had the intention of causing the cheque to be treated as the property of the person by whom it was to be obtained, to dispose of, regardless of the rights of the true owner".

18. Lord Lane then referred to further academic scholarship, that of Professor Griew, to the effect that s 6 should be referred to in exceptional cases only, since in the vast majority of cases it need not be referred to or considered at all at 835H. A third distinguished academic, Professor Glanville Williams, was then cited with approval at 836B for this observation:

"... a trial judge would be well advised not to introduce it to the jury unless he reaches the conclusion that it will assist them, and even then (it may be suggested) the question he leaves to the jury should not be worded in terms of the generalities of the subsection but should reflect those generalities as applied to the alleged facts."

19. Lord Lane then referred to the law as it had been before the Theft Act. He said this (at 836C) ". . . we would try to interpret the section in such a way as to ensure that nothing is construed as an intention permanently to deprive which would not prior to the 1968 Act have been so construed." In that connection he said that the section seemed to be aimed at the sort of case where a Defendant takes things and then offers them back to the owner for the owner to buy if he wishes. He referred to the 19th century case of *R v Hall* 2 Car & Kir 947, 1 Den 381. He also referred to the early case of *R v Beecham* (1851) 5 Cox CC 181, where railway tickets had been stolen with the intention that they should be returned to the railway company in the usual way only after the journeys had been completed. Another example given was the taking of a torch battery with the intention of returning it only when its power was exhausted.

20. Turning in the light of those examples to the case of the films, Lord Lane concluded thus (836H – 837B):

"That being the case, we turn to inquire whether the feature films in this case can fall within that category. Our view is that they cannot. The goodness, the virtue, the practical value of the films to the owners has not gone out of the article. The film could still be projected to paying audiences, and, had everything gone according to the conspirators' plans, would have been projected in the ordinary way to audiences at the Odeon Cinema, Barking, who had paid for their seats. Our view is that those particular films which were the subject of this alleged conspiracy had not themselves diminished in value at all. What had happened was that the borrowed film had been used or was going to be used to perpetrate a copyright swindle on the owners whereby their commercial interests were grossly and adversely affected in the way that we have endeavoured to describe at the outset of this judgment. That borrowing, it seems to us, was not for a period, or in such circumstances, as made it equivalent to an outright taking or disposal. There was still virtue in the film."

21. The next case is *R v Coffey* [1987] Crim LR 498. That concerned the obtaining of machinery by a worthless cheque. The Defendant had obtained the machinery in order to put pressure upon someone with whom he had a dispute. The appeal was again allowed because the summing-up was defective but in the course of this court's judgment it was observed that this was one of those rare cases where s 6(1) could usefully be deployed before the jury, but the jury should have been invited to consider whether the taking of the machinery in the circumstances obtaining in that case was equivalent to an outright taking or disposal.

22. In *R v Cahill* [1993] Crim LR 141 a package of newspapers had been taken by the Defendant and, he said, put outside the front door of a friend of his as a joke.

Section 6(1) had been brought into play at the trial but in summing up the matter to the jury the recorder in that case had dropped from his directions the statutory words in their place "to dispose of". That was held to be a misdirection because this court approved what Professor Smith had said of those words in his book on The Law of Theft as follows:

"The attribution of an ordinary meaning to the language of section 6 presents some difficulties. It is submitted, however, that an intention merely to use the thing as one's own is not enough and that 'dispose of' is not used in the sense in which a general might 'dispose of' his forces but rather in the meaning given by the Shorter Oxford dictionary: To deal with definitely; to get rid of; to get done with, finish. To make over by way of sale or bargain, sell."

So that appeal was allowed as well. A note by Professor Smith followed the extract of that report by way of commentary. Professor Smith pointed out that that case could have been dealt with without mentioning s 6 at all since the question was "Did the Defendant intend the package of newspapers to be lost to the newsagent forever?" – as might well have been the case where that package had disappeared to some strange doorstep. If, however, s 6 was to be invoked at all, the question would be whether the virtue had gone out of the thing, even if the Defendant had believed that the newsagent would get his papers back the following day, but at a time when they would be quite useless to him. So upon that basis s 6 might have been correctly deployed.

23. Finally, in *R v Fernandes* [1996] 1 Cr App Rep 175 this jurisprudence was revisited in the context of a case where a solicitor had invested client's money at his disposal in his colleague's back street money-lending business where it was lost. It was argued that s 6 should not have been deployed in that case. But in his judgment Auld LJ accepted that this was a case of proper use of it, saying at 188E:

"We consider that section 6 may apply to a person in possession or control of another's property who, dishonestly and for his own purpose, deals with that property in such a manner that he knows he is risking its loss.

In the circumstances alleged here, an alleged dishonest disposal of someone else's money on an obviously insecure investment, we consider that the judge was justified in referring to section 6. His direction, looked at as a whole, did not water down the requirement that the jury should be sure of an intention permanently to deprive as illustrated by that provision."

24. It is in the light of that jurisprudence that we have to consider the ruling of the judge on the application of no case to answer. What was said to the judge was that in the circumstances of this case there was no intention permanently to deprive Mr or Mrs Davis of their BMW, nor was there an intention within s 6, which the prosecution also relied upon, to treat the thing as the Defendant's own to dispose of regardless of the owner's rights. The car had only been driven for a few miles before being abandoned. The fact of abandonment showed that there was no intention permanently to deprive the owners of it or to dispose of it

irrespective of the owner's rights. The judge, however, considered that there was either in the taking or in the use or in the abandonment of the vehicle evidence capable of amounting to a disposal under s 6(1). Of those three matters – the taking, the use and the abandonment – the judge in particular had emphasised the abandonment where he said "It appears to me that abandonment in those circumstances might amount to a disposal. That is a matter which in my judgment should be decided by a jury."

25. In our judgment the judge erred in these considerations. So far as the abandonment itself of the car was concerned, a matter which on this appeal Mr Jackson on behalf of the Crown has not relied upon, that of course operated as a factor in favour of the defence. Moreover, the fact that its hazard lights were left on emphasized that there was no intention to avoid drawing attention to the car. So far as the use of the vehicle is concerned, again a matter not relied upon on this appeal by Mr Jackson, its use amounted to being driven just a few miles before its abandonment. So far as the taking is concerned, that was the one matter which Mr Jackson stressed in his submissions to the court. Those submissions proceeded in this way. When he was asked whether the red Fiesta, which was the car into which Mrs Davis' assailants had decamped from the BMW later that night, had been stolen Mr Jackson answered that question with the answer "No". He was then asked to state what the difference was between the taking of the Fiesta and the taking of the BMW. His first response was to say that the difference was the removal of Mrs Davis by force from the BMW and also the breaking of its windows. Subsequently in his submissions he abandoned the breaking of the windows as being a critical difference. Ultimately he took his stand upon the removal of Mrs Davis by force. This for him was the critical and distinguishing feature. This was the feature which showed that her assailants intended to treat the car as their own to dispose of regardless of the other's rights.

26. At some point during his submissions Mr Jackson, before being reminded of the words "to dispose of", which Professor Smith had emphasised in his Law of Theft (see above) and which this court similarly picked up in Cahill, omitted those words and emphasised, as we can well understand him saying, that the treatment of Mrs Davis showed an intention to treat the BMW as the Defendant's own regardless of the other's rights (but omitting the words "to dispose of"). Of course, everything about the taking and use of the BMW, like any car taken away without the owner's authority, indicates an intention to treat such a car regardless of the owner's rights. That is the test of conversion in the civil law. But not every conversion is a theft. Theft requires the additional intention of permanently depriving the owner or the substituted intention under s 6(1). The fact that the taking becomes more violent, thereby setting up a case of robbery, if there is an underlying case of theft, does not in itself turn what would be a robbery, if there was a theft, into a case of robbery without theft. The theft has to be there without the violence which would turn the theft into robbery.

[He then considered evidence that the gang had intended to destroy the BMW, and found this to be inconclusive]

28. In our judgment the facts of this case simply do not support a case to go before a jury of theft and therefore robbery of the BMW. The BMW was plainly taken for the purposes of a getaway. There was nothing about its use or subsequent abandonment to suggest otherwise. Indeed, its brief use and subsequent abandonment show very clearly what was the obvious prima facie inference to be drawn from its taking which was that the occupants of the Subaru needed another conveyance that evening. We therefore consider that the judge erred in being beguiled by s 6 into leaving this count of robbery to the jury.

29. In those circumstances, we need spend little time on ground 2 of this appeal, which was a complaint about the circumstances in which the ingredients of robbery were summed up in the judge's directions to the jury. We think that the factors for the jury to consider were put before the jury but of course the recorder never directed them, for the purposes of s 6(1) and the jurisprudence which we have considered, to ask themselves whether those factors amounted to such an outright taking or disposal or an intention within the words of s 6(1) as to amount to the equivalence of an intention permanently to deprive. We consider that the authorities which we have reviewed in this judgment show that the purpose of s 6 is not greatly to widen the requirement of s 1's intention permanently to deprive. A slightly broader definition of that intention is there provided in order to deal with a small number of difficult cases which had either arisen in the past under the common law or might arise in the future where, although it might be hard to put the matter strictly in terms of an intention permanently to deprive, in the sense of meaning the owner permanently to lose the thing itself, nevertheless something equivalent to that could be obtained through the intention to treat the thing as his own to dispose of, regardless of the other's rights, remembering Professor Smith's Oxford English dictionary use of the words "to dispose of". Thus, the newspaper taken but only returned on the next day when it is out of date, or a ticket which had been used, or a cheque which is paid, or something which has been substantially used up or destroyed, or something which would only be returned to its owner subject to a condition, all these are the sorts of examples to be found in the jurisprudence which discusses s 6. All of these cases are of ready equivalence to an intention permanently to deprive. None of them go any way towards extending the scope of s 6 to a case, however violent, of the taking of a car for the purposes of its brief use before being abandoned with its lights on. It must be remembered of course that a car with its licence plates on, left on the road, is utterly unlike a bundle of newspapers which have disappeared from a newsagents shop to a place where they would not be found.

30. For these reasons this appeal must be allowed. Given the overall criminality displayed in this case, we regret the conclusion to which we have felt constrained to come. However, the prosecution could have laid other charges against the Defendant – charges such as affray or malicious damage, of course assault, possibly even assault occasioning actual bodily harm. It may be that if a prosecution on that basis had arrived at a conviction, the gravamen of what was charged under the offence of robbery could have been adequately dealt with in

the sentencing of the court. As it is, by charging the wrong offence this prosecution could not succeed and ought not to have succeeded. We therefore allow this appeal. Mr Kelly, your referred application against sentence does not arise.

R v Vinall and J [2011] EWCA Crim 2652

Panel: Lord Justice Pitchford , Mr Justice Andrew Smith and Mr Justice Popplewell

Statute: Theft Act 1968 s 6(1)

Facts: The defendants had punched a man on a bicycle. They then took his bicycle, which they later abandoned at a bus shelter 50 yards away. They were charged with robbery and the question arose whether the defendants had the intention to permanently deprive the victim of the bicycle at the time of the punch, so that the force could be said to have been used in order to steal. The judge gave a confusing direction to the jury on the meaning of s 6(1) and an appeal was allowed on this point. The Court of Appeal judgment shows that what a defendant does is good evidence of what he intended, but ultimately the relevant issue is his intention. It was also noted that for theft it was not necessary for the defendant to have the relevant intention at the time of the initial appropriation.

PITCHFORD LJ

[W]e would draw attention to an unreported decision of the Divisional Court of the Queen's Bench Division in *Chief Constable of Avon and Somerset Constabulary v Smith* and another unreported November, 20 1984 (Goff LJ and McCullough J.). The defendants broke into a parked car and removed a briefcase and an attaché case. Having searched them they concealed the briefcase in a nearby hedge and the attaché case in a public lavatory cubicle. In giving the leading judgment with which Goff LJ agreed, McCullough J. said:

"In my judgment, there plainly was evidence capable of establishing intent, at the time the briefcases were taken from the car, permanently to deprive the owner of them. There was clearly evidence capable of amounting to an intention, at that moment, to treat the briefcases as the respondent's own, to dispose of regardless of the true owner's rights. They were in fact so disposed of. They were not taken back to the car; one was thrown into a hedge and the other was left in the public lavatory. This evidence of disposal was, in my judgment, evidence from which one might infer an intention within the terms of section 6(1) at the time of the disposal and, having regard to considerations of time and distance, it was evidence from which one might also infer that the same intention existed at the time the articles were removed from the motor car."

As to the possibility of a later appropriation with the requisite intent McCullough J. said:

"In any event, there is an alternative way in which the Crown Court could have thought there was sufficient evidence of theft, even if it was of the view that the original appropriation which began when the briefcases were first seized was over by the time of their disposal. At that time there was, in my judgment, evidence that the respondents were assuming a right to deal with them as owners. If so, there was evidence of an appropriation at the time of disposal: section 3(1). There was also sufficient evidence of an intention at that moment permanently to deprive and of dishonesty. So, even if there was no evidence that the original appropriation was still at that moment continuing, it would have been open to the court to say that there was evidence that all three elements of theft were present at the time of disposal."

In our view this decision represents the plain common sense of most cases of alleged theft of property. If the prosecution is unable to establish an intent permanently to deprive at the moment of taking it may nevertheless establish that the defendant exercised such a dominion over the property that it can be inferred that at the time of the taking he intended to treat the property as his own to dispose of regardless of the owner's rights (c.f. Easom in which the handbag was replaced approximately in the position from which it had been removed). Subsequent "disposal" of the property may be evidence either of an intention at the time of the taking or evidence of an intention at the time of the disposal. When the allegation is theft a later appropriation will suffice; when the allegation is robbery it almost certainly will not. In Smith the manner in which the property was disposed of was evidence supporting the inference of the s 6(1) intention; in Mitchell the manner in which the car was abandoned, and in Easom the replacement of the handbag, could not support the inference.

Conclusion

20 In the present case, we conclude that it was open to the judge to invite the jury to consider whether the later abandonment of Mr De-Nijs' bicycle was evidence from which they could infer that the appellants intended at the time of the taking to treat the bicycle as their own to dispose of regardless of his rights. If that was the way the judge had chosen to leave the issue of intent to the jury, an explicit direction would have been required explaining that an intention formed only upon abandonment of the bicycle at the bus shelter was inconsistent with and fatal to the allegation of robbery. In the absence of such an explanation, it seems to this court that the verdicts were unsafe and must be quashed.

Further Reading

Cross R 'Protecting Confidential Information under the Criminal Law of Theft and Fraud' (1991) 11 *OJLS* 264

Griew E J 'Dishonesty, the Objections to *Feely* and *Ghosh*' [1985] *Crim LR* 341

Shute S 'Appropriation and the law of theft' [2002] *Crim LR* 445

Spencer J R 'The Metamorphosis of Section 6 of the Theft Act' [1977] *Crim LR* 653

7

Robbery and Blackmail

Topic List

9.1 Robbery

Robbery is made a crime by the Theft Act 1968 s 8. Its distinguishing feature is the requirement of 'force', however the degree of 'force' required for robbery is not defined. Case law illustrates that simply nudging the victim so as to cause him to lose his balance is sufficient.

R v Dawson and James (1977)] 64 Cr App R 170

Panel: Lawton LJ, Mackenna and Swanick JJ

Statute: Theft Act 1968 s 8(1)

Facts: The two defendants were jointly convicted of robbery. One of them nudged the victim causing him to lose his balance, while the other stole his wallet. The defendants' appeal against conviction on the basis that there had been no force was dismissed by the Court of Appeal.

LORD JUSTICE LAWTON

The object of that Act was to get rid of all the old technicalities of the law of larceny and to put the law into simple language which juries would understand and which they themselves would use. That is what has happened in section 8 which defines "robbery." That section is in these terms: "A person is guilty of robbery if he steals, and immediately before or at the time of doing so, and in order to do so, he uses force on any person or puts or seeks to put any person in fear of being then and there subjected to force."

The choice of the word "force" is not without interest because under the Larceny Act 1916 the word "violence" had been used, but Parliament deliberately on the advice of the Criminal Law Revision Committee changed that word to "force." Whether there is any difference between "violence" or "force" is not relevant for the purposes of this case; but the word is "force." It is a word in ordinary use. It is a word which juries understand. The learned judge left it to the jury to say whether jostling a man in the way which the victim described to such an extent that he had difficulty in keeping his balance could be said to be the use of force. The learned judge, because of the argument put forward by Mr Locke, went out of his way to explain to the jury that force in these sort of circumstances must be substantial to justify a verdict.

Whether it was right for him to put that adjective before the word "force" when Parliament had not done so we will not discuss for the purposes of this case. It was a matter for the jury. They were there to use their common sense and knowledge of the world. We cannot say that their decision as to whether force was used was wrong. They were entitled to the view that force was used.

Other points were discussed in the case as to whether the force had been used for the purpose of distracting the victim's attention or whether it was for the purpose of overcoming resistance. Those sort of refinements may have been relevant under the old law, but so far as the new law is concerned the sole question is whether the accused

 Alert

used force on any person in order to steal. That issue in this case was left to the jury. They found in favour of the Crown.

We cannot say that this verdict was either unsafe or unsatisfactory. Accordingly the appeal is dismissed.

Thus, "force" is an ordinary word. It does not require violence.

R v Clouden [1987] Crim LR 56

Panel: Lloyd LJ, Eastham and French JJ

Statute: Theft Act 1968 s 8

Facts: The defendant approached the victim from behind and wrenched a bag from her grasp. One of the defendant's grounds of appeal against his conviction was that there was insufficient evidence of resistance to the snatching of the bag to constitute force on the person under s 8 of the Theft Act 1968 s 8.

MR JUSTICE EASTHAM

Prior to the enactment of the Theft Act 1968 there had been numerous decisions, including *R v Gnosill*, (1824) 1 C & P 304, where the law then sought to distinguish cases where force was actually directed against the person from those where it was used merely to get possession of the property. We have been reminded that the Law Commission, when making their recommendations to Parliament, indicated that in their view it was undesirable for simple bag-snatching to amount to robbery.

However, in *R v Dawson and James*, 64 Cr App Rep 170, which is a post-Act case, this Court held that in directing a jury where the charge is robbery the judge should direct his attention to the words of the statute and not refer to the old authorities, because the object of the Theft Act was to get rid of all the former technicalities of the law of larceny and to put the law in simple language which juries would understand and which they themselves would use. Whether the defendant used force on any person in order to steal is an issue that should be left to the jury. In *Dawson and James*, where the force was limited to the extent that the person was jostled and lost his balance, it was held that that amounted to force within s 8.

Section 8 (1) of the Theft Act provides:

> "A person is guilty of robbery if he steals, and immediately before or at the time of doing so, and in order to do so, he uses force on any person or puts or seeks to put any person in fear of being then and there subjected to force."

The latter part of the subsection has no application here, because the appellant approached the victim from behind and she had no knowledge of his presence until with both hands he managed to break her grasp on the bag in her left hand.

In support of the first of the two grounds of appeal we have been referred to a number of textbooks the learned authors of which would certainly like the law to be as recommended by the Law Commission to Parliament. But there is the case to which we

Alert

have already referred which in our judgment makes it quite plain that, in the view of this Court, the distinctions which formerly undoubtedly existed between force on the actual person and force on the property which in fact causes force on the person have all gone.

In our judgment the learned judge, on the evidence of the two police officers, was wholly justified and indeed right to leave the issue of robbery or not for the jury, providing that he adequately directed them on the law. Although criticism has been made of the learned judge, this was a case in which almost certainly the jury had copies of the indictment. The learned judge followed the advice given by this Court per Lawton LJ in *Dawson and James* 64 Cr App Rep 170 (supra) and repeated to the jury the precise wording of s 8 of the Theft Act. True, thereafter he did not use the expression, "on the person", and merely the word "force"; but he told them quite clearly at the outset what the statutory definition was.

The question of whether force has been used or a person has been put in fear of force is one of fact for the jury to determine.

The force must be used or threatened immediately before or at the time of stealing. There is no robbery where force is used or threatened after the theft.

R v Hale (1979) 68 Cr App R 415

Panel: Waller and Eveleigh LJJ and Tudor Evans J

Statute: Theft Act 1968 s 8(1)

Facts: The defendant and a co-accused went to the victim's house. When she answered the door they rushed in. The defendant put a hand over the victim's mouth to stop her screaming. The co-accused went upstairs and found a jewellery box. Both accused then tied up the victim and warned her not to call the police within five minutes. The defendant was convicted of robbery and appealed on the basis that the trial judge had misdirected the jury by indicating to the jury that if an accused used force in order to effect his escape with the stolen goods that would be sufficient to constitute robbery.

LORD JUSTICE EVELEIGH

In so far as the facts of the present case are concerned, counsel submitted that the theft was completed when the jewellery box was first seized and any force thereafter could not have been "immediately before or at the time of stealing" and certainly not " in order to steal." The essence of the submission was that the theft was completed as soon as the jewellery box was seized. ...

Section 8 of the Theft Act 1968 begins: "A person is guilty of robbery if he steals..." He steals when he acts in accordance with the basic definition of theft in section 1 of the Theft Act; that is to say when he dishonestly appropriates property belonging to another with the intention of permanently depriving the other of it. It thus becomes necessary to consider what is "appropriation" or, according to section 3, "any assumption by a person of the rights of an owner." An assumption of the rights of an owner describes the conduct of a person towards a particular article. It is conduct which usurps the rights of the owner. To say that the conduct is over and done with as soon as he lays hands upon the property, or when he first manifests an intention to deal with it as his, is contrary to common-sense and to the natural meaning of words. A thief who steals a motor car first opens the door. Is it to be said that the act of starting up the motor is no more a part of the theft?

In the present case there can be little doubt that if the appellant had been interrupted after the seizure of the jewellery box the jury would have been entitled to find that the appellant and his accomplice were assuming the rights of an owner at the time when the jewellery box was seized. However, the act of appropriation does not suddenly cease. It is a continuous act and it is a matter for the jury to decide whether or not the act of appropriation has finished. Moreover, it is quite clear that the intention to deprive the owner permanently, which accompanied the assumption of the owner's rights was a continuing one at all material times. This Court therefore rejects the contention that the theft had ceased by the time the lady was tied up. As a matter of common-sense the appellant was in the course of committing theft; he was stealing.

There remains the question whether there was robbery. Quite clearly the jury were at liberty to find the appellant guilty of robbery relying upon the force used when he put his hand over Mrs Carrett's mouth to restrain her from calling for help. We also think that they were also entitled to rely upon the act of tying her up provided they were satisfied (and it is difficult to see how they could not be satisfied) that the force so used was to enable them to steal. If they were still engaged in the act of stealing the force was clearly used to enable them to continue to assume the rights of the owner and permanently to deprive Mrs Carrett of her box, which is what they began to do when they first seized it.

Taking the summing-up as a whole, and in relation to the particular facts of this case, the jury could not have thought that they were entitled to convict if the force used was not at the time of the stealing and for the purpose of stealing. The learned judge said "In order to be sure that the person is guilty of robbery you have to be sure they were stealing." While the use of the words complained of would not serve as an alternative definition of robbery and could, if standing alone, be open to the criticism that the learned judge was arriving at a conclusion of fact which the jury had to decide, those words did not stand alone and this Court is satisfied that there was no misdirection. This appeal is accordingly dismissed.

Thus, appropriation may be a continuing act. The Court of Appeal held that it is for the jury to decide whether the appropriation is still continuing at the time that force is used or threatened.

Ashworth, "Robbery reassessed" [2002] Crim LR 851

The point of departure for any re-assessment of robbery must be the statutory definition of the offence, in section 8 of the Theft Act 1968:

"(1) A person is guilty of robbery if he steals and, immediately before or at the time of doing so, and in order to do so, he uses force on any person or puts or seeks to put any person in fear of being then and there subjected to force.

(2) A person guilty of robbery, or of an assault with intent to rob, shall on conviction on indictment be liable to imprisonment for life."

Several features of the offence require comment.

First, there are three ways of committing robbery–using force, putting someone in fear, or seeking to put someone in fear. This leaves no doubt about the relevance of imitation weapons to the definition of robbery; but, on the other hand, the various ways of committing the offence are not ranked in order of relative seriousness.

Secondly, and echoing a point already made in relation to statistical classification, the dividing line between robbery and theft is anything but robust. This is not necessarily a criticism of the legal definition, since many offences inevitably have fuzzy edges. But the term " uses force" has been interpreted so as to include relatively slight force, such as barging into someone or tugging at a handbag in such a way that the owner's hand is pulled downwards. The effect is to label such offences as robbery rather than theft, and to put them in a category which has life imprisonment as the maximum penalty.

And thirdly, robbery is a single offence: "robbery with violence" and armed robbery are not legal terms of art, however often they may appear in crime novels. The single offence is also extraordinarily broad. The maximum penalty for theft is seven years' imprisonment; but, where force or the threat of force is used in order to steal, the category of robbery covers everything from a push or a raised hand in order to snatch a bag, to the most violent robbery of a security vehicle with guns fired and so forth. The single maximum penalty, life imprisonment, covers the whole range. The contrast with other offences involving violence is stark. Although English law remains in a rather antiquated state, the Offences Against the Person Act 1861 provides a ladder of non-fatal crimes–common assault, assault occasioning actual bodily harm, unlawful wounding or grievous bodily harm, and wounding or grievous bodily harm with intent. The structure is desperately in need of modernisation: most modern penal codes grade their offences of violence according to differences in the seriousness of the harm done and differences in culpability, but current English law does so only imperfectly. However, no one has been heard to suggest that we should have a single offence of violence, such as "using force on another person", to replace everything from common assault to wounding with intent. That would be rejected on many grounds–sentencing would be at large rather than graduated according to different maxima, the label would fail to distinguish the serious from the not-so-serious, the label would be useless for classification purposes (e.g. when assessing an offender's criminal record), and so on.

If we (rightly) reject a single offence of violence, should we not also object to such a broad and undifferentiated offence as robbery, based on using or threatening force of any degree? I would argue that the offence of robbery is objectionable because it fails to mark in a public way the distinction between a mere push and serious violence, and because the label "robbery" is therefore too vague and too liable to stereotypical interpretations–some may assume that serious violence, or a weapon, was involved when this was not necessarily the case. It is often said that robbery is a serious offence, but that applies only to some robberies. There are some offences that involve a small theft with only slight violence that would not warrant more than a charge of assault or battery. Consideration must be given to dividing the offence, so as to mark out as particularly serious those robberies which involve the use or threat of significant violence.

Such an approach could also have a worthwhile practical and procedural consequence. At present all robberies are triable only on indictment. Again, this results in some offences being tried at a higher level than their separate elements (assault, theft) might warrant. Offences of assault occasioning actual bodily harm and section 20 wounding or grievous bodily harm are triable either way, as are offences of theft. If the essence of the offence would not otherwise justify a higher charge, it is surely questionable whether all robberies should go to the Crown Court. If some offences against the person are summary only or triable either way, why should robberies involving similar force be triable only on indictment? No doubt the prospect of dividing the offence of robbery would be unattractive to prosecutors, who would prefer the latitude of the present definition of robbery to being required to specify the degree of violence or to argue in court that the degree of force amounted to "grievous bodily harm". Of course, the existing law does not compel prosecutors to charge only robbery. Where injury has been caused, they may also charge the defendant with whatever offence they think has been committed. This rarely happens, except where a firearm is carried, when it is good practice to charge an offence under the Firearms Act 1968 as well as robbery. Beyond that, the evidence is that a very small proportion of robbery cases involve a separate charge of an offence against the person (usually, grievous bodily harm with intent). ...

The starting point should be to review the definition of the offence. Violence can be a serious matter, and the law distinguishes serious from less serious degrees. Robbery can also be serious, but the law fails to distinguish very serious from less serious degrees. The result is that the label "robbery" carries connotations that sometimes grossly misrepresent the seriousness of an offence. A radical approach would be to abolish the offence of robbery, leaving its ingredients to be charged separately. Another approach would be to divide the offence into at least two degrees, using the law of offences against the person as the basis. This would have the procedural benefit of ensuring that lesser offences become triable either way, rather than sending all offenders aged 18 and over to the Crown Court.

9.2 Blackmail

9.2.1 Actus Reus: Demand

Blackmail is created as an offence in the Theft Act 1968 s 21(1). It requires proof of an unwarranted demand made with menaces with a view to gain or intent to cause loss. The demand can be express or implied.

R v Collister (1955) 39 Cr App R 100

Panel: Hilbery, Gorman and Havers JJ

Facts: The defendants were police officers who implied that the victim would be arrested for an offence unless he met them the following evening and gave them money. The defendants were charged with demanding money by menaces under the Larceny Act 1916 s 30 (now blackmail under the Theft Act 1968 s 21(1)). They were convicted and appealed.

> MR JUSTICE HILBERY
>
> Mr Platts-Mills has argued that the learned judge left to the jury a case of demanding money by menaces when there was no demand and no menace. …
>
> There remains the point which Mr Platts-Mills has argued whether there were threats or a demand of money. He has argued strongly that there must be some actual substantive demand, either express or by an unequivocal gesture. As early as *Jackson and Randall* (1783) 1 Leach 267, the court held that an actual demand is not necessary and that it is a fact for the consideration of the jury whether in all the circumstances of the case there was a demand. … In our view, that correctly expresses precisely what the jury had to decide. It was quite clear from the account which the appellants themselves were giving that on the night before there had been, according to them, statements by Jeffries which would have led them to consider that he was importuning for homosexual purposes. It is quite clear that there would have been talk of his being in danger of arrest and criminal proceedings for such conduct, and that he was agitated, emotional and frightened by it. It is clear that there was talk of money, that a meeting had been appointed after talk about a report being prepared on the case, and that next day the meeting was attended by the two appellants, at which— if the jury accepted the story— one of them undoubtedly received money from Jeffries. … There was abundant evidence on which the jury could find, from the circumstances, that there was a demand intended and conveyed, as the judge pointed out, and it was a demand accompanied by instilling into the person to whom it was made the fear of a prosecution for importuning for an immoral purpose. In the circumstances this court is unable to do other than dismiss the appeals.

9.2.2 Actus Reus: Menaces

The term "menaces" was defined by the House of Lords in *Thorne v Motor Trade Association* [1937] AC 797.

Thorne v Motor Trade Association [1937] AC 797

Panel: Lord Atkin, Lord Thankerton, Lord Russell of Killowen, Lord Wright and Lord Roche

Facts: The claimant was a member of the Motor Trade Association (a certified trade union). The Association had a "Stop List" on which the names of those members who had infringed an Association rule were placed. However, one rule of the constitution of the Association stated that a name would not be put on the Stop List if the relevant member paid a fine within 21 days. The claimant sued the Association, claiming a declaration that this rule was illegal and an injunction. The action failed and the claimant appealed to the Court of Appeal and then to the House of Lords. The appeal was dismissed.

LORD WRIGHT

 Alert

There must be… a demand for money, which is property or a valuable thing. I think the word "menace" is to be liberally construed and not as limited to threats of violence but as including threats of any action detrimental to or unpleasant to the person addressed. It may also include a warning that in certain events such action is intended. Thus it might ordinarily include such a threat as the threat to place on the Stop List, which for a motor trader has serious consequences. The crucial question is whether there is an absence of reasonable or probable cause. I find it difficult to give a precise meaning to "probable," as distinguished from "reasonable," and I shall assume that it adds nothing beyond what is meant by "reasonable." The question then is whether there is reasonable cause for the demand. A demand to satisfy the sub-section must be not merely with menaces but with an absence of reasonable cause. Is the liberty in law, which the respondent Association possesses, to put a trader's name on the Stop List, capable in law of constituting a reasonable cause for demanding the money? I have stated the question in this form because I now feel I must observe on a peculiar difficulty in answering the questions put in the statement of claim. … The facts would in that event be before the jury, who would, as I think, in general be asked to find a verdict of guilty or not guilty. For that purpose they would have to decide, after being duly directed in law, if there was a demand in writing, if it was with menaces, if it was without reasonable or probable cause. The last direction would in my opinion need to be carefully explained. I think the jury should be directed by the judge that the respondent Association had a legal right to put the person's name on the Stop List, so long as they did so in order to promote the trade interests of the Association and its members and not with intent to injure, and so long as the money, fine or penalty demanded was reasonable and not extortionate. In other words the jury would have to answer the question … "whether there was a conspiracy to injure or only a set of acts dictated by business interests." The question of reasonable cause would have to be applied to the amount of the penalty or fine, as well as to the menace of inserting on the Stop List. If the amount demanded is beyond reason in all the circumstances, there could not be a reasonable cause for demanding that amount regarded merely from the aspect of quantum. There must be a reasonable cause for demanding the particular amount.

Thus, "menaces" is construed widely and is not limited to threats of violence, but includes threats of any action detrimental or unpleasant to the victim.

R v Clear [1968] 1 QB 670

Panel: Sellers LJ, John Stephenson and James JJ

Facts: The defendant was a driver at a transit company. He was in charge of a vehicle containing £3,000 worth of goods which was stolen. The defendant had locked the vehicle and set the alarms. However, when asked by the managing director of the transit company to give evidence to this effect, he refused to do so unless he was paid £300. The defendant was convicted of demanding money with menaces under the Larceny Act 1916 s 30 and appealed against his conviction.

LORD JUSTICE SELLERS

Turning now to the ingredients of the offence, there was no doubt a demand made by the defendant for money from Mr Chapman and the summing-up in that respect was not challenged. A demand may be implicit or explicit. The argument before the trial judge and on this appeal has been in relation to the other two vital elements in the offence, a demand with menaces and with an intent to steal the money.

It was not suggested and could not be that there was a right or justification in claiming £300 to give evidence and the jury were entitled to hold, notwithstanding that there were no express words, that the defendant was threatening either to withhold his evidence that care had been taken of the lorry and its contents or to give evidence to the contrary and that it would be detrimental to the defence of the action in which the D & C Carriers' Company as well as the insurers were interested. Mr Chapman himself may have been at no financial loss. No evidence was given of his interest in the company save as managing director. ...

It was submitted first that ... there had been a misdirection by the trial judge; that ... there was no evidence to go to the jury as Mr Chapman was not intimidated or influenced by any menaces or threats and, second, that ... what the appellant said and did was not making a demand with menaces, as no reasonable and fair-minded man in the situation in which Mr Chapman found himself would have been intimidated or influenced to hand over the money involuntarily. It was contended that although the menaces need not necessarily be of duress or of personal violence and may be of injury to person or property they should not be trivial but of some gravity. ...

In our opinion the offence under section 30 relates to the acts and the intent of the accused. The intent to steal must be derived from the whole of the circumstances. Words or conduct which would not intimidate or influence anyone to respond to the demand would not be menaces and might negative any intent to steal, but threats and conduct of such a nature and extent that the mind of an ordinary person of normal stability and courage might be influenced or made apprehensive so as to accede unwillingly to the demand would be sufficient for a jury's consideration. The demand must be accompanied both by menaces and by an intent to steal, and there is no intent to steal unless there is an intent to take without the true consent of the person to whom the demand is made. ...

There was a further submission that the summing-up did not go far enough in explaining that any threat must be such as to unsettle the mind of an ordinary person to whom the threat and demand were made so as to take away his freedom of action. These precise words perhaps were not used, but we are of opinion that the tenor of the judge's direction was to that effect.

 Alert

Thus, an objective test is applied: the threats must be such that the mind of an ordinary person of normal stability and courage might be influenced or made apprehensive so as to accede unwillingly to the demand.

Where a defendant is charged with blackmail under the Theft Act 1968 s 21(1), no explanation of the meaning of "menaces" need usually be given to the jury because it is an ordinary word. However, a special direction should be given where because of special knowledge in special circumstances what would be a menace to an ordinary person is not a menace to the person to whom it is addressed.

R v Lawrence and Pomroy (1973) 57 Cr App R 64

Panel: Cairns and Orr LJJ and Bean J

Statute: Theft Act 1968 s 21(1)

Facts: The defendants threatened to use force to enforce a debt owed by the victim. They were convicted of blackmail under the Theft Act 1968 s 21(1) and appealed.

LORD JUSTICE CAIRNS

As to the blackmail charge, the first point we deal with is the contention that the judge gave the jury no definition of what constitutes a menace. It is said that they should have been directed in accordance with *Clear* (1968) 52 Cr App R 78... that they must consider what the effect would be in the mind of a reasonable man of the words and actions of the two defendants. The word "menaces" is an ordinary English word which any jury can be expected to understand. In exceptional cases where because of special knowledge in special circumstances what would be a menace to an ordinary person is not a menace to the person to whom it is addressed, or where the converse may be true, it is no doubt necessary to spell out the meaning of the word. But, in our view, there was no such necessity here. The judge made it abundantly clear that the issue for the jury was whether the two men had gone to Thorn's house merely to ask reasonably for payment, on Pomroy's part to ask reasonably for payment and on Lawrence's part merely as a companion, or whether they had gone to threaten and frighten him into paying. That was quite a sufficient explanation of what is meant by menaces.

 Alert

"Menaces" exist where threats, which would not have affected the mind of a person of normal stability, did in fact effect the mind of the victim, provided that the accused was aware of the likely effect of his actions on the victim.

In *R v Harry* [1974] Crim LR 32 the defendant had written to a number of shopkeepers on behalf of his college Rag Committee asking each of them buy a poster in aid of charity to "protect you from any Rag Activity which could in any way cause you inconvenience." Some shopkeepers, none of whom paid, complained about the letter. The shopkeepers complaint was that he believed the letter contained a veiled threat.

The prosecution submitted that the letter contained 'the clearest threat or menace however nicely it was crouched, and that there was no need for direct evidence that anyone thought it was a threat.' Defence counsel submitted that there was no, or no *sufficient* evidence to leave to the jury. Not every threat, veiled or otherwise, was within the section but only of it satisfied the test in *Clear* [1968] 2 WLR 122 at 130 of being 'of such a nature and extent that the mind of an ordinary person of normal stability and courage might be influenced or made apprehensive so as to accede unwillingly to the demand.' There was no evidence from any victim or possible victim that the letter had that effect at all.

The trial judge, Judge Francis Petre, ruled that he was not satisfied there were any menaces within the definition in *Clear*. That case had stiffened the law as previously laid down in *Thorne v Motor Trade Association* [1937] AC 797 at 817. Normally a demand with menaces was made to one person; in this case it was made to over 100 people. To some extent one could be guided by their reaction. Exercising a broad general judgment commonsense indicated that no menaces had been proved such as fell within the Act. In directing the jury to return verdicts of not guilty on both counts, Judge Petre said, 'Menaces is a strong word. You may think that menaces must be of a fairly stern nature to fall within this definition.'

R v Garwood [1987] 1 WLR 319

Panel: Lord Lane CJ, Caulfield and McCowan JJ

Statute: Theft Act 1968 s 21(1)

Facts: The defendant accused the victim of having "done over" his house. He asked the victim if he had a television or some jewellery and told him that he wanted something "to make it quits". He then became aggressive. The victim went home and got £10 which he gave to the defendant. The defendant then demanded the victim give him £20 three days later as protection money. The defendant was charged with blackmail under the Theft Act 1968 s 21(1). The jury sent a note to the judge stating that they thought the victim was unusually timid and that the defendant would appear more menacing than he would have been to the ordinary person. They asked whether it was sufficient for "menaces" that the victim found the defendant menacing even if the reasonable man would not have. The jury convicted the defendant and he appealed on the basis that the recorder had misdirected the jury.

LORD LANE CJ

[T]he definition which the recorder had given to [the jury] of the word menaces... was:

> "The definition which I give you of the word 'menaces,' which is satisfactory for this case is as follows: that threats or conduct of such a nature and extent that the mind of an ordinary person of normal stability and courage might be influenced or made apprehensive so as to accede unwillingly to a demand upon him is menaces; that is a demand with menaces."

In answer to the jury's question the recorder gave the following further direction:

> "May I first of all remind you of the definition of menaces which I gave you for the purposes of your deliberation as follows." — He then repeated

the definition of the word menaces which he had given in the body of the summing up. — "Now, you must give that definition a very liberal and common sense interpretation because it is a fact very often that people who are influenced by menaces, who are practised upon, as lawyers say, are very often people who are not of average firmness and courage. They are the sort of people upon whom blackmailers prey; vulnerable people. So, give those words a liberal and commonsense interpretation and if at the end of the day when you have come to a conclusion as to what you are satisfied so that you are sure of as having happened, if you get to that stage, so that you have decided what the facts are, you must acquit the defendant if your decision about the facts leads you to the conclusion that nothing that was said or done to Mr Sayed was capable of influencing or making apprehensive the mind of an ordinary, normal person."

In the judgment of this court those words might have led the jury to believe that the prosecution had proved the existence of menaces even though a person of normal ability would not have been influenced by the words or actions of the accused and the accused was not aware that the victim was thus unduly susceptible to threats. To that extent we think there was a misdirection.

In our judgment it is only rarely that a judge will need to enter upon a definition of the word menaces. It is an ordinary word of which the meaning will be clear to any jury. As Cairns LJ said in *Reg. v Lawrence (Rodney)* (1971) 57 Cr App R 64 , 72:

"In exceptional cases where because of special knowledge in special circumstances what would be a menace to an ordinary person is not a menace to the person to whom it is addressed, or where the converse may be true, it is no doubt necessary to spell out the meaning of the word."

It seems to us that there are two possible occasions upon which a further direction on the meaning of the word menaces may be required. The first is where the threats might affect the mind of an ordinary person of normal stability but did not affect the person actually addressed. In such circumstances that would amount to a sufficient menace: see Reg. v Clear [1968] 1 QB 670.

Alert

The second situation is where the threats in fact affected the mind of the victim, although they would not have affected the mind of a person of normal stability. In that case, in our judgment, the existence of menaces is proved providing that the accused man was aware of the likely effect of his actions upon the victim.

Alert

If the recorder had told the jury that Sayed's undue timidity did not prevent them from finding "menaces" proved, providing that the appellant realised the effect his actions were having on Sayed, all would have been well. The issue before the jury was clear-cut. If they felt sure that Sayed's version of events was true, there were plainly menaces. If they thought that the appellant's version might be true, there were equally plainly no menaces. There was no need for the recorder to have embarked upon any definition of the word. It only served to confuse, as the jury's question showed.

However, if he had given a proper and full answer to the jury's question in the terms which we suggested earlier, the jury could have been in no doubt at all that if Sayed's version was correct — which they must have felt that it was — the appellant must have realised from the moment that the conversation started the effect which his actions and words were having upon Sayed.

This is accordingly eminently a case for the application of the proviso. The appeal against conviction is accordingly dismissed.

9.2.3 Mens Rea: Unwarranted

The courts have directed that accompanying a demand with a threat which itself amounts to a criminal offence, will never be warranted.

R v Harvey (1981) 72 Cr App R 139

Panel: Shaw LJ, Wien and Bingham JJ

Statute: Theft Act 1968 s 21(1)

Facts: The appellant had ordered £20,000 worth of cannabis from the victim. The victim actually delivered a 'load of rubbish'. The defendant in an effort to get his money back, kidnapped the victim and his family. The defendant threatened to harm the victim and his family if his money was not returned.

MR JUSTICE BINGHAM

The learned judge in his direction to the jury quoted the terms of the subsection and then continued as follows: "Now where the defence raise this issue, in other words, where they say that the demand is warranted and where they say they believe they had reasonable cause for making the demand and that the use of the menaces was a proper way of reinforcing the demand, it is for the prosecution to negative that allegation. It is not for the defendants to prove it once they have raised it. It is for the prosecution to prove that they had no such belief. Now is that clear? It is not easy and I do not want to lose you on the way. It has been raised in this case so you have got to ask yourself this. Has the prosecution disproved that these defendants or those who have raised the matter believed that they had *reasonable* grounds for making the demand? Certainly you may say to yourselves that they had been ripped off to the tune of £20,000. They had been swindled ... As I say, on this question of reasonable ground for making a demand, you may say to yourselves: 'Well, they did have reasonable ground for making the demand in this sense, that they had put money into this deal, they had been swindled by Scott, and it was reasonable to demand the return of their money.' So you may say: 'Well, the prosecution have not negatived that but what about the second leg of the proviso, the belief that the use of menaces is a proper method of reinforcing the demand?' Now it is for you to decide what, if any, menaces were made, because that is a question of evidence. If you decide that the threats or menaces made by these accused, or any of them, were to kill or to maim or to rape, or any of the other matters that have been mentioned in evidence—I mention about three that come into my mind—then those menaces or threats are threats to

Alert

commit a criminal act, a threat to murder, a threat to rape, or a threat to blow your legs or kneecaps off, those are threats to commit a criminal offence and surely everybody in this country, including the defendants, knows those are criminal offences. The point is that this is a matter of law. It cannot be a proper means of reinforcing the demand to make threats to commit serious criminal offences. So I say to you that if you look at these two counts of blackmail and you decide that these defendants, or any of them, used menaces, dependent upon the menaces you decide were used, the threats that were used, but if you decide that these threats were made by these men to commit criminal offences against Scott, they cannot be heard to say on this blackmail charge that they had reasonable belief that the use of those threats was a proper method of reinforcing their demand."

Later, when prosecuting counsel drew attention to the learned judge's erroneous reference to "reasonable" belief, he added the following: "I do not think it affects the point I was seeking to make, that where the demand or the threat is to commit a criminal offence, and a serious criminal offence like murder and maiming and rape, or whatever it may be, it seems hard for anybody to say that the defendants had a belief that was a proper way of reinforcing their demand. That is the point."

For the appellants it was submitted that the learned judge's direction, and in particular the earlier of the passages quoted, was incorrect in law because it took away from the jury a question properly falling within their province of decision, namely, what the accused in fact believed. He was wrong to rule as a matter of law that a threat to perform a serious criminal act could never be thought by the person making it to be a proper means. While free to comment on the unlikelihood of a defendant believing threats such as were made in this case to be a proper means, the judge should nonetheless (it was submitted) have left the question to the jury. For the Crown it was submitted that a threat to perform a criminal act can never as a matter of law be a proper means within the subsection, and that the learned judge's direction was accordingly correct. Support for both these approaches is to be found in academic works helpfully brought to the attention of the Court.

The answer to this problem must be found in the language of the subsection, from which in our judgment two points emerge with clarity: (1) The subsection is concerned with the belief of the individual defendant in the particular case: "... a demand with menaces is unwarranted unless the person making it does so in the belief ..." (added emphasis). It matters not what the reasonable man, or any man other than the defendant, would believe save in so far as that may throw light on what the defendant in fact believed. Thus the factual question of the defendant's belief should be left to the jury. To that extent the subsection is subjective in approach, as is generally desirable in a criminal statute. (2) In order to exonerate a defendant from liability his belief must be that the use of the menaces is a "proper" means of reinforcing the demand. "Proper" is an unusual expression to find in a criminal statute. It is not defined in the Act, and no definition need be attempted here. It is, however, plainly a word of wide meaning, certainly wider than (for example) "lawful." But the greater includes the less and no act which was not believed to be lawful could be believed to be proper within the meaning of the subsection. Thus no assistance is given to any defendant, even a fanatic or a

 Alert

deranged idealist, who knows or suspects that his threat, or the act threatened, is criminal, but believes it to be justified by his end or his peculiar circumstances. The test is not what he regards as justified, but what he believes to be proper. And where, as here, the threats were to do acts which any sane man knows to be against the laws of every civilised country no jury would hesitate long before dismissing the contention that the defendant genuinely believed the threats to be a proper means of reinforcing even a legitimate demand.

It is accordingly our conclusion that the direction of the learned judge was not strictly correct. If it was necessary to give a direction on this aspect of the case at all (and in the absence of any evidence by the defendants as to their belief we cannot think that there was in reality any live issue concerning it) the jury should have been directed that the demand with menaces was not to be regarded as unwarranted unless the Crown satisfied them in respect of each defendant that the defendant did not make the demand with menaces in the genuine belief both—(a) that he had had reasonable grounds for making the demand; and (b) that the use of the menaces was in the circumstances a proper (meaning for present purposes a lawful, and not a criminal) means of reinforcing the demand.

The learned judge could, of course, make appropriate comment on the unlikelihood of the defendants believing murder and rape or threats to commit those acts to be lawful or other than criminal.

On the facts of this case we are quite satisfied that the misdirection to which we have drawn attention could have caused no possible prejudice to any of the appellants. Accordingly, in our judgment, it is appropriate to apply the proviso to section 2(1) of the Criminal Appeal Act 1968, and the appeals are dismissed.

Further Reading

Block W 'The Logic of the Argument of Legalising Blackmail' [2001] Bracton *LJ* 61

MacKenna B 'Blackmail' [1966] *Crim LR* 467

8

Burglary

Topic List

10.1 Burglary

Burglary is made an offence in the Theft Act 1968 s 9. There are two different ways in which burglary can be committed under s 9(1)(a) and 9(1)(b), You should refer to those sections of the statute when reading this chapter.

10.1.1 Entry

The word "entry" is not defined in the Theft Act 1968. The courts have attempted to explain the meaning of "entry" in the following cases.

R v Collins [1973] QB 100

Panel: Edmund Davies and Stephenson LJJ and Boreham J

Statute: Theft Act 1968 s 9(1)

Facts: The defendant was charged with burglary under the Theft Act 1968 s 9(1)(a). He climbed up a ladder in order to enter the bedroom window of a woman whom he intended to rape (n.b. an intention to rape was sufficient for a charge under s 9(1)(a) until 2004 when the Sexual Offences Act 2003 amended the Theft Act 1968). When the defendant was on the window sill, the woman invited the defendant in and they had sex. The defendant was convicted of burglary and appealed. The issue on appeal was whether or not the defendant had entered the building as a trespasser or whether he only entered after being invited in (and thus, was not trespassing on entry).

LORD JUSTICE EDMUND DAVIES

This is about as extraordinary a case as my brethren and I have ever heard either on the bench or while at the bar.

…

Let me relate the facts. Were they put into a novel or portrayed on the stage, they would be regarded as being so improbable as to be unworthy of serious consideration and as verging at times on farce. At about 2 o'clock in the early morning of Saturday, July 24, 1971, a young lady of 18 went to bed at her mother's home in Colchester. She had spent the evening with her boyfriend. She had taken a certain amount of drink, and it may be that this fact affords some explanation of her inability to answer satisfactorily certain crucial questions put to her at the trial.

She has the habit of sleeping without wearing night apparel in a bed which is very near the lattice-type window of her room which, in accordance with her practice, was wide open.

…

At about 3.30 or 4 o'clock she awoke and she then saw in the moonlight a vague form crouched in the open window. She was unable to remember, and this is important, whether the form was on the outside of the window sill or on that part of the sill which was inside the room, and for reasons which will later become clear, that seemingly narrow point is of crucial importance.

The young lady then realised several things: first of all that the form in the window was that of a male; secondly that he was a naked male and thirdly that he was a naked male with an erect penis. She also saw in the moonlight that his hair was blond. She thereupon leapt to the conclusion that her boyfriend, with whom for some time she had been on terms of regular and frequent sexual intimacy, was paying her an ardent nocturnal visit. She promptly sat up in bed, and the man descended from the sill and joined her in bed and they had full sexual intercourse. But there was something about him which made her think that things were not as they usually were between her and her boyfriend. The length of his hair, his voice as they had exchanged what was described as "love talk," and other features led her to the conclusion that somehow there was something different. So she turned on the bed-side light, saw that her companion was not her boyfriend and slapped the face of the intruder, who was none other than the defendant. He said to her, "Give me a good time tonight," and got hold of her arm, but she bit him and told him to go. She then went into the bathroom and he promptly vanished.

The complainant said that she would not have agreed to intercourse if she had known that the person entering her room was not her boyfriend. But there was no suggestion of any force having been used upon her, and the intercourse which took place was undoubtedly effected with no resistance on her part.

The defendant was seen by the police at about 10.30 later that same morning. ... He was very lustful the previous night. He had taken a lot of drink. ...[H]e knew the complainant because he had worked around her house. On this occasion, desiring sexual intercourse - and according to the police evidence he added that he was determined to have a girl, by force if necessary, although that part of the police evidence he challenged - he went on to say that he walked around the house, saw a light in an upstairs bedroom, and he knew that this was the girl's bedroom. He found a step ladder, leaned it against the wall and climbed up and looked into the bedroom. He could see through the wide-open window a girl who was naked and asleep. So he descended the ladder and stripped off all his clothes, with the exception of his socks, because apparently he took the view that if the girl's mother entered the bedroom it would be easier to effect a rapid escape if he had his socks on than if he was in his bare feet. That is a matter about which we are not called upon to express any view, and would in any event find ourselves unable to express one.

Having undressed, he then climbed the ladder and pulled himself up on to the window sill. His version of the matter is that he was pulling himself in when she awoke. She then got up and knelt on the bed, she put her arms around his neck and body, and she seemed to pull him into the bed.

...

Now, one feature of the case which remained at the conclusion of the evidence in great obscurity is where exactly Collins was at the moment when, according to him, the girl manifested that she was welcoming him. Was he kneeling on the sill outside the window or was he already inside the room, having climbed through the window frame, and kneeling upon the inner sill? It was a crucial matter, for there were certainly three ingredients that it was incumbent upon the Crown to establish. Under section 9 of the Theft Act 1968, which renders a person guilty of burglary if he enters any building or part of a building as a trespasser and with the intention of committing rape, the entry of the accused into the building must first be proved. Well, there is no doubt about that, for it is common ground that he did enter this girl's bedroom. Secondly, it must lie proved that he entered as a trespasser. We will develop that point a little later. Thirdly, it must be proved that he entered as a trespasser with intent at the time of entry to commit rape therein.

...

We hold that, for the purposes of section 9 of the Theft Act, a person entering a building is not guilty of trespass if he enters without knowledge that he is trespassing or at least without acting recklessly as to whether or not he is unlawfully entering.

 Alert

...

[T]he pivotal point of this appeal is whether the Crown established that this defendant at the moment that he entered the bedroom knew perfectly well that he was not welcome there or, being reckless as to whether he was welcome or not, was nevertheless determined to enter. That in turn involves consideration as to where he was at the time that the complainant indicated that she was welcoming him into her bedroom.

...

[W]hat the accused had said was, "She knelt on the bed, she put her arms around me and then I went in." If the jury thought he might be truthful in that assertion, they would need to consider whether or not, although entirely surprised by such a reception being accorded to him, this young man might not have been entitled reasonably to regard her action as amounting to an invitation to him to enter. If she in fact appeared to be welcoming him, the Crown do not suggest that he should have realised or even suspected that she was so behaving because, despite the moonlight, she thought he was someone else. Unless the jury were entirely satisfied that the defendant made an effective and substantial entry into the bedroom without the complainant doing or saying anything to cause him to believe that she was consenting to his entering it, he ought not to be convicted of the offence charged. The point is a narrow one, as narrow maybe as the window sill which is crucial to this case. But this is a criminal charge of gravity and, even though one may suspect that his intention was to commit the offence charged, unless the facts show with clarity that he in fact committed it he ought not to remain convicted.

 Alert

We have to say that this appeal must be allowed on the basis that the jury were never invited to consider the vital question whether this young man did enter the premises as a trespasser, that is to say knowing perfectly well that he had no invitation to enter or reckless of whether or not his entry was with permission. ... For the reasons we have stated, the outcome of the appeal is that this young man must be acquitted of the charge preferred against him. The appeal is accordingly allowed and his conviction quashed.

Thus, the Court of Appeal held that "entry" must be "effective and substantial". However following *R v Ryan* [1996] Crim LR 320 this is no longer necessary and it suggested that we are back to the previous common law position where entry was satisfied by insertion of any part of your body, however small, into the building.

R v Ryan [1996] Crim LR 320

Panel: Hirst LJ, Judge and Steel JJ

Statute: Theft Act 1968 s 9(1)(a)

Facts: An elderly householder found the defendant stuck in a window. His head and one arm were inside the window but he was trapped and unable to move. He was charged with burglary under the Theft Act 1968 s 9(1)(a) and convicted. He appealed, arguing that he had not entered the building because he was stuck and unable to steal anything. The Court of Appeal dismissed his appeal.

COMMENTARY

Held, dismissing the appeal, that it was clear from *Brown* [1985] Crim LR 212 that for the purposes of section 9 of the 1968 Act a person could enter a building even if only part of his body was actually within the premises and it was totally irrelevant whether he was or was not capable of stealing anything because he was trapped halfway through the window.

The decision is only that there was evidence on which a jury could find that R had entered; but, if a magistrates' court had found on these facts that a defendant had not entered, the Divisional Court would surely have told the justices that they were wrong. In the light of *Brown* and the present case, it seems impossible to insist that the entry must be "effective" or "substantial" as Edmund Davies LJ suggested in *Collins* [1973] QB 100 at 106. It is in principle unsatisfactory that it should be left open to a jury to find that there was no entry in a case like the present; and it would be better to recognise that the 1968 Act leaves unaltered the rule of the common law that the insertion of any part of the body, however small, is sufficient. *Cf.* Griew, *The Theft Acts* (7th edn), page 103; JC Smith, *The Law of Theft* (7th edn), para. 11-03 and ATH. Smith, *Property Offences*, para. 28-28. [*JCS*]

 Alert

10.1.2 Building or Part of a Building

A partial definition of a "building" is provided in the Theft Act 1968 s 9(4). What constitutes a building or part of a building is a question of fact for the jury to decide. A "part of a building" was considered in *R v Walkington* [1979] 1 WLR 1169

R v Walkington [1979] 1 WLR 1169

Panel: Geoffrey Lane LJ, Swanwick and Wien JJ

Statute: Theft Act 1968 s 9(1)(a)

Facts: The defendant entered a department store and found an unattended till on a three-sided moveable counter. He went behind the counter and looked inside the till. He was charged with burglary under the Theft Act 1968 s 9(1)(a) on the basis that he entered a part of a building with an intent to steal. He was convicted and appealed against his conviction.

LORD JUSTICE GEOFFREY LANE

The basis of the defence at the Crown Court was that the defendant had not been a trespasser for the purposes of burglary. ...

The defendant at the trial gave evidence ... claiming that he had gone to the store originally as a bona fide customer. He had gone to look at the dresses on the first floor and had given way to the temptation of opening the drawer. He had no idea that he was trespassing and he had not looked at the tills on the ground floor before he went to the first floor as the store detective had said. ...

[T]he judge, as this court thinks, [explained] in clear and accurate language to the jury what it is they have to decide: first of all, so far as the store was concerned, was this area prohibited, was it off limits? Secondly, if so, did the defendant realise when he crossed the limit that that area was off limits? Thirdly, at the time when he crossed that limit, the first two questions having been decided against the defendant, did he have an intent to steal? The first ground of appeal ... was on the basis that the judge was wrong in refusing to withdraw the matter from the jury. The way it is put in the notice of appeal is:

> "It would be wrong to divide the store artificially into 'parts' in the way that
> would be necessary to make a case of burglary out of the situation presented
> by the prosecution. That being so, the defendant could not be said to have
> trespassed behind the counter and the count of burglary must fail."

As Mr Osborne put it before us this morning, what he submits is that the counter area could not have constituted a part of the building for the purposes of burglary. ...

What the prosecution had to prove here was that the defendant had entered a part of a building as a trespasser with intent to steal anything in that part of the building. Mr Osborne submitted that this could not be said to be a part of a building. It was a submission which we confess we found a little difficult to follow. But it transpired that what Mr Osborne was principally relying upon was a passage in a publication by Professor Griew entitled *The Theft Acts* 1968 *and* 1978, 3rd edn (1978). He made particular reference to paragraph 4 – 16 at page 68, which reads:

> "D has the licence that all customers have in a shop to move from counter
> to counter. He has lawfully entered the shop and bought something at
> counter one. He now moves to counter two, intending to steal at it. If in
> doing so he is entering a different 'part' of the shop, he may be guilty of
> burglary, for entry for a purpose other than that for which a licence to
> enter is granted is a trespassory entry. But it does not seem likely that the
> courts will be hasty to divide buildings artificially into 'parts' in the way
> that would be necessary to make a case of burglary out of the situation
> presented here."

With respect to Mr Osborne it seems to us that that passage is not dealing with the present situation at all. It is dealing with a situation where there is no physical demarcation at all and the only matter which may cause the man to be a trespasser is a change of intention in his own mind. This is not the situation here. Here there is a physical demarcation, and if one turns to the passage where Professor Griew is dealing with the situation which exists here, we find, at page 64:

> "A licence to enter a building may extend to part of the building only. If so, the licensee will trespass if he enters some other part not within the scope of the licence. To do so with intent to commit in that other part one of the specified offences, or to do so and then to commit or attempt to commit one of those offences therein, will be burglary."

That seems to us precisely to fit the circumstances of the present case and really deals the death blow to this part of Mr Osborne's submission.

If support is required, it is to be found in Professor Smith's publication, The Law of Theft, 3rd edn (1977), page 152, para. 329 (i), where he says:

Alert

"A customer in a shop who goes behind the counter and takes money from the till during a short absence of the shopkeeper would be guilty of burglary even though he entered the shop with the shopkeeper's permission. The permission did not extend to his going behind the counter."

Alert

There are similar passages at paragraphs 331 and 334. Paragraph 331 is the only one to which I need refer: "It would seem that the whole reason for the words 'or part of a building,' is that D may enter or be in part of a building without trespass and it is desirable that he should be liable as a burglar if he trespasses in the remainder of the building with the necessary intent. It is submitted that the building need not be physically divided into 'parts.' It ought to be sufficient if a notice in the middle of a hall stated, 'No customers beyond this point.' These considerations suggest that, for present purposes, a building falls into two parts only: first, that part in which D was lawfully present and, second, the remainder of the building. This interpretation avoids anomalies which arise if physical divisions within a building are held to create 'parts.'"

One really gets two extremes, as it seems to us. First of all you have the part of the building which is shut off by a door so far as the general public is concerned, with a notice saying "Staff Only" or "No admittance to customers." At the other end of the scale you have for example a single table in the middle of the store, which it would be difficult for any jury to find properly was a part of the building into which the licensor prohibited customers from moving.

Here, it seems to us, there was a physical demarcation. Whether it was sufficient to amount to an area from which the public were plainly excluded was a matter for the jury. It seems to us that there was ample evidence on which they could come to the conclusion (a) that the management had impliedly prohibited customers entering that area and (b) that this particular defendant knew of that prohibition. Whether the jury came to the conclusion that the prosecution made out their case was a matter for them,

Alert

but there is no dispute that the judge, in those two careful passages which I have read, left the matter fairly and correctly to the jury.

The appeal was dismissed and the conviction upheld.

10.1.3 As a Trespasser

The defendant must enter the building or part of a building as a trespasser. There can be no burglary where the defendant is not trespassing on entry.

R v Laing [1995] Crim LR 395

Panel: Lord Taylor of Gosforth CJ, Scott Baker and Longmore JJ

Statute: Theft Act 1968 s 9(1)(a)

Facts: The defendant was found in the stock area of a department store after closing time. The trial judge directed the jury that even though the defendant may have not been trespassing when he entered the building, it was for the jury to decide whether he was a trespasser when found. The defendant was convicted of burglary under the Theft Act 1968 s 9(1)(a). He appealed against conviction. The Court of Appeal allowed the appeal.

COMMENTARY

Held, allowing the appeal, (1) the court doubted that there was a case to answer. There was no evidence he was a trespasser when he entered the store and it was not suggested that he became a trespasser by moving from one part of the building to another.

(2) In any event, the judge clearly misdirected the jury. The proper question was, was the appellant a trespasser when he entered the store? It may be that a case could have been constructed by the Crown on the basis of later entry into a part of the building as a trespasser, although there would still have been difficulties on the evidence. They did not, however, and the conviction could not stand.

It is completely clear that, for burglary, whether under section 9(1)(a) or 9(1)(b) of the Act, it must be proved that the defendant entered the building or part of a building as a trespasser. It is not sufficient that, after a non-trespassory entry into a building or part of a building, he became a trespasser. [JCS]

Where the defendant is invited into the building but enters with an intention which exceeds the implied permission of his entry, he has entered as a trespasser.

R v Jones and Smith [1976] 1 WLR 672

Panel: James and Geoffrey Lane LJJ and Cobb J

Statute: Theft Act 1968 s 9(1)(b)

Facts: The defendants entered the house belonging to Smith's father. They stole two television sets. The defendants were convicted of burglary under the Theft Act 1968 s

9(1)(b) and appealed against conviction on the grounds that they were not trespassing on entry. The Court of Appeal dismissed the appeal.

LORD JUSTICE JAMES

The argument is based upon the wording of the Theft Act 1968, section 9 (1) (b) which is this:

> "(1) A person is guilty of burglary if — ...
> (b) having entered any building or part of a building as a trespasser he steals or attempts to steal anything in the building or that part of it or inflicts or attempts to inflict on any person therein any grievous bodily harm."

The important words from the point of view of the arguments in this appeal are "having entered any building ... as a trespasser." This is a section of an Act of Parliament which introduced a novel concept. Entry as a trespasser was new in 1968 in relation to criminal offences of burglary. It was introduced in substitution for, as an improvement upon, the old law which required considerations of breaking and entering and involved distinctions of nicety which had bedevilled the law for some time.

Mr Rose argues that a person who had a general permission to enter premises of another person cannot be a trespasser. His submission is as short and as simple as that. Related to this case he says that a son to whom a father has given permission generally to enter the father's house cannot be a trespasser if he enters it even though he had decided in his mind before making the entry to commit a criminal offence of theft against the father once he had got into the house and had entered that house solely for the purpose of committing that theft. It is a bold submission. Mr Rose frankly accepts that there has been no decision of the court since this statute was passed which governs this particular point. ...

We were also referred to *Reg. v Collins* [1973] Q. B. 100 and in particular to the long passage, commencing at page 104 where Edmund Davies LJ commenced the consideration of what is involved by the words "the entry must be 'as a trespasser.'" It is unnecessary to cite the passage in full; suffice it to say that this court on that occasion at page 104 expressly approved the view expressed in Professor Smith's book, *The Law of Theft*, 1st edn (1968), and also the view of Professor Griew in his publication, The Theft Act 1968, upon this aspect of what is involved in being a trespasser.

In our view the passage there referred to is consonant with the passage in the well-known case, *Hillen and Pettigrew v ICI (Alkali) Ltd.* [1936] AC 65, 69, where Lord Atkin said:

> "My Lords, in my opinion this duty to an invitee only extends so long as and so far as the invitee is making what can reasonably be contemplated as an ordinary and reasonable use of the premises by the invitee for the purposes for which he has been invited. He is not invited to use any part of the premises for purposes which he knows are wrongfully dangerous

and constitute an improper use. As Scrutton LJ has pointedly said: 'When you invite a person into your house to use the staircase you do not invite him to slide down the banisters.' "

That case, of course, was a civil case in which it was sought to make the defendant liable for a tort.

The decision in *Reg. v Collins* [1973] QB 100 in this court, a decision upon the criminal law, added to the concept of trespass as a civil wrong only the mental element of mens rea, which is essential to the criminal offence. Taking the law as expressed in *Hillen and Pettigrew v ICI (Alkali) Ltd.* and in *Reg. v Collins* it is our view that a person is a trespasser for the purpose of section 9(1)(b) of the Theft Act 1968 if he enters premises of another knowing that he is entering in excess of the permission that has been given to him, or being reckless as to whether he is entering in excess of the permission that has been given to him to enter. Provided the facts are known to the accused which enable him to realise that he is acting in excess of the permission given or that he is acting recklessly as to whether he exceeds that permission, then that is sufficient for the jury to decide that he is in fact a trespasser.

 Alert

In this particular case it was a matter for the jury to consider whether, on all the facts, it was shown by the prosecution that the defendants, entered with the knowledge that entry was being effected against the consent or in excess of the consent that had been given by Mr Smith senior to his son, the defendant Smith. The jury were, by their verdict satisfied of that. It was a novel argument that we heard, interesting but one without, in our view, any foundation.

Thus, the defendants were guilty because they had entered the house in excess of the authority granted to them.

10.1.4 Mens Rea

R v Collins held that the defendant must know or be reckless to the fact that he is a trespasser.

For s 9(1)(a) burglary the defendant must enter the building with the intention to commit one of the ulterior offences contained within s 9(2)

In respect of s 9(1)(b) once inside the building as a trespasser the defendant must commit or attempt to commit the offence of stealing or inflicting grievous bodily harm.

10.1.5 Theft

This requires an analysis of the Theft Act 1968 s 1. (See Chapter 8.)

10.1.6 Grievous Bodily Harm

In *R v Jenkins* [1983] 1 All ER 1000 it was determined that grievous bodily harm in the Theft Act 1968 did not require an assault. The judgment of the Court of Appeal is extracted below. While the decision was ultimately overruled on appeal (see [1984] AC 242) this aspect of the judgment was not.

R v Jenkins [1983] 1 All ER 1000

Panel: Purchas LJ, Talbot and Staughton JJ

Statute: Theft Act 1968 s 9(1)(b)

Facts: The victim was attempting to visit his estranged wife who was now living with one of the defendants. A serious altercation followed causing the victim to drive away in a hurry. He was followed by the defendants to his home address where they forced entry into the victims house and serious assaulted him. During the course of the defendants appeal against their convictions, the Court of Appeal considered the meaning of the wording contained within s 9(1)(b) of the Theft Act 1968.

LORD JUSTICE PURCHAS

In the instant appeal two specific questions arise. (1) Is the meaning of the phrase 'inflict … grievous bodily harm' in s 9(1)*(b)*, and presumably s 9(2), the same as its meaning in s 20 of the Offences against the Person Act 1861? (2) Does the expression 'inflict grievous bodily harm' necessarily involve an assault by the accused on the victim?

If the judgments of the majority of the judges in *R v Clarence* (1988) 22 QBD, [1886-90] All ER Rep 133 are correct, as was accepted by the Court of Appeal, Criminal Division in *R v Snewing* [1972] Crim LR 267 and *R v Carpenter* (30 July 1979, unreported), to give a proper interpretation of s 9(1)(b) of the Theft Act 1968 the answer to the first question may have to be in the negative; but if the judgments of the minority, including Wills J in *R v Clarence*, are right, the meaning of the expression in the two Acts will be the same.

The intention of Parliament in enacting s 9 of the Theft Act 1968, as appears from a consideration of the section as a whole within the context of s 1 (ordinary theft) with a maximum term of imprisonment of 10 years, s 9 (burglary) with a maximum sentence of 14 years, and s 10 (aggravated burglary) and s 8 (robbery), both offences carrying a maximum sentence of imprisonment for life, would indicate that, where a person enters a building as a trespasser, either with an intent to commit any of a number of specified offences, or, having entered as a trespasser, steals or attempts to steal (itself an offence, but one of lesser gravity), then that person should be liable to the greater penalty provided by s 9. Where he inflicts or attempts to inflict on any person grievous bodily harm then this of itself, in conjunction with the trespass which is the essential ingredient of an offence under s 9 would, if committed unlawfully and maliciously, be of itself an offence under s 20 of the Offences against the Person Act 1861. If, however, it is committed by a trespasser in a dwelling, then again under s 9 of the 1968 Act the extra penalty is incurred.

It seems unlikely that in this context Parliament intended to restrict the expression 'inflict grievous bodily harm' to the narrow area of assault. To test this proposition it may be helpful to consider a set of circumstance that could not be described as fanciful. An intruder gains access to the house without breaking in (where there is an open window, for instance). He is on the premises as a trespasser, and his intrusion is observed by

 Alert

someone in the house of whom he may not even be aware, and as a result that person suffers severe shock, with a resulting stroke. In such a case it is difficult to see how an assault could be alleged; but nevertheless his presence would have been a direct cause of the stroke, which must amount to grievous bodily harm. Should such an event fall outside the provisions of s 9, when causing some damage to the property falls fairly within it? We cite this as merely one example. For other examples, all of which would be relevant, we refer to the judgments in cases where the meaning of the words 'inflict grievous bodily harm' are considered in relation to s 20 of the 1861 Act.

10.2 Aggravated Burglary

In order to be guilty of aggravated burglary under s 10, the prosecution must prove that the defendant had with him at the time of the burglary a firearm, imitation firearm, weapon of offence or explosive.

R v Stones [1989] 1 WLR 156

Panel: Glidewell LJ, Owen and Ian Kennedy JJ

Statute: Theft Act 1968 s 10(1)(b)

Facts: The defendant was seen running away from a house which had just been burgled. He was in possession of a knife which he claimed was for self-defence. He was convicted of aggravated burglary under the Theft Act 1968 and appealed against his conviction.

LORD JUSTICE GLIDEWELL

Mr Lowe, who appeared for the appellant, submitted that the prosecution had to prove first, that at the time of committing the burglary the defendant had a weapon with him; secondly, that he knew he had it; and thirdly, that he intended to use it to cause injury to or incapacitate a person in the course of a burglary if it became necessary.

...

The prosecution accepted that they had to prove that it was intended by the person having it with him (the defendant) for such use.

...

As I have said, the defence submission was that it had to be proved that it was intended to use it to cause injury to or incapacitate a person in the course of the burglary if it became necessary. The prosecution submission to the contrary was that if the jury were sure that the defendant intended to use the knife to cause injury to or incapacitate any person, that was sufficient. Thus his answer to the police, saying that he in effect intended to use it in self-defence, if necessary, on the lads from Blyth, was evidence of such an intention.

I have referred to "if it became necessary" because counsel for the appellant conceded that if the jury found that the appellant hoped not to use the knife during the course of the burglary, but intended to do so if necessary, for instance if he were challenged by the householder, that would constitute the necessary intent.

...

It is agreed by counsel that the prosecution must prove that the appellant knew that he had a knife with him at the relevant time. Clearly that is right, because otherwise he cannot have the relevant intent. As I have said, the prosecution submit that if he knowingly had the knife with him at the time of the burglary with the intention of using it to cause injury to or incapacitate the lads from Blyth if he met them, the offence is proved. It is not necessary to prove the intention to use the knife to cause injury etc. during the course of the burglary.

In our view that submission is correct. The mischief at which the section is clearly aimed is that if a burglar has a weapon which he intends to use to injure some person unconnected with the premises burgled, he may nevertheless be tempted to use it if challenged during the course of the burglary and put under sufficient pressure.

...

On a correct interpretation of the section there clearly was evidence, which the jury equally clearly accepted, of intention to use the knife to injure or incapacitate some person, i.e. one or other of the lads from Blyth if he thought it was necessary to use the knife in self-defence.

...

The appeal was dismissed and the conviction upheld.

R v Kelly (1993) 97 Cr App R 245

Panel: Lord Taylor of Gosforth CJ, Potts and Judge JJ

Statute: Theft Act 1968 s 10(1)(b)

Facts: The defendant used a screwdriver to break into a house. He was disturbed by two occupants. He was arrested leaving the house, carrying a video recorder and the screwdriver. The prosecution charged him with aggravated burglary on the basis that he jabbed the screwdriver at one of the occupants. The defendant denied this. He was convicted of aggravated burglary and appealed on the ground that it was necessary to prove that he had the screwdriver with him with intent to cause injury before the incident with the occupants occurred.

MR JUSTICE POTTS

[T]he charge derives from section 9(1)(b) of the Act and the time at which the appellant must be proved to have had with him a weapon of offence to make him guilty of aggravated burglary was the time he actually stole. The screwdriver would become a weapon of offence on proof that the appellant intended to use it for causing injury to, or incapacitating Mr Sheterline or Ms Matthews at the time of the theft, thereby aggravating the burglary: section 10(1)(b). This construction follows from the clear language of section 10 of the Theft Act , and is consistent with its purpose.

...

The Court of Appeal dismissed the appeal and held that the relevant time for consideration of the appellant's intent to use the weapon for causing injury was the time he actually stole the goods. It had been proved that the defendant has used the screwdriver at the time of the theft with the requisite intent to injure if the need arose.

R v O'Leary (1986) 82 Cr App R 341

Panel: Lord Lane CJ, Leggatt and Simon Brown JJ

Statute: Theft Act 1968 s 10(1)(b)

Facts: The defendant broke into a house unarmed. He picked up a knife in the kitchen and went upstairs, where he was disturbed by the occupants. After a struggle, the occupants and the defendant were all injured and the defendant demanded items such as jewellery and money. He was ultimately charged with aggravated burglary. He initially pleaded not guilty, but changed his plea to guilty after the trial judge dismissed a submission that he could not be guilty of aggravated burglary because he did not have the knife with him at the time of entry. He appealed on the basis that the trial had been wrong to reject the submission.

LORD LANE CJ

Counsel for the appellant submitted to the judge that in those circumstances, where the appellant at the time of entering the house, probably aiming to steal, was not equipped with a knife, he could not be guilty of aggravated burglary under section 10(1) of the Theft Act 1968. That submission was rejected by the learned Judge. ...

In order to get this point out of the way, the appellant having pleaded guilty to this offence, quite plainly any question whether or not the knife was intended by him for use as a weapon of offence can be disposed of: he has admitted that it was.

So we come to the question of whether this man, on the facts as indicated, was guilty of aggravated burglary.

There are, as already indicated in section 9(1)(a) and (b) two means by which the prosecution can make out a charge of burglary: first of all by proving that the defendant entered as a trespasser with intent to steal, and secondly, by proving that the defendant having entered as a trespasser, actually stole. In order to discover whether aggravated burglary had been committed or not, it is necessary to determine which of those two limbs is the one which applies in the instant case. ...

If he had been charged under subsection (1)(a), the offence of burglary would be completed and committed when he entered and it would be at that point that one would have to consider whether or not he was armed. But in the case of subsection (1)(b), which is the one under which he was charged, the offence is complete when, and not until, the stealing is committed, provided again of course that he has trespassed in the first place. The prosecution did not have to prove an intent to steal at the time of entry as the charge is laid here. Indeed such an intent is irrelevant to the charge as laid.

 Alert

Alert

It follows that under this particular charge, the time at which the defendant must be proved to have had with him a weapon of offence to make him guilty of aggravated burglary was the time at which he actually stole. As already indicated, at that moment, when he confronted the householders and demanded their cash and jewellery, which was the theft, he still had the kitchen knife in his hand. No one alleged that he entered with the intent to steal, and that would not have been, had this matter proceeded to trial before a jury, a matter for the jury to consider at all. Indeed such evidence would, strictly speaking, be inadmissible and irrelevant.

The judge ruled, as this Court has indicated he should have ruled, namely that the material time in this charge for the possession of the weapon was the time when he confronted the householders and stole.

We have had our attention referred to passages in two textbooks: Professor JC Smith on the Law of Theft, 5th edn, paragraph 366 at page 380 which, insofar as it goes, bears out the ruling which we have just made, and also Professor Griew, *The Theft Act* 1968 – 1978 4th edn paragraph 4 – 36, at page 85, a passage which was written before the decision of this Court in the case of Francis (unreported, save in the Crim LR, dated February 19, 1982). Insofar as Professor Griew's conclusions do not accord with the views that we have expressed, Professor Griew, if we may respectfully say so, is wrong.

In short the learned judge was correct in the ruling that he gave in this case, and this appeal consequently is dismissed.

The appeal was dismissed. Thus, the relevant time at which the defendant must be proved to have the weapon of offence under s 9(1)(b) is the time of the theft, attempted theft or GBH or attempted GBH.

Further Reading

Herring J 'Burglary and Blackmail: Theory', *Criminal Law Text, Cases and Materials* (2008)

Pace P 'Burglarious Trespass', *Crim LR* 716

9

Criminal Damage

Topic List

12.1 Destroy or Damage

There is no definition of what constitutes 'damage' in the Criminal Damage Act 1971. However, this was decided in *Samuels v Stubbs* [1972] 4 SASR 200 soon after the Act came into force, where the court held that a reduction in the value of property and/or its usefulness, was likely to mean that damage had been caused. The case of *Hardman v Chief Constable of Avon* [1986] *Crim LR* 220 also suggested that if expenditure were incurred to restore the property to the condition before the defendant's act, then damage was likely to have been caused.

Hardman v Chief Constable of Avon [1986] Crim LR 330

Panel: A Judge and two Magistrates

Facts: The defendants, who were members of the Campaign for Nuclear Disarmament, painted white figures on the pavement to draw attention to their cause. The paint was soluble in water and would eventually have been washed away by rain. Before this had happened, the local authority employed a "Graffiti Squad" using high pressure hoses to clean the pavement. The defendants were convicted in the magistrates' court and appealed against conviction.

Held: Notwithstanding the fact that the markings could be washed away there had nonetheless been damage, which had caused expense and inconvenience to the Local Authority. An unduly narrow definition of damage was not appropriate. The approach of Walters J. in *Samuels v Stubbs*, 4 SASR 200 was approved when he said at page 203

> "It seems to me that it is difficult to lay down any very general and, at the same time, precise and absolute rule as to what constitutes "damage". One must be guided in a great degree by the circumstances of each case, the nature of the article, and the mode in which it is affected or treated. Moreover, the meaning of the word "damage" must as I have already said, be controlled by its context. The word may be used in the sense of "mischief done to property."

Morphis v Salmon (1990) 154 JP 365, below, is another which shows that it is necessary to look at the context in which the damage is alleged, to consider the type of property and also what was done to it. Hence, scratches to a scaffolding bar would not constitute damage, because such a bar has no ascetic value, while scratches to another item might well be damage.

This case also reaffirmed that an item of property could be damaged by removing its parts, even though there is no damage to each individual part.

Morphitis v Salmon (1990) 154 JP 365

Panel: Lloyd LJ and Auld J

Facts: The respondent had erected a barrier across a road leading to premises shared by himself and the appellant. The barrier consisted of an upright and a scaffold bar, joined to the upright by a clip. The appellant had removed the bar and clip. The bar had been scratched. The appellant was convicted in a magistrates' court of criminal damage to the bar and clip. The Divisional Court of the Queen's Bench overturned the conviction.

MR JUSTICE AULD

The essential question in this case is whether the scaffold clip and scaffold bar, although not physically damaged as individual objects, were nevertheless damaged within the meaning of s 1(1) of the Criminal Damage Act 1971 if, by their separation from the other part making up the barrier, their use as part of that barrier was impaired. The question is not whether the barrier as a whole was damaged by the removal of the scaffold clip and the scaffold bar, for that is not what was charged.

The authorities to which we have been referred in the very helpful skeleton argument produced on behalf of the appellant show that what constitutes damage for the purpose of this provision is not always clear. Undoubtedly, as Cantley, J observed, giving the judgment of the Court of Appeal in the unreported case of *R v Henderson and Batley* on November 29, 1984, whether damage is done in any particular case is a question of fact and degree and it can be of various kinds. That pragmatic approach was cited with approval by Stephen Brown, LJ, giving the leading judgment in this court, in *Cox v Riley* (1986) 83 Cr App R 54.

The authorities show that the term "damage" for the purpose of this provision, should be widely interpreted so as to include not only permanent or temporary physical harm, but also permanent or temporary impairment of value or usefulness.

 Alert

He then noted that no conclusion had been reached in the magistrates' court as to whether the appellant had caused the scratches on the bar.

Even if the scratches had been capable of being attributed to the appellant, it is apparent from the case stated and the findings of the magistrates, that there was no evidence before them upon which they could have found that it constituted damage in the sense of impairment of value or usefulness on what were, after all, scaffolding components. The scratching of a scaffolding bar is an ordinary incident of its existence and it is unlikely that the magistrates, if they had considered the matter, would have been entitled to find that it constituted damage in the sense that I have described.

The main question for this court is whether the dismantling of the barrier constituted damage to the bar and to the clip in the wide sense of impairment in their value or usefulness as part of the barrier.

Many of the reported cases concern allegations of criminal damage to an article by reason only of the removal of some part of it although no physical damage was caused to the article in question or to the part removed. In such case, where the owner is left, albeit temporarily, with an incomplete article which does not fully serve the purpose that it did before the removal of the part, there has clearly been damage to the article as a whole. Thus, in *R v Tacey* (1821) Russ & Ry 452, there was held to be damage to a stocking frame where a part was removed from it rendering it inoperative. In *R v*

Fisher (1865) 29 JP 804; (1865) LR 1 CCR 7, the mere tampering with a machine so that it would not work was held to be damaged although no part of it was removed or broken. And in *Getty v Antrim County Council* (1950) NIR 114, the dismantling of a plough without damage to any of the dismantled parts, was held to be damage to the plough.

A more up-to-date example of criminal damage is *Cox v Riley* (1986) 83 Cr App R 54. In that case, the Court of Appeal upheld a conviction where the appellant had deliberately erased a computer programme from a plastic circuit card of a computerized sort so as to render it inoperable.

However, the matter is different, as in this case, if the charge is one of criminal damage to the part removed from some other object and not to the larger object itself and where there is no physical damage to the part removed. See e.g. *R v Woodcock* [1977] Crim LR 104 and 161.

In para 7 of the case stated, the magistrates were clearly of the view that the dismantling and removal by the appellant of the scaffold bar and clip from the upright, which together had formed a barrier, impaired the use to which they had been put by the respondent. Therefore, they had been damaged.

In my view, the magistrates, in deciding the matter on the basis of the use to which the scaffold clip and the scaffold bar had been put before removal from the upright, were in effect relying on the impairment of use of, that is to say, damage to, the barrier as a whole. But that was not what had been charged. If the charge had been framed so as to allege criminal damage to the barrier, then, on the authorities, their reasoning could not have been faulted.

12.1.1 Mens Rea

The mens rea for criminal damage is intention or recklessness as to damaging property. From 1982 – 2003 the test for recklessness was that given in the case of *R v Caldwell* [1982] AC 341. That cause caused much debate in the academic literature and was eventually overturned in the case below.

R v G and Another [2003] UKHL 50, [2004] 1 AC 1034

Panel: Lord Bingham of Cornhill, Lord Browne-Wilkinson, Lord Steyn, Lord Hutton and Lord Rodger of Earlsferry

Facts: The appellants were boys of 11 and 12 years old who had been camping out for the night. In the early hours of the morning they went to a yard behind a supermarket and set some piles of newspapers alight. They thought the papers would burn out on the concrete floor and left the yard whilst the papers were still burning. The fire spread to the shop and did £1 million pounds worth of damage. The boys were convicted of arson under the Criminal Damage Act using the test for recklessness for criminal damage, which at the time was that from *R v Caldwell*. The House of Lords overturned their conviction, giving a new test for recklessness.

LORD BINGHAM OF CORNHILL

41 For the reasons I have given I would allow this appeal and quash the appellants' convictions. I would answer the certified question obliquely, basing myself on clause 18(c) of the Criminal Code Bill annexed by the Law Commission to its Report on Criminal Law: A Criminal Code for England and Wales and Draft Criminal Code Bill, vol 1 (*Law Com* No 177, April 1989):

"A person acts recklessly within the meaning of section 1 of the Criminal Damage Act 1971 with respect to—(i) a circumstance when he is aware of a risk that it exists or will exist; (ii) a result when he is aware of a risk that it will occur; and it is, in the circumstances known to him, unreasonable to take the risk."

The defendant must intend or be reckless not only as to the destruction or damage of the property, but also to the fact that the property belongs to another.

R v Smith (David) [1974] QB 354

Panel: Roskill and James LJJ and Talbot J

Facts: The appellant was the tenant of a flat which he shared with his brother. The appellant, with his landlord's permission, installed wiring for his music system, together with some roofing, wall panels and floor boards. The roofing, wall panels and floor boards became fixtures and fittings and part of the house. They therefore belonged to the landlord. When the appellant gave notice to quit, he asked if his brother could continue as the tenant. The landlord refused. The appellant then damaged the roofing, wall panels and floorboards he had installed. He said this was to remove the wiring. He believed all this property was his, as he had installed it in the house. He was convicted and appealed to the Court of Appeal.

LORD JUSTICE JAMES

Construing the language of section 1 (1) we have no doubt that the actus reus is "destroying or damaging any property belonging to another." It is not possible to exclude the words "belonging to another" which describes the "property." Applying the ordinary principles of mens rea, the intention and recklessness and the absence of lawful excuse required to constitute the offence have reference to property belonging to another. It follows that in our judgment no offence is committed under this section if a person destroys or causes damage to property belonging to another if he does so in the honest though mistaken belief that the property is his own, and provided that the belief is honestly held it is irrelevant to consider whether or not it is a justifiable belief.

It should be noted that the appellant's mistake which prevented him from committing the crime was a mistake of civil law. A mistake as to the criminal law, such as not knowing it was a crime to damage another's property, would not have helped him.

12.2 Lawful Excuse

The general criminal law defences, such as duress and self defence, apply to criminal damage offences, but the Act provides two further defences in s 5(2). It can be seen from s 5(3) that these defences are subjective. It is clear that they were intended to apply in cases where the defendant has made an unreasonable mistake.

12.2.1 Consent: s 5(2)(a)

The defence in s 5(2)(a) has been held to apply where the defendant's unreasonable mistake arose from self-induced intoxication despite the fact that criminal damage is a basic intent crime.

Jaggard v Dickinson [1981] QB 527

Panel: Donaldson LJ and Mustill J

Facts: Mrs Jaggard had been given permission to use a friend's house 'as if it were her own'. One evening, while in a state of self-induced intoxication, she asked a taxi to deliver her to this house. The taxi dropped her off at another house, which was of identical appearance. Mrs Jaggard was confronted by the owner, but believing it to be the house she had permission to enter, broke two window panes and damaged a net curtain. She was convicted of criminal damage on the basis that criminal damage was a basic intent crime to which self induced intoxication was no defence. She appealed to the Divisional Court of The Queen's Bench.

MR JUSTICE MUSTILL

Whilst this is an attractive submission [the prosecution had argued that 'drunkenness does not negative mens rea in crimes of basic intent, it cannot be relied upon as part of a defence based on section 5(2)'], we consider it to be unsound, for the following reasons. Firstly, the argument transfers the distinction between offences of specific and of basic intent to a context in which it has no place. The distinction is material where the accused relies upon his own drunkenness as a ground for denying that he had the degree of intention or recklessness required in order to constitute the offence. Here, by contrast, the defendant does not rely upon her drunkenness to displace an inference of intent or recklessness; indeed she does not rely upon it at all. Her defence is founded on the state of belief called for by section 5 (2). True, the fact of the defendant's intoxication was relevant to the defence under section 5 (2), for it helped to explain what would otherwise have been inexplicable, and hence lent colour to her evidence about the state of her belief. This is not the same as using drunkenness to rebut an inference of intention or recklessness. Belief, like intention or recklessness, is a state of mind: but they are not the same states of mind.

Can it nevertheless be said that, even if the context is different, the principles established by *Reg. v Majewski* [1977] A.C. 443 ought to be applied to this new situation? If the basis of the decision in *Reg. v Majewski* had been that drunkenness does not prevent a person from having an intent or being reckless, then there would be grounds for saying that it should equally be left out of account when deciding on his state of belief. But this is not in our view what *Reg. v Majewski* decided. The House of Lords did not conclude that intoxication was irrelevant to the fact of the accused's state of mind, but rather that, whatever might have been his actual state of mind, he should for reasons of policy be precluded from relying on any alteration in that state brought about by self-induced intoxication. The same considerations of policy apply to the intent or recklessness which is the mens rea of the offence created by section 1 (1), and that offence is accordingly regarded as one of basic intent: *Reg. v Stephenson* [1979] QB 695. It is indeed essential that this should be so, for drink so often plays a part in offences of criminal damage; and to admit drunkenness as a potential means of escaping liability would provide much too ready a means of avoiding conviction. But these considerations do not apply to a case where Parliament has specifically required the court to consider the accused's actual state of belief, not the state of belief which ought to have existed. It seems to us that the court is required by section 5 (3) to focus on the existence of the belief, not its intellectual soundness; and a belief can be just as much honestly held if it is induced by intoxication, as if it stems from stupidity, forgetfulness or inattention. It was, however, urged that we could not properly read section 5 (2) in isolation from section 1 (1), which forms the context of the words, "without lawful excuse," partially defined by section 5 (2). Once the words are put in context, so it is maintained, it can be seen that the law must treat drunkenness in the same way in relation to lawful excuse (and hence belief) as it does to intention and recklessness: for they are all part of the mens rea of the offence. To fragment the mens rea, so as to treat one part of it as affected by drunkenness in one way, and the remainder as affected in a different way, would make the law impossibly complicated to enforce.

If it had been necessary to decide whether, for all purposes, the mens rea of an offence under section 1 (1) extends as far as an intent (or recklessness) as to the existence of a lawful excuse, I should have wished to consider the observations of James LJ delivering the judgment of the Court of Appeal in *Reg. v Smith (David)* [1974] QB 354, 360. I do not however find it necessary to reach a conclusion on this matter, and will only say that I am not at present convinced that, when these observations are read in the context of the judgment as a whole, they have the meaning which the prosecutor has sought to put upon them. In my view, however, the answer to the argument lies in the fact that any distinction which has to be drawn as to the effect of drunkenness arises from the scheme of the Act of 1971 itself. No doubt the mens rea is in general indivisible, with no distinction being possible as regards the effect of drunkenness. But Parliament has specifically isolated one subjective element, in the shape of honest belief, and has given it separate treatment, and its own special gloss in section 5 (3). This being so, there is nothing objectionable in giving it special treatment as regards drunkenness, in accordance with the natural meaning of the words.

In these circumstances, I would hold that the justices were in error when they decided that the defence furnished to the defendant by section 5 (2) was lost because the defendant was drunk at the time. I would therefore allow the appeal.

The motive of the defendant in damaging the property, or the owner in consenting to that damage is irrelevant.

R v Denton [1981] 1 WLR 1446

Panel: Lord Lane CJ, Mustill and McCullough JJ

Facts: Denton set fire to machinery in the cotton mill where he worked. He gave evidence that he had done this because his employer had asked him to put the machines out of action. The company was in financial difficulties and Denton claimed the employer had said "There is nothing like a good fire for improving the financial circumstances of a business." Denton claimed that he had the defence in s 5(2)(a) as he believed that he acted with the consent of the owner. The trial judge ruled that "entitled" in section s 5(2)(a) carried a connotation of general lawfulness and that the owner could not be said to have been entitled to consent to damage for a fraudulent purpose, i.e. insurance fraud.

LORD LANE CJ

It was agreed on all hands for the purpose of this case that T [the owner of the cotton mill] was the person who, any evil motives apart, was entitled to consent to the damage. It was likewise conceded that the appellant Denton honestly believed that T occupied that position and was entitled to consent.

It is plain from the way that the judge put the matter in his certificate, that he had come to the conclusion that the word "entitled" was in some way qualified by a word which does not appear in the section, namely "honestly". It is upon that basis that Mr Fawcus for the Crown here seeks to support the judge's direction.

In order perhaps to see what the scheme of the Criminal Damage Act 1971 entails, it is necessary to have regard to the earlier Act, namely the Malicious Damage Act 1861. Under that Act certainly by section 3, and also by two other sections (ss 13 and 59), a man's right to do what he likes to his own property was restricted, and it was, amongst other things, an offence to set fire to certain buildings, if there was an intent to injure or defraud, even if those buildings were in the possession of the defendant. It is very striking to observe that the words "with intent to injure or defraud" are absent in the terms of the 1971 Act which I have just read. It is quite apparent from that, indeed in this Court it is not argued to the contrary, that in so far as the 1971 Act is concerned, it is not an offence for a man to damage or injure or destroy or set fire to his own premises.

One therefore turns to see what the situation would have been had T made a confession in the same, or similar, terms to that made by Denton, and to see what would have happened on the Crown's argument if the two of them, T and Denton, stood charged under section 1 (1) of the 1971 Act at the Crown Court at Wigan. It is not an offence for a man to set light to his own property. So T would have been acquitted. But if the Crown is correct, Denton, the man who had been charged with the task of actually putting the match to the polystyrene, and setting the fire alight, would have been convicted.

Alert

Quite apart from any other consideration, that is such an anomalous result that it cannot possibly be right. The answer is this, that one has to decide whether or not an offence is committed at the moment that the acts are alleged to be committed. The fact that somebody may have had a dishonest intent which in the end he was going to carry out, namely to claim from the insurance company, cannot turn what was not originally a crime into a crime. There is no unlawfulness under the 1971 Act in burning a house. It does not become unlawful because there may be an inchoate attempt to commit fraud contained in it; that is to say it does not become a crime under this Act, whatever may be the situation outside of the Act.

However, the courts have put a limit to the subjectivity of the defence.

Blake v DPP [1993] Crim LR 586

Panel: Otton J

Facts: The appellant, a vicar, had written a biblical quotation in marker pen on a pillar by the Houses of Parliament. He was protesting against the Iraq war to liberate Kuwait in 1991. He claimed that he was carrying out the instructions of God, and that he had a lawful excuse under s 5(2)(a), in that he believed God to be the person entitled to consent to the damage of the property. He was convicted and appealed to the Divisional Court of The Queen's Bench.

Divine command as a defence. There would be obvious difficulties in accepting a defence that the accused was acting in pursuance of a divine command. However sincere the belief of the accused and the court repeatedly acknowledged the complete sincerity of the present appellant it is impossible to produce any evidence other than the accused's own belief that the command was in fact given. Religious beliefs vary greatly and may run counter to the policy of the law. If the defence were accepted in a case like the present, how could it be distinguished in principle from that where a person killed in pursuance of a fatwah which he believed to emanate from God? It is not practicable to distinguish between one religion and another and, as recent events in Waco, Texas, remind us, some religious cults believe in divine requirements which are repulsive to the great majority of people and contrary to the policy of the law. Stephen J. had no doubts about the matter, remarking (History of the Criminal Law, II, 160, n.1) with uncharacteristic frivolity, "My own opinion is that if a special divine order were given to a man to commit murder, I should certainly hang him for it, unless I got a special divine order not to hang him."

A belief that God is entitled to consent. As for the belief that God was the person entitled to consent to the damage to the property, one answer might be that "person" in the Act must mean a human being or a corporate body; but that would not avail if a defendant said that he believed that the person was God's vicar on earth, a prophet, who spoke with the authority of God. "Entitled" might reasonably be read as meaning "entitled by the law of England," but even that would not defeat the claim to a defence of one who believes the law of God to be part of the law of England. He might, after all, rely on no less an authority than Blackstone (Commentaries on the Laws of England, Introduction):

"This law of nature being coeval with mankind and dictated by God himself, is of course superior in obligation to any other. It is binding all over the globe in all countries and at all times; no human laws are of any validity, if contrary to this."

This is not the law, but that is not the point. If Blackstone could believe it, why not the defendant?

12.2.2 Protection of Property: s 5(2)(b)

The courts, presumably for policy reasons, have introduced an objective element into the defence in s 5(2)(b). It has been decided that whether the property was damaged 'in order to protect property' is to be judged objectively.

R v Hunt (1978) 66 Cr App R 105

Panel: Roskill LJ, Wien and Slynn JJ

Facts: Hunt's wife was the deputy warden of a block of old people's flats. The fire alarm and emergency alarm did not work and the council had done nothing to repair it. Hunt set fire to a bed in an isolated part of the block and telephoned the fire brigade. He claimed he had done so to draw attention to the defective alarm system. The trial judge withdrew the defence in s 5(2)(b) from the jury and Hunt was convicted. He appealed on the grounds that this defence should have been left to the jury.

LORD JUSTICE ROSKILL

Mr Marshall-Andrews' submission can be put thus: If this man honestly believed that that which he did was necessary in order to protect this property from the risk of fire and damage to the old people's home by reason of the absence of a working fire alarm, he was entitled to set fire to that bed and so to claim the statutory defence accorded by section 5 (2).

I have said we will assume in his favour that he possessed the requisite honest belief. But in our view the question whether he was entitled to the benefit of the defence turns upon the meaning of the words "in order to protect property belonging to another." It was argued that those words were subjective in concept, just like the words in the latter part of section 5 (2) (b) which are subjective.

We do not think that is right. The question whether or not a particular act of destruction or damage or threat of destruction or damage was done or made in order to protect property belonging to another must be, on the true construction of the statute, an objective test. Therefore we have to ask ourselves whether, whatever the state of this man's mind and assuming an honest belief, that which he admittedly did was done in order to protect this particular property, namely the old people's home in Hertfordshire?

 Alert

If one formulates the question in that way, in the view of each member of this Court, for the reason Slynn J. gave during the argument, it admits of only one answer: this was not done in order to protect property; it was done in order to draw attention to the defective state of the fire alarm. It was not an act which in itself did protect or was capable of protecting property. The learned trial judge, during the argument, mentioned quite correctly, that one, though not necessarily the only, purpose of this subsection was to make provision whereby a person, in order to protect his own property, might destroy or damage the property of another without being guilty of criminal damage. There are cases of which it is easy to think of examples, in which a person, in order to protect his property in actual or imminent danger of damage, will take steps, maybe drastic steps, legitimately protecting either his property or the property of another. It is that kind of protective action to which this particular subsection is directed though we do not suggest that that is exhaustive. But the subsection, on its proper construction, cannot possibly extend to the situation which arose in this present case.

During the argument after the adjournment Slynn J. gave an example of the position which might arise were the argument for the appellant to succeed. Let it be supposed that the roof of some famous cathedral or building, like Westminster Abbey, was in danger due to a defective beam suffering from dry rot; let it be supposed that the authorities are doing nothing to repair it; let it be supposed that some person, acting in good faith, is horrified at this lack of attention. In order to draw attention to what he regards as a dangerous position, he goes and sets fire to a hassock. Is that seriously to be said not to be an offence of criminal damage because it is done to draw attention to the defective beam on the roof of the Abbey? Mr Marshall-Andrews says that the section would, on those facts, provide a defence. We think that the question has only to be asked to be answered in the negative.

In those circumstances the learned judge was absolutely right in his decision and for the reasons which he gave. As Slynn J. pointed out, even if, contrary to our view, the test were subjective, the appellant did not set fire to the bed in order to protect property: he merely did that act in order to draw attention to what was in his view an immediate need for protection by repairing the alarm.

Whether an objective or subjective test should be employed to discover Hunt's purpose in acting, the court appears to have only considered the most immediate result of Hunt's damage; that is the fire. It didn't consider the further consequences of the damage, one of which would probably be the repair of the fire alarm.

It is difficult to see how Slynn J's analogy with the defective beam in Westminster Abbey is applicable. While the fire that Hunt started drew attention to the fact that the fire alarm did not work, how would setting fire to the hassock draw attention to the dry rot in the beam?

The Court of Appeal has reaffirmed in *R v Ashford* [1988] Crim LR 682 and *R v Hill and Hall* (1988) 89 Cr App R 74 that whether the defendant acted in order to protect property is to be judged objectively. In both these cases the defendants were convicted of possessing articles with intend to damage property belonging to another, specifically perimeter fences surrounding military bases.

It has been coherently argued that a person's purpose in acting can only be judged subjectively.

Professor Sir John Smith: Criminal Damage: lawful excuse – objective test [1988] Crim LR 682

Though the Court expresses its agreement with the reasoning in *Hunt*, it is submitted that that reasoning is indefensible. As was pointed out in the commentary on *Hunt*, [1977] Crim LR 741, the question whether the defendant acted "in order to protect property belonging to another" can be answered only by determining the purpose with which the defendant acted. If D shoots a dog which is harassing P's sheep, the question whether he did so in order to protect property cannot be answered simply by observing what he did. D might have shot the dog in order to protect the sheep. Alternatively, he might have shot it purely out of malice against its owner, or because he hates dogs, in either case not caring a rap about the sheep. If, as the citation in the present case of the headnote to *Hunt* suggests, the test is the purely objective one of whether the act which was done was one which did protect or was capable of protecting property, the killer of the dog would have been acting "in order to protect property" even if he was acting out of malice or hatred of dogs or the dog's owner, even, indeed, if he was intending to go on and shoot a few sheep as well, which is absurd. Surely the court did not intend that. Of course it is necessary to look into the defendant's mind in order to decide whether he acted "in order" to produce a particular consequence, i.e. it is necessary to apply a subjective, not an objective, test. This can be avoided only by a gross distortion of the words of the statute, reading it as if the words, "in order to," read, "by an act likely to." The commentary on *Hunt*, referred to above, and the discussion of that case in Smith & Hogan, Criminal Law, (6th edn) 690 are probably too charitable.

The courts may be influenced by fear that the wide terms of section 5(2), if applied in their natural and proper sense, will lead to acquittals in cases of such a kind that the public interest requires conviction. The subsection is certainly excessively subjective insofar as it allows a defence where the defendant believes, justifiably or not, that the means adopted by him "in order to" protect property are reasonable. This departs from the general principle of the criminal law that standards are set by the law, i.e. in effect, the jury or magistrates, not by each person for himself. But this is not a good reason for giving a statute a meaning which it cannot reasonably bear, making a mockery of the often-proclaimed principle that statutes are to be construed strictly in favour of the defendant. Moreover, such a fear would appear to be entirely groundless in a case such as the present. The defendants had a defence only if they believed that the property they claimed to be defending was "in immediate need of protection." Would any sensible jury accept that the defendants believed, or (if the onus of proof was on the prosecution see *Jaggard v Dickinson* [1981] QB 527 and cf. s 101 of the Magistrates' Court Act 1980) may have believed, that there was an immediate need to cut the fence in order to protect property? Could the defendants really have said to any effect that they believed that damage to property by the nuclear missiles was imminent? Or that, if it was, cutting the wire would have had any effect in preventing it?

To conclude, for the defence in s 5(2)(b) to apply three things which must be established: (i) the damage or destruction of the property must be objectively capable of protecting property belonging to the defendant or another, (ii) the defendant must believe that the property was in immediate need of protection (a subjective test) and (iii) the defendant must believe that the means of protection were reasonable in the circumstances (a subjective test).

12.3 Aggravated Criminal Damage

Aggravated criminal damage is defined in s 1(2).

12.3.1 Mens Rea

For the aggravated form of the criminal damage offence to be committed there is no need for life to actually be endangered. It forms a part of the mens rea only. It has been held that the intention or recklessness as to endangering life must be from the damage intended or foreseen, rather than the damage actually caused.

R v Dudley [1989] Crim LR 57

Facts: Dudley had a grievance against the J family. He consumed drink and drugs and threw a fire bomb at their house. The fire was extinguished by the J family and only trivial damage was caused. D's counsel claimed that it must be proved that he intended to endanger life or had been reckless as to whether life was endangered by the actual damaged caused and that as the damage caused was not great, he could not have been reckless as to endangering life. The Court of Appeal disagreed.

Held, the appeal would be dismissed. The words "destruction or damage" in section 1(2)(b) of the Act (endangering life) referred back to the destruction or damage intended, or as to which there was recklessness, in section 1(2)(a) (damaging property). The words did not refer to the destruction or damage actually caused; if they did, injustice would be done in the converse case where someone was reckless only as to trivial damage but by some mishap caused danger to life. *R v Steer* [1988] A.C. 111 was distinguishable because the House of Lords in that case was considering a different question, viz. whether the danger to life had to be caused by the destruction or damage to property or by the act of the defendant (in firing a rifle at a window); and in that case the actual damage and the intended damage coincided. In the present case the judge's ruling was correct and D. changed his plea, no doubt after advice, on the basis of his state of mind.

Professor Sir John Smith Criminal Damage - Intending by the Destruction or Damage to Endanger Life [1989] *Crim LR 57*

For an offence under section 1(2), property must be destroyed or damaged; but the destruction and damage which occurs in fact may be quite different from that envisaged by the defendant when he did the act causing it and, indeed, the property destroyed or damaged may be different. Where there is such a difference, it is obvious that it is to the destruction or damage which the defendant envisaged that we must have regard in determining whether he was "intending by the destruction or damage to endanger the life of another or being reckless whether the life of another would be thereby endangered," as section 1(2)(b) has it. The question is as to the defendant's state of mind when he did the act and we cannot, at that point, know for certain what, if any, destruction or damage will be caused. The offence is not committed unless the act results in some destruction of, or some damage to, some property. That is a condition of liability; but whether the terms of section 1(2)(b), above, are satisfied has been predetermined though, of course, the nature of the destruction or damage actually caused will frequently be very good evidence of the defendant's intention to endanger life or his recklessness whether life be endangered.

It must be intended that, or a risk must be foreseen of, life being endangered by damaged property, rather than the means of damaging the property.

R v Steer [1988] AC 111

Panel: Lord Bridge of Harwich, Lord Griffiths, Lord Ackner, Lord Oliver of Aylmerton and Lord Goff of Chieveley

Facts: Steer had a grudge against his business partner, Mr Gregory. He went to Mr Gregory's bungalow in the middle of the night, armed with a .22 automatic rifle and rang the door bell. Mr and Mrs Gregory looked out of their bedroom window. Steer then fired a shot at the bedroom window, a shot at another window and one at the front door. He did not aim at the Gregorys. He was convicted under the Criminal Damage Act 1971 s 1(2). The conviction was overturned by the Court of Appeal. An appeal by the Crown to the House of Lords was dismissed.

LORD BRIDGE OF HARWICH

It is to be observed that the offence created by subsection (2), save that it may be committed by destroying or damaging one's own property, is simply an aggravated form of the offence created by subsection (1), in which the prosecution must prove, in addition to the ingredients of the offence under subsection (1), the further mental element specified by subsection (2)(b). In this case presumably count 2 was intended to relate to the damage done by the shot fired at the bedroom window and count 3 to the damage done by one or other or both of the other two shots. It is also significant to note the maximum penalties attaching to the three offences charged. For an offence under section 16 of the Act of 1968 it is 14 years' imprisonment, for an offence under section 1(2) of the Act of 1971 life imprisonment, for an offence under section 1(1) of the Act of 1971 10 years' imprisonment.

At some stage in the trial the particulars of count 2 were amended by deleting the words alleging an intent to endanger life and leaving only recklessness in that regard as the mental element relied on to establish the offence under section 1(2). The prosecution, it appears, presented the case on the footing that counts 1 and 2 were alternatives and, if the case had been left to the jury, the judge would presumably have directed them that, if they found that the respondent intended to endanger the lives of Mr and Mrs Gregory they should convict on count 1, but if they found that he was merely reckless with regard to such danger, they should acquit on count 1 and convict on count 2.

At the conclusion of the case for the prosecution, however, counsel for the respondent submitted that there was no case to answer on count 2 on the ground that, in so far as the lives of Mr and Mrs Gregory had been endangered, the danger had not been caused by the damage done to the bungalow, but by the shot fired from the respondent's rifle. Of course, it is obvious that any danger to life in this case was caused by the shot from the rifle itself, not by any trifling damage done to the bedroom window or to any property in the bedroom. But the judge rejected counsel's submission and accepted the submission made for the Crown that the phrase in section 1(2)(b) of the Act of 1971 "by the destruction or damage" refers on its true construction not only to the destruction or damage to property as the cause of the danger to life on which the mental element in the aggravated offence under the subsection depends, but also to the act of the defendant which causes that destruction or damage. On the basis of the judge's ruling the respondent changed his plea to guilty on count 2. He appealed against conviction on the ground that the judge's ruling was erroneous. The Court of Appeal (Criminal Division) (Neill LJ, Peter Pain and Gatehouse JJ.) allowed the appeal, but certified that their decision involved a question of law of general public importance in the following terms:

 Alert

> "Whether, upon a true construction of section 1(2)(b) of the Criminal Damage Act 1971, the prosecution are required to prove that the danger to life resulted from the destruction of or damage to the property, or whether it is sufficient for the prosecution to prove that it resulted from the act of the defendant which caused the destruction or damage."

The Crown now appeals by leave of your Lordships' House.

We must, of course, approach the matter on the footing, implicit in the outcome of the trial, that the respondent, in firing at the bedroom window, had no intent to endanger life, but accepts that he was reckless as to whether life would be endangered.

Under both limbs of section 1 of the Act of 1971 it is the essence of the offence which the section creates that the defendant has destroyed or damaged property. For the purpose of analysis it may be convenient to omit reference to destruction and to concentrate on the references to damage, which was all that was here involved. To be guilty under subsection (1) the defendant must have intended or been reckless as to the damage to property which he caused. To be guilty under subsection (2) he must additionally have intended to endanger life or been reckless as to whether life would be endangered "by the damage" to property which he caused. This is the context in which the words must be construed and it seems to me impossible to read the words "by the damage" as meaning "by the damage or by the act which caused the damage." Moreover, if the language of the statute has the meaning for which the Crown contends, the words "by the destruction or damage" and "thereby" in subsection (2)(b) are mere surplusage. If the Crown's submission is right, the only additional element necessary to convert a subsection (1) offence into a subsection (2) offence is an intent to endanger life or recklessness as to whether life would be endangered simpliciter.

It would suffice as a ground for dismissing this appeal if the statute were ambiguous, since any such ambiguity in a criminal statute should be resolved in favour of the defence. But I can find no ambiguity. It seems to me that the meaning for which the respondent contends is the only meaning which the language can bear.

The contrary construction leads to anomalies which Parliament cannot have intended. If A and B both discharge firearms in a public place, being reckless as to whether life would be endangered, it would be absurd that A, who incidentally causes some trifling damage to property, should be guilty of an offence punishable with life imprisonment, but that B, who causes no damage, should be guilty of no offence. In the same circumstances, if A is merely reckless but B actually intends to endanger life, it is scarcely less absurd that A should be guilty of the graver offence under section 1(2) of the Act of 1971, B of the lesser offence under section 16 of the Firearms Act 1968.

Counsel for the Crown did not shrink from arguing that section 1(2) of the Act of 1971 had created, in effect, a general offence of endangering life with intent or recklessly, however the danger was caused, but had incidentally included as a necessary, albeit insignificant, ingredient of the offence that some damage to property should also be caused. In certain fields of legislation it is sometimes difficult to appreciate the rationale of particular provisions, but in a criminal statute it would need the clearest language to persuade me that the legislature had acted so irrationally, indeed perversely, as acceptance of this argument would imply.

It was further argued that to affirm the construction of section 1(2)(b) adopted by the Court of Appeal would give rise to problems in other cases in which it might be difficult or even impossible to distinguish between the act causing damage to property and the ensuing damage caused as the source of danger to life. In particular it was suggested that in arson cases the jury would have to be directed that they could only convict if the danger to life arose from falling beams or similar damage caused by the fire, not if the danger arose from the heat, flames or smoke generated by the fire itself. Arson is, of course, the prime example of a form of criminal damage to property which, in the case of an occupied building, necessarily involves serious danger to life and where the gravity of the consequence which may result as well from recklessness as from a specific intent fully justifies the severity of the penalty which the Act of 1971 provides for the offence. But the argument in this case is misconceived. It is not the match and the inflammable materials, the flaming firebrand or any other inflammatory agent which the arsonist uses to start the fire which causes danger to life, it is the ensuing conflagration which occurs as the property which has been set on fire is damaged or destroyed. When the victim in the bedroom is overcome by the smoke or incinerated by the flames as the building burns, it would be absurd to say that this does not result from the damage to the building.

Further Reading

Elliott D 'Endangering Life by Destroying or Damaging Property' [1997] *Crim LR* 382

Watson M 'Graffiti – Popular Art Anti Social Behaviour or Criminal Damage:' (200X4) 168 JP 668

Williams G 'Two Nocturnal Blunders' (1990) 140 *NLJ* 1564

10

Defences I:
Intoxication and Consent

Topic List

13.1 Intoxication

Although intoxication is not a defence per se, evidence of intoxication may negate the mens rea for an offence. Where a defendant was so intoxicated that he did not form the mens rea of an offence, he will not be convicted of that offence (although he may be convicted of a lesser offence). Where a defendant forms the necessary mens rea of an offence despite being intoxicated, he may not use evidence of his intoxication to negate that mens rea.

R v Kingston [1995] 2 AC 355

Panel: Lord Keith of Kinkel, Lord Goff of Chieveley, Lord Browne-Wilkinson, Lord Mustill and Lord Slynn of Hadley

Facts: The defendant, who had paedophiliac tendencies, was charged with indecent assault on a 15-year old boy. He claimed that he had been set up by a business partner, with whom he had had a dispute, in order that the business partner might blackmail the defendant. His defence was that he had been drugged by a co-defendant who had then lured him back to his flat and photographed and taped him in a compromising situation with the 15-year old boy. The prosecution alleged that both the defendant and the co-defendant had indecently assaulted the boy. The co-defendant pleaded guilty. The defendant argued that had he not been drugged, he would not have acted as he did. The trial judge directed the jury that a drugged intent is still an intent and the defendant was convicted. He appealed and the Court of Appeal quashed his conviction on the grounds that the intention to assault the boy arose out of circumstances for which the defendant was not responsible and that he would not have formed such an intent had he not been surreptitiously drugged. The Crown appealed.

LORD MUSTILL

... [T]he general nature of the case is clear enough. In ordinary circumstances the respondent's paedophiliac tendencies would have been kept under control, even in the presence of the sleeping or unconscious boy on the bed. The ingestion of the drug (whatever it was) brought about a temporary change in the mentality or personality of the respondent which lowered his ability to resist temptation so far that his desires overrode his ability to control them. Thus we are concerned here with a case of disinhibition. The drug is not alleged to have created the desire to which the respondent gave way, but rather to have enabled it to be released. ...

On these facts there are three grounds on which the respondent might be held free from criminal responsibility. First, that his immunity flows from general principles of the criminal law. Secondly, that this immunity is already established by a solid line of authority. Finally, that the court should, when faced with a new problem acknowledge the justice of the case and boldly create a new common law defence.

It is clear from the passage already quoted that the Court of Appeal adopted the first approach. The decision was explicitly founded on general principle. There can be no doubt what principle the court relied upon, for at the outset the court [1994] QB 81, 87, recorded the submission of counsel for the respondent:

> "the law recognises that, exceptionally, an accused person may be entitled to be acquitted if there is a possibility that although his act was intentional, the intent itself arose out of circumstances for which he bears no blame."

The same proposition is implicit in the assumption by the court that if blame is absent the necessary mens rea must also be absent.

My Lords, with every respect I must suggest that no such principle exists or, until the present case, had ever in modern times been thought to exist. Each offence consists of a prohibited act or omission coupled with whatever state of mind is called for by the statute or rule of the common law which creates the offence. In those offences which are not absolute the state of mind which the prosecution must prove to have underlain the act or omission - the "mental element" - will in the majority of cases be such as to attract disapproval. The mental element will then be the mark of what may properly be called a "guilty mind." The professional burglar is guilty in a moral as well as a legal sense; he intends to break into the house to steal, and most would confidently assert that this is wrong. But this will not always be so. In respect of some offences the mind of the defendant, and still less his moral judgment, may not be engaged at all. In others, although a mental activity must be the motive power for the prohibited act or omission the activity may be of such a kind or degree that society at large would not criticise the defendant's conduct severely or even criticise it at all. Such cases are not uncommon. Yet to assume that contemporary moral judgments affect the criminality of the act, as distinct from the punishment appropriate to the crime once proved, is to be misled by the expression "mens rea," the ambiguity of which has been the subject of complaint for more than a century. Certainly, the "mens" of the defendant must usually be involved in the offence; but the epithet "rea" refers to the criminality of the act in which the mind is engaged, not to its moral character. ...

Alert

I would therefore reject that part of the respondent's argument which treats the absence of moral fault on the part of the appellant as sufficient in itself to negative the necessary mental element of the offence.

... His second ground is more narrow, namely that involuntary intoxication is already recognised as a defence by authority which the House ought to follow. ...

Alert

My Lords, I cannot find... any sufficient grounds for holding that the defence relied upon is already established by the common law, any more than it can be derived from general principles. Accordingly I agree with the analysis of Professor Griew, Archbold News, 28 May 1993, pages 4-5:

> "What has happened is that the Court of Appeal has recognised a new *defence* to criminal charges in the nature of an exculpatory excuse. It is precisely because the defendant acted in the prohibited way with the

intent (the mens rea) required by the definition of the offence that he needs this defence."

There is thus a crucial difference between the issue raised by the second line of argument and that now under scrutiny. As to the former, the Law Commission aptly said, in Consultation Paper No. 127 (1993) on Intoxication and Criminal Liability, pages 4-5, para. 1.12:

"The person who commits criminal acts while he is intoxicated, at least when he is voluntarily so intoxicated, does not therefore appeal to excuse; but rather raises the prior question of whether, because of his intoxicated state, he can be proved to have been in the (subjective) state of mind necessary for liability. Issues of intoxication are, thus, intimately bound up with the prosecution's task of proving the primary guilt of the defendant: that he did indeed do the act prohibited by the definition of the offence with the relevant state of mind."

By contrast, the excuse of involuntary intoxication, if it exists, is superimposed on the ordinary law of intent.

To recognise a new defence of this type would be a bold step. ...I suspect that the recognition of a new general defence at common law has not happened in modern times. Nevertheless, the criminal law must not stand still, and if it is both practical and just to take this step, and if judicial decision rather than legislation is the proper medium, then the courts should not be deterred simply by the novelty of it. ...

My Lords,... the defence appears to run into difficulties at every turn. In point of theory, it would be necessary to reconcile a defence of irresistible impulse derived from a combination of innate drives and external disinhibition with the rule that irresistible impulse of a solely internal origin (not necessarily any more the fault of the offender) does not in itself excuse although it may be a symptom of a disease of the mind... . Equally, the state of mind which founds the defence superficially resembles a state of diminished responsibility, whereas the effect in law is quite different. It may well be that the resemblance is misleading, but these and similar problems must be solved before the bounds of a new defence can be set.

On the practical side there are serious problems. Before the jury could form an opinion on whether the drug might have turned the scale witnesses would have to give a picture of the defendant's personality and susceptibilities, for without it the crucial effect of the drug could not be assessed; pharmacologists would be required to describe the potentially disinhibiting effect of a range of drugs whose identity would, if the present case is anything to go by, be unknown; psychologists and psychiatrists would express opinions, not on the matters of psychopathology familiar to those working within the framework of the Mental Health Acts but on altogether more elusive concepts. No doubt as time passed those concerned could work out techniques to deal with these questions. Much more significant would be the opportunities for a spurious defence. Even in the field of road traffic the "spiked" drink as a special reason for not disqualifying from driving is a regular feature. Transferring this to the entire range of criminal offences is a disturbing prospect. The defendant would only have to assert, and support by the evidence of well-wishers, that he was not the sort of person to have done this kind of thing, and to suggest an occasion when by some means a drug might have been administered to him for the jury to be sent straight to the question of a possible disinhibition. The judge would direct the jurors that if they felt any legitimate doubt on the matter - and by its nature the defence would be one which the prosecution would often have no means to rebut - they must acquit outright, all questions of intent, mental capacity and the like being at this stage irrelevant.

My Lords, the fact that a new doctrine may require adjustment of existing principles to accommodate it, and may require those involved in criminal trials to learn new techniques, is not of course a ground for refusing to adopt it, if that is what the interests of justice require. Here, however, justice makes no such demands, for the interplay between the wrong done to the victim, the individual characteristics and frailties of the defendant, and the pharmacological effects of whatever drug may be potentially involved can be far better recognised by a tailored choice from the continuum of sentences available to the judge than by the application of a single yea-or-nay jury decision. To this, there is one exception. The mandatory life sentence for murder, at least as present administered, leaves no room for the trial judge to put into practice an informed and sympathetic assessment of the kind just described. It is for this reason alone that I have felt any hesitation about rejecting the argument for the respondent. In the end however I have concluded that this is not a sufficient reason to force on the theory and practice of the criminal law an exception which would otherwise be unjustified. For many years mandatory sentences have impelled juries to return merciful but false verdicts, and have stimulated the creation of partial defences such as provocation and diminished responsibility whose lack of a proper foundation has made them hard to apply in practice. I do not think it right that the law should be further distorted simply because of this anomalous relic of the history of the criminal law.

Thus, the appeal was allowed. The House of Lords held that where a defendant forms the necessary intention despite being intoxicated, then his drugged (or drunken) intent is sufficient mens rea for the offence charged. This confirmed the view in the earlier case of *R v Sheehan and Moore* [1975] 1 WLR 739 that "a drunken intent is nevertheless an intent". However, where, due to involuntary intoxication, the defendant does not form the *mens rea* of an offence, evidence of his intoxication will be relevant in negating the *mens rea* of the offence. The courts have distinguished between dangerous drugs and non-dangerous drugs. Thus, where a drug is commonly known to be dangerous and likely to cause the taker to become aggressive or do unpredictable things, the drug is treated in the same way as alcohol is. Where the drug is not commonly known to have such an effect, it is a non-dangerous drug and different rules apply (see *R v Hardie* [1985] 1 WLR 64 below).

R v Hardie [1985] 1 WLR 64

Panel: Parker LJ, McCowan and Stuart-Smith JJ

Statute: Criminal Damage Act 1971 s 1(2),(3)

Facts: The defendant was charged with arson, contrary to s 1(2) and (3) of the Criminal Damage Act 1971 after he started a fire at his girlfriend's flat. His relationship with his girlfriend had broken down and she had previously asked him to leave the flat. On the day in question, the defendant packed a suitcase to leave. He took a Valium tablet to calm his nerves. As it appeared to have no effect on him, the defendant took more tablets. The tablets belonged to his girlfriend, who told him that the tablets would do him no harm. The defendant later started a fire in the wardrobe in the bedroom and was charged with arson on the basis that he had intended to damage property belonging to his girlfriend or had been reckless as to whether such property would be damaged and that he intended by the same damage to endanger the life of another or was reckless as to whether that life would be thereby endangered. The trial judge directed the jury that evidence of the defendant's intoxication was no defence because he voluntarily took the drug, thus it could not negate the *mens rea* of a basic intent offence (applying *DPP v Majewski* [1977] AC 443). The defendant was convicted and appealed to the Court of Appeal.

LORD JUSTICE PARKER

...It is clear from *Reg. v Caldwell* [1982] AC 341 that self-induced intoxication can be a defence where the charge is only one of specific intention. It is equally clear that it cannot be a defence where, as here, the charge included recklessness. Hence, if there was self-intoxication in this case the judge's direction was correct. The problem is whether, assuming that the effect of the Valium was to deprive the appellant of any appreciation of what he was doing it should properly be regarded as self-induced intoxication and thus no answer.

...There can be no doubt that the same rule applies both to self-intoxication by alcohol and intoxication by hallucinatory drugs, but this is because the effects of both are well-known and there is therefore an element of recklessness in the self-administration of the drug. ...

"Intoxication" or similar symptoms may, however, arise in other circumstances. ...

In the present instance the defence was that the Valium was taken for the purpose of calming the nerves only, that it was old stock and that the appellant was told it would do him no harm. There was no evidence that it was known to the appellant or even generally known that the taking of Valium in the quantity would be liable to render a person aggressive or incapable of appreciating risks to others or have other side effects such that its self-administration would itself have an element of recklessness. It is true that Valium is a drug and it is true that it was taken deliberately and not taken on medical prescription, but the drug is, in our view, wholly different in kind from drugs which are liable to cause unpredictability or aggressiveness. It may well be that the taking of a sedative or soporific drug will, in certain circumstances, be no answer, for example in a case of reckless driving, but if the effect of a drug is merely soporific or sedative the taking of it, even in some excessive quantity, cannot in the ordinary way raise a conclusive presumption against the admission of proof of intoxication for the purpose of disproving mens rea in ordinary crimes, such as would be the case with

 Alert

alcoholic intoxication or incapacity or automatism resulting from the self-administration of dangerous drugs.

In the present case the jury should not, in our judgment, have been directed to disregard any incapacity which resulted or might have resulted from the taking of Valium. They should have been directed that if they came to the conclusion that, as a result of the Valium, the appellant was, at the time, unable to appreciate the risks of (sic) property and persons from his actions they should then consider whether the taking of the Valium was itself reckless. We are unable to say what would have been the appropriate direction with regard to the elements of recklessness in this case for we have not seen all the relevant evidence, nor are we able to suggest a model direction, for circumstances will vary infinitely and model directions can sometimes lead to more rather than less confusion. It is sufficient to say that the direction that the effects of Valium were necessarily irrelevant was wrong.

 Alert

The Court of Appeal allowed the appeal on the basis that the defendant had not been reckless in his self-administration of the Valium. The commonly understood effect of Valium was that it was a sedative and there was no evidence that the defendant knew that the drug would have any other effect on him.

The leading authority on voluntary intoxication is *DPP v Majewski* [1977] AC 443. In this case, the House of Lords confirmed that voluntary intoxication could only be a defence to crimes of "specific intent", provided that the defendant did not form the necessary intention. Voluntary intoxication would never provide a defence to offences of "basic intent".

DPP v Majewski [1977] AC 443

Panel: Lord Elwyn-Jones LC, Lord Diplock, Lord Simon of Glaisdale, Lord Kilbrandon, Lord Salmon, Lord Edmund-Davies and Lord Russell of Killowen

Statutes: Criminal Justice Act 1967 s 8, Offences Against the Person Act 1861 s 47

Facts: The defendant was involved in a fight at a pub in which he attacked the landlord. He was charged with three counts of assault occasioning actual bodily harm, contrary to s 47 of the Offences Against the Person Act 1861, amongst other offences. He argued that he had committed the offences while intoxicated. The trial judge directed the jury that the defendant's voluntary intoxication could not be a defence to the offences because no specific intent was required. The defendant was convicted and appealed. The Court of Appeal dismissed the appeal and the defendant appealed to the House of Lords.

LORD ELWYN-JONES LC

...If a man consciously and deliberately takes alcohol and drugs not on medical prescription, but in order to escape from reality, to go "on a trip," to become hallucinated, whatever the description may be and thereby disables himself from taking the care he might otherwise take and as a result by his subsequent actions causes injury to another – does our criminal law enable him to say that because he did not know what he was doing he lacked both intention and recklessness and accordingly is entitled to an acquittal?

Originally the common law would not and did not recognise self-induced intoxication as an excuse. Lawton LJ spoke of the "merciful relaxation" to that rule which was introduced by the judges during the 19th century, and he added, at page 411:

> "Although there was much reforming zeal and activity in the 19th century, Parliament never once considered whether self-induced intoxication should be a defence generally to a criminal charge. It would have been a strange result if the merciful relaxation of a strict rule of law had ended, without any Parliamentary intervention, by whittling it away to such an extent that the more drunk a man became, provided he stopped short of making himself insane, the better chance he had of an acquittal.... The common law rule still applied but there were exceptions to it which Lord Birkenhead LC tried to define by reference to specific intent."

There are, however, decisions of eminent judges in a number of Commonwealth cases in Australia and New Zealand, (but generally not in Canada nor in the United States) as well as impressive academic comment in this country, to which we have been referred, supporting the view that it is illogical and inconsistent with legal principle to treat a person who of his own choice and volition has taken drugs and drink, even though he thereby creates a state in which he is not conscious of what he is doing, any differently from a person suffering from the various medical conditions like epilepsy or diabetic coma and who is regarded by the law as free from fault. However our courts have for a very long time regarded in quite another light the state of self-induced intoxication. The authority which for the last half century has been relied upon in this context has been the speech of the Earl of Birkenhead LC in *Director of Public Prosecutions v Beard* [1920] AC 479, who stated, at page 494:

"Under the law of England as it prevailed until early in the 19th century voluntary drunkenness was never an excuse for criminal misconduct; and indeed the classic authorities broadly assert that voluntary drunkenness must be considered rather an aggravation than a defence. This view was in terms based upon the principle that a man who by his own voluntary act debauches and destroys his will power shall be no better situated in regard to criminal acts than a sober man."

Lord Birkenhead LC made a historical survey of the way the common law from the 16th century on dealt with the effect of self-induced intoxication upon criminal responsibility. This indicates how, from 1819 on, the judges began to mitigate the severity of the attitude of the common law in such cases as murder and serious violent crime when the penalties of death or transportation applied or where there was likely to be sympathy for the accused, as in attempted suicide. Lord Birkenhead LC concluded, at page 499, that (except in cases where insanity is pleaded) the decisions he cited

"establish that where a specific intent is an essential element in the offence, evidence of a state of drunkenness rendering the accused incapable of forming such an intent should be taken into consideration in order to determine whether he had in fact formed the intent necessary to constitute the particular crime. If he was so drunk that he was incapable of forming the intent required he could not be convicted of a crime which was committed only if the intent was proved.... In a charge of murder based upon intention to kill or to do grievous bodily harm, if the jury are satisfied that the accused was, by reason of his drunken condition, incapable of forming the intent to kill or to do grievous bodily harm... he cannot be convicted of murder. But nevertheless unlawful homicide has been committed by the accused, and consequently he is guilty of unlawful homicide without malice aforethought, and that is manslaughter: *per* Stephen J. in *Reg. v Doherty* (1887)16 Cox CC 306 , 307."

He concludes the passage:

"...the law is plain beyond all question that in cases falling short of insanity a condition of drunkenness at the time of committing an offence causing death can only, when it is available at all, have the effect of reducing the crime from murder to manslaughter."

From this it seemed clear - and this is the interpretation which the judges have placed upon the decision during the ensuing half century - that it is only in the limited class of cases requiring proof of specific intent that drunkenness can exculpate. Otherwise in no case can it exempt completely from criminal liability. ...

The seal of approval is clearly set on the passage at page 499 of the *Beard* decision. In no case has the general principle of English law as described by Lord Denning in *Gallagher's case* [1963] AC 349 and exposed again in *Bratty's case* [1963] AC 386 been overruled in this House and the question now to be determined is whether it should be.

I do not for my part regard that general principle as either unethical or contrary to the principles of natural justice. If a man of his own volition takes a substance which causes him to cast off the restraints of reason and conscience, no wrong is done to him by holding him answerable criminally for any injury he may do while in that condition. His course of conduct in reducing himself by drugs and drink to that condition in my view supplies the evidence of mens rea, of guilty mind certainly sufficient for crimes of basic intent. It is a reckless course of conduct and recklessness is enough to constitute the necessary mens rea in assault cases... . The drunkenness is itself an intrinsic, an integral part of the crime, the other part being the evidence of the unlawful use of force against the victim. Together they add up to criminal recklessness. On this I adopt the conclusion of Stroud in 1920, 36 L Q.R. 273 that:

 Alert

"... it would be contrary to all principle and authority to suppose that drunkenness" (and what is true of drunkenness is equally true of intoxication by drugs) "can be a defence for crime in general on the ground that 'a person cannot be convicted of a crime unless the mens was rea.' By allowing himself to get drunk, and thereby putting himself in such a condition as to be no longer amenable to the law's commands, a man shows such regardlessness as amounts to mens rea for the purpose of all ordinary crimes."

...The final question that arises is whether section 8 of the Act of 1967 has had the result of abrogating or qualifying the common law rule. That section emanated from the consideration the Law Commission gave to the decision of the House in *Director of Public Prosecutions v Smith* [1961] AC 290. Its purpose and effect was to alter the law of evidence about the presumption of intention to produce the reasonable and probable consequences of one's acts. It was not intended to change the common law rule. In referring to "all the evidence" it meant all the *relevant* evidence. But if there is a substantive rule of law that in crimes of basic intent, the factor of intoxication is irrelevant (and such I hold to be the substantive law), evidence with regard to it is quite irrelevant. Section 8 does not abrogate the substantive rule and it cannot properly be said that the continued application of that rule contravenes the section. ...

LORD SIMON OF GLAISDALE

I still have the temerity to think that the concept of "crime of basic intent" is a useful tool of analysis... . It stands significantly in contrast with "crime of specific intent" as that term was used in Stephen's *Digest* and by the Earl of Birkenhead in *Beard*. The best description of "specific intent" in this sense that I know is contained in the judgment of Fauteux J. in *Reg. v George* (1960) 128 Can CC 289, 301:

"In considering the question of mens rea, a distinction is to be made between (i) intention as applied to acts considered in relation to their purposes and (ii) intention as applied to acts apart from their purposes. A general intent attending the commission of an act is, in some cases, the only intent required to constitute the crime while, in others, there must be, in addition to that general intent, a specific intent attending the purpose for the commission *(sic)* of the act."

In short, where the crime is one of "specific intent" the prosecution must in general prove that the purpose for the commission of the act extends to the intent expressed or implied in the definition of the crime. ...

As I have ventured to suggest, there is nothing unreasonable or illogical in the law holding that a mind rendered self-inducedly insensible (short of *M'Naghten* insanity), through drink or drugs, to the nature of a prohibited act or to its probable consequences is as wrongful a mind as one which consciously contemplates the prohibited act and foresees its probable consequences (or is reckless as to whether they ensue). The latter is all that is required by way of mens rea in a crime of basic intent. But a crime of specific intent requires something more than contemplation of the prohibited act and foresight of its probable consequences. The mens rea in a crime of specific intent requires proof of a purposive element. This purposive element either exists or not; it cannot be supplied by saying that the impairment of mental powers by self-induced intoxication is its equivalent, for it is not. So that the 19th century development of the law as to the effect of self-induced intoxication on criminal responsibility is juristically entirely acceptable; and it need be a matter of no surprise that Stephen stated it without demur or question.

LORD SALMON

...[A]n assault committed accidentally is not a criminal offence.

...A man who by voluntarily taking drink and drugs gets himself into an aggressive state in which he does not know what he is doing and then makes a vicious assault can hardly say with any plausibility that what he did was a pure accident which should render him immune from any criminal liability. Yet this in effect is precisely what Mr Tucker contends that the learned judge should have told the jury.

The decision of the House of Lords in this case was heavily based on policy considerations and it has been criticised by commentators for violating fundamental principles of criminal law. The House confirmed a distinction between offences of "specific intent" and those of "basic intent". The House held that evidence of voluntary intoxication may negate the *mens rea* of an offence of specific intent, but would provide no defence to an offence of basic intent. This distinction has been criticised and was given further consideration in the more recent case of *R v Heard* [2008] QB 43.

R v Heard [2007] EWCA Crim 125, [2008] QB 43

Panel: Hughes LJ, Henriques and Field JJ

Statute: Sexual Offences Act 2003 s 3

Facts: The defendant, who was very drunk, rubbed his penis against the thigh of a police officer. He was charged with sexual assault, contrary to the Sexual Offences Act 2003 s 3. The defendant claimed that due to his intoxication, he could not remember the incident. He argued that due to his voluntary intoxication he did not form the intention required for the offence under s 3(1)(a), namely, the intentional touching of another person. The trial judge ruled that the offence was one of basic intent, so voluntary intoxication was no defence. The defendant was convicted and appealed to the Court of Appeal.

LORD JUSTICE HUGHES

14. The first thing to say is that it should not be supposed that every offence can be categorised simply as either one of specific intent or of basic intent. So to categorise an offence may conceal the truth that different elements of it may require proof of different states of mind. ...

15. The offence of sexual assault, with which this case is concerned, is an example. The different elements of the offence, identified in paragraphs (a) to (d) of section 3 of the 2003 Act, do not call for proof of the same state of mind. ...It is accordingly of very limited help to attempt to label the offence of sexual assault, as a whole, one of either basic or specific intent, because the state of mind which must be proved varies with the issue. For this reason also, it is unsafe to reason (as at one point the Crown does) directly from the state of mind required in relation to consent to the solution to the present question.

16. Since it is only the touching which must be intentional, whilst the sexual character of the touching is, unless equivocal, to be judged objectively, and a belief in consent must be objectively reasonable, we think that it will only be in cases of some rarity that the question which we are posed in this appeal will in the end be determinative of the outcome.

17. We do not think that it determines this appeal. On the evidence the defendant plainly did intend to touch the policeman with his penis. That he was drunk may have meant either: (i) that he was disinhibited and did something which he would not have done if sober; and/or (ii) that he did not remember it afterwards. But neither of those matters (if true) would destroy the intentional character of his touching. In the homely language employed daily in directions to juries in cases of violence and sexual misbehaviour, "a drunken intent is still an intent". And for the memory to blot out what was intentionally done is common, if not perhaps quite as common as is the assertion by offenders that it has done so. In the present case, what the defendant did and said at the time, and said in interview afterwards, made it perfectly clear that this was a case of drunken intentional touching. ...

23. Because the offence is committed only by intentional touching, we agree that the judge's direction that the touching must be deliberate was correct. To flail about, stumble or barge around in an unco-ordinated manner which results in an unintended touching, objectively sexual, is not this offence. If to do so when sober is not this offence, then nor is it this offence to do so when intoxicated. It is also possible that such an action would not be judged by the jury to be objectively sexual, on the basis that it was clearly accidental, but whether that is so or not, we are satisfied that in such a case this offence is not committed. The intoxication, in such a situation, has not impacted on intention. Intention is simply not in question. What is in question is impairment of control of the limbs. ... We would expect that in some cases where this was in issue the judge might well find it useful to add to the previously-mentioned direction that "a drunken intent is still an intent", the corollary that "a drunken accident is still an accident". To the limited, and largely theoretical, extent that a reckless sexual touching is possible the same would apply to that case also. Whether, when a defendant claims accident, he is doing so truthfully, or as a means of disguising the reality that he intended to touch, will be what the jury has to decide on the facts of each such case.

24. The remaining question is whether the judge was also correct to direct the jury that drunkenness was not a defence.

25. We do not agree with Mr Stern's submission for the defendant that the fact that reckless touching will not suffice means that voluntary intoxication can be relied upon as defeating intentional touching. We do not read the cases, including *R v Majewski* [1977] AC 443, as establishing any such rule. As we shall show, we would hold that it is not open to a defendant charged with sexual assault to contend that his voluntary intoxication prevented him from intending to touch. The judge was accordingly correct, not only to direct the jury that the touching must be

deliberate, but also to direct it that the defence that voluntary drunkenness rendered him unable to form the intent to touch was not open to him.

...

31. It is necessary to go back to *R v Majewski* [1977] AC 443 in order to see the basis for the distinction there upheld between crimes of basic and of specific intent. It is to be found most clearly in the speech of Lord Simon, at pp 478 b – 479 b. Lord Simon's analysis had been foreshadowed in his speech in *R v Morgan* [1976] AC 182, 216 (dissenting in the result), which analysis was cited and approved in *R v Majewski* [1977] AC 443 by Lord Elwyn-Jones LC, at page 471. It was that crimes of specific intent are those where the offence requires proof of purpose or consequence, which are not confined to, but amongst which are included, those where the purpose goes beyond the actus reus (sometimes referred to as cases of "ulterior intent"). ...

That explanation of the difference is consistent with the view of Lord Edmund-Davies that an offence contrary to section 1(2)(b) of the Criminal Damage Act 1971 is one of specific intent in this sense, even though it involves no more than recklessness as to the endangering of life; the offence requires proof of a state of mind addressing something beyond the prohibited act itself, namely its consequences. We regard this as the best explanation of the sometimes elusive distinction between specific and basic intent in the sense used in *R v Majewski*, and it seems to us that this is the distinction which the judge in the present case was applying when he referred to the concept of a "bolted-on" intent. By that test, element (a) (the touching) in sexual assault contrary to section 3 of the Sexual Offences Act 2003 is an element requiring no more than basic intent. It follows that voluntary intoxication cannot be relied upon to negate that intent.

...

33. ...Sexual touching must be intentional, that is to say deliberate. But voluntary intoxication cannot be relied upon as negating the necessary intention. If, whether the defendant is intoxicated or otherwise, the touching is unintentional, this offence is not committed.

Thus, the Court of Appeal expressed its disapproval of the simplicity of the distinction between specific intent and basic intent offences. The Court held that sexual assault was not a specific intent offence and thus voluntary intoxication was no defence to it. Hughes LJ stated *obiter* that an offence of specific intent is one of ulterior intent, requiring proof of purpose or consequence, including offences where the purpose goes beyond the actus reus of the offence.

13.2 Consent

The general rule is that consent is a defence to assault and battery only. The leading case on the general rule is *Attorney General's Reference (No 6 of 1980)* [1981] QB 715.

Attorney General's Reference (No 6 of 1980) [1981] QB 715

Panel: Lord Lane CJ, Phillips and Drake JJ

Facts: This case involved two men who decided to settle an argument by having a fist fight. The victim sustained injuries amounting to actual bodily harm and the defendant was charged with assault occasioning actual bodily harm, contrary to the Offences Against the Person Act 1861 s 47. The jury were directed that the defendant might not be guilty if the victim agreed to fight and only reasonable force was used. The jury acquitted the defendant and the Attorney General referred the case to the Court of Appeal for the Court's judgment as to whether:

"Where two persons fight (otherwise than in the course of sport) in a public place can it be a defence for one of those persons to a charge of assault arising out of the fight that the other consented to fight?"

LORD LANE CJ

We think that it can be taken as a starting point that it is an essential element of an assault that the act is done contrary to the will and without the consent of the victim; and it is doubtless for this reason that the burden lies on the prosecution to negative consent. Ordinarily, then, if the victim consents, the assailant is not guilty.

But the cases show that the courts will make an exception to this principle where the public interest requires: *Reg. v Coney* (1882) 8 QBD 534 ("the prize fight case"). The 11 judges were of opinion that a prize fight is illegal, that all persons aiding and abetting were guilty of assault, and that the consent of the actual fighters was irrelevant'. Their reasons varied as follows: Cave J., that the blow was struck in anger and likely to do corporal hurt, as opposed to one struck in sport, not intended to cause bodily harm; Mathew J., the dangerous nature of the proceedings; Stephen J., what was done was injurious to the public, depending on the degree of force and the place used; Hawkins J., the likelihood of a breach of the peace, and the degree of force and injury; Lord Coleridge CJ, breach of the peace and protection of the public.

The judgment in *Rex v Donovan* [1934] 2 KB 498 (beating for the purposes of sexual gratification), the reasoning in which seems to be tautologous, proceeds upon a different basis, starting, at page 507, with the proposition that consent is irrelevant if the act complained of is "unlawful ... in itself," which it will be if it involves the infliction of bodily harm.

...[S]tarting with the proposition that ordinarily an act consented to will not constitute an assault, the question is: at what point does the public interest require the court to hold otherwise? ...

The answer to this question, in our judgment, is that it is not in the public interest that people should try to cause, or should cause, each other actual bodily harm for no good reason. Minor struggles are another matter. So, in our judgment, it is immaterial whether the act occurs in private or in public; it is an assault if actual bodily harm is intended and/or caused. This means that most fights will be unlawful regardless of consent.

 Alert

> Nothing which we have said is intended to cast doubt upon the accepted legality of properly conducted games and sports, lawful chastisement or correction, reasonable surgical interference, dangerous exhibitions, etc. These apparent exceptions can be justified as involving the exercise of a legal right, in the case of chastisement or correction, or as needed in the public interest, in the other cases.

 Alert

> Our answer to the point of law is No, but not, as the reference implies, because the fight occurred in a public place, but because, wherever it occurred, the participants would have been guilty of assault, subject to self-defence, if, as we understand was the case, they intended to and/or did cause actual bodily harm.

This general rule is subject to a number of exceptions set out above. The rule was confirmed by the House of Lords in the case of *R v Brown* [1994] AC 212.

R v Brown [1994] AC 212

Panel: Lord Templeman, Lord Jauncey of Tullichettle, Lord Lowry, Lord Mustill and Lord Slynn of Hadley

Statute: Offences Against the Person Act 1861 ss 47, 20

Facts: The defendants were a group of homosexual men who willingly consented to participating in sadomasochistic sexual acts. The acts involved the giving and receiving of pain for sexual pleasure and they caused injuries to one another. None of the injuries required medical treatment. The trial judge refused to leave the defence of consent to the jury, so the defendants pleaded guilty to of offences under ss 47 and 20 of the Offences Against the Person Act 1861. They appealed to the Court of Appeal on the basis that the trial judge was wrong in law. The Court of Appeal dismissed the appeal, but certified a question on a point of law of general public importance for the House of Lords:

"Where A wounds or assaults B occasioning him actual bodily harm in the course of a sado-masochistic encounter, does the prosecution have to prove lack of consent on the part of B before they can establish A's guilt under section 20 or section 47 of the Offences Against the Person Act 1861?"

LORD TEMPLEMAN

In some circumstances violence is not punishable under the criminal law. When no actual bodily harm is caused, the consent of the person affected precludes him from complaining. There can be no conviction for the summary offence of common assault if the victim has consented to the assault. Even when violence is intentionally inflicted and results in actual bodily harm, wounding or serious bodily harm the accused is entitled to be acquitted if the injury was a foreseeable incident of a lawful activity in which the person injured was participating. Surgery involves intentional violence resulting in actual or sometimes serious bodily harm but surgery is a lawful activity. Other activities carried on with consent by or on behalf of the injured person have been accepted as lawful notwithstanding that they involve actual bodily harm or may cause serious bodily harm. Ritual circumcision, tattooing, ear-piercing and violent sports including boxing are lawful activities.

...My Lords, the authorities dealing with the intentional infliction of bodily harm do not establish that consent is a defence to a charge under the Act of 1861. They establish that the courts have accepted that consent is a defence to the infliction of bodily harm in the course of some lawful activities. The question is whether the defence should be extended to the infliction of bodily harm in the course of sado-masochistic encounters. The Wolfenden Committee did not make any recommendations about sado-masochism and Parliament did not deal with violence in 1967. The Act of 1967 is of no assistance for present purposes because the present problem was not under consideration.

The question whether the defence of consent should be extended to the consequences of sado-masochistic encounters can only be decided by consideration of policy and public interest. Parliament can call on the advice of doctors, psychiatrists, criminologists, sociologists and other experts and can also sound and take into account public opinion. But the question must at this stage be decided by this House in its judicial capacity in order to determine whether the convictions of the appellants should be upheld or quashed.

Alert

Counsel for some of the appellants argued that the defence of consent should be extended to the offence of occasioning actual bodily harm under section 47 of the Act of 1861 but should not be available to charges of serious wounding and the infliction of serious bodily harm under section 20. I do not consider that this solution is practicable. Sado-masochistic participants have no way of foretelling the degree of bodily harm which will result from their encounters. The differences between actual bodily harm and serious bodily harm cannot be satisfactorily applied by a jury in order to determine acquittal or conviction.

Counsel for the appellants argued that consent should provide a defence to charges under both section 20 and section 47 because, it was said, every person has a right to deal with his body as he pleases. I do not consider that this slogan provides a sufficient guide to the policy decision which must now be made. It is an offence for a person to abuse his own body and mind by taking drugs. Although the law is often broken, the criminal law restrains a practice which is regarded as dangerous and injurious to individuals and which if allowed and extended is harmful to society generally. In any event the appellants in this case did not mutilate their own bodies. They inflicted bodily harm on willing victims. Suicide is no longer an offence but a person who assists another to commit suicide is guilty of murder or manslaughter.

Alert

The assertion was made on behalf of the appellants that the sexual appetites of sadists and masochists can only be satisfied by the infliction of bodily harm and that the law should not punish the consensual achievement of sexual satisfaction. There was no evidence to support the assertion that sado-masochist activities are essential to the happiness of the appellants or any other participants but the argument would be acceptable if sado-masochism were only concerned with sex, as the appellants contend. In my opinion sado-masochism is not only concerned with sex. Sado-masochism is also concerned with violence. The evidence discloses that the practices of the appellants were unpredictably dangerous and degrading to body and mind and were developed with increasing barbarity and taught to persons whose consents were dubious or worthless.

A sadist draws pleasure from inflicting or watching cruelty. A masochist derives pleasure from his own pain or humiliation. The appellants are middle-aged men. The victims were youths some of whom were introduced to sado-masochism before they attained the age of 21. ...

The evidence disclosed that drink and drugs were employed to obtain consent and increase enthusiasm. The victim was usually manacled so that the sadist could enjoy the thrill of power and the victim could enjoy the thrill of helplessness. The victim had no control over the harm which the sadist, also stimulated by drink and drugs might inflict. In one case a victim was branded twice on the thigh and there was some doubt as to whether he consented to or protested against the second branding. The dangers involved in administering violence must have been appreciated by the appellants because, so it was said by their counsel, each victim was given a code word which he could pronounce when excessive harm or pain was caused. The efficiency of this precaution, when taken, depends on the circumstances and on the personalities involved. No one can feel the pain of another. The charges against the appellants were based on genital torture and violence to the buttocks, anus, penis, testicles and nipples. The victims were degraded and humiliated sometimes beaten, sometimes wounded with instruments and sometimes branded. Bloodletting and the smearing of human blood produced excitement. There were obvious dangers of serious personal injury and blood infection. Prosecuting counsel informed the trial judge against the protests of defence counsel, that although the appellants had not contracted Aids, two members of the group had died from Aids and one other had contracted an HIV infection although not necessarily from the practices of the group. Some activities involved excrement. The assertion that the instruments employed by the sadists were clean and sterilised could not have removed the danger of infection, and the assertion that care was taken demonstrates the possibility of infection. Cruelty to human beings was on occasions supplemented by cruelty to animals in the form of bestiality. It is fortunate that there were no permanent injuries to a victim though no one knows the extent of harm inflicted in other cases. It is not surprising that a victim does not complain to the police when the complaint would involve him in giving details of acts in which he participated. Doctors of course are subject to a code of confidentiality.

In principle there is a difference between violence which is incidental and violence which is inflicted for the indulgence of cruelty. The violence of sado-masochistic encounters involves the indulgence of cruelty by sadists and the degradation of victims. Such violence is injurious to the participants and unpredictably dangerous. I am not prepared to invent a defence of consent for sado-masochistic encounters which breed and glorify cruelty and result in offences under sections 47 and 20 of the Act of 1861.

 Alert

... The violence of sadists and the degradation of their victims have sexual motivations but sex is no excuse for violence.

... Society is entitled and bound to protect itself against a cult of violence. Pleasure derived from the infliction of pain is an evil thing. Cruelty is uncivilised. I would answer the certified question in the negative and dismiss the appeals of the appellants against conviction.

LORD JAUNCEY OF TULLICHETTLE

...[I]n considering the public interest it would be wrong to look only at the activities of the appellants alone, there being no suggestion that they and their associates are the only practitioners of homosexual sado-masochism in England and Wales. This House must therefore consider the possibility that these activities are practised by others and by others who are not so controlled or responsible as the appellants are claimed to be. Without going into details of all the rather curious activities in which the appellants engaged it would appear to be good luck rather than good judgment which has prevented serious injury from occurring. Wounds can easily become septic if not properly treated, the free flow of blood from a person who is HIV positive or who has Aids can infect another and an inflicter who is carried away by sexual excitement or by drink or drugs could very easily inflict pain and injury beyond the level to which the receiver had consented. Your Lordships have no information as to whether such situations have occurred in relation to other sado-masochistic practitioners. It was no doubt these dangers which caused Lady Mallalieu to restrict her propositions in relation to the public interest to the actual rather than the potential result of the activity. In my view such a restriction is quite unjustified. When considering the public interest potential for harm is just as relevant as actual harm. As Mathew J. said in *Reg. v Coney*, 8 QBD 534 , 547: "There is, however, abundant authority for saying that no consent can render that innocent which is in fact dangerous." Furthermore, the possibility of proselytisation and corruption of young men is a real danger even in the case of these appellants and the taking of video recordings of such activities suggests that secrecy may not be as strict as the appellants claimed to your Lordships. If the only purpose of the activity is the sexual gratification of one or both of the participants what then is the need of a video recording?

My Lords I have no doubt that it would not be in the public interest that deliberate infliction of actual bodily harm during the course of homosexual sado-masochistic activities should be held to be lawful. ...If it is to be decided that such activities as the nailing by A of B's foreskin or scrotum to a board or the insertion of hot wax into C's urethra followed by the burning of his penis with a candle or the incising of D's scrotum with a scalpel to the effusion of blood are injurious neither to B, C and D nor to the public interest then it is for Parliament with its accumulated wisdom and sources of information to declare them to be lawful.

LORD LOWRY

Sado-masochistic homosexual activity cannot be regarded as conducive to the enhancement or enjoyment of family life or conducive to the welfare of society. A relaxation of the prohibitions in sections 20 and 47 can only encourage the practice of homosexual sado-masochism, with the physical cruelty that it must involve (which can scarcely be regarded as a "manly diversion"), by withdrawing the legal penalty and giving the activity a judicial imprimatur. As well as all this, one cannot overlook the physical danger to those who may indulge in sado-masochism. In this connection, and also generally, it is idle for the appellants to claim that they are educated exponents of "civilised cruelty." A proposed *general* exemption is to be tested by considering the likely *general* effect. This must include the probability that some sado-masochistic activity, under the powerful influence of the sexual instinct, will get out of hand and result in serious physical damage to the participants and that some activity will involve a danger of infection such as these particular exponents do not contemplate for themselves. When considering the danger of infection, with its inevitable threat of Aids, I am not impressed by the argument that this threat can be discounted on the ground that, as long ago as 1967, Parliament, subject to conditions, legalised buggery, now a well known vehicle for the transmission of Aids.

Thus, sexual gratification is not an exception to the general rule that consent is only a defence to assault and battery. The decision of the House of Lords to reject the defence of consent in this case was a majority one. Lord Templeman, Lord Jauncey and Lord Lowry were in the majority, dismissing the appeals. Lord Mustill and Lord Slynn delivered dissenting opinions, allowing the appeals.

LORD MUSTILL

... I ask myself, not whether as a result of the decision in this appeal, activities such as those of the appellants should *cease* to be criminal, but rather whether the Act of 1861 (a statute which I venture to repeat once again was clearly intended to penalise conduct of a quite different nature) should in this new situation be interpreted so as to *make* it criminal. Why should this step be taken? Leaving aside repugnance and moral objection, both of which are entirely natural but neither of which are in my opinion grounds upon which the court could properly create a new crime, I can visualise only the following reasons.

(1) Some of the practices obviously created a risk of genito-urinary infection, and others of septicaemia. These might indeed have been grave in former times, but the risk of serious harm must surely have been greatly reduced by modern medical science.

(2) The possibility that matters might get out of hand, with grave results. ... If this happened, those responsible would be punished according to the ordinary law, in the same way as those who kill or injure in the course of more ordinary sexual activities are regularly punished. But to penalise the appellants' conduct even if the extreme consequences do not ensue, just because they might have done so would require an assessment of the degree of risk, and the balancing of this risk against the interests of individual freedom. Such a balancing is in my opinion for Parliament, not the courts...

(3) I would give the same answer to the suggestion that these activities involved a risk of accelerating the spread of auto-immune deficiency syndrome, and that they should be brought within the Act of 1861 in the interests of public health. The consequence would be strange, since what is currently the principal cause for the transmission of this scourge, namely consenting buggery between males, is now legal...

(4) There remains an argument to which I have given much greater weight. As the evidence in the present case has shown, there is a risk that strangers (and especially young strangers) may be drawn into these activities at an early age and will then become established in them for life. This is indeed a disturbing prospect, but I have come to the conclusion that it is not a sufficient ground for declaring these activities to be criminal under the Act of 1861. The element of the corruption of youth is already catered for by the existing legislation; and if there is a gap in it which needs to be filled the remedy surely lies in the hands of Parliament, not in the application of a statute which is aimed at other forms of wrongdoing. As regards proselytisation for adult sado-masochism the argument appears to me circular. For if the activity is not itself so much against the public interest that it ought to be declared criminal under the Act of 1861 then the risk that others will be induced to join in cannot be a ground for making it criminal.

Leaving aside the logic of this answer, which seems to me impregnable, plain humanity demands that a court addressing the criminality of conduct such as that of the present should recognise and respond to the profound dismay which all members of the community share about the apparent increase of cruel and senseless crimes against the defenceless. Whilst doing so I must repeat for the last time that in the answer which I propose I do not advocate the decriminalisation of conduct which has hitherto been a crime; nor do I rebut a submission that a new crime should be created, penalising this conduct... The only question is whether these consensual private acts are offences against the existing law of violence. To this question I return a negative response.

Consideration was given to the issue of consent and sexually transmitted diseases in the case of *R v Dica* [2004] QB 1257.

R v Dica [2004] EWCA Crim 1103, [2004] QB 1257

Panel: Lord Woolf CJ, Judge LJ and Forbes J

Statute: Offences Against the Person Act 1861 s 20

Facts: The defendant knew that he was HIV positive. He had consensual sexual intercourse with two women but he did not tell them that he was HIV positive. The women later tested positive for HIV. The defendant was charged with two counts of unlawfully and maliciously inflicting grievous bodily harm, contrary to the Offences Against the Person Act 1861 s 20. He was convicted and appealed to the Court of Appeal.

LORD JUSTICE JUDGE

41. As a general rule, unless the activity is lawful, the consent of the victim to the deliberate infliction of serious bodily injury on him or her does not provide the perpetrator with any defence. Different categories of activity are regarded as lawful. Thus no one doubts that necessary major surgery with the patient's consent, even if likely to result in severe disability (eg an amputation) would be lawful. However the categories of activity regarded as lawful are not closed, and equally, they are not immutable. Thus, prize fighting and street fighting by consenting

participants are unlawful: although some would have it banned, boxing for sport is not. Coming closer to this case, in *Bravery v Bravery* [1954] 1 WLR 1169, 1180, Denning LJ condemned in the strongest terms, and as criminal, the conduct of a young husband who, with the consent of his wife, underwent a sterilisation operation, not so as to avoid the risk of transmitting a hereditary disease, or something similar, but to enable him to "have the pleasure of sexual intercourse, without shouldering the responsibilities attaching to it". He thought that such an operation, for that reason, was plainly "injurious to the public interest". This approach sounds dated, as indeed it is. Denning LJ's colleagues expressly and unequivocally dissociated themselves from it. However, judges from earlier generations, reflecting their own contemporary society, might have agreed with him. We have sufficiently illustrated the impermanence of public policy in the context of establishing which activities involving violence may or may not be lawful.

42. The present policy of the law is that, whether or not the violent activity takes place in private, and even if the victim agrees to it, serious violence is not lawful merely because it enables the perpetrator (or the victim) to achieve sexual gratification. Judge Philpot was impressed with the conclusions to be drawn from the well-known decision in *R v Brown (Anthony)* [1994] 1 AC 212. Sado-masochistic activity of an extreme, indeed horrific kind, which caused grievous bodily harm, was held to be unlawful, notwithstanding that those who suffered the cruelty positively welcomed it. This decision of the House of Lords was supported in the European Court of Human Rights on the basis that although the prosecution may have constituted an interference with the private lives of those involved, it was justified for the protection of public health: *Laskey, Jaggard and Brown v United Kingdom* (1997) 24 EHRR 39.

43. The same policy can be seen in operation in *R v Donovan* [1934] 2 KB 498, where the violence was less extreme and the consent of the victim, although real, was far removed from the enthusiastic co-operation of the victims in *Brown*.

44. *R v Boyea* (1992) 156 JP 505 represents another example of the application of the principle in *Donovan*. If she consented to injury by allowing the defendant to put his hand into her vagina and twist it, causing, among other injuries, internal and external injuries to her vagina and bruising on her pubis, the woman's consent (if any) would have been irrelevant. Recognising that social attitudes to sexual matters had changed over the years, a contemporaneous approach to these matters was appropriate. However, "the extent of the violence inflicted ... went far beyond the risk of minor injury to which, if she did consent, her consent would have been a defence": page 513. On close analysis, however, this case was decided on the basis that the victim did not in fact consent.

45. In *R v Emmett* The Times, 15 October 1999, as part of their consensual sexual activity, the woman agreed to allow her partner to cover her head with a plastic bag, tying it tightly at the neck. On a different occasion, she agreed that he could pour fuel from a lighter onto her breasts and set fire to the fuel. On the first occasion, she was at risk of death, and lost consciousness. On the second, she

suffered burns, which became infected. This court did not directly answer the question posed by the trial judge in his certificate, but concluded that *Brown* [1994] 1 AC 212 demonstrated that the woman's consent to these events did not provide a defence for her partner.

46. These authorities demonstrate that violent conduct involving the deliberate and intentional infliction of bodily harm is and remains unlawful notwithstanding that its purpose is the sexual gratification of one or both participants. Notwithstanding their sexual overtones, these cases were concerned with violent crime, and the sexual overtones did not alter the fact that both parties were consenting to the deliberate infliction of serious harm or bodily injury on one participant by the other. To date, as a matter of public policy, it has not been thought appropriate for such violent conduct to be excused merely because there is a private consensual sexual element to it. The same public policy reason would prohibit the deliberate spreading of disease, including sexual disease.

 Alert

47. In our judgment the impact of the authorities dealing with sexual gratification can too readily be misunderstood. It does not follow from them, and they do not suggest, that consensual acts of sexual intercourse are unlawful merely because there may be a known risk to the health of one or other participant. These participants are not intent on spreading or becoming infected with disease through sexual intercourse. They are not indulging in serious violence for the purposes of sexual gratification. They are simply prepared, knowingly, to run the risk—not the certainty—of infection, as well as all the other risks inherent in and possible consequences of sexual intercourse, such as, and despite the most careful precautions, an unintended pregnancy. At one extreme there is casual sex between complete strangers, sometimes protected, sometimes not, when the attendant risks are known to be higher, and at the other, there is sexual intercourse between couples in a long-term and loving, and trusting relationship, which may from time to time also carry risks.

...

50. ... Modern society has not thought to criminalise those who have willingly accepted the risks, and we know of no cases where one or other of the consenting adults has been prosecuted, let alone convicted, for the consequences of doing so.

51. The problems of *criminalising* the consensual taking of risks like these include the sheer impracticability of enforcement and the haphazard nature of its impact. The process would undermine the general understanding of the community that sexual relationships are pre-eminently private and essentially personal to the individuals involved in them. And if adults were to be liable to prosecution for the consequences of taking known risks with their health, it would seem odd that this should be confined to risks taken in the context of sexual intercourse, while they are nevertheless permitted to take the risks inherent in so many other aspects of everyday life, including, again for example, the mother or father of a child suffering a serious contagious illness, who holds the child's hand, and comforts or kisses him or her goodnight.

52. In our judgment, interference of this kind with personal autonomy, and its level and extent, may only be made by Parliament.

...

59. The effect of this judgment in relation to section 20 is to remove some of the outdated restrictions against the successful prosecution of those who, knowing that they are suffering HIV or some other serious sexual disease, recklessly transmit it through consensual sexual intercourse, and inflict grievous bodily harm on a person from whom the risk is concealed and who is not consenting to it. In this context, *Clarence* 22 QBD 23 has no continuing relevance. Moreover, to the extent that Clarence suggested that consensual sexual intercourse of itself was to be regarded as consent to the risk of consequent disease, again, it is no longer authoritative. If however, the victim consents to the risk, this continues to provide a defence under section 20. Although the two are inevitably linked, the ultimate question is not knowledge, but consent. We shall confine ourselves to reflecting that unless you are prepared to take whatever risk of sexually transmitted infection there may be, it is unlikely that you would consent to a risk of major consequent illness if you were ignorant of it. That said, in every case where these issues arise, the question whether the defendant was or was not reckless, and whether the victim did or did not consent to the risk of a sexually transmitted disease is one of fact, and case specific.

60. In view of our conclusion that the trial judge should not have withdrawn the issue of consent from the jury, the appeal is allowed.

Alert

Where a complainant consents to sexual intercourse with a partner who he or she knows to be HIV positive, he or she consents to the risk of contracting the virus. Thus, consent will be a defence to any charge under the Offences Against the Person Act 1861 s 20.

Further Reading

Gough S 'Surviving without *Majewski*' [2002] *Crim LR* 719

Giles M 'Consensual Harm and the Public Interest"' (1994) *57 MLR* 101

Law Commission Report No. 314, *Intoxication and Criminal Liability* (2009)

Weait M 'Criminal Law and the Sexual Transmission of HIV: *R v Dica*' (2005) 68 *MLR* 121

11

Defences II:
Self Defence and Duress

Topic List

14.1 Self Defence

Under common law a defendant may use such force as is reasonable in the circumstances as he believed them to be in defending himself, others or property. It does not matter whether or not he defendant's belief was reasonable, as long as it was honestly held. Thus, the defendant is judged on the facts as he subjectively believed them to be. The Criminal Justice and Immigration Act 2008 s 76 placed much of the common law defence on a statutory footing, but an understanding of the relevant case law will assist in applying the new statutory provisions.

R v Gladstone Williams (1984) 78 Cr App R 276

Panel: Lord Lane CJ, Skinner and McCowan JJ

Facts: The victim witnessed a youth committing a robbery by snatching a handbag from a woman. The victim chased the youth and caught him, planning to take him to the police station. The youth escaped and the victim gave chase again, this time knocking the youth to the floor in order to immobilise him. The defendant had witnessed the last part of this and approached the victim. The victim falsely informed the defendant that he was a police officer. When the defendant asked to see the victim's warrant card, the victim was obviously unable to show one. The defendant thought that the victim was assaulting the youth, so the defendant punched the victim. The victim sustained a number of injuries. The defendant was charged with assault occasioning actual bodily harm contrary to the Offences Against the Person Act 1861 s 47. His defence was that he was acting the in the defence of another because he honestly believed that the victim was attacking the youth. The trial judge directed the jury that the defendant's belief must be both honest and reasonable. The defendant appealed against his conviction.

LORD LANE CJ

…"Assault" in the context of this case,… is an act by which the defendant, intentionally or recklessly, applies unlawful force to the complainant. There are circumstances in which force may be applied to another lawfully. Taking a few examples:… Secondly, where the defendant is acting in self-defence: the exercise of any necessary and reasonable force to protect himself from unlawful violence is not unlawful. Thirdly, by virtue of section 3 of the Criminal Law Act 1967, a person may use such force as is reasonable in the circumstances in the prevention of crime or in effecting or assisting in the lawful arrest of an offender or suspected offender or persons unlawfully at large. In each of those cases the defendant will be guilty if the jury are sure that first of all he applied force to the person of another, and secondly that he had the necessary mental element to constitute guilt.

The mental element necessary to constitute guilt is the intent to apply unlawful force to the victim. We do not believe that the mental element can be substantiated by simply showing an intent to apply force and no more.

What then is the situation if the defendant is labouring under a mistake of fact as to the circumstances? What if he believes, but believes mistakenly, that the victim is consenting, or that it is necessary to defend himself, or that a crime is being committed which he intends to prevent? He must then be judged against the mistaken facts as he believes them to be. If judged against those facts or circumstances the prosecution fail to establish his guilt, then he is entitled to be acquitted.

The next question is, does it make any difference if the mistake of the defendant was one which, viewed objectively by a reasonable onlooker, was an unreasonable mistake? In other words should the jury be directed as follows: "Even if the defendant may have genuinely believed that what he was doing to the victim was either with the victim's consent or in reasonable self-defence or to prevent the commission of crime, as the case may be, nevertheless if you, the jury, come to the conclusion that the mistaken belief was unreasonable, that is to say that the defendant as a reasonable man should have realised his mistake, then you should convict him."

...

The reasonableness or unreasonableness of the defendant's belief is material to the question of whether the belief was held by the defendant at all. If the belief was in fact held, its unreasonableness, so far as guilt or innocence is concerned, is neither here nor there. It is irrelevant. Were it otherwise, the defendant would be convicted because he was negligent in failing to recognise that the victim was not consenting or that a crime was not being committed and so on. In other words the jury should be directed first of all that the prosecution have the burden or duty of proving the unlawfulness of the defendant's actions; secondly, if the defendant may have been labouring under a mistake as to the facts, he must be judged according to his mistaken view of the facts; thirdly, that is so whether the mistake was, on an objective view, a reasonable mistake or not.

 Alert

In a case of self-defence, where self-defence or the prevention of crime is concerned, if the jury came to the conclusion that the defendant believed, or may have believed, that he was being attacked or that a crime was being committed, and that force was necessary to protect himself or to prevent the crime, then the prosecution have not proved their case. If however the defendant's alleged belief was mistaken and if the mistake was an unreasonable one, that may be a powerful reason for coming to the conclusion that the belief was not honestly held and should be rejected.

Even if the jury come to the conclusion that the mistake was an unreasonable one, if the defendant may genuinely have been labouring under it, he is entitled to rely upon it.

The Court of Appeal held that the trial judge had misdirected the jury and allowed the appeal.

There is no duty to retreat in English law. This was confirmed in the case of *R v Bird* [1985] 1 WLR 816.

R v Bird [1985] 1 WLR 816

Panel: Lord Lane CJ, Skinner and Simon Brown JJ

Facts: The appellant threw a party to celebrate her 17th birthday. Her ex-boyfriend brought his new girlfriend to the party and an argument broke out. The appellant told her ex-boyfriend to leave and he did, but he later returned and another argument ensued. The appellant poured a drink over her ex-boyfriend and he slapped her in the face. The appellant claimed that the ex-boyfriend held her up against a wall, at which point she lunged at him with her hand which was holding a glass. The ex-boyfriend lost an eye as a result. The appellant was convicted of unlawfully wounding her ex-boyfriend contrary to the Offences Against the Person Act 1861 s 20. She had raised self defence but the trial judge directed the jury that before they could find that the appellant had acted in self defence they must be satisfied that she had demonstrated by her action that she did not want to fight. She appealed against her conviction.

LORD LANE CJ

...The matter is dealt with accurately and helpfully in *Smith and Hogan Criminal Law*, 5th edn (1983), page 327:

> "There were formerly technical rules about the duty to retreat before using force, or at least fatal force. This is now simply a factor to be taken into account in deciding whether it was necessary to use force, and whether the force was reasonable. If the only reasonable course is to retreat, then it would appear that to stand and fight must be to use unreasonable force. There is, however, no rule of law that a person attacked is bound to run away if he can; but it has been said that- '...what is necessary is that he should demonstrate by his actions that he does not want to fight. He must demonstrate that he is prepared to temporise and disengage and perhaps to make some physical withdrawal.' [*Reg. v Julien* [1969] 1 WLR 839, 842]. It is submitted that it goes too far to say that action of this kind is *necessary*. It is scarcely consistent with the rule that it is permissible to use force, not merely to counter an actual attack, but to ward off an attack honestly and reasonably believed to be imminent. A demonstration by [the defendant] at the time that he did not want to fight is, no doubt, the best evidence that he was acting reasonably and in good faith in self-defence; but it is no more than that. A person may in some circumstances so act without temporising, disengaging or withdrawing; and he should have a good defence."

Alert

We respectfully agree with that passage. If the defendant is proved to have been attacking or retaliating or revenging himself, then he was not truly acting in self-defence. Evidence that the defendant tried to retreat or tried to call off the fight may be a cast-iron method of casting doubt on the suggestion that he was the attacker or retaliator or the person trying to revenge himself. But it is not by any means the only method of doing that.

Alert

...The real problem for the jury to decide in this case was whether the appellant realised that she had a glass in her hand when she, in her reaction, struck the blow that she did. It may very well have been, in all the circumstances of the case, that the jury came to the conclusion that they were doubtful as to whether she realised that or not. Of course if they were doubtful, then the judgment on that aspect of the case had to come down in favour of the appellant. If the jury thought that she did not realise that she had a glass in her hand, then they might very well have turned to the next problem, namely, to consider what the judge had been telling them about the "necessity" for the appellant to demonstrate by her actions that she did not want to fight.

In those circumstances this misdirection might very well have caused them to come to a wrong conclusion. ...This was a material misdirection and consequently this appeal must be allowed and the conviction quashed.

According to the case of *Beckford v R* [1988] AC 130, a pre-emptive strike does not preclude self defence.

Beckford v R [1988] AC 130

Panel: Lord Keith of Kinkel, Lord Elwyn-Jones, Lord Templeman, Lord Griffiths, Lord Oliver of Aylmerton

Facts: This case took place in Jamaica. The appellant was a police officer. He was called out to a house where a man (the deceased) was allegedly terrorizing his mother and family with a gun. When the deceased tried to escape, the appellant chased the deceased. The deceased was holding a gun and shooting at the officers. The appellant shot and killed the deceased. At his trial for murder, the appellant raised self defence. The trial judge directed the jury that self defence would be available if the appellant reasonably believed that his life was in danger. The defendant was convicted. His appeal to the Court of Appeal in Jamaica was dismissed, so the appellant appealed to the Privy Council.

LORD GRIFFITHS

In *Reg. v Williams (Gladstone)*, 78 Cr App R 276, the decision in *Reg. v Morgan* [1976] AC 182 was carried a step further and in their Lordships' view to its logical conclusion.

...

The common law recognises that there are many circumstances in which one person may inflict violence upon another without committing a crime, as for instance, in sporting contests, surgical operations or in the most extreme example judicial execution. The common law has always recognised as one of these circumstances the right of a person to protect himself from attack and to act in the defence of others and if necessary to inflict violence on another in so doing. If no more force is used than is reasonable to repel the attack such force is not unlawful and no crime is committed. Furthermore a man about to be attacked does not have to wait for his assailant to strike the first blow or fire the first shot; circumstances may justify a pre-emptive strike.

 Alert

It is because it is an essential element of all crimes of violence that the violence or the threat of violence should be unlawful that self-defence, if raised as an issue in a criminal trial, must be disproved by the prosecution. If the prosecution fail to do so the accused is

entitled to be acquitted because the prosecution will have failed to prove an essential element of the crime namely that the violence used by the accused was unlawful.

If then a genuine belief, albeit without reasonable grounds, is a defence to rape because it negatives the necessary intention, so also must a genuine belief in facts which if true would justify self-defence be a defence to a crime of personal violence because the belief negatives the intent to act unlawfully. Their Lordships therefore approve the following passage from the judgment of Lord Lane CJ in *Reg. v Williams (Gladstone)*, 78 Cr App R 276, 281, as correctly stating the law of self-defence.

...

"...if the defendant may have been labouring under a mistake as to the facts, he must be judged according to his mistaken view of the facts; thirdly, that is so whether the mistake was, on an objective view, a reasonable mistake or not..."

There may be a fear that the abandonment of the objective standard demanded by the existence of reasonable grounds for belief will result in the success of too many spurious claims of self-defence. The English experience has not shown this to be the case. The Judicial Studies Board with the approval of the Lord Chief Justice has produced a model direction on self-defence which is now widely used by judges when summing up to juries. The direction contains the following guidance:

"Whether the plea is self-defence or defence of another, if the defendant may have been labouring under a mistake as to the facts he must be judged according to his mistaken belief of the facts. That is so whether the mistake was, on an objective view, a reasonable mistake or not."

Alert

Their Lordships have heard no suggestion that this form of summing up has resulted in a disquieting number of acquittals. This is hardly surprising for no jury is going to accept a man's assertion that he believed that he was about to be attacked without testing it against all the surrounding circumstances. In assisting the jury to determine whether or not the accused had a genuine belief the judge will of course direct their attention to those features of the evidence that make such a belief more or less probable. Where there are no reasonable grounds to hold a belief it will surely only be in exceptional circumstances that a jury will conclude that such a belief was or might have been held.

Their Lordships therefore conclude that the summing up in this case contained a material misdirection ...the test to be applied for self-defence is that a person may use such force as is reasonable in the circumstances as he honestly believes them to be in the defence of himself or another... .

While this case may be cited as an authority for the principle that a pre-emptive strike does not preclude self defence, it also confirms that a defendant's belief that the use of force is necessary need only be honestly held; it need not be reasonable.

14.2 Duress by Threat

The test for duress was laid down by the Court of Appeal in the case of *R v Graham* [1982] 1 All ER 801. This was approved by the House of Lords in *R v Howe* [1987]

AC 147. The test was revised more recently by the House of Lords in the case of *R v Hasan* [2005] UKHL 22, [2005] 2 AC 467.

R v Graham [1982] 1 WLR 294

Panel: Lord Lane CJ, Taylor and McCullough JJ

Facts: The defendant was a homosexual man living in a "ménage a trois" with his wife and his male lover, King. King was a violent and jealous man who bullied the defendant. The defendant was vulnerable as he was taking Valium for anxiety. One day, while the defendant's wife was at her mother's house, King suggested that they kill her. The defendant persuaded her to return home and when she did, King put flex around her neck and told the defendant to pull on the end of the flex. The wife died and the defendant was charged with her murder. He raised a defence in two parts, claiming first that he did not have the necessary intention for murder (he drew attention to the drink and drugs that he had consumed on the night of the murder), and secondly he pleaded duress. He was convicted and appealed to the Court of Appeal.

LORD LANE CJ

...The Crown at the trial conceded that,... it was open to the defence to raise the issue of duress. In other words, they were not prepared to take the point that the defence of duress is not available to a principal in the first degree to murder. Consequently, the interesting question raised by the decisions in *Lynch v DPP for Northern Ireland* [1975] 1 All ER 913, [1975] AC 653, and *Abbott v R* [1976] 3 All ER 140, [1977] AC 755 was not argued before us. We do not have to decide it. We pause only to observe that the jury would no doubt have been puzzled to learn that whether the appellant was to be convicted of murder or acquitted altogether might depend on whether the plug came off the end of the percolator flex when he began to pull it...

The direction which the judge gave to the jury required them to ask themselves two questions. First, a subjective question which the judge formulated thus: 'Was this man at the time of the killing taking part because he feared for his own life or personal safety as a result of the words or the conduct on the part of King, either personally experienced by him, or genuinely believed in by him?' Neither side in the present appeal has taken issue with the judge on this question. We feel, however, that for purposes of completeness, we should say that the direction appropriate in this particular case should have been in these words: 'Was this man at the time of the killing taking part because he held a well-grounded fear of death (or serious physical injury) as a result of the words or conduct on the part of King?' The bracketed words may be too favourable to the defendant. The point was not argued before us.

The judge then went on to direct the jury that if the answer to that first question was 'Yes', or 'He may have been', the jury should then go on to consider a second question importing an objective test of reasonableness. This is the issue which arises in this appeal. Counsel for the appellant contends that no second question arises at all; the test is purely subjective. He argues that if the appellant's will was in fact overborne by threats of the requisite cogency, he is entitled to be acquitted and no question arises as to whether a reasonable man, with or without his characteristics, would have reacted similarly.

Counsel for the Crown, on the other hand, submits that such dicta as can be found on the point are in favour of a second test; this time an objective test. He argues that public policy requires this and draws an analogy with provocation. He submits that while the judge was right to pose a second question, he formulated it too favourably to the appellant. The question was put to the jury in the following terms:

> 'Taking into account all the circumstances of the case, including the age, sex, sexual propensities and other characteristics personal to the defendant, including his state of mind and the amount of drink or drugs he had taken, was it reasonable for the defendant to behave in the way he did, that is to take part in the murder of his wife as a result of the fear present at the time in his mind? The test of reasonableness in this context is: would the defendant's behaviour in all the particular circumstances to which I have just referred reflect the degree of self-control and firmness of purpose which everyone is entitled to expect that his fellow citizens would exercise in society as it is today?'

If the references to drink and drugs had been omitted, the judge's phraseology would have been in line with the direction given in cases of provocation (see *DPP v Camplin* [1978] 2 All ER 168, [1978] AC 705 and *R v Newell* (1980) 71 Cr App R 331). By using those words the judge introduced, says counsel for the Crown, transitory factors and self-induced factors peculiar to the appellant and having no place in an objective test.

There is no direct binding authority on the questions whether the test is solely subjective or, if objective, how it is to be formulated... .

Smith and Hogan's *Criminal Law* (4th edn, 1978) page 205 states the law in this way:

> '*Subjective or Objective?* Since duress is a concession to human frailty and some are more frail than others so, it is arguable, the standard should vary. Probably, however, the standard of resolution and fortitude required is fixed by the law. It is for the law to lay down standards of conduct. Under provocation, D must display a reasonable degree of self-restraint. When actually attacked, D may use only a reasonable degree of force in self-defence. In blackmail, P is expected to display a measure of fortitude and not to be affected by trivial threats. Probably, then, a person under duress must display reasonable fortitude and has no defence unless the threat is one which might have affected a reasonably resolute man.'

As a matter of public policy, it seems to us essential to limit the defence of duress by means of an objective criterion formulated in terms of reasonableness. Consistency of approach in defences to criminal liability is obviously desirable. Provocation and duress are analogous. In provocation the words or actions of one person break the self-control of another. In duress the words or actions of one person break the will of another. The law requires a defendant to have the self-control reasonably to be expected of the ordinary citizen in his situation. It should likewise require him to have the steadfastness reasonably to be expected of the ordinary citizen in his situation. So too with self-defence, in which the law permits the use of no more force than is reasonable in the circumstances. And, in general, if a mistake is to excuse what would otherwise be criminal, the mistake must be a reasonable one.

It follows that we accept counsel for the Crown's submission that the direction in this case was too favourable to the appellant. The Crown having conceded that the issue of duress was open to the appellant and was raised on the evidence, the correct approach on the facts of this case would have been as follows: (1) was the defendant, or may he have been, impelled to act as he did because, as a result of what he reasonably believed King had said or done, he had good cause to fear that if he did not so act King would kill him or (if this is to be added) cause him serious physical injury? (2) if so, have the prosecution made the jury sure that a sober person of reasonable firmness, sharing the characteristics of the defendant, would not have responded to whatever he reasonably believed King said or did by taking part in the killing? The fact that a defendant's will to resist has been eroded by the voluntary consumption of drink or drugs or both is not relevant to this test.

 Alert

We doubt whether the Crown were right to concede that the question of duress ever arose on the facts of this case. The words and deeds of King relied on by the defence were far short of those needed to raise a threat of the requisite gravity. However, the Crown having made the concession, the judge was right to pose the second objective question to the jury. His only error lay in putting it too favourably to the appellant.

The Court of Appeal dismissed the appeal.

R v Hasan [2005] UKHL 22, [2005] 2 AC 467

Panel: Lord Bingham of Cornhill, Lord Steyn, Lord Rodger of Earlsferry, Baroness Hale of Richmond and Lord Brown of Eaton-Under-Heywood

Facts: The defendant was charged with aggravated burglary contrary to the Theft Act 1968 s 10. He pleaded duress on the basis that he had been coerced into committing the burglary by a drug dealer. He claimed that the drug dealer had threatened both him and his family with violence unless the defendant committed the burglary. He further claimed that he had no chance to escape to go to the police. His appeal against conviction was dismissed by the Court of Appeal. The House of Lords considered the scope of the defence of duress.

LORD BINGHAM OF CORNHILL

17. The commonsense starting point of the common law is that adults of sound mind are ordinarily to be held responsible for the crimes which they commit. To this general principle there has, since the fourteenth century, been a recognised but limited exception in favour of those who commit crimes because they are forced or compelled to do so against their will by the threats of another. Such persons are said, in the language of the criminal law, to act as they do because they are subject to duress.

18. Where duress is established, it does not ordinarily operate to negative any legal ingredient of the crime which the defendant has committed. Nor is it now

regarded as justifying the conduct of the defendant, as has in the past been suggested... . Duress is now properly to be regarded as a defence which, if established, excuses what would otherwise be criminal conduct... .

19. Duress affords a defence which, if raised and not disproved, exonerates the defendant altogether. It does not, like the defence of provocation to a charge of murder, serve merely to reduce the seriousness of the crime which the defendant has committed. And the victim of a crime committed under duress is not, like a person against whom a defendant uses force to defend himself, a person who has threatened the defendant or been perceived by the defendant as doing so. The victim of a crime committed under duress may be assumed to be morally innocent, having shown no hostility or aggression towards the defendant. The only criminal defences which have any close affinity with duress are necessity, where the force or compulsion is exerted not by human threats but by extraneous circumstances, and, perhaps, marital coercion under s 47 of the Criminal Justice Act 1925.

20. Where the evidence in the proceedings is sufficient to raise an issue of duress, the burden is on the prosecution to establish to the criminal standard that the defendant did not commit the crime with which he is charged under duress... .

21. Having regard to these features of duress, I find it unsurprising that the law in this and other jurisdictions should have been developed so as to confine the defence of duress within narrowly defined limits...,

(1) Duress does not afford a defence to charges of murder..., attempted murder... and, perhaps, some forms of treason... . The Law Commission has in the past... recommended that the defence should be available as a defence to all offences, including murder, and the logic of this argument is irresistible. But their recommendation has not been adopted, no doubt because it is felt that in the case of the gravest crimes no threat to the defendant, however extreme, should excuse commission of the crime... . **Alert**

(2) To found a plea of duress the threat relied on must be to cause death or serious injury...

(3) The threat must be directed against the defendant or his immediate family or someone close to him. ...[T]he threat must be directed, if not to the defendant or a member of his immediate family, to a person for whose safety the defendant would reasonably regard himself as responsible... . **Alert**

(4) The relevant tests pertaining to duress have been largely stated objectively, with reference to the reasonableness of the defendant's perceptions and conduct and not, as is usual in many other areas of the criminal law, with primary reference to his subjective perceptions... .

(5) The defence of duress is available only where the criminal conduct which it is sought to excuse has been directly caused by the threats which are relied upon.

(6) The defendant may excuse his criminal conduct on grounds of duress only if, placed as he was, there was no evasive action he could reasonably have been expected to take... .

(7) The defendant may not rely on duress to which he has voluntarily laid himself open... .

After considering the existing limitations of the defence of duress, Lord Bingham discussed the law relating to four questions which the trial judge had directed the jury to answer in their deliberations. The first two questions were:

Was the defendant driven or forced to act as he did by threats which, rightly or wrongly, he genuinely believed that if he did not burgle the house, his family would be seriously harmed or killed?

Would a reasonable person of the defendant's age and background have been driven or forced to act as the defendant did?

In relation to these questions, Lord Bingham stated:

23. ...Save in one respect those directions substantially followed the formulation propounded by the Court of Appeal... in *R v Graham* [1982] 1 All ER 801 at 806,... approved by the House of Lords in *R v Howe* [1987] 1 All ER 771 at 783, 784-785, 790-791, 800,... . It is evident that the judge, very properly, based himself on the JSB's specimen direction as promulgated in August 2000. That specimen direction included the words, adopted by the judge, 'he genuinely believed'. But the words used in *R v Graham* and approved in *R v Howe* were 'he reasonably believed'. It is of course essential that the defendant should genuinely, i.e. actually, believe in the efficacy of the threat by which he claims to have been compelled. But there is no warrant for relaxing the requirement that the belief must be reasonable as well as genuine. There can of course be no complaint of this departure from authority, which was favourable to the defendant.

 Alert

Thus, the House of Lords confirmed that the threat must be one of death or serious injury and held that the defendant's belief in the threat must be reasonable as well as genuine.

The third question posed by the trial judge was:

Could the defendant have avoided acting as he did without harm coming to his family?

24. ...[T]he Court of Appeal held that the judge had misdirected the jury on question 3 because, it was held, there was no suggestion that the defendant could have taken evasive action. ... [T]here may be an area of overlap between questions 2 and 3: a reasonable person of a defendant's age and background would not have been forced and driven to act as the defendant did if there was any evasive action reasonably open to him to take in order to avoid committing the crime... .

26. The recent English authorities have tended to lay stress on the requirement that a defendant should not have been able, without reasonably fearing execution of the

threat, to avoid compliance. Thus Lord Morris in *Lynch v DPP for Northern Ireland* [1975] 1 All ER 913 at 918..., emphasised that duress—

'must never be allowed to be the easy answer of those who can devise no other explanation of their conduct nor of those who readily could have avoided the dominance of threats nor of those who allow themselves to be at the disposal and under the sway of some gangster-tyrant.'

Lord Simon gave as his first example of a situation in which a defence of duress should be available ([1975] 1 All ER 913 at 932...): 'A person, honestly and reasonably believing that a loaded pistol is at his back which will in all probability be used if he disobeys ...' In the view of Lord Edmund-Davies ([1975] 1 All ER 913 at 949...) there had been 'for some years an unquestionable tendency towards progressive latitude in relation to the plea of duress'.

27. In making that observation Lord Edmund-Davies did not directly criticise the reasoning of the Court of Appeal in its then recent judgment in *R v Hudson, R v Taylor* [1971] 2 All ER 244,... but that was described by Professor Glanville Williams as 'an indulgent decision' (*Textbook of Criminal Law* (2nd edn, 1983) page 636), and it has in my opinion had the unfortunate effect of weakening the requirement that execution of a threat must be reasonably believed to be imminent and immediate if it is to support a plea of duress. The appellants were two teenage girls who had committed perjury at an earlier trial by failing to identify the defendant. When prosecuted for perjury they set up a plea of duress, on the basis that they had been warned by a group, including a man with a reputation for violence, that if they identified the defendant in court the group would get the girls and cut them up. They resolved to tell lies, and were strengthened in their resolve when they arrived at court and saw the author of the threat in the public gallery. The trial judge ruled that the threats were not sufficiently present and immediate to support the defence of duress but was held by the Court of Appeal to have erred, since although the threats could not be executed in the courtroom they could be carried out in the streets of Salford that same night. It was argued for the Crown that the appellants should have neutralised the threat by seeking police protection, but this argument was criticised as failing to distinguish between cases in which the police would be able to provide effective protection and those when they would not... .

The appeal was allowed because evidence relied on by the appellant to show that he had had a reasonable apprehension of instant death was wrongly excluded. It is hard to read that decision as authority for the Court of Appeal's conclusion. I can understand that the Court of Appeal in *R v Hudson* had sympathy with the predicament of the young appellants but I cannot, consistently with principle, accept that a witness testifying in the Crown Court at Manchester has no opportunity to avoid complying with a threat incapable of execution then or there. When considering necessity in *R v Cole* (1994) Independent, 21 February, Simon Brown LJ, giving the judgment of the court, held that the peril relied on to support the plea of necessity lacked imminence and the degree of directness and immediacy required of the link between the suggested peril and the offence charged, but in *R v Abdul-Hussain* (1999) Times, 26

January, the Court of Appeal declined to follow these observations to the extent that they were inconsistent with *R v Hudson*, by which the court regarded itself as bound.

28. The judge's direction on question 3... is not in my opinion open to criticism. It should however be made clear to juries that if the retribution threatened against the defendant or his family or a person for whom he reasonably feels responsible is not such as he reasonably expects to follow immediately or almost immediately on his failure to comply with the threat, there may be little if any room for doubt that he could have taken evasive action, whether by going to the police or in some other way, to avoid committing the crime with which he is charged.

 Alert

On this point, Lord Bingham held that the defence of duress is unlikely to succeed where the defendant had an opportunity to take evasive action to avoid the consequences of the threat.

The fourth question addressed by the trial judge was:

Did the defendant voluntarily put himself in the position in which he knew he was likely to be subjected to threats?

31. The issue might have been raised in *Lynch v DPP for Northern Ireland* [1975] 1 All ER 913,... but the argument in that case was largely directed to the question whether the defence of duress was open to a defendant charged as a secondary party to murder. It was in *R v Fitzpatrick* [1977] NI 20, another IRA case, that the Court of Criminal Appeal in Northern Ireland had occasion to consider the matter in depth. The ratio of the decision is found in the judgment of the court delivered by Lowry LCJ (at 33):

'A person may become associated with a sinister group of men with criminal objectives and coercive methods of ensuring that their lawless enterprises are carried out and thereby voluntarily expose himself to illegal compulsion, whether or not the group is or becomes a proscribed organisation ... if a person voluntarily exposes and submits himself, as the appellant did, to illegal compulsion, he cannot rely on the duress to which he has voluntarily exposed himself as an excuse either in respect of the crimes he commits against his will or in respect of his continued but unwilling association with those capable of exercising upon him the duress which he calls in aid.'

32. That statement was no doubt drafted with the peculiar character of the IRA in mind. *R v Sharp* [1987] 3 All ER 103,... arose from criminal activity of a more routine kind committed by a gang of robbers. The trial judge's direction which was challenged on appeal is fully quoted in *R v Shepherd* (1987) 86 Cr App R 47 at 51, and was to this effect:

'but in my judgment the defence of duress is not available to an accused who voluntarily exposes and submits himself to illegal compulsion.

It is not merely a matter of joining in a criminal enterprise; it is a matter of joining in a criminal enterprise of such a nature that the defendant appreciated the nature of the enterprise itself and the attitudes of those in charge of it, so that when he was in fact subjected to compulsion he could fairly be said by a jury to have voluntarily exposed himself and submitted himself to such compulsion.'

The Court of Appeal (Lord Lane CJ, Farquharson and Gatehouse JJ) upheld that direction in *R v Sharp*, expressing the principle ([1987] 3 All ER 103 at 109,...):

'where a person has voluntarily, and with knowledge of its nature, joined a criminal organisation or gang which he knew might bring pressure on him to commit an offence and was an active member when he was put under such pressure, he cannot avail himself of the defence of duress.'

In *R v Shepherd*, the criminal activity was of a less serious kind: the question which the jury should have been (but were not) directed to consider (see (1987) 86 Cr App R 47 at 51) was 'whether the appellant could be said to have taken the risk of P's violence simply by joining a shoplifting gang of which he [P] was a member'.

33. *R v Ali* is summarised at [1995] Crim LR 303, but the ratio of the decision more clearly appears from the transcript of the judgment given by the Court of Appeal (Lord Taylor of Gosforth CJ, Alliott and Rix JJ) on 14 November 1994. The appellant claimed to have become involved in drug dealing and to have become indebted to his supplier, X, who (he said) had given him a gun and told him to obtain the money from a bank or building society the following day, failing which he would be killed. The appellant accordingly committed the robbery of which he was convicted. In directing the jury on the defence of duress advanced by the defendant the trial judge had said:

'The final question is this: did he, in obtaining heroin from Mr X and supplying it to others for gain, after he knew of Mr X's reputation for violence, voluntarily put himself in a position where he knew that he was likely to be forced by Mr X to commit a crime?'

It was argued by the appellant that the judge should have said 'forced by Mr X to commit armed robbery', but this was rejected, and the court held that by 'a crime' the jury could only have understood the judge to be referring to a crime other than drug dealing. The principle stated by the court on page 7 of the transcript was this:

'The crux of the matter, as it seems to us, is knowledge in the defendant of either a violent nature to the gang or the enterprise which he has joined, or a violent disposition in the person or persons involved with him in the criminal activity he voluntarily joined. In our judgment, if a defendant voluntarily participates in criminal offences with a man "X", whom he knows to be of a violent disposition and likely to require him to perform other criminal acts, he cannot rely upon duress if "X" does so.'

...

34. In its Working Paper no 55 of 1974, the Law Commission favoured (page 18 (para 26))—

'a limitation upon the defence [of duress] which would exclude its availability where the defendant had joined an association or conspiracy which was of such a character that he was aware that he might be compelled to participate in offences of the type with which he is charged.'

This reference to 'offences of the type with which he is charged' was, in substance, repeated in the Law Commission's *Criminal Law: Report on Defences of General Application* (1977) (Law Com no 83), pages 13-14, 17 (paras 2.38 and 2.46(8)), in cl 1(5) of the draft bill appended to that report, in cl 45(4) of the draft bill appended to the Law Commission's Report on *Codification of the Criminal Law* (1985) (Law Com no 143), as explained in para 13.19 (page 118) of the Report, and in cl 42(5) of the Law Commission's draft *Criminal Code Bill* (Law Com no 177) published in 1989. But there was no warrant for this gloss in any reported British authority until the Court of Appeal (Roch LJ, Richards J and Judge Colston QC) gave judgment in *R v Baker* [1999] 2 Cr App R 335. The facts were very similar to these in *R v Ali*, save that the appellants claimed that they had been specifically instructed to rob the particular store which they were convicted of robbing. The trial judge had directed the jury (see 341):

'A person cannot rely on the defence of duress if he has voluntarily and with full knowledge of its nature joined a criminal group which he was aware might bring pressure on him of a violent kind or require him if necessary to commit offences to obtain money where he himself had defaulted to the criminal group in payment to the criminal group.'

This was held (at 344) to be a misdirection:

'What a defendant has to be aware of is the risk that the group might try to coerce him into committing criminal offences of the type for which he is being tried by the use of violence or threats of violence.'

At 346 this ruling was repeated: 'The purpose of the pressure has to be to coerce the accused into committing a criminal offence of the type for which he is being tried.' The appeals were accordingly allowed and the convictions quashed.

35. Counsel for the defendant in the present case contends (as the Court of Appeal accepted) that this ruling was correct and that the trial judge in the present case misdirected the jury because he did not insist on the need for the defendant to foresee pressure to commit the offence of robbery of which he was convicted.

36. In *R v Heath* (1999) Times, 15 October (Court of Appeal: Kennedy LJ, Turner and Smedley JJ) the appellant again claimed that he had become indebted to a drug supplier, and claimed that he had been compelled by threats of physical violence to collect the consignment of drugs which gave rise to his conviction. His defence of duress failed at trial, rightly as the Court of Appeal held. In its judgment, Kennedy LJ said:

'The appellant in evidence conceded that he had put himself in the position where he was likely to be subjected to threats. He was therefore, in our judgment, not entitled to rely on those same threats as duress to excuse him from liability for subsequent criminal conduct.'

The court found it possible to distinguish *R v Baker*, observing:

'It is the awareness of the risk of compulsion which matters. Prior awareness of what criminal activity those exercising compulsion may offer as a possible alternative to violence is irrelevant.'

The facts in *R v Harmer* [2001] EWCA Crim 2930 (Court of Appeal: May LJ, Goldring and Gross JJ) were very similar to those in *R v Heath*, which the court followed. It does not appear from the court's judgment given by Goldring J whether *R v Baker* was directly cited, but it would seem that counsel for the appellant did not rely on it. He argued that the appellant did not foresee that he might be required to commit crimes for the supplier. But the court did not accept this argument:

> 'We cannot accept that where a man voluntarily exposes himself to unlawful violence, duress may run if he does not foresee that under the threat of such violence he may be required to commit crimes. There is no reason in principle why that should be so.'

37. The principal issue between the Crown on one side and the appellant and the Court of Appeal on the other is whether *R v Baker* correctly stated the law. To resolve that issue one must remind oneself of the considerations outlined in paras [18]-[22], above. The defendant is seeking to be wholly exonerated from the consequences of a crime deliberately committed. The prosecution must negative his defence of duress, if raised by the evidence, beyond reasonable doubt. The defendant is, ex hypothesi, a person who has voluntarily surrendered his will to the domination of another. Nothing should turn on foresight of the manner in which, in the event, the dominant party chooses to exploit the defendant's subservience. There need not be foresight of coercion to commit crimes, although it is not easy to envisage circumstances in which a party might be coerced to act lawfully. In holding that there must be foresight of coercion to commit crimes of the kind with which the defendant is charged, *R v Baker* mis-stated the law.

38. There remains the question, which the Court of Appeal left open in their judgment ([2003] 1 WLR 1489 at [75]), whether the defendant's foresight must be judged by a subjective or an objective test: ie does the defendant lose the benefit of a defence based on duress only if he actually foresaw the risk of coercion or does he lose it if he ought reasonably to have foreseen the risk of coercion, whether he actually foresaw the risk or not? I do not think any decided case has addressed this question, and I am conscious that application of an objective reasonableness test to other ingredients of duress has attracted criticism: see, for example, Elliott, 'Necessity, Duress and Self-Defence' [1989] Crim LR 611, pages 614-615, and the commentary by Professor Ashworth on *R v Safi* [2003] Crim LR 721, page 723. The practical importance of the distinction in this context may not be very great, since if a jury concluded that a person voluntarily associating with known criminals ought reasonably to have foreseen the risk of future coercion they would not, I think, be very likely to accept that he did not in fact do so. But since there is a choice to be made, policy in my view points towards an objective test of what

the defendant, placed as he was and knowing what he did, ought reasonably to have foreseen. I am not persuaded otherwise by analogies based on self-defence or provocation for reasons I have already given. The policy of the law must be to discourage association with known criminals, and it should be slow to excuse the criminal conduct of those who do so. If a person voluntarily becomes or remains associated with others engaged in criminal activity in a situation where he knows or ought reasonably to know that he may be the subject of compulsion by them or their associates, he cannot rely on the defence of duress to excuse any act which he is thereafter compelled to do by them. It is not necessary in this case to decide whether or to what extent that principle applies if an undercover agent penetrates a criminal gang for bona fide law enforcement purposes and is compelled by the gang to commit criminal acts.

39. I would answer this certified question by saying that the defence of duress is excluded when as a result of the accused's voluntary association with others engaged in criminal activity he foresaw or ought reasonably to have foreseen the risk of being subjected to any compulsion by threats of violence. ...

 Alert

This last question was the issue which formed the point of law which had been certified for consideration by the House of Lords in *R v Hasan*. The House stated that a defendant who has voluntarily associated with those engaged in criminal activity should not be able to rely upon the defence of duress if he foresaw or ought reasonably to have foreseen the risk of being subjected to such threats. Thus, an objective test is applied here.

14.3 Characteristics of the Reasonable Man

R v Bowen [1997] 1 WLR 372

Panel: Stuart-Smith LJ, Buckley J and Judge Hyam

Facts: The appellant, Cecil Bowen, was arrested and charged in relation to a number of deception offences. Although the appellant accepted that he had obtained goods on credit and not made full payment for them, he claimed, at his trial, that he had been acting under duress. The issue which arose within his appeal against his conviction was what characteristics could the jury take into account when determining whether a reasonable person would have acted in the same way.

LORD JUSTICE STUART-SMITH

But the question remains, what are the relevant characteristics of the accused to which the jury should have regard in considering the second objective test? This question has given rise to considerable difficulty in recent cases. It seems clear that age and sex are, and physical health or disability may be, relevant characteristics. But beyond that it is not altogether easy to determine from the authorities what others may be relevant.

In *R v Emery* (1992) 14 Cr App R the female defendant was convicted of cruelty which had resulted in the death of her child aged 11 months. On the same occasion the father of the child was convicted both of cruelty and assault causing actual bodily harm. At the trial each of the accused maintained that the other was responsible for abusing the child. Emery was allowed to call expert evidence in support of the defence of duress. She claimed that because of her fear of the father she had totally lost her capacity to act independently of him. The effect of the expert's evidence was that medical science recognised a condition known as "post-traumatic stress disorder" which can result from prolonged serious violence and abuse. The features of this disorder, also termed "learnt helplessness," include an inability to resist or stand up to the abuser coupled with a dependence on the abuser which made the victim unable to seek help. The defence of duress was rejected by the jury; but the Court of Appeal, in deciding whether the sentence of four years was correct, had occasion to consider whether the medical evidence was rightly admitted. Lord Taylor of Gosforth CJ said, at page 397:

> "The nature of the condition for which Miss Emery's advisers contended was something with which juries would not necessarily be familiar. The medical expertise relating to this form of stress disorder is of comparatively recent development. It is complex and it is not known by the public at large. Accordingly we are quite satisfied that it was appropriate for the judge to decide that this evidence should be allowed. Of course there must be limits on the nature of the evidence which can be given by medical experts in this context."

It appears, however, that the evidence of the doctors went further than elucidating the nature of post-traumatic stress disorder and sought to support the credibility of Miss Emery. Lord Taylor of Gosforth CJ said, at page 398:

> "The evidence should have gone no further than allowing for the doctors to give an expert account of the causes of the condition of dependent helplessness, the circumstances in which it might arise and what level of abuse would be required to produce it; what degree of isolation of the person in question one would expect to find before it appeared and what sort of personality factors might be involved. The issue the jury had to decide in regard to Miss Emery was, whether or not the prosecution had negatived duress, and therefore the question for the doctors was whether a woman of reasonable firmness with the characteristics of Miss Emery, if abused in the manner which she said, would have had her will crushed so that she could not have protected her child. It was not for the experts to go into the question whether what she had said by way of history as to what abuse had taken place was true or not."

In *R v Hegarty* [1994] Crim LR 353 the appellant sought to call before the jury evidence of medical witnesses to testify to his mental instability; their reports described him as "emotionally unstable" and in a "grossly elevated neurotic state." The judge refused to admit the evidence and his decision was upheld on appeal.

Questions of duress and provocation are similar, in that the twofold test applies in each case. So far as the objective test in provocation is concerned, the question is that posed by Lord Goff to which we have referred. In the case of duress, the question is: "Would an ordinary person sharing the characteristics of the defendant be able to resist the threats made to him?"

What principles are to be derived from these authorities? We think they are as follows. (1) The mere fact that the defendant is more pliable, vulnerable, timid or susceptible to threats than a normal person is not a characteristic with which it is legitimate to invest the reasonable/ordinary person for the purpose of considering the objective test. (2) The defendant may be in a category of persons whom the jury may think less able to resist pressure than people not within that category. Obvious examples are age, where a young person may well not be so robust as a mature one; possibly sex, though many women would doubtless consider they had as much moral courage to resist pressure as men; pregnancy, where there is added fear for the unborn child; serious physical disability, which may inhibit self protection; recognised mental illness or psychiatric condition, such as post-traumatic stress disorder leading to learnt helplessness. (3) Characteristics which may be relevant in considering provocation, because they relate to the nature of the provocation itself, will not necessarily be relevant in cases of duress. Thus homosexuality may be relevant to provocation if the provocative words or conduct are related to this characteristic; it cannot be relevant in duress, since there is no reason to think that homosexuals are less robust in resisting threats of the kind that are relevant in duress cases. (4) Characteristics due to self-induced abuse, such as alcohol, drugs or glue-sniffing, cannot be relevant. (5) Psychiatric evidence may be admissible to show that the defendant is suffering from some mental illness, mental impairment or recognised psychiatric condition provided persons generally suffering from such condition may be more susceptible to pressure and threats and thus to assist the jury in deciding whether a reasonable person suffering from such a condition might have been impelled to act as the defendant did. It is not admissible simply to show that in the doctor's opinion a defendant, who is not suffering from such illness or condition, is especially timid, suggestible or vulnerable to pressure and threats. Nor is medical opinion admissible to bolster or support the credibility of the accused.

 Alert

How are these principles to be applied in this case? Miss Levitt accepts, rightly in our opinion, that the evidence that the appellant was abnormally suggestible and a vulnerable individual is irrelevant. But she submits that the fact that he had, or may have had, a low IQ of 68 is relevant since it might inhibit his ability to seek the protection of the police. We do not agree. We do not see how low IQ, short of mental impairment or mental defectiveness, can be said to be a characteristic that makes those who have it less courageous and less able to withstand threats and pressure. Moreover, we do not think that any such submission as is now made, based solely on the appellant's low IQ, was ever advanced at the trial. Furthermore, it is to be noted that in two places in the summing up the judge told the jury that if they thought the appellant passed the subjective test they should acquit him. We are quite satisfied that in the circumstances of this case the judge's direction was sufficient. He directed the jury to consider the only two relevant characteristics, namely age and sex. It would not have assisted them, and might well have confused them, if he had added, without qualification, that the person of reasonable firmness was one who shared the characteristics of the appellant. For these reasons, the appeal will be dismissed.

14.4 Duress of Circumstances

The defence of duress of circumstances has developed into a separate defence over the years. This defence arises where the defendant is forced to act by force of circumstances, rather than by threats.

R v Martin [1989] 1 All ER 652

Panel: Lord Lane CJ, Simon Brown and Roch JJ

Facts: The defendant drove his car while disqualified and was charged accordingly. His wife had suicidal tendencies. On the day in question, the defendant's step son had overslept and was late for work. The defendant's wife became distraught and threatened to commit suicide unless the defendant drove the stepson to work. Genuinely believing her threats, the defendant did so. The trial judge held that the defence of duress of circumstances was not available. Consequently, the defendant pleaded guilty to the charge but then appealed on a point of law, raising the defence of duress of circumstances.

MR JUSTICE SIMON BROWN

The principles may be summarised thus. First, English law does, in extreme circumstances, recognise a defence of necessity. Most commonly this defence arises as duress, that is pressure upon the accused's will from the wrongful threats or violence of another. Equally, however, it can arise from other objective dangers threatening the accused or others. Arising thus it is conveniently called "duress of circumstances."

 Alert

Secondly, the defence is available only if, from an objective standpoint, the accused can be said to be acting reasonably and proportionately in order to avoid a threat of death or serious injury.

 Alert

Thirdly, assuming the defence to be open to the accused on his account of the facts, the issue should be left to the jury, who should be directed to determine these two questions: first, was the accused, or may he have been, impelled to act as he did because as a result of what he reasonably believed to be the situation he had good cause to fear that otherwise death or serious physical injury would result? Second, if so, may a sober person of reasonable firmness, sharing the characteristics of the accused, have responded to that situation by acting as the accused acted? If the answer to both those questions was yes, then the jury would acquit: the defence of necessity would have been established.

 Alert

That the defence is available in cases of reckless driving is established by *Conway*... itself and indeed by an earlier decision of the court in *Willer* (1986) 83 Cr App R 225. *Conway* is authority also for the proposition that the scope of the defence is no wider for reckless driving than for other serious offences. As was pointed out in the judgment, (1988) 88 Cr App R at 164 ...: " reckless driving can kill."

We see no material distinction between offences of reckless driving and driving whilst disqualified so far as the application of the scope of this defence is concerned'. Equally we can see no distinction in principle between various threats of death: it matters not whether the risk of death is by murder or by suicide or, indeed, by accident. One can illustrate the matter by considering a disqualified driver being driven by his wife, she suffering a heart attack in remote countryside and he needing instantly to get her to hospital.

It follows from this that the judge quite clearly did come to a wrong decision on the question of law, and the appellant should have been permitted to raise this defence for what it was worth before the jury.

It is in our judgment a great pity that that course was not taken. It is difficult to believe that any jury would in fact have swallowed the improbable story which this defendant desired to advance. There was, it emerged when evidence was given in mitigation, in the house at the time a brother of the boy who was late for work, who was licensed to drive, and available to do so; the suggestion was that he would not take his brother because of "a lot of aggravation in the house between them." It is a further striking fact that when apprehended by the police the appellant was wholly silent as to why on this occasion he had felt constrained to drive. But those considerations, in our judgment, were essentially for the jury, and we have concluded, although not without hesitation that it would be inappropriate here to apply the proviso.

Thus, the appeal was allowed and the defendant's conviction was quashed.

14.5 Necessity

There is a question mark over the issue of whether the defence of necessity applies to the offence of murder. It was long thought that necessity did not apply to such a serious offence; however, the courts appear to have circumvented making a definitive statement on this issue in recent years (see *Re A (children) (conjoined twins: separation)* [2000] EWCA Civ 254, [2001] FLR 267).

R v Dudley and Stephens (1884) 14 QBD 273

Panel: Lord Coleridge CJ, Grove and Denman JJ, Pollock and Huddleston BB

Facts: Five men, including the two defendants, were shipwrecked at sea over 1,000 miles from land. They survived for eight days without food and six days without water. They then decided to kill and eat the youngest and weakest member of the group, the 17 year old cabin boy. Days later they were rescued. On returning to land, the defendants were charged with the murder of the cabin boy. The jury found on a special verdict that the defendants were guilty of murder and that they could not escape liability by relying on a plea of necessity. The case was referred to the Queen's Bench Division.

LORD COLERIDGE CJ

...Now it is admitted that the deliberate killing of this unoffending and unresisting boy was clearly murder, unless the killing can be justified by some well-recognised excuse admitted by the law. It is further admitted that there was in this case no such excuse, unless the killing was justified by what has been called "necessity." But the temptation to the act which existed here was not what the law has ever called necessity. Nor is this to be regretted. Though law and morality are not the same, and many things may be immoral which are not necessarily illegal, yet the absolute divorce of law from morality would be of fatal consequence; and such divorce would follow if the temptation to murder in this case were to be held by law an absolute defence of it. It is not so. To preserve one's life is generally speaking a duty, but it may be the plainest and the highest duty to sacrifice it. War is full of instances in which it is a man's duty not to live, but to die. The duty, in case of shipwreck, of a captain to his crew, of the crew to the passengers, of soldiers to women and children, as in the noble case of the *Birkenhead*; these duties impose on men the moral necessity, not of the preservation, but of the sacrifice of their lives for others, from which in no country, least of all, it is to be hoped, in England, will men ever shrink, as indeed, they have not shrunk. It is not correct, therefore, to say that there is any absolute or unqualified necessity to preserve one's life. ... It is not needful to point out the awful danger of admitting the principle which has been contended for. Who is to be the judge of this sort of necessity? By what measure is the comparative value of lives to be measured? Is it to be strength, or intellect, or what? It is plain that the principle leaves to him who is to profit by it to determine the necessity which will justify him in deliberately taking another's life to save his own. In this case the weakest, the youngest, the most unresisting, was chosen. Was it more necessary to kill him than one of the grown men? The answer must be " No"...

Alert

Alert

[I]t is quite plain that such a principle once admitted might be made the legal cloak for unbridled passion and atrocious crime. There is no safe path for judges to tread but to ascertain the law to the best of their ability and to declare it according to their judgment; and if in any case the law appears to be too severe on individuals, to leave it to the Sovereign to exercise that prerogative of mercy which the Constitution has intrusted to the hands fittest to dispense it.

It must not be supposed that in refusing to admit temptation to be an excuse for crime it is forgotten how terrible the temptation was; how awful the suffering; how hard in such trials to keep the judgment straight and the conduct pure. We are often compelled to set up standards we cannot reach ourselves, and to lay down rules which we could not ourselves satisfy. But a man has no right to declare temptation to be an excuse, though he might himself have yielded to it, nor allow compassion for the criminal to change or weaken in any manner the legal definition of the crime. It is therefore our duty to declare that the prisoners' act in this case was wilful murder, that the facts as stated in the verdict are no legal justification of the homicide; and to say that in our unanimous opinion the prisoners are upon this special verdict guilty of murder.

Further Reading

Clarkson C 'Necessary Action: A New Defence' [2004] *Crim LR* 81

Elliott D 'Necessity, Duress and Self-defence' [1989] *Crim LR* 611

Rogers J 'Necessity, Private Defence and the Killing of Mary' [2001] *Crim LR* 515

Inchoate Offences: Incitement, Conspiracy and Attempt

15.1 Encouraging or Assisting Crime (Incitement)

The Serious Crime Act 2007 provides for three offences of encouraging or assisting crime. The Act also abolished the common law offence of incitement. These reforms arose as a result of the Law Commission Report in 2006 into *Inchoate Liability for Assisting and Encouraging Crime*. The Report criticised the offence of incitement for being "unsatisfactory for a number of reasons" (para. 1.5). The main reason for the reforms was to fill a loophole in the old common law which meant that a person who assisted the commission of an offence which did not ultimately take place faced no liability, while encouraging the commission of an offence which did not take place amounted to the common law offence of incitement.

Law Commission Report, No. 300, *Inchoate Liability for Assisting and Encouraging Crime* (2006)

1.1　The issue of criminal liability for encouraging or assisting another person to commit an offence is important, complex and difficult. It is important because it is very common for offences to involve two or more participants only some of whom are actual perpetrators of the offence as opposed to encouraging or assisting its commission.

1.2　The issue is also important because it is often the prime movers behind criminal ventures, for example drug or people traffickers, who take good care to distance themselves from the commission of the offences that they seek to encourage or assist. Recent advances in technology, together with the enhanced financial resources of career criminals, have facilitated this process.

1.3　This is the first of two reports in which we consider the circumstances in which a person ("D") ought to be criminally liable for encouraging or assisting another person ("P") to commit an offence. A substantial portion of this report focuses on what we consider to be a major defect of the common law. At common law if D encourages P to commit an offence that subsequently P does not commit or attempt to commit, D may nevertheless be criminally liable. By contrast, if D assists P to commit an offence, D incurs no criminal liability at common law if subsequently P, for whatever reason, does not commit or attempt to commit the offence:

Alert

Example 1A

D, in return for payment, lends a van to P believing that P will use the van in order to commit a robbery. The police arrest P in connection with another matter before P can even attempt to commit the robbery.

D is not criminally liable despite the fact that he or she intended to bring about harm and, by lending the van to P, has manifested that intention. If, however, in addition to giving P the van, D had uttered words encouraging P to rob V, D would be guilty of incitement to commit robbery. The common law appears to treat words more seriously than deeds. Yet, it might be thought that seeking to bring about harm by assisting a person to commit an offence is as culpable as seeking to do so by means of encouragement.

1.4 Increasingly, the police, through the gathering of intelligence, are able to identify preliminary acts of assistance by D before P commits or attempts to commit the principal offence. Yet, the common law only partially reflects this significant development. As a result, if D assists but does not encourage P to commit an offence, the police may have to forego at least some of the advantages of more sophisticated and effective methods of investigation by having to wait until P commits or attempts to commit the offence before they can proceed against D.

1.5 In contrast to acts of assistance, if D encourages P to commit an offence which P does not go on to commit, D will be guilty of incitement provided he or she satisfies the fault element of the offence. However, the offence of incitement has a number of unsatisfactory features:

 Alert

   (1) there is uncertainty as to whether it must be D's purpose that P should commit the offence that D is inciting;

   (2) the fault element of the offence has been distorted by decisions of the Court of Appeal. These decisions have focused, wrongly, on the state of mind of P rather than on D's state of mind;

   (3) there is uncertainty as to whether and, if so, to what extent it is a defence to act in order to prevent the commission of an offence or to prevent or limit the occurrence of harm;

   (4) there is uncertainty as to the circumstances in which D is liable for inciting P to do an act which, if done by P, would not involve P committing an offence, for example because P is under the age of criminal responsibility or lacks a guilty mind;

   (5) the rules governing D's liability in cases where D incites P to commit an inchoate offence have resulted in absurd distinctions;

   (6) D may have a defence if the offence that he or she incites is impossible to commit whereas impossibility is not a defence to other inchoate offences, apart from common law conspiracies.

The offence of incitement is therefore in need of clarification and reform.

...

4.25 ... If D sells P a weapon that D correctly believes P will use to murder V, D has done everything that that he or she intends to do. Nothing more turns on D's subsequent conduct whereas P has yet to take the step of attempting to commit the offence. Professor Spencer has described P as:

   "... still a long way from his objective, and [having] a number of psychological barriers to cross before he reaches it, at any one of which he may change his mind and abandon his wicked plan".

The case of *Race Relations Board v Applin* [1973] QB 815 was formerly the leading authority on the meaning of "incitement" and may still be a useful point of reference today.

Race Relations Board v Applin [1973] QB 815

Panel: Lord Denning MR, Buckley and Stephenson LJJ

Facts: Mr and Mrs Watson were foster parents who generally took four or five children into their home at a time. Over half of the children they fostered were not white. The neighbours objected to the Watsons fostering children who were not white. An organisation calling itself the National Front put pressure on the Watsons to adopt only children who were white. Mr Applin was the branch organiser of the National Front and he sent a circular to the neighbours which referred to the enlargement of the Watsons' house for use as a foster home for largely non-British children. It also accused Mr and Mrs Watson of making "malicious and disgraceful attacks" on their neighbours. The National Front also organised a public meeting complaining about the fostering of non-white children. The Race Relations Board brought an action in the civil courts seeking a declaration that the acts done by Mr Applin and the National Front were unlawful.

LORD DENNING MR

It is not easy to apply the Act to the situation before us, but I will try and explain it. It is quite clear that Mr and Mrs Watson were acting perfectly lawfully. They were fostering children without making any difference between them on the ground of colour. Mr Applin and Mr Taylor were bringing pressure to bear on Mr and Mrs Watson to get them to take white children only, and not coloured ones. That pressure did not succeed. Mr and Mrs Watson have resisted it. They have continued to take white and coloured children without making any difference. They continue so to take them. But, the point is this: suppose the pressure had succeeded. Suppose that Mr and Mrs Watson had stipulated "We will only take white children". Would that conduct of Mr and Mrs Watson have been unlawful? If it would have been unlawful, then it was unlawful of Mr Applin and Mr Taylor to bring pressure to bear on Mr and Mrs Watson to do an unlawful act. This follows from section 12 of the Act of 1968, which says:

> "Any person who deliberately aids, induces or incites another person to do an act which is unlawful by virtue of any provision of this Part of this Act shall be treated for the purposes of this Act as doing that act."

If, therefore, Mr Applin and Mr Taylor "incited" Mr and Mrs Watson to do an unlawful act, i.e., to take white children only, they are to be treated as themselves doing that act, even though the incitement did not succeed. Here I may mention a small point. [Defence counsel] suggested that to "incite" means to urge or spur on by advice, encouragement, and persuasion, and not otherwise. I do not think the word is so limited, at any rate in this context. A person may "incite" another to do an act by threatening or by pressure, as well as by persuasion. Mr Applin and Mr Taylor undoubtedly brought pressure to bear on Mr and Mrs Watson to take white children only, and thus "incited" them to do so.

 Alert

So the question is this: if Mr and Mrs Watson had stipulated: "We will take white children only," and acted accordingly, would their conduct have been unlawful? This depends on section 2 (1) of the Act of 1968, which says:

> "It shall be unlawful for any person concerned with the provision to the public or a section of the public (whether on payment or otherwise) of any goods, facilities or services, to discriminate against any person seeking to obtain or use those goods, facilities or services by refusing or deliberately omitting to provide him with any of them or to provide him with goods, services or facilities of the like quality, in the like manner and on the like terms in and on which the former normally makes them available to other members of the public."

...

In my opinion,... it would be unlawful for Mr and Mrs Watson to stipulate with the local authority that they would take white children only. ... It was, therefore, unlawful for Mr Applin and Mr Taylor to incite Mr and Mrs Watson to take white children only by bringing pressure on them to do so.

Lord Denning MR allowed the appeal and granted the declaration that the conduct of Mr Applin and the National Front was unlawful. His Lordship provided a wide interpretation of the *actus reus* of incitement which covered anything from advice and persuasion to threats and pressure.

15.2 Statutory Conspiracy

Conspiracy is a statutory offence under the Criminal Law Act 1977 s 1(1). The *actus reus* of conspiracy is relatively straightforward and requires proof of an agreement between two or more people to pursue a course of conduct which amounts to a criminal offence. By contrast, the *mens rea* elements of statutory conspiracy have caused the courts some problems. It is clear that the prosecution must prove that the defendant intended to reach the agreement. However, confusion has arisen over whether the defendant must intend to agree that the offence be committed and whether he must intend to play a part in carrying out the agreement. The House of Lords' decision in *R v Anderson* [1986] AC 27 can be identified as the root cause of the confusion.

R v Anderson [1986] AC 27

Panel: Lord Scarman, Lord Diplock, Lord Keith of Kinkel, Lord Bridge of Harwich and Lord Brightman

Statute: Criminal Law Act 1977 s 1(1)

Facts: The defendant agreed with X to participate in a plan to secure the escape of X from prison. The defendant was to supply diamond wire which was capable of cutting through metal bars. He was to be paid £20,000 for his part in the plan. Before the escape could be put into effect, the defendant was charged with conspiracy to effect the escape of a prisoner contrary to the Criminal Law Act 1977 s 1(1). Defence counsel made a submission of no case to answer on the basis that the defendant did not have the necessary *mens rea* for the offence since he did not intend the escape plan to actually take place, and even if it did, he did not think that it would succeed. This submission was rejected by the trial judge. The defendant appealed against conviction to the Court of Appeal and then to the House of Lords.

LORD BRIDGE OF HARWICH

The Act of 1977, subject to exceptions not presently material, abolished the offence of conspiracy at common law. It follows that the elements of the new statutory offence of conspiracy must be ascertained purely by interpretation of the language of section 1(1) of the Act of 1977. For purposes of analysis it is perhaps convenient to isolate the three clauses each of which must be taken as indicating an essential ingredient of the offence as follows: (1) "if a person agrees with any other person or persons that a course of conduct shall be pursued" (2) "which will necessarily amount to or involve the commission of any offence or offences by one or more of the parties to the agreement" (3) "if the agreement is carried out in accordance with their intentions".

Clause (1) presents, as it seems to me, no difficulty. It means exactly what it says and what it says is crystal clear. To be convicted, the party charged must have agreed with one or more others that "a course of conduct shall be pursued". What is important is to resist the temptation to introduce into this simple concept ideas derived from the civil law of contract. Any number of persons may agree that a course of conduct shall be pursued without undertaking any contractual liability. The agreed course of conduct may be a simple or an elaborate one and may involve the participation of two or any larger number of persons who may have agreed to play a variety of roles in the course of conduct agreed.

Again, clause (2) could hardly use simpler language. Here what is important to note is that it is not necessary that more than one of the participants in the agreed course of conduct shall commit a substantive offence. It is, of course, necessary that any party to the agreement shall have assented to play his part in the agreed course of conduct, however innocent in itself, knowing that the part to be played by one or more of the others will amount to or involve the commission of an offence.

It is only clause (3) which presents any possible ambiguity. The heart of the submission for the appellant is that in order to be convicted of conspiracy to commit a given offence the language of clause (3) requires that the party charged should not only have agreed that a course of conduct shall be pursued which will necessarily amount to or involve the commission of that offence by himself or one or more other parties to the agreement, but must also be proved himself to have intended that that offence should be committed. Thus, it is submitted here that the appellant's case that he never intended that Andaloussi should be enabled to escape from prison raised an issue to be left to the jury, who should have been directed to convict him only if satisfied that he did so intend. I do not find it altogether easy to understand why the draftsman of this provision chose to use the phrase "in accordance with their intentions". But I suspect the answer may be that this seemed a desirable alternative to the phrase "in accordance with its terms" or any similar expression, because it is a matter of common experience in the criminal courts that the "terms" of a criminal conspiracy are hardly ever susceptible of proof. The evidence from which a jury may infer a criminal conspiracy is almost invariably to be found in the conduct of the parties. This was so at common law and remains so under the statute. If the evidence in a given case justifies the inference of an agreement that a course of conduct should be pursued, it is a not inappropriate formulation of the test of the criminality of the inferred agreement to ask whether the further inference can be drawn that a crime would necessarily have been committed if the agreed course of conduct had been pursued in accordance with the *several* intentions of the parties. Whether that is an accurate analysis or not, I am clearly driven by consideration of the diversity of roles which parties may agree to play in criminal conspiracies to reject any construction of the statutory language which would require the prosecution to prove an intention on the part of each conspirator that the criminal offence or offences which will necessarily be committed by one or more of the conspirators if the agreed course of conduct is fully carried out should in fact be committed. A simple example will illustrate the absurdity to which this construction would lead. The proprietor of a car hire firm agrees for a substantial payment to make available a hire car to a gang for use in a robbery and to make false entries in his books relating to the hiring to which he can point if the number of the car is traced back to him in connection with the robbery. Being fully aware of the circumstances of the robbery in which the car is proposed to be used he is plainly a party to the conspiracy to rob. Making his car available for use in the robbery is as much a part of the relevant agreed course of conduct as the robbery itself. Yet, once he has been paid, it will be a matter of complete indifference to him whether the robbery is in fact committed or not. In these days of highly organised crime the most serious statutory conspiracies will frequently involve an elaborate and complex agreed course of conduct in which many will consent to play necessary but subordinate roles, not involving them in any direct participation in the commission of the offence or offences at the centre of the conspiracy. Parliament cannot have intended that such parties should escape conviction of conspiracy on the basis that it cannot be proved against them that they intended that the relevant offence or offences should be committed.

 Alert

There remains the important question whether a person who has agreed that a course of conduct will be pursued which, if pursued as agreed, will necessarily amount to or involve the commission of an offence is guilty of statutory conspiracy irrespective of his intention, and, if not, what is the mens rea of the offence. I have no hesitation in answering the first part of the question in the negative. There may be many situations in which perfectly respectable citizens, more particularly those concerned with law enforcement, may enter into agreements that a course of conduct shall be pursued which will involve commission of a crime without the least intention of playing any part in furtherance of the ostensibly agreed criminal objective, but rather with the purpose of exposing and frustrating the criminal purpose of the other parties to the agreement. To say this is in no way to encourage schemes by which police act, directly or through the agency of informers, as agents provocateurs for the purpose of entrapment. That is conduct of which the courts have always strongly disapproved. But it may sometimes happen, as most of us with experience in criminal trials well know, that a criminal enterprise is well advanced in the course of preparation when it comes to the notice either of the police or of some honest citizen in such circumstances that the only prospect of exposing and frustrating the criminals is that some innocent person should play the part of an intending collaborator in the course of criminal conduct proposed to be pursued. The mens rea implicit in the offence of statutory conspiracy must clearly be such as to recognise the innocence of such a person, notwithstanding that he will, in literal terms, be obliged to agree that a course of conduct be pursued involving the commission of an offence.

I have said already, but I repeat to emphasise its importance, that an essential ingredient in the crime of conspiring to commit a specific offence or offences under section 1(1) of the Act of 1977 is that the accused should agree that a course of conduct be pursued which he knows must involve the commission by one or more of the parties to the agreement of that offence or those offences. But, beyond the mere fact of agreement, the necessary mens rea of the crime is, in my opinion, established if, and only if, it is shown that the accused, when he entered into the agreement, intended to play some part in the agreed course of conduct in furtherance of the criminal purpose which the agreed course of conduct was intended to achieve. Nothing less will suffice; nothing more is required.

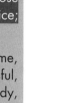

Alert

Alert

Applying this test to the facts which, for the purposes of the appeal, we must assume, the appellant, in agreeing that a course of conduct be pursued that would, if successful, necessarily involve the offence of effecting Andaloussi's escape from lawful custody, clearly intended, by providing diamond wire to be smuggled into the prison, to play a part in the agreed course of conduct in furtherance of that criminal objective. Neither the fact that he intended to play no further part in attempting to effect the escape, nor that he believed the escape to be impossible, would, if the jury had supposed they might be true, have afforded him any defence.

The appeal was unanimously dismissed by the House of Lords. Lord Bridge stated that there is no requirement that a defendant intend that the offence be committed, but he must intend to "play some part in the agreed course of conduct". Despite its binding status as a House of Lords authority, the *dicta* of Lord Bridge on both of these points has been criticised and overlooked in later cases (see *R v McPhillips* [1990] 6 BNIL (NICA), *Yip Chiu-Cheung v R* [1994] 2 All ER 924 and *R v Siracusa* (1990) 90 Cr App R 340 below). The case was also addressed recently by the Law Commission in its Consultation Paper on *Conspiracy and Attempts*.

Law Commission Consultation Paper No. 183, *Conspiracy and Attempts* (2007)

1.38 Section 1(1) of the 1977 Act appears unambiguously to require that for a person to be convicted of conspiracy he or she must intend that the conduct element of the principal offence be perpetrated and that the consequence element (if any) of the substantive offence materialise. However, the well-known and much criticized decision of the House of Lords in *Anderson* detracts from the clarity of this position. On the one hand, it requires that D must intend "to play some part in the agreed course of conduct". On the other hand, it does not require that D should intend that the agreement be carried through to completion. In both respects, the decision is troublesome.

1.39 First, there is no reason, in terms of statutory language or policy, for insisting that D must intend to play some part in implementing the agreement. If D1 and D2 agree to murder V, D1 ought to be convicted of conspiracy to murder even if it was not his or her intention to play any part in V's murder. Secondly, an agreement to commit an offence implies an intention that it should be committed, as section 1(1) of the 1977 Act seems to make clear. The idea of a conspiracy that the conspirators agree to take part in but which none intends to see carried out is very unsatisfactory.

R v McPhillips [1990] 6 BNIL (NICA)

Panel: Lord Lowry, O'Donnell and Kelly LJJ

Statute: Criminal Attempts and Conspiracy (Northern Ireland) Order 1983 Article 9(1)

Facts: The appellant was in a car which was stopped by the police. A search revealed that the car contained explosives and the appellant admitted being part of a conspiracy to plant a bomb on the roof of a hotel, timed to go off during a disco. The appellant claimed that he intended to give a warning before the bomb went off but that he was not going to tell his co-conspirators about this. The appellant was convicted of conspiracy to murder and appealed.

LORD LOWRY

To be guilty at common law of conspiracy to murder the accused must agree with another that murder will be committed and must intend that this will happen. The guilty act is the agreement that the crime contemplated will be committed; the guilty mind is the intention that that crime will be committed. Both elements were needed in order to render the accused guilty: *DPP v Nock* [1978] AC 979, 994E.... In regard to the offence of statutory conspiracy section 1(1) "assumes the existence of an intention of the parties to carry out the agreement": Smith & Hogan, Criminal Law (6th ed 1988) 259. The wording of the identical article 9(1) makes this clear: the agreed course of conduct was the planting of a "no warning" bomb at the Seagoe Hotel and persons who had agreed to that course of conduct intending it to be carried out would be guilty of conspiracy to murder because, if the agreement had been carried out in accordance with their intentions it would (unless all the patrons of the disco had gone home or had a miraculous escape) necessarily involve the commission of murder. But, on the facts found here, this result would not have been in accordance with the intention of the appellant. Therefore he was not guilty of conspiracy to murder. So, although, by going to the Seagoe in Drumm's car, the appellant up to a point acted in accordance with the agreed course of conduct (and was thereby guilty of conspiracy to cause an explosion), he was not guilty as an alleged conspirator in respect of count 1. This result is consistent with the doctrine that, if a joint enterprise goes beyond the agreed or authorised act, a party to that enterprise is not guilty beyond the acts which he agreed to or authorised. To put the matter simply, there must be a common criminal design

 Alert

and, in order to be guilty of a conspiracy to carry out that design, the accused must be a party to the design. That condition is not satisfied in this case.

The Crown's alternative proposition is that the appellant was guilty of aiding and abetting a conspiracy to murder on the part of the conspirators and was therefore liable to be tried, indicted and punished (as happened in the instant case) as a principal offender. The need, and the ability, to rely on this proposition must stem from the hypothesis that the appellant was not a party to the conspiracy to murder, and that hypothesis (having regard to the appellant's ostensible acquiescence in the murder plan) must be based on the fact that the appellant did not intend or authorise the commission of murder. But how then, say the appellant's counsel, did he aid and abet a conspiracy to murder? The Crown's answer is that the appellant assisted the conspirators by his presence when the murder plan was devised and by accompanying Drumm in the car which was conveying the bomb to the intended scene of the crime...

The common law offence of aiding and abetting involves an act of assisting the principal (actus reus) and a guilty intention (mens rea) that the crime will be committed. This intention is not to be confused with purpose, motive or desire (although those elements may be and often are present) but can be inferred from, and has been in the recent past wrongly identified with, the probability, overwhelming probability or certainty (known to the aider and abettor) that the crime will be committed. Conspiracy is a crime which it is possible to aid and abet and thus the ingredients of aiding and abetting a conspiracy remain as we have described them: a person aids and abets a conspiracy to commit a crime when, not being a party to the conspiracy (otherwise he would be a principal offender) and knowing of the agreement and at least its general object, he assists the principal offenders (by an actus reus, such as supplying a vehicle or a weapon) with the guilty intention (mens rea) that the object of the conspiracy should be achieved.

...[T]he decisive point here is that ...the fact that the appellant had the intention, which he could reasonably have expected to implement, that murder would not take place destroys the possibility of finding the necessary mens rea on his part.

The appellant's acts and intentions were sufficient to render him guilty of conspiracy to cause an explosion, and the same acts are relied on to prove him guilty of aiding and abetting the conspiracy to murder. This overlooks the fact that his intentions differed between causing an explosion and aiding the commission of a murder. ...The action proposed by the conspirators, namely, to plant a bomb with no warning (and thereby to extend a property damaging explosion into a murder) was something which the appellant did not authorise and had actually made up his mind to prevent. And the fact that the extension of the crime involved a negative, that is, a failure to warn, cannot obscure the reality that this proposed failure was to be an aggravation of the crime, since the distinction between a warning bomb and a no warning bomb is well understood.

As we have said, the Crown also relied on *R v Anderson* [1986] AC 27, in which the appellant was convicted of conspiracy to effect the escape of a prisoner. Stress has been laid on Anderson's undisclosed intention not to carry out the second part of his agreed role (that is, the supply of a car to facilitate the prisoner's getaway) and on his avowed belief that the escape attempt was doomed to failure, notwithstanding all of which his conviction was affirmed. The conclusion which the court has been invited to draw is that a person can and should be found guilty of conspiracy to effect an escape (or of aiding and abetting such a conspiracy: see the judgment in the Court of Appeal in *R v Anderson* (1985) 80 Cr App R 64, 76).

The case has given rise to some interesting discussion in the learned legal periodicals, to which, however, we deem it unnecessary to contribute, since we consider the case to be readily distinguishable. The appellant there conspired to effect the escape of a remand prisoner and, pursuant to the agreement reached, supplied "diamond lace" to help the prisoner to cut his way out. Up to that stage he could be said to have agreed to help and to have actually helped in the escape and to have contemplated that, if the conspiracy went according to plan, the object would be achieved and the offence of prison breach would be committed. Neither his intention not to fulfil the second part of his allotted role nor his avowed opinion that the escape could not succeed can detract from his guilt already proved. Nor could Anderson be saved by the fact that he did not intend the "agreement" to be performed, in the sense that he would participate in stage 2. The judgment in the Court of Appeal cites *R v Thomson* (1965) 50 Cr App R 1 and *Churchill v Walton* [1967] 2 AC 224, both being cases consistent with what we have already said on the subject of mens rea in conspiracy, and the conclusion reached appears to us to be consistent both with those cases and with what we have said in this judgment.

So far as concerns the hearing before the House of Lords, we find it necessary only to recall what Lord Bridge of Harwich, who delivered the leading speech, said at 39D:

> "I have said already, but I repeat to emphasise its importance, that an essential ingredient in the crime of conspiring to commit a specific offence or offences under section 1(1) of the Act of 1977 is that the accused should agree that a course of conduct be pursued which he knows must involve the commission by one or more of the parties to the agreement of that offence or those offences."

It is obvious, for the reasons already given, that, so far as count 1 is concerned, the conduct of the appellant does not satisfy that test. It is equally clear that R v Anderson is not an authority for the proposition that someone who at all times intends to frustrate the commission of the crime "agreed upon" is guilty of conspiracy to commit that crime or of aiding and abetting such a conspiracy.

...[T]he appellant was not guilty of conspiracy to murder either as a principal offender or as an accomplice because his mind did not go with his acts, but on the contrary was directed towards frustrating the conspiracy to murder. The mere fact that the appellant had already committed terrorist offences and was a member of a terrorist organisation does not disable him from relying on the absence of the necessary intent and the principle enunciated in *R v Fitzpatrick* [1977] NI 20 is not in point.

While the conviction on counts 2 and 3 will stand, the conviction appealed against in relation to count 1 must therefore be quashed.

The appellant's conviction was quashed on the basis that he did not intend that the agreement be carried out. This was clearly evidenced from the fact that he planned to telephone through a warning without the knowledge of his co-conspirators. The House of Lords' decision in *R v Anderson* was not followed, but was distinguished. The Privy Council has also refused to follow *R v Anderson*.

Yip Chiu-Cheung v R [1995] 1 AC 111

Panel: Lord Jauncey of Tullichettle, Lord Griffiths, Lord Browne-Wilkinson, Lord Mustill and Lord Slynn of Hadley

Facts: This case took place in Hong Kong, where the appellant was convicted of conspiracy to traffic in heroin. The conspiracy involved an undercover drug enforcement agent who arranged to meet the appellant in Hong Kong in order to be supplied with heroin which he was to carry on a flight to Australia. The agent was trying to break a drug ring. The authorities had known about the conspiracy and had agreed not to stop the agent. The agent claimed that he had intended to carry out the agreement but that he abandoned the agreed course of action after he missed his flight. The trial judge directed the jury that if the agent had intended to carry the heroin on the flight, he was a co-conspirator and they could convict the appellant of conspiracy with the agent. The appellant appealed against his conviction on the ground that the agent lacked the *mens rea* necessary for conspiracy. The Court of Appeal of Hong Kong dismissed the appeal on the basis that the trial judge's direction was correct and the agent was capable of being a co-conspirator. The appellant appealed to the Privy Council.

LORD GRIFFITHS

On the principal ground of appeal it was submitted that the trial judge and the Court of Appeal were wrong to hold that Needham, the undercover agent, could be a conspirator because he lacked the necessary mens rea or guilty mind required for the offence of conspiracy. It was urged upon their Lordships that no moral guilt attached to the undercover agent who was at all times acting courageously and with the best of motives in attempting to infiltrate and bring to justice a gang of criminal drug dealers. In these circumstances it was argued that it would be wrong to treat the agent as having any criminal intent, and reliance was placed upon a passage in the speech of Lord Bridge of Harwich in *Reg. v Anderson (William Ronald)* [1986] AC 27 , 38-39; but in that case Lord Bridge was dealing with a different situation from that which exists in the present case. There may be many cases in which undercover police officers or other law enforcement agents pretend to join a conspiracy in order to gain information about the plans of the criminals, with no intention of taking any part in the planned crime but rather with the intention of providing information that will frustrate it. It was to this situation that Lord Bridge was referring in *Reg. v Anderson*. The crime of conspiracy requires an agreement between two or more persons to commit an unlawful act with the intention of carrying it out. It is the intention to carry out the crime that constitutes the necessary mens rea for the offence. As Lord Bridge pointed out, an undercover agent who has no intention of committing the crime lacks the necessary mens rea to be a conspirator.

 Alert

The facts of the present case are quite different. Nobody can doubt that Needham was acting courageously and with the best of motives; he was trying to break a drug ring. But equally there can be no doubt that the method he chose and in which the police in Hong Kong acquiesced involved the commission of the criminal offence of trafficking in drugs by exporting heroin from Hong Kong without a licence. Needham intended to commit that offence by carrying the heroin through the customs and on to the aeroplane bound for Australia.

Neither the police, nor customs, nor any other member of the executive have any power to alter the terms of the Ordinance forbidding the export of heroin, and the fact that they may turn a blind eye when the heroin is exported does not prevent it from being a criminal offence.

The High Court of Australia in *A. v Hayden (No. 2)* (1984) 156 CLR 532 declared emphatically that there was no place for a general defence of superior orders or of Crown or executive fiat in Australian criminal law. Gibbs CJ said, at page 540:

'It is fundamental to our legal system that the executive has no power to authorise a breach of the law and that it is no excuse for an offender to say that he acted under the orders of a superior officer.'

This statement of the law applies with the same force in England and Hong Kong as it does in Australia.

Naturally, Needham never expected to be prosecuted if he carried out the plan as intended. But the fact that in such circumstances the authorities would not prosecute the undercover agent does not mean that he did not commit the crime albeit as part of a wider scheme to combat drug dealing.

The judge correctly directed the jury that they should regard Needham as a conspirator if they found that he intended to export the heroin.

The Privy Council dismissed the appeal and held that the *mens rea* of conspiracy required an intention to carry out the crime. Thus, the Privy Council refused to follow *R v Anderson*.

In *R v Anderson*, Lord Bridge stated that the prosecution must prove that the defendant intended to play a part in the agreement. This was not strictly followed by O'Connor LJ in the Court of Appeal in *R v Siracusa* (1990) 90 Cr App R 340.

R v Siracusa (1990) 90 Cr App R 340

Panel: O'Connor LJ, Boreham and Ian Kennedy JJ

Statute: Criminal Law Act 1977 s 1(1)

Facts: This case involved the mass importation of cannabis and heroin from Thailand and Kashmir to Canada via England. The drugs were hidden in secret compartments in specially constructed furniture. The defendant was involved in the operation and was charged with conspiracy to contravene the Customs and Excise Management Act 1979 s 170(2)(b) (conspiracy to import controlled drugs) contrary to the Criminal Law Act 1977 s 1(1). The defendant was convicted and appealed.

O'CONNOR LJ

We think it obvious that Lord Bridge [in R v Anderson] cannot have been intending that the organiser of a crime who recruited others to carry it out would not himself be guilty of conspiracy unless it could be proved that he intended to play some active part himself thereafter. Lord Bridge had pointed out at pages 259 and 38 respectively that

 Alert

> "...in these days of highly organised crime the most serious statutory conspiracies will frequently involve an elaborate and complex agreed course of conduct in which many will consent to play necessary but subordinate roles, not involving them in any direct participation in the commission of the offence or offences at the centre of the conspiracy."

The present case is a classic example of such a conspiracy. It is the hallmark of such crimes that the organisers try to remain in the background and more often than not are not apprehended. Secondly, the origins of all conspiracies are concealed and it is usually quite impossible to establish when or where the initial agreement was made, or when or where other conspirators were recruited. The very existence of the agreement can only be inferred from overt acts. Participation in a conspiracy is infinitely variable: it can be active or passive. If the majority shareholder and director of a company consents to the company being used for drug smuggling carried out in the company's name by a fellow director and minority shareholder, he is guilty of conspiracy. Consent, that is the agreement or adherence to the agreement, can be inferred if it is proved that he knew what was going on and the intention to participate in the furtherance of the criminal purpose is also established by his failure to stop the unlawful activity. Lord Bridge's *dictum* does not require anything more.

 Alert

 Alert

We return to... Lord Bridge's speech. ...when he goes on to say:

> "...an essential ingredient in the crime of conspiring to commit a specific offence or offences under section 1(1) of the Act of 1977 is that the accused should agree that a course of conduct be pursued which he knows must involve the commission by one or more of the parties to the agreement of that offence or those offences,"

he plainly does not mean that the prosecution have to prove that persons who agree to import prohibited drugs into this country know that the offence which will be committed will be a contravention of section 170(2) of the Customs and Excise Act . He is not to be taken as saying that the prosecution must prove that the accused knew the name of the crime. We are satisfied that Lord Bridge was doing no more than applying the words of section 1 of the Criminal Law Act 1977, namely, that when the accused agreed to the course of conduct, he knew that it involved the commission of an offence.

The *mens rea* sufficient to support the commission of a substantive offence will not necessarily be sufficient to support a charge of conspiracy to commit that offence. An intent to cause grievous bodily harm is sufficient to support the charge of murder, but is not sufficient to support a charge of conspiracy to murder or of attempt to murder.

We have come to the conclusion that if the prosecution charge a conspiracy to contravene section 170(2) of the Customs and Excise Management Act by the importation of heroin, then the prosecution must prove that the agreed course of conduct was the importation of heroin. This is because the essence of the crime of conspiracy is the agreement and in simple terms, you do not prove an agreement to import heroin by proving an agreement to import cannabis.

We are confident that in coming to this conclusion, we are not making the enforcement of the anti-drug laws more difficult. If the facts suggest that the agreement was to import prohibited drugs of more than one class, that can be appropriately laid because section 1(1) of the Criminal Law Act expressly provides for the agreed course of conduct to involve the commission of more than one offence.

Thus, O'Connor LJ interpreted Lord Bridge's *dicta* in *R v Anderson* very loosely. Lord Bridge stated that the defendant must intend to "play a part" in the agreed course of conduct, thus implying that the defendant must intend to have an active role in the commission of the offence. However, O'Connor LJ held that a defendant could intend to play an active part or a passive part in the offence and that even failing to stop the unlawful activity would be sufficient.

15.3 Attempt

The law on attempts is governed by the Criminal Attempts Act 1981 s 1(1). The *actus reus* of the offence is defined as doing an act which is more than merely preparatory towards the commission of the offence. Prior to the 1981 Act, the courts found this a difficult element to define. The question of whether or not the defendants' acts were more than merely preparatory is a question of fact to be determined by the jury: the Criminal Attempts Act 1981 s 4(3).

R v Gullefer [1990] 3 All ER 82

Panel: Lord Lane CJ, Kennedy and Owen JJ

Statute: Criminal Attempts Act 1981 s 1(1)

Facts: The defendant placed a bet of £18 on a dog in a greyhound race. When he realised that his dog was losing, he jumped onto the race track in order to disrupt the race. The defendant's intention was to get the race declared void and then to claim back his stake. He was convicted of attempted theft of the £18 stake contrary to the Criminal Attempts Act 1981 s 1(1) and sentenced to six months' imprisonment.

LORD LANE CJ

We have been referred to a number of decisions, many of them of respectable antiquity, which show, if nothing else, the difficulties which abound in this branch of the criminal law. ...

...[T]he judge's task is to decide whether there is evidence upon which a jury could reasonably come to the conclusion that the appellant had gone beyond the realm of mere preparation and had embarked upon the actual commission of the offence. If not, he must withdraw the case from the jury. If there is such evidence, it is then for the jury to decide whether the defendant did in fact go beyond mere preparation. That is the way in which the judge approached this case. He ruled that there was sufficient evidence. Mr Copeman submits that he was wrong in so ruling.

The first task of the court is to apply the words of the Act of 1981 to the facts of the case. Was the appellant still in the stage of preparation to commit the substantive offence, or was there a basis of fact which would entitle the jury to say that he had embarked on the theft itself? Might it properly be said that when he jumped on to the track he was trying to steal £18 from the bookmaker?

Alert

Our view is that it could not properly be said that at that stage he was in the process of committing theft. What he was doing was jumping on to the track in an effort to distract the dogs, which in its turn, he hoped, would have the effect of forcing the stewards to declare "no race," which would in its turn give him the opportunity to go back to the bookmaker and demand the £18 he had staked. In our view there was insufficient evidence for it to be said that he had, when he jumped on to the track, gone beyond mere preparation.

So far at least as the present case is concerned, we do not think that it is necessary to examine the authorities which preceded the Act of 1981...

However, ...we venture to make the following observations. Since the passing of the Act of 1981, a division of this court in *Reg. v Ilyas* (1983) 78 Cr App R 17, has helpfully collated the authorities. As appears from the judgment in that case, there seem to have been two lines of authority. The first was exemplified by the decision in *Reg. v Eagleton* (1854) 5 Dears CC 515. That was a case where the defendant was alleged to have attempted to obtain money from the guardians of a parish by falsely pretending to the relieving officer that he had delivered loaves of bread of the proper weight to the outdoor poor, when in fact the loaves were deficient in weight.

Park B., delivering the judgment of the court of nine judges, said, at page 538:

> "Acts remotely leading towards the commission of the offence are not to be considered as attempts to commit it, but acts immediately connected with it are; and if, in this case, after the credit with the relieving officer for the fraudulent overcharge, any *further step* on the part of the defendant had been necessary to obtain payment, as the making out a further account or producing the vouchers to the Board, we should have thought that the obtaining credit in account with the relieving officer would not have been sufficiently proximate to the obtaining the money. But, on the statement in this case, no other act on the part of the defendant would have been required. It was the last act, *depending on himself,* towards the payment of the money, and therefore it ought to be considered as an attempt."

Lord Diplock in *Director of Public Prosecutions v Stonehouse* [1978] AC 55, 68, having cited part of that passage from *Reg. v Eagleton*, added: "In other words the offender must have crossed the Rubicon and burnt his boats."

The other line of authority is based on a passage in *Stephen's Digest of the Criminal Law*, 5th ed. (1894), art. 50: "An attempt to commit a crime is an act done with intent to commit that crime, and forming part of a series of acts which would constitute its actual commission if it were not interrupted." As Lord Edmund-Davies points out in *Director of Public Prosecution v Stonehouse*, at page 85, that definition has been repeatedly cited with judicial approval.... However, as Lord Parker CJ in the latter case points out, at p. 370G, *Stephen's* definition falls short of defining the exact point of time at which the series of acts can be said to begin.

It seems to us that the words of the Act of 1981 seek to steer a midway course. They do not provide, as they might have done, that the *Reg. v Eagleton* test is to be followed, or that, as Lord Diplock suggested, the defendant must have reached a point from which it was impossible for him to retreat before the actus reus of an attempt is proved. On the other hand the words give perhaps as clear a guidance as is possible in the circumstances on the point of time at which *Stephen's* "series of acts" begin. It begins when the merely preparatory acts come to an end and the defendant embarks upon the crime proper. When that is will depend of course upon the facts in any particular case.

Alert

The appeal was allowed and the defendant's conviction was quashed.

R v Jones (1990) 91 Cr App R 351

Panel: Taylor LJ, Mars-Jones and Waite JJ

Statute: Criminal Attempts Act 1981 s 1(1)

Facts: The defendant bought a shot gun, cut off the end and went to meet the victim. He then climbed into a car with the victim, pointed the gun at the victim and said, "You are not going to like this". The safety catch was on the gun, but it was unclear whether the defendant had his finger on the trigger. The victim grabbed the gun and there was a struggle. The victim managed to escape unharmed. The defendant was convicted of attempted murder contrary to the Criminal Attempts Act 1981 s 1(1). He appealed against conviction.

LORD JUSTICE TAYLOR

We do not accept Mr Farrer's contention that section 1(1) of the 1981 Act in effect embodies the "last act" test derived from *Eagleton*. Had Parliament intended to adopt that test, a quite different form of words could and would have been used.

It is of interest to note that the 1981 Act followed a report from the Law Commission on Attempt, and Impossibility in Relation to Attempt, Conspiracy and Incitement (1980 No. 102 dated June 25). At paragraph 2.47 the report states:

"The definition of sufficient proximity must be wide enough to cover two varieties of cases; first, those in which a person has taken all the steps towards the commission of a crime which he believes to be necessary as far as he is concerned for that crime to result, such as firing a gun at another and missing. Normally such cases cause no difficulty. Secondly, however, the definition must cover those instances where a person has to take some further step to complete the crime, assuming that there is evidence of the necessary mental element on his part to commit it; for example, when the defendant has raised the gun to take aim at another but has not yet squeezed the trigger. We have reached the conclusion that, in regard to these cases, it is undesirable to recommend anything more complex than a rationalisation of the present law."

In paragraph 2.48 the report states:

"The literal meaning of 'proximate' is 'nearest, next before or after (in place, order, time, connection of thought, causation, et cetera.' Thus, were this term part of a statutory description of the actus reus of attempt, it would clearly be capable of being interpreted to exclude all but the 'final act'; this would not be in accordance with the policy outlined above."

Clearly, the draftsman of section 1(1) must be taken to have been aware of the two lines of earlier authority and of the Law Commission's report. The words "an act which is more than merely preparatory to the commission of the offence" would be inapt if they were intended to mean "the last act which lay in his power towards the commission of the offence".

Looking at the plain natural meaning of section 1(1) in the way indicated by the Lord Chief Justice, the question for the judge in the present case was whether there was evidence from which a reasonable jury, properly directed, could conclude that the appellant had done acts which were more than merely preparatory. Clearly his actions in obtaining the gun, in shortening it, in loading it, in putting on his disguise, and in going to the school could only be regarded as preparatory acts. But, in our judgment, once he had got into the car, taken out the loaded gun and pointed it at the victim with the intention of killing him, there was sufficient evidence for the consideration of the jury on the charge of attempted murder. It was a matter for them to decide whether they were sure those acts were more than merely preparatory. In our judgment, therefore, the learned judge was right to allow the case to go to the jury, and the appeal against conviction must be dismissed.

The mens rea of an attempt is an intention to commit the full offence. Thus, the mens rea for attempted murder is intention to kill.

R v Whybrow [1951] 35 Cr App R 141

Panel: Lord Goddard CJ, Hilber, Finnemore, Slade and Devlin JJ

Facts: The defendant was convicted of the attempted murder of his wife. He had been on bad terms with his wife and had been having an affair with another woman. His wife had received an electric shock while in the bath. The prosecution case was that the defendant had wired the soap dish to the mains power. The defendant denied the allegation, claiming that the purpose of the wiring apparatus was to provide an earth for the wireless set in the bedroom. He claimed that any electric shock his wife received was due to accident. He appealed against conviction.

LORD GODDARD CJ

The case lasted two days and the learned Judge's summing-up, so far as the facts were concerned, was meticulously careful and meticulously accurate, but unfortunately he did, in charging the jury, confuse in his mind for a moment the direction given to a jury in a case of murder with the direction given to a jury in a case of attempted murder. In murder the jury is told—and it has always been the law—that if a person wounds another or attacks another either intending to kill or intending to do grievous bodily harm, and the person attacked dies, that is murder, the reason being that the requisite malice aforethought, which is a term of art, is satisfied if the attacker intends to do grievous bodily harm. Therefore, if one person attacks another, inflicting a wound in such a way that an ordinary, reasonable person must know that at least grievous bodily harm will result, and death results, there is the malice aforethought sufficient to support the charge of murder. But, if the charge is one of attempted murder, the intent becomes the principal ingredient of the crime. It may be said that the law, which is not always logical, is somewhat illogical in saying that, if one attacks a person intending to do grievous bodily harm and death results, that is murder, but that if one attacks a person and only intends to do grievous bodily harm, and death does not result, it is not attempted murder, but wounding with intent to do grievous bodily harm. It is not really illogical because, in that particular case, the intent is the essence of the crime while, where the death of another is caused, the necessity is to prove malice aforethought, which is supplied in law by proving intent to do grievous bodily harm....

...the jury should have been told that the essence of the offence was the intent to murder...

 Alert

The Law Commission have recently considered reforming the law on attempts.

Law Commission Consultation Paper No. 183, *Conspiracy and Attempts (2007)*

12.14   First of all, in the absence of clear, consistent guidelines the 'more than merely preparatory' test of proximity has proved to be too vague and uncertain a basis for a court to determine whether an attempt has been committed. ... We provisionally propose that specific guidance should be provided on the kinds of conduct that should be regarded as 'criminal' preparation, for the purposes of the proposed new offence of that name...

12.15   Secondly, because of the absence of any clear, consistent guidance, the Court of Appeal has had to determine where the line between mere preparation and attempt is to be drawn. As a result too much emphasis has on occasion been placed on the offence's label ('attempt') – and therefore on the notion of 'trying' to commit an offence. Too little regard has correspondingly been paid to the underlying rationale for the offence. Under our provisional proposals, clarity would be introduced to the law of attempt in this respect, because the offence of 'attempt' would be confined to the last acts D needs to do to bring about the commission of the offence. The key distinction would become one between 'mere' preparation and 'criminal' preparation, for the purposes of that proposed new offence.

12.16   In that regard, we take the view that there are a number of sound policy reasons for imposing criminal liability for some preparatory conduct occurring before D actually completes or all-but completes an attempt to commit another offence.

These are:

(1)   The need for effective intervention by the police;

(2)   The desirability of imposing criminal liability in relation to conduct associated with a sufficiently vivid danger of intentional harm; and

(3)   The high moral culpability associated with preparatory acts closely linked in time with (what would be) the last act towards the commission of an intended offence....

12.24   Our third reason for believing section 1(1) of the 1981 Act to be unsatisfactory is that it would appear omissions are currently excluded from the scope of the offence. We take the view that there is no reason in principle, or indeed as a matter of policy, why attempts should be limited to the commission of positive acts, particularly as the Crown must always prove D's intention. If D deliberately starves his or her baby to death, this is murder even though the death is achieved through 'doing nothing' rather than by a positive act of killing. Suppose, however, that someone overhears D admitting that he or she is endeavouring to starve his or her baby to death and has already denied the baby food for a couple of days. We believe it would be wrong if D could avoid liability for attempted murder in such circumstances, but it may well be that this is the present legal position. We ...provisionally propose ...that the law be clarified to ensure that D will incur inchoate liability in such circumstances.

12.25   Our fourth reason relates to the current requirement that the jury should be directed to determine whether D's proven or admitted conduct amounts to an 'attempt' for the purposes of the 1981 Act, even when the trial judge has already made a ruling on this issue. This is difficult to reconcile with the general division of roles between judge and jury in criminal proceedings. More worryingly, lay triers of fact may have an insufficient understanding of the scope of the offence, or of the policy considerations underpinning it, to be able to apply it in the way it was intended to be applied. The present test may give rise to inconsistent or perverse verdicts.... Under our provisional proposal..., the relevant question will be one of law for the trial judge. ...that question will be whether an act it is alleged that D has engaged in can amount to criminal preparation. The role of the jury will be to decide whether an act ruled capable of amounting to criminal preparation in fact took place.

12.26 Finally, there is a lack of clarity in relation to the fault element required for circumstance elements of an attempt to commit an offence. It may be that inchoate liability can now arise for attempting an (indictable) offence of strict liability regardless of whether the accused 'intended' to do anything unlawful (and even regardless of whether he or she had any culpable state of mind at all). ...we provisionally propose that the fault element for attempt should be intention in relation to conduct and consequence elements..., and at least subjective recklessness in relation to a circumstance element.... However, where a substantive offence requires a higher form of fault than recklessness in relation to a circumstance element, that higher element should be required for an attempt to commit that offence....

15.4 Impossibility

Impossibility in fact is no defence to an attempt. In *R v Shivpuri* [1987] AC 1, the House of Lords overruled the previous House of Lords' authority of *Anderton v Ryan* [1985] 2 WLR 23.

R v Shivpuri [1987] AC 1

Panel: Lord Hailsham of St. Marylebone LC, Lord Elwyn-Jones, Lord Scarman, Lord Bridge of Harwich and Lord Mackay of Clashfern

Statute: Criminal Attempts Act 1981 s 1(1)

Facts: The defendant was convicted of attempting to be knowingly concerned in dealing with and harbouring a controlled drug, heroin, contrary to the Criminal Attempts Act 1981 s 1(1). He was arrested while carrying a package which he believed to contain drugs. In fact, the package contained a vegetable matter. He appealed against his conviction, arguing that he could not be guilty as the substance was not a controlled drug.

LORD BRIDGE OF HARWICH

...[T]he first question to be asked is whether the appellant intended to commit the offences of being knowingly concerned in dealing with and harbouring drugs of Class A or Class B with intent to evade the prohibition on their importation. ...did the appellant intend to receive and store (harbour) and in due course pass on to third parties (deal with) packages of heroin or cannabis which he knew had been smuggled into England from India? The answer is plainly yes, he did. Next, did he in relation to each offence, do an act which was more than merely preparatory to the commission of the offence? The act relied on in relation to harbouring was the receipt and retention of the packages found in the lining of the suitcase. The act relied on in relation to dealing was the meeting at Southall station with the intended recipient of one of the packages. In each case the act was clearly more than preparatory to the commission of the *intended* offence; it was not and could not be more than merely preparatory to the commission of the *actual* offence, because the facts were such that the commission of the actual offence was impossible. Here then is the nub of the matter. Does the "act which is more than merely preparatory to the commission of the offence" in section 1 (1) of the Act of 1981... require any more than an act which is more than merely preparatory to the commission of the offence which the defendant intended to commit? Section 1 (2) must surely indicate a negative answer; if it were otherwise, whenever the facts were such that the commission of the actual offence was impossible, it would be impossible to prove an act more than merely preparatory to the commission of that offence and subsections (1) and (2) would contradict each other.

This very simple, perhaps over simple, analysis leads me to the provisional conclusion that the appellant was rightly convicted of the two offences of attempt with which he was charged. But can this conclusion stand with *Anderton v Ryan*? The appellant in that case was charged with an attempt to handle stolen goods. She bought a video recorder believing it to be stolen. On the facts as they were to be assumed it was not stolen. By a majority the House decided that she was entitled to be acquitted. I have re-examined the case with care. If I could extract from the speech of Lord Roskill or from my own speech a clear and coherent principle distinguishing those cases of attempting the impossible which amount to offences under the statute from those which do not, I should have to consider carefully on which side of the line the instant case fell. But I have to confess that I can find no such principle....

If we fell into error, it is clear that our concern was to avoid convictions in situations which most people, as a matter of common sense, would not regard as involving criminality....

...any attempt to commit an offence which involves "an act which is more than merely preparatory to the commission of the offence" but for any reason fails, so that in the event no offence is committed, must ex hypothesi, from the point of view of the criminal law, be "objectively innocent." What turns what would otherwise, from the point of view of the criminal law, be an innocent act into a crime is the intent of the actor to commit an offence. ... A puts his hand into B's pocket. Whether or not there is anything in the pocket capable of being stolen, if A intends to steal, his act is a criminal attempt; if he does not so intend, his act is innocent. A plunges a knife into a bolster in a bed. To avoid the complication of an offence of criminal damage, assume it to be A's bolster. If A believes the bolster to be his enemy B and intends to kill him, his act is an attempt to murder B; if he knows the bolster is only a bolster, his act is innocent. These considerations lead me to the conclusion that the distinction sought to be drawn in *Anderton v Ryan* between innocent and guilty acts considered "objectively" and independently of the state of mind of the actor cannot be sensibly maintained.

...I am thus led to the conclusion that there is no valid ground on which *Anderton v Ryan* can be distinguished. I have made clear my own conviction, which as a party to the decision (and craving the indulgence of my noble and learned friends who agreed in it) I am the readier to express, that the decision was wrong....

I cannot conclude this opinion without disclosing that I have had the advantage, since the conclusion of the argument in this appeal, of reading an article by Professor Glanville Williams entitled "The Lords and Impossible Attempts, or Quis Custodiet Ipsos Custodes?" [1986] C.L.J. 33. The language in which he criticises the decision in

Anderton v Ryan is not conspicuous for its moderation, but it would be foolish, on that account, not to recognise the force of the criticism and churlish not to acknowledge the assistance I have derived from it.

Further Reading

Dennis I 'The Rationale of Criminal Conspiracy' (1977) 93 *LQR* 39

Ormerod D and Forston R 'The Serious Crime Act 2007: The Part 2 Offences' [2009] *Crim LR* 389

Smith K 'Proximity in Attempt: Lord Lane's Midway Course' [1991] *Crim LR* 576

Notes

Notes

Notes

Notes

Notes

Notes

Notes

Notes